a-z
of careers
& jobs

THE ✚ TIMES

a-z
of careers & jobs

14th edition

Edited by:
Susan Hodgson

**KOGAN
PAGE**

Publisher's note

Every possible effort has been made to ensure that the information contained in this book is accurate at the time of going to press. Neither Kogan Page nor the editor can accept responsibility for any errors or omissions, however caused. No responsibility for loss or damage occasioned to any person acting, or refraining from action, as a result of the material in this publication can be accepted by the editor, the publisher or any of the authors.

First published in Great Britain in 1984 by Kogan Page Limited
Fourteenth edition 2007

Apart from any fair dealing for the purposes of research or private study, or criticism or review, as permitted under the Copyright, Designs and Patents Act 1988, this publication may only be reproduced, stored or transmitted, in any form or by any means, with the prior permission in writing of the publishers, or in the case of reprographic reproduction in accordance with the terms and licences issued by the CLA. Enquiries concerning reproduction outside these terms should be sent to the publishers at the undermentioned address:

Kogan Page Limited
120 Pentonville Road
London N1 9JN
www.kogan-page.co.uk

© Kogan Page, 1984, 1986, 1988, 1991, 1992, 1994, 1995, 1997, 2000, 2002, 2004, 2005, 2006, 2007

The views expressed in this book are those of the author, and are not necessarily the same as those of Times Newspapers Ltd.

British Library Cataloguing in Publication Data

A CIP record for this book is available from the British Library.

ISBN-10 0 7494 4977 2
ISBN-13 978 0 7494 4977 3

Typeset by Saxon Graphics Ltd, Derby
Printed and bound in Great Britain by Bell & Bain, Glasgow

gap year
working holidays

Make the most of your long summer holidays or 'year out' with BUNAC's wide range of exciting work and travel programmes. With the benefit of BUNAC's support, you'll be able to gain useful work experience while exploring another country. It also looks great on your CV!

- Work and travel for up to twelve months in Canada, Australia or South Africa or, up to two years in New Zealand

- Volunteer or teach in Ghana, South Africa, Costa Rica, Peru, Cambodia or China

- Summer camp jobs in the US on *Summer Camp USA*

For further information or to download an application form, please visit the BUNAC website.

Preface

Choice can be daunting or desirable, marvellous or muddling. What helps a confusing plethora of options to become a wealth of exciting opportunities is clear information upon which to base your choices. At present the job market is relatively buoyant and there are plenty of pathways from which to choose. Education and training and training options are perhaps the most extensive they have ever been. All this is, of course, good news, but it does mean that anyone entering the employment market at whatever level must undertake considerable research. It is also true that having plenty to choose from does not mean that every choice is easy. Much of the job market, for example work in the media, is fiercely competitive.

This guide will help you access all the information you need to inform your decision making. It is useful whether you are at the stage where you think you know what you want, but would like to check entry requirements, or whether you just want to flick through to give yourself some ideas. If you really are unsure where to begin, flick through some of the 'Personal Qualities and Skills' sections to see what matches your experience and ambitions. If you read a 'Qualifications and Training' section and are in any doubt as to whether you have what is required, check directly with an employer, a course provider or a relevant professional body. The information on salaries can only be a guide, because different types of employer have different types of salary structure. It is worth noting that at present the national minimum wage is £5.35 per hour for people aged 22 or over. For workers aged 18 to 21 the minimum wage is £4.45 per hour and for workers aged 16 to17 the minimum rate is £3.30 per hour. These rates are due to rise in October 2007. The new rates are likely to be agreed in April/May 2007. The Info panels at the end of each career entry will lead you to a wealth of sources of further information. Websites are especially useful, providing details of training, education and vacancy sources and linking you to further sources of information.

Susan Hodgson
Careers Adviser

Abbreviations

A level	Advanced level
AS level	Advanced Special level
AVCE	Vocational A level
CAM	Communication, Advertising and Marketing Foundation
Edexcel	Edexcel Foundation
Edexcel (BTEC)	Comprises ULEAC (University of London Examination and Assessment Council) and BTEC (Business and Technology Education Council)
GCE	General Certificate of Education
GCSE	General Certificate of Secondary Education
GNVQ	General National Vocational Qualification
GSVQ	General Scottish Vocational Qualification
H grade	Higher grade (SCE)
HNC/HND	Higher National Certificate/Higher National Diploma
HTC	Higher Technical Certificate
LSC	Learning Skills Council
NC/ND	National Certificate/National Diploma
NVQ	National Vocational Qualification
QCA	Qualifications and Curriculum Authority
SCE	Scottish Certificate of Education (equivalent to GCSE)
SNC/SND	Scottish National Certificate/Scottish National Diploma
SQA	Scottish Qualifications Authority
SVQ	Scottish Vocational Qualification
SWAS	Social Work Admissions System
TEC	Training and Enterprise Council
UCAS	Universities and Colleges Admissions System

'50% of school children to enter higher education'

And the other 50%?

Think...
...about
Podiatry

Podiatry is a healthcare profession, which has developed from its origins in Chiropody. It involves assessment, diagnosis and treatment of patients with foot and lower limb disorders.

Who do Podiatrists treat?

It is not only the elderly who have problems with their feet! Podiatrists treat patients of all ages, and from all walks of life.

Training

- To become Registered you must complete a degree in Podiatry. This can be done at one of 13 institutions across the UK.

- Places for UK Residents are funded by the NHS and SHEFC. They will pay your tuition fees and offer you a means tested bursary.

- Entry requirements for the degree courses vary but generally applicants need to have 2 A Levels or equivalent, one of which must be science based.

- Following the degree most students find employment very quickly in a variety of environments, including the health service, private practice and the retail sector.

If you would like further detailed information please visit our website at:

www.feetforlife.org

or contact:

The Society of Chiropodists & Podiatrists
1 Fellmongers Path, Tower Bridge Road, London SE1 3LY
Telephone: 020 7234 8620 E-mail: enq@scpod.org

 The Society of Chiropodists & Podiatrists (SCP)

Are you thinking about working in health care?

Did you know:
- The person in the health care team responsible for providing comprehensive management of foot and lower limb problems is the podiatrist.
- Podiatrists work in many professional sports clubs including football and cricket clubs.
- Working in the NHS, private practice, commerce & industry or in Universities is possible as a podiatrist.
- If you are have been a UK resident for at least 3 years you will have no tuition fees to pay while studying your podiatry degree at University.
- In the NHS salaries for podiatrists start at around £18,000
- Qualified podiatrists can undertake further training to become Podiatric Surgeons.
- There are only 13 places in the UK you can study for a podiatry degree.
- As a podiatrist you work along side lots of other health care professionals including doctors, physiotherapists, specialist nurses and consultants.
- Podiatry is practiced in many countries around the world so podiatrists have the opportunity to travel & work overseas.

What do Podiatrists do?
- When a child has a problem with pains in their legs or tripping, the assessment and prescription of orthotics (insoles) can be done by a podiatrist.
- When a patient with diabetes is having problems with numb feet a podiatrist can assess the problem.
- When a teenager has an in growing toe nail, the surgery to resolve the problem can be done by a podiatrist.
- When an elderly or disabled person is unable to reach their own feet, podiatrists are able to provide simple foot care.
- When an athlete has a recurring knee problem a podiatrist can undertake the assessment and management.

Think about it:
How many times do you use your feet every day? Multiply that by the number of people in the UK. Then think what happens when they go wrong and the things that you and everyone else wouldn't be able to do.

There is an important role for you to play as a podiatrist.

A Podiatrist keep you walking – for life!

For further information please visit **www.feetforlife.org**

Qualifications

Scottish readers should be aware that in order to simplify the text the editor has referred to qualifications required in terms of GCSEs, A levels and NVQs or equivalent. NVQs are directly equivalent to SVQs but Scottish National and Higher Qualifications are not equivalent to GCSEs and A levels. A new qualification, the Advanced Higher, does equate to A level but most universities still express their entry requirements in terms of the Higher. Full details of all Scottish qualifications can be found on the SQA website. The easiest way to compare the points awarded for A levels and Highers is using the Universities and Colleges Admissions Service (UCAS) tariff calculator. Relevant Scottish sources of further information have been included where appropriate.

Overseas international qualifications

The National Recognition Centre (comparability of international qualifications) (NARIC) can provide a letter outlining how your overseas qualifications equate to UK qualifications. There is a charge for this service: £42 for paper applications, £35 if you apply online. Large organisations that deal with many overseas applicants may be able to give you some guidance too.

National Recognition Centre (comparability of international qualifications) (NARIC) Oriel House, Oriel Road, Cheltenham, Gloucestershire GL50 1XP; 0870 990 4088; www.naric.org.uk

Financing your future

A further period of academic study or vocational training can really make a job applicant stand out from the crowd. But, whilst finding a suitable course may not be a problem, finding the money to pay for it could be.

That's where a Career Development Loan can help. Designed as the result of a government initiative, Career Development Loans have helped tens of thousands of people over the last 17 years to make sure that a lack of money doesn't get in the way of vocational training.

Whilst you can't use a Career Development Loan to pay for a three or four year university undergraduate course, it could help you to cover the cost of a vocational course of up to two years. You can also include a further year's practical experience if it is part of the course.

So how do Career Development Loans work? Well it's simple. You borrow between £300 and £8,000 to help pay for your training from a Career Development Loan provider such as The Co-operative Bank. You don't need to be a customer to apply.

The Department for Education and Skills then pays the interest on your Career Development Loan whilst you are on your course and for up to one month afterwards. After that, you repay the loan over an agreed period of one to five years, at a rate of interest that was fixed before you started the course.

For example, say you are applying for a 12 month course which starts on 1 October 2007. You don't pay anything for 13 months as the government pays the interest for you. After that, you can pay off your loan over the agreed period of 1 to 5 years.

If you arrange your Career Development Loan with The Co-operative Bank, you can be certain that the money you borrow has not come from the profits of unnecessary pollution, human rights abuses or tobacco manufacture. That's because The Co-operative Bank is the only UK high street bank which works to a strict Ethical Policy that says where it will – and where it won't – invest its customers' money.

To find out more about a Career Development Loan from The Co-operative Bank, simply phone **08457 212 212**, call into your local Co-operative Bank branch or visit **www.co-operativebank.co.uk**

Useful points of contact

www.ucas.com
Details of, and current entry requirements for most higher education courses in the UK. The tariff calculator that can be found in the News section removes the need to grapple with the new points system (www.ucas.com/higher/tariff/calc/index.html).

www.statistics.gov.uk
This site includes various surveys about the labour market, including the New Earnings surveys, which are published annually. These are retrospective, but they still provide helpful information on relative salaries in different fields of employment.

www.ssda.org.uk
Information about the 25 existing sector skills councils and any aspirant sector skills likely to be licensed in the near future.

www.qca.org.uk
The Qualifications and Curriculum Authority accredit and monitor qualifications in schools, colleges and at work in England, Wales and Northern Ireland. Details of the national qualifications framework showing the equivalence between all qualifications are available here.

www.sqa.org.uk
The Scottish Qualifications Authority is responsible for the development, accreditation, assessment and certification of qualifications other than degrees in Scotland. Information on these and their equivalence to qualifications in the rest of the UK can be found on this site.

The national minimum wage

The current minimum wage for people over 22 is £5.35 per hour. For workers aged 18–21 the minimum wage is £4.45 per hour, and for workers aged 16–17 the minimum rate is £3.30 per hour.

Vision...

...can take you places you've never dreamed of, make a career choice second to none.

Opportunities...

...to become a leading professional in one of today's fastest growing professions.

Support...

...at the moment you need it most, we'll give you the confidence to keep moving forward, taking your career to new heights.

CIPS – one organisation, 42,000 members, infinite benefits
CIPS runs a graduate level diploma qualification for its members which is recognised worldwide demonstrating that the holder has achieved a sound technical knowledge and understanding of the subject.

THE
CHARTERED INSTITUTE OF
PURCHASING & SUPPLY

For more information on a career in purchasing visit: www.cips.org
email: info@cips.org
Tel: 01780 756777

The right path for you?

What is purchasing & supply?

Have you ever fancied being in charge of spending an organisation's money...welcome to a career in purchasing and supply.
People have been purchasing or 'procuring' things for thousands of years, striking agreements or arrangements between two parties for the provision of a desired object or service and in receipt of that object or service there is a form of payment made by the receiver. It sounds very simple and obviously in today's global economy this is an integral business function that, if done well can help bring considerable success to an organisation. Essentially purchasing and supply management involves buying the goods and services that enable an organisation to operate on a short term basis and succeed on a long term basis.

A purchaser may be responsible for sourcing raw materials from suppliers worldwide, bringing them into the organisation, to enable production of goods for customers. Additionally this could involve the purchasing of marketing, advertising or IT related services. Purchasing and supply management is the link in that chain which manages the interface between the supply market and the organisation. Its importance lies in the fact that a company can spend more than two thirds of its revenue buying its goods and services, so even a modest reduction in purchasing costs have a significant effect on profit.

What personal skills do I need?
To succeed in purchasing you will need to demonstrate a wide variety of skills such as good business sense, financial management, good communication skills as wells as creativity and innovation.

The right skill set is obviously reflected by the salary offered by an organisation. Average salary entry levels for individuals with no purchasing experience can be up to about £17k. However salaries are rising rapidly and a good graduate moving into purchasing and supply management could expect a quick promotion. Many purchasing directors especially in a large organisation can command salaries well in excess of £100k.

Where could I work?

One of the most beneficial things about a career in purchasing is that a well-qualified purchasing professional can walk into a wide range of environments where they can use their skills to buy a whole variety of products and services. For example in a project team responsible for building a football stadium, the purchaser will have a fundamental role. They could be involved not only in the construction of the stadium but also in buying the seats, turn styles, turf, stands, catering and interior facilities, fixtures and fittings as well as marketing and advertising services needed to launch the new stadium.

There is no standard formula as to how purchasing and supply chain departments should be set up and organised and most companies will have a 'model' that works best for them, but just to highlight the variety of roles available depending on the type of sector you choose to work in, some of the list includes:

- Procurement Officer
- Buyer
- Supply Chain Manager
- Procurement Performance Manager
- Contract Manager
- Category Buyer
- E-procurement Manager
- Travel Buyer
- Business Service Buyer
- Trading Manager
- Supplier Relationship Manager
- Procurement Analyst
- Purchasing Manager

The Chartered Institute of Purchasing & Supply (CIPS)

The role of CIPS is to support, represent and service the interest of its members worldwide and to promote best practice in purchasing and supply management. CIPS runs a graduate level diploma qualification for its members which is recognised worldwide demonstrating that the holder has achieved a sound technical knowledge and understanding of the subject.

For more information on a career in purchasing visit: **www.cips.org**
or contact **info@cips.org** Tel: **01780 740986**

MORE than a thousand further and higher education courses are on offer at two magnificent campuses in Doncaster.

Students could study anything from English to construction and tourism management to engineering at either the new Waterfront campus in the centre of town or the idyllic countryside campus six miles west of the town.

Both sites, operated by Doncaster College, give students a superb learning experience in readiness for employment.

The College has full-time and part-time courses at a variety of different levels – right from certificate to masters.

The new campus, a new multi-million pound development on Doncaster's Waterfront opened in September 2006 and houses some of the best educational facilities in the country. It includes a 200-seat drama studio, a 100-seat lecture theatre, a huge two-floor Learning Resource Centre, excellent sporting facilities and a beauty salon complete with nail bar, hairdressers, Jacuzzi, flotation bed, steam room and sauna.

State-of-the-art technology is at the heart of the building with most classrooms fitted with electronic whiteboards and electronic door systems. More than 30 plasma screens are also dotted around the campus, informing students of the latest College, local, national and international news.

The Hub, as it is known, is in the heart of Doncaster town centre and is in walking distance of the shops and transport interchange.

In contrast, the countryside campus at High Melton is surrounded by 126 acres of greenery and offers learners the perfect place to unwind while learning.

It is home to the town's School of Intermedia and Performance Art, Doncaster Business School, The Stables Conference Centre and Britain's first centre of excellence for relationship studies – The Relate Institute.

This wonderful campus also houses a jogging trail and a nine-hole golf course.

It all makes for the perfect learning experience. There has never been a better time to learn in South Yorkshire.

For more information on the courses offered at Doncaster College, please call **0800 358 7575** or visit **www.don.ac.uk** to order a prospectus online.

Reward yourself. The British Council takes an active interest in the welfare and careers of its teachers and there are many other rewards for teaching English abroad. Discovering and engaging with other cultures makes all our teachers richer people. If you would like more information about a rewarding career teaching English as a Foreign Language, please e-mail us on teacher. vacancies@britishcouncil.org, telephone 020 7389 4931 or visit our website at **http://trs.britishcouncil.org**

BRITISH COUNCIL

Welcome to the European Business School London

Since its establishment in 1979, the European Business School London has become a centre of excellence in international business and management education.

Our mission is to educate future leading managers in the world of international business. We provide programmes that are both academically rigorous and practical through a combination of business subjects, business language skills, study abroad, work experience and entrepreneurial and networking skills. EBS London delivers these in a dynamic international environment, where you are supported by a caring, professional academic and administrative staff.

For more than twenty years, our vision of a business school has been a resounding success. Each year, our new graduates offer employers something unique – a world-class business education combined with excellence in languages, study abroad and intensive work experience in blue-chip companies. The tremendous success our graduates have achieved as entrepreneurs, consultants, international managers and finance specialists has spread the word around the world about our unique approach to business education.

Dean
Professor Michael Scriven

Tailor Your Degree

The EBS degree offers over 300 possible pathways. Students tailor the main BA (Hons) in International Business with a choice of one or two languages, and by selecting a specific major.

The first three semesters comprise core business subjects, covering key concepts in economics, marketing, finance, management and international business. Students will also study their language options from the first semester.

During this time you will choose your Major. Your personal tutor will be at hand to assist you in this selection, you will also use knowledge gained on the course and through your work experience to select the major that complements your future goals.

The choices you make will build on your greatest strengths, and will offer your future employers the special EBS London combination of skills and experience.

The six areas in which you can take a Major are:

Economics
Finance
Law
Management (Entrepreneurship)
Management (Human Resource Management)
Marketing

Why study physics?

A degree in physics opens the doors to a wider range of careers than almost any other subject and yet many people are unaware of the opportunities it can offer. Physics is the most fundamental of the sciences and therefore underpins almost every area of our lives and indeed many advances in the other sciences. Physicists are involved in an enormous range of areas including:

- cancer treatment
- computers and computer games design
- mobile phones
- sports wear
- renewable energy
- weather forecasting/climate change research.

The advantage of a physics degree, however, is that while a career in science is possible you are also gain many transferable skills valued by all employers in all sectors; you learn to think logically and solve problems, gain experience of working in a team and in computing. This means that all the usual graduate training schemes love physicists and many can even be found in the city modelling financial markets. In fact, according to a report by PricewaterhouseCoopers, physics graduates earn around £187,000 more during their career than someone with A-levels but no degree, whereas history and English graduates increase their earnings by only about half as much. In the UK, graduates in physics earn more than those in most other disciplines.

The prospect of a well paid career is great but what about the cost of going to university and the debt you might accumulate, especially if you choose a four year MPhys degree over a BSc? The Institute of Physics provides bursaries to selected physics undergraduates. These bursaries, administered through participating universities are worth £3000 over the duration of a bachelor's degree and £4000 over the duration of and MPhys/MSci degree. Many universities also have their own schemes.

For more information about the Institute's bursary scheme, see **www.iop.org**

Institute *of* Physics
Undergraduate Bursaries

The Institute of Physics is providing 300 bursaries for students who intend to study physics at university at the start of the 2007 academic year. These bursaries, administered through participating universities will be worth £3000 over the duration of a bachelors degree and £4000 over the duration of an MPhys/MSci degree.

Why study physics?

Getting to grips with the latest discoveries in physics is intellectually challenging and at the same time gives you skills highly valued by employers. You can:

- learn to think logically and solve problems;
- learn how to work in a team;
- pick up high-level computing skills.

This means that as well as being able to work in research there are also a wide range of other jobs available to you. You can for example:

- design computer games;
- monitor the environment;
- invent life-saving medical equipment;
- model financial markets.

According to a report by PricewaterhouseCoopers, physics graduates earn around £187 000 more during their career than non-graduates. This is double the advantage you would gain as a history or English graduate.

So, studying physics is stimulating, leads to a wide range of careers and gives you good earning potential.

Details of our bursaries can be found at: **www.iop.org**

As the only business school in the world to hold triple accreditation from the Association to Advance Collegiate Schools of Business (AACSB), The UN World Travel Organization (WTO) and the Association of MBAs (AMBA), the University of Surrey's School of Management offers a world-class management education, providing qualifications relevant to and valued by today's global community. In preparing future leaders to think creatively and practically within a rapidly changing environment, the School promotes an appreciation of both the science and art of management.

The School has a strong international reputation for its service sector management research and teaching. With over 40 years experience in tourism and hospitality education, it was the first UK institution to be awarded UN World Tourism Organization (WTO) TedQual recognition for all of its tourism degree programmes.

The AACSB, WTO and AMBA acknowledgment of the high quality of its programmes gives assurance that the School of Management provides an excellent education for anyone seeking to start or further their management career.

The School offers BSc (Hons) undergraduate degree programmes in:
- Accounting and Finance*
- Business Management
- International Hospitality Management
- International Hospitality and Tourism Management
- Retail Management
- Tourism Management

MSc postgraduate degree programmes are offered in:
- Change Agent Skills and Strategies
- Entrepreneurship
- e-Tourism*
- Financial Services Management
- Food Management
- Health Care Management
- Human Resource Management
- International Business Management
- International Hotel Management
- International Marketing Management
- International Retail Marketing (subject to validation)*
- Management
- Management Information Systems
- Marketing Management
- Retail Management
- Technology Management
- Tourism Development/Management/Marketing

Other postgraduate study options include:
- Doctor of Business Administration (DBA)
- Master of Business Administration (MBA)
- MBA Hospitality
- MBA Retail (subject to validation)*
- MBA Tourism (subject to validation)*
- MA Intercultural Communication with International Business
- Postgraduate Certificate in Spiritual Development and Facilitation
- Master Entry Programme

* Programme commences in September 2007

Situated within a purpose built building on the University of Surrey's Guildford campus, the School is just 40 minutes from London by train. Full details can be found at
www.som.surrey.ac.uk

Think of it as your business card

BSc Management Programmes
Business Management • Tourism • Retail • Hospitality • Accounting and Financial Services

With an internationally recognised degree from The School of Management – something we've been successfully awarding for 40 years – who knows where you could be a few years from now?

Our distinguished history has earned us a global reputation for quality and excellence in our specialist fields including Tourism, Retail, Hospitality and Business Management.

Enrolling with us guarantees you an innovative, industry-relevant approach to learning that will later see you and your skills greatly valued by employers. Our undergraduate programmes offer a professional training year – giving you important employment experience and making our graduates some of the most sought-after in the UK and internationally.

We offer undergraduate programmes in:
BSc (Hons) Accounting and Financial Services Management*
BSc (Hons) Business Management
BSc (Hons) International Hospitallity Management
BSc (Hons) International Hospitality & Tourism Management
BSc (Hons) Retail Management
BSc (Hons) Tourism Management

Our postgraduate programmes include an MBA and a wide range of business and specialised management MSc programmes. Please see our website for more details.

* Programme commences in September 2007

Give your career the best possible start.

Call +44 (0) 1483 686 300, or write to: The Admissions Team,
School of Management, University of Surrey, Guildford, Surrey GU2 7XH.
You can also email som@surrey.ac.uk
www.som.surrey.ac.uk

UniS

University of Surrey

Teach First

Teach First transforms outstanding graduates into inspiring leaders, ready to excel in any management career. It's an intensive two-year leadership development programme that combines qualifying and working as a teacher with business skills training, coaching and networking opportunities. Teach First is a unique opportunity for you both to be different and to make a difference.

High-profile recruiters from all sectors recognise that the skills and strategies developed in teaching are highly relevant and applicable to management careers. That's why over 80 companies, government agencies and public bodies are backing Teach First to develop top talent for the future.

How it works

Teach First recruits high-calibre graduates from all disciplines to train and qualify as teachers. Before being assigned to a school you will attend six weeks of intensive education training. At the end of year one you achieve Qualified Teacher Status – a qualification that means you can return to teaching at any point in the future. In tandem with your teaching role, you will contribute to the extracurricular life of your school and its students, and participate in courses in strategy, marketing and finance, and skills master classes. You will also have the opportunity to attend regular Teach First networking events with industry leaders and benefit from the support of an experienced network of advisers and coaches.

The challenge

Joining Teach First means spending two years preparing and delivering real lessons to real pupils in a challenging school in London, Manchester or the Midlands. Make no mistake, this is no soft option. But if Teach First is uniquely demanding, it is also uniquely satisfying. No other career choice offers the same degree of responsibility so early or the chance to make such an important difference. And after Teach First? Whether you choose finance, management, public service or education, you will stand out as an exceptional individual with something special to offer.

For more information and to apply visit www.teachfirst.org.uk

Closing date: 30 March 2007.

Teach First's graduate programme is a unique opportunity to be different and to make a difference. It's an innovative combination of teaching with management skills training and leadership development, plus unparalleled internship, networking and coaching opportunities.

Whatever you aim to do with your career, Teach First.

APPLY NOW
DEADLINE: 30th March 2007
(including Deloitte Teach First Scheme)

SUBJECTS: MATHS, SCIENCE, ENGLISH, ICT, D&T, BUSINESS STUDIES, RE, ART, MUSIC

taught first

www.teachfirst.org.uk

Teach First
LEARNING TO LEAD

ACCOUNTANCY

(*see also* Taxation)

Members of the accountancy profession are involved in the financial transactions of businesses, including the preparation and verification of accounts, auditing and analysis.

Accountants

Accountants work with and have expert understanding of a wide range of financial questions, issues and procedures. They work in many different settings, including small high street offices, local and central government offices, for management consultants and for the finance departments of commercial and industrial organisations from small to huge multinationals. They deal with such questions as taxation, business forecasting, monitoring financial performance, advising on investments, acquisitions and mergers and good daily financial management. They also audit paperwork and computer records of organisations to make sure that all financial transactions are accounted for and comply with the law.

Because accountants cover such a wide area of expertise, there are several different specialist branches within the profession. There are four main groups of accountants.

Management accountants
Chartered management accountants, usually referred to as management accountants, work in commerce and industry. They work with a company or organisation monitoring and planning budgets, preparing information for external auditors, overseeing credit control, monitoring financial performance and making suggestions about future business development. They work closely with other members of the management team.

Accountants in private practice
Accountants working in private practice assess, monitor and advise on the financial status of private businesses. They work for freelances, for small firms or for large practices offering their services to fee-paying clients.

Practitioners are either qualified as Associate Members of the Institute of Chartered Accountants in England and Wales (ICAEW), the Institute of Chartered Accountants of Scotland (ICAS), the Institute of Chartered Accountants in Ireland (ICAI), or the Association of Chartered Certified Accountants (ACCA). Members of the Association of International Accountants (AIA) also do private practice work.

One specific role within accountancy is that of the auditor. Auditors are responsible for checking the financial records of every kind of business and organisation and they are not employees of that organisation. External auditors must be qualified chartered accountants or international accountants.

Accountants in the public sector

Chartered public finance accountants (public sector accountants) control and assess the efficiency of public spending. Working, for example, in health trusts, local authorities, universities and central government departments, they examine the cost-effectiveness of policies, manage budgets, conduct internal audits and advise on policy.

Knowing in what kind of environment you would work and what specialist knowledge you wish to apply will help you choose which of the branches of accountancy is most appropriate for you.

Qualifications and Training

Because it is such a complex profession comprising several professional bodies, it is important that you check individual requirements with the branch that interests you. It is possible, however, to give some useful general guidelines.

It is an 80 per cent graduate profession and you need a good honours degree, often a 2.1 in any subject. A degree in a mathematical subject may offer you some exemptions from professional exams. You should have five GCSEs grades A or B and two A levels. Many accountancy firms require you to have 280 to 300 UCAS points. Most organisations prefer to offer training to applicants aged 21 or over. There are some exceptions: occasionally if you are aged 18 and have three good A levels including maths you may be offered a contract. All the accounting professional bodies offer alternative entry routes for mature students and for applicants who are already qualified accounting technicians.

Management accountants do not have to be graduates, but a good honours degree in a mathematical or business subject may offer exemptions from some of the professional examinations.

Accountants qualified with any of the professional accountancy bodies can work in the public sector, but the most relevant organisation is the Chartered Institute of Public Finance and Accountancy (CIPFA). If you don't have another accountancy qualification you must have three GCSEs grades A to C and two A levels and you must have maths and English at either GCSE or A level.

All the accountancy professions offer similar training routes where you have to complete three years' supervised work and take professional exams at two levels.

Personal Qualities and Skills

Accountants have to be good at working with numbers but they must also be very good communicators. They have to be able to understand complex information and also to explain complicated information to people who don't have detailed financial knowledge. They must be persistent, and assertiveness is as important as tact and discretion.

Starting Salary

Starting salaries vary considerably, depending on location and size of firm, but can reach £24,000 for trainees in London and the South-East. £18,000 to £23,000 is more typical.

On qualifying, salaries can increase quite significantly. Salary packages can also include benefits such as pay bonuses, share options and pension and private health plans.

The Association of Accounting Technicians (AAT), 154 Clerkenwell Road, London EC1R 5AD; 020 7415 7500; www.aat.org.uk

Association of Chartered Certified Accountants (ACCA), ACCA Connect, 2 Central Quay, 89 Hydepark Street, Glasgow G3 8BW; 0141 582 2000; www.accaglobal.com

Association of International Accountants, South Bank Building, Kingsway, Team Valley, Newcastle upon Tyne NE11 0JS; 0191 482 4409; www.aia.org.uk

Chartered Institute of Management Accountants (CIMA), 26 Chapter Street, London SW1P 4NP; 020 8849 2251; www.cimaglobal.com

Chartered Institute of Public Finance and Accountancy (CIPFA), 3 Robert Street, London WC2N 6RL; 020 7543 5600; www.cipfa.org.uk

Financial Training Company (FTC), 7–13 Melior Street, London SE1 3QP; 020 7407 5000; www.financial-training.com

Financial Services Skills Council, 51 Gresham Street, London EC2V 7HQ; 020 7216 7366; www.fssc.org.uk

HM Revenue & Customs (HMRC); www.hmrc.gov.uk

The Insolvency Service, 21 Bloomsbury Street, London WC1B 3QW; 020 7291 6895; www.insolvency.gov.uk

Institute of Chartered Accountants in England and Wales (ICAEW), Chartered Accountants' Hall, PO Box 433, London EC2P 2BJ; 020 7920 8100; www.icaew.co.uk

Institute of Chartered Accountants in Ireland (ICAI), CA House, 83 Pembroke Road, Dublin 4; +3531 637 7200; www.icai.ie

Institute of Chartered Accountants of Scotland (ICAS), CA House, 21 Haymarket Yards, Edinburgh EH12 5BH; 0131 347 0100; www.icas.org.uk

Institute of Public Finance, 7th Floor, NLA Tower, 12–16 Addiscombe Road, Croydon CR0 0XT; 020 8667 1144; www.ipf.co.uk

National Audit Office, 157–197 Buckingham Palace Road, London SW1W 9SP; 020 7798 7000; www.nao.gov.uk

info

Accounting for every profession

Accountancy and finance have always been at the heart of every business, but now the profession holds more challenges and opportunities than ever before. There are a wide range of exciting career paths throughout the corporate, public and practice sectors that can lead up to senior positions.

Any company that you name will employ accountants either working in the firm full time or as a consultant asked to come in to advise the company. Either way accountants are there to feed into the senior managers and directors to help them make decisions about the future direction of the company. The role of an accountant is so much more than writing reports and counting money – they have to be good at communicating with a wide range of people; at managing teams of people; and be able to come up with solutions to problems.

Becoming an accountant takes hard work and commitment but the rewards at the end are worth it. Individuals need to study towards a professional accountancy qualification and it is important that you choose a qualification that suits you and your needs from a respected and recognised professional body. The advantage of having a recognised qualification is that throughout your career any company you want to work for will know that you have the skills and knowledge to do your job to the highest standard.

ACCA (Association of Chartered Certified Accountants) is the largest and fastest-growing international accountancy body with 260,000 students and 110,000 members in 170 countries. Each year, over 19,000 graduates register with ACCA because it opens the door to a future that is diverse, challenging and constantly surprising. Our mission is to be the leading global professional accountancy body by reputation, influence and size, offering first choice qualifications to people of application, ability and ambition around the world who seek a rewarding career in accountancy, finance and management.

ACCA is committed to providing students and members the knowledge and expertise needed to remain competitive and successful. ACCA has always been associated with flexibility and freedom of choice. Entry into the accountancy profession can begin at 16, by registering onto the CAT (Certified Accounting Technician) scheme. Accounting technicians support the work of qualified accountants in areas such as audit, taxation and maintaining financial records. Obtaining a CAT qualification acts as an ideal stepping stone to registering to the ACCA Qualification to become a fully qualified accountant.

Alternatively, registration onto the ACCA Qualification can take place after A Levels or even after completing a degree. Certain relevant degrees are eligible to exemptions from some of the ACCA exams which enables the student to complete the qualification a lot quicker. As well as completing the exams students must also complete three years relevant work experience as an accountant before they are awarded with the ACCA Qualification.

Once you complete your exams and professional experience you become a member of ACCA and can use these initials after your name. You can choose to work in any type of industry around the world. Having an ACCA accountancy qualification will mark you out to employers as being highly skilled with the right experience. The opportunities for career progression are limitless.

get the complete picture

The ACCA Qualification is more than a set of exams. We believe that what you learn on the journey is as important as the qualification itself. Through a blend of experience and theory, you'll see the full picture – preparing you to make a contribution from day one.

ACCA. Accountants with **perspective.**
www.accaglobal.com/theview

Accounting technician

Accounting technicians work in a variety of roles, often alongside professionally qualified Chartered Accountants. They are involved in the day-to-day practical work of accountancy and finance, including the preparation of information and accounts and the interpretation of computer information, such as audit tax and payroll. Accounting technicians are widely employed in public finance, industry and commerce, and private practice. Their roles range from accounts clerks to finance managers. A growing number of accounting technicians provide a range of services direct to the public and manage their own practice. Many go on to qualify with the senior chartered accountancy bodies.

Qualifications and Training

There are no set entry qualifications, but you must be confident with maths. Some employers may prefer you to have GCSEs (A–C) or equivalent in English and maths. Previous experience of office work and good IT skills, especially experience of spreadsheets and databases, is also valuable.

You could begin as an accounts clerk doing basic duties, and take work-based training or a part-time college course to qualify as a technician with the Association of Accounting Technicians (AAT) or Association of Chartered Certified Accountants (ACCA). You may not have to do the first stages of accounting technician training if you already have an A level or equivalent in accounting, previous relevant work experience or a basic bookkeeping qualification. AAT and ACCA qualifications comprise a foundation, an intermediate and a technician stage. The AAT or the ACCA can advise you about where to find a training place. It is also sometimes possible to do an apprenticeship as an accounting technician.

Personal Qualities and Skills

You must be thorough and methodical and enjoy working with figures. Good IT skills and the ability to work as part of a team are also very important. Some positions involve considerable responsibility and/or the pressure of deadlines.

Starting Salary

There are often significant differences between salaries in London and the South-East compared to other regions. Starting salaries for trainees range from £10,000 to £18,500. Qualified technicians earn from £18,000 to £25,000. Accounting technicians with other management responsibilities can earn far more than this.

The Association of Accounting Technicians (AAT), 154 Clerkenwell Road, London EC1R 5AD; 020 7415 7500; www.aat.org.uk

Association of Chartered Certified Accountants (ACCA), ACCA Connect, 2 Central Quay, 89 Hydepark Street, Glasgow G3 8BW; 0141 582 2000; www.accaglobal.com

Financial Services Skills Council, 51 Gresham Street, London EC2V 7HQ; 020 7216 7366; www.fssc.org.uk

info

ACTOR

see Performing Arts

ACTUARY

Actuaries use their knowledge of mathematics, statistics, economics and business to assess financial risks and probabilities. Traditionally their work is mainly concerned with pensions, life assurance and other types of insurance, but they may also work in investment and other business areas where major financial risks are involved.

They create statistical and mathematical models to analyse past events and predict the financial outcome of different situations. For example, in insurance they may study accident rates or medical data to develop and price new insurance policies, making sure that there are sufficient funds to cover liabilities but still make a profit for the insurance company. Insurance companies are required by law to employ at least one actuary to advise on financial management.

Nearly half of actuaries work for consultancies providing specialist actuarial services to businesses of every kind. They advise on business recovery, acquisitions and employee benefit schemes. Central government also has its own actuarial departments, which provide actuarial support and information across central government, its agencies and the National Health Service.

Qualifications and Training

To qualify as an actuary you must become a student member of one of the professional bodies; either the Faculty or Institute of Actuaries. Minimum entry qualifications are three GCSEs grades A–C including English and two A levels one of which must be maths and for which you must have a grade B. If you have a second class honours degree in any subject, A level maths grade C is acceptable. If you have a degree in maths or actuarial science you do not need a maths A level. If your degree is in maths or a highly numerate discipline a third class honours degree is acceptable. In practice, entry to the profession is competitive, so the majority of recruits are graduates. Once you have completed your professional training, study and examinations you become a Fellow of either the Institute or Faculty.

To qualify as a Fellow of the Faculty or Institute of Actuaries, you must pass 15 professional examinations. After one year's work experience and appropriate examinations you should reach associate membership and after three years' work experience and appropriate exams you should reach fellowship.

If you have a degree or postgraduate qualification in actuarial science, statistics or economics, you may be exempt from some or all of the exams at the Core Technical Stage and some at the next stage. Please contact the Institute of Actuaries for further details of exemptions.

Personal Qualities and Skills

You must have excellent maths and statistical skills and be able to understand and explain complex information. You should have a thorough understanding of business and economics, be a great communicator and be aware of the bigger picture while paying attention to fine detail.

Starting Salary

Graduate trainees earn between £23,000 and £26,000 and this rises to between £26,000 and £40,000 for part-qualified associate actuaries. Qualified actuaries with at least five years' experience can earn up to £75,000 and some salaries in the profession reach more than £100,000.

The Actuarial Education Company, 31 Bath Street, Abingdon, Oxfordshire OX14 3FF; 01235 550005; www.acted.co.uk

The Association of Consulting Actuaries, Warnford Court, 29 Throgmorton Street, London EC2N 2AT; 020 7382 4954; www.aca.org.uk

Faculty of Actuaries, Maclaurin House, 18 Dublin Street, Edinburgh EH1 3PP; 0131 240 1300; www.actuaries.org.uk

Institute of Actuaries, Napier House, 4 Worcester Street, Oxford OX1 2AW; 01865 268200; www.actuaries.org.uk

Financial Services Skills Council, 51 Gresham Street, London EC2V 7HQ; 020 7216 7366; www.fssc.org.uk

Government Actuary's Department (GAD), Finlaison House, 15–17 Furnival Street, London EC4A 1AB; 020 7211 2601; www.gad.gov.uk

Insurance Careers; www.insurancecareers.org

info

ADVERTISING

(*see also* Marketing, Market Researcher *and* Public Relations Officer)
Communication is the heart of this complex industry, providing a wide range of openings, many with agencies that plan, organise and run advertising campaigns. Working on behalf of clients, advertising agencies study the product or service to be advertised and its market. They then plan how it should be sold and distributed, and how the media might be used to the best advantage in this process.

Account executive

Account executives are responsible within the agency for a particular client or group of clients. They interpret the client's wishes; coordinate and supervise the work of others within the agency, such as creatives, account planners, copywriters and scriptwriters; seek advice from other experts such as media executives; and then present the ideas most likely to meet with the client's approval.

Account planner

Account planners consider the client's brief and work to identify the ideal audience and optimum method of getting the client's message across. They analyse market research and other data and provide the creative team with the information that will help them develop the most effective campaign. They may also work on forward planning for the agency, identifying likely future clients based on market data they have researched.

Art editor/executive director

This position involves coordinating the work of the creative department, which converts the client's original intentions into a visual form for approval. Others, including copywriters, may elaborate upon this.

Artist

(*see also* Art and Design)
Agency artists prepare initial visual layouts of adverts, posters and displays, and produce final artwork for printing. They need to be competent in using design software.

Copywriter and scriptwriter

The writers in the agency produce headings, text, jingles and copy for articles in journals, and scripts for films and commercials. Copywriters often work closely with the Art Editor and visualisers.

Media executive

Media executives provide expert advice on the advertising medium – for example, television, cinema, posters, newspapers, journals – that will best suit a particular campaign, and negotiate the most economical rates.

Qualifications and Training

Advertising is a fiercely competitive sector. Most entrants to jobs in advertising have either a degree or an HND. Any subject is acceptable, but some employers prefer degrees or HNDs in advertising, business studies, marketing, English or consumer science. Smaller agencies may take you without a degree, particularly if you have some relevant work experience. Work experience is extremely valuable, helping you to understand how agencies work, but even this experience is hard to come by, so you may have to consider doing voluntary work. Some agencies offer formal work experience schemes and details of these appear on the Institute of Practitioners in Advertising website. There are many courses in marketing, communications and media studies at many levels. These may provide useful background, but they won't necessarily make you more employable. There are a few highly respected postgraduate courses in advertising including a diploma in copy-writing at West Herts College and a postgraduate diploma in advertising at Falmouth College of Art and Design.

Most of the training is on the job, learning from colleagues, and you are usually considered to be a trainee for about two years. The IPA offers induction courses and continuing professional development courses and the Chartered Institute of Marketing offers a range of part-time and distance learning courses for those who are already working in the sector.

Personal Qualities and Skills

Excellent communication skills at every level are extremely important. Being able to deal with people, write clearly and work creatively are all essential skills. Many roles require you to be persuasive and tactful, and to be a media planner you need to be highly numerate. Advertising is a highly pressured business so you have to be thick skinned and keep calm when chasing deadlines.

info

Account Planning Group, 16 Creighton Avenue, London N10 1NU; 020 8444 3692; www.apg.org.uk

The Advertising Association (AA), 7th Floor North, Artillery House, 11–19 Artillery Row, London SW1P 1RT; 020 7340 1100; www.adassoc.org.uk

British Interactive Media Association (BIMA), Briarlea House, Southend Road, South Green, Billericay, Essex CM11 2PR; www.bima.co.uk

Chartered Institute of Marketing (CIM), Moor Hall, Cookham, Maidenhead, Berks SL6 9QH; 01628 427500; www.cim.co.uk

The Communication Advertising and Marketing Education Foundation (CAM), Moor Hall, Cookham, Maidenhead, Berkshire SL6 9QH; 01628 427120; www.camfoundation.com

The Creative Circle, 22 Poland Street, London W1F 8QQ; 020 7734 9334; www.creativecircle.co.uk

Creative and Cultural Skills, 4th Floor, Lafone House, The Leathermarket, Weston Street, London SE1 3HN; 020 7015 1800; www.ccskills.org.uk

Design and Art Directors Association (D&AD), 9 Graphite Square, Vauxhall Walk, London SE11 5EE; 020 7840 1111; www.dandad.org

Institute of Practitioners in Advertising (IPA), 44 Belgrave Square, London SW1X 8QS; 020 7235 7020; www.ipa.co.uk

The Media Circle, 44 Belgrave Square, London SW1X 8QS; 020 7201 8252; www.mediacircle.org

Starting Salary

Starting salaries range from £12,000 to £24,000 depending on your job title and the size of the agency. Many agencies are based in London and the South-East. Where there are jobs in the regions, starting salaries range from £9,500 to £16,000.

AERIAL ERECTOR

Aerial erectors fix aerials to roof structures along with the necessary cabling to feed televisions, VCRs and radio receivers. Many installers also offer cable and satellite dish installation, and a number of businesses specialise in these areas as well as offering standard communication aerial installation.

Qualifications and Training

No formal qualifications are necessary, but many employers would expect a good general standard of education; some companies like you to have three or four GCSEs grades A–C. Training is on the job, but the main trade organisation in the sector, the CAI, has developed a good range of basic and more advanced training courses. It offers short courses in basic radio and TV installation, basic satellite installation and motorised dish installation. It also offers courses on customer relations and training in working safely at heights. Through the CAI you can work for NVQ levels 2 and 3. Level 2 is aimed at installing aerials and communications equipment on individual private properties. The level 3 qualification is for technicians who are installing systems to blocks of flats, commercial premises and large organisations such as hospitals or schools. For aerial installers, there is a City & Guilds Certificate in Digital Television Aerial Installation at level 2. Many installers go on to do other courses in electronics engineering, maintenance engineering or communications engineering. There is a wide range of courses, full and part time, in all these areas.

Personal Qualities and Skills

You have to be very practical, have good numeracy skills and be quite happy working up high. You should be able to get on well with people. You need to be a good problem solver and a thorough and meticulous worker.

Starting Salary

Trainees earn between £12,000 and £15,000 and with three years' experience you can earn £16,000 to £19,000. Technicians with management or planning responsibilities can earn £25,000 plus.

info

Confederation of Aerial Industries (CAI), Fulton House, Fulton Road, Wembley, Middlesex HA9 0TF; 020 8902 8998; www.cai.org.uk; e-mail: office@cai.org.uk

Local Job Centre Plus and Careers/ Connexions Centres

AGRICULTURE

(*see also* Farming)

The work in agriculture involves cultivating crops and raising livestock for food, energy and raw materials.

Agricultural contractor

Agricultural contractors employ experienced workers and managers to provide specific help to farmers at certain times of the year. About 60 per cent of farms use contractors from time to time.

Qualifications and Training

While qualifications are not essential, NVQs are available in relevant subjects. These, together with certificates at national or advanced national level in agriculture or agricultural contracting, from a college of agriculture, improve chances of finding employment.

Personal Qualities and Skills

Agricultural contractors must have an appreciation of farmers' needs, combined with efficiency, reliability and a good business sense.

Starting Salary

Variable, depending on whether or not the contractor is an employee or running his or her own concern, and the size of the operation, but in the region of £10,000 to £25,000.

Lantra is the Sector Skills Council for the environmental and land-based sector. For further information on training, education and careers within the environmental and land-based sector contact: Lantra Connect, Lantra House, Stoneleigh, Kenilworth, Warwickshire CV8 2LG; 0845 707 8007; www.lantra.co.uk; e-mail: connect@lantra.co.uk

Agricultural engineering

see Engineering

Agricultural surveying

see Surveying

AMBULANCE SERVICE

Most of the work in the ambulance service is directly with patients, providing pre-hospital care and transportation in response to emergency and urgent calls, or providing transport for those unable, for medical reasons, to make their own way to hospital. There are two distinct areas of front-line work: Accident and Emergency and Patient Transport Services.

Ambulance care assistants

Ambulance care assistants are mainly concerned with transporting elderly, infirm or handicapped people to hospital. They work within Patient Transport Services (PTS) and are mainly involved in routine transportation work. Such work does not involve emergency duties but staff are trained in Basic Life Support Skills, First Aid and Patient Care. Staff may also work in hospital units.

Ambulance control and communication

Staff requirements vary among ambulance services, although most require a good general standard of education. Control staff can move to ambulance duties providing they meet the entry requirements and successfully complete the selection process.

Ambulance paramedics

Paramedics are trained to use advanced life support techniques and administer a range of drugs for the emergency treatment of a number of conditions. In order for paramedics to maintain their qualification, they must update their skills regularly and prove their competence through examination, and are only allowed to practise if they are state registered. They must comply with Council for Professions Supplementary to Medicine (CPSM) regulations. There has to be a paramedic on each emergency ambulance.

Ambulance technicians

Ambulance technicians work alongside paramedics responding to 999 and urgent calls. They make decisions on the treatment and transportation of ill and injured patients. Their work involves a wide range of skills, including resuscitation, oxygen and some drug therapy, fracture splintage, wound dressing and pain relief. The type of work undertaken by both technicians and paramedics is varied and demanding. Both paramedics and technicians are trained in advanced driving skills and may work in ambulance motor vehicles, air ambulances or on motorcycles.

Emergency medical dispatcher

Emergency medical dispatchers work in central control rooms answering calls from GPs and the public, and ensuring that resources are deployed effectively and efficiently. Some ambulance services run a despatch prioritising system for emergency calls, which are analysed and placed in order of priority. When a caller gives information about a life-threatening situation, staff give advice over the phone while the ambulance travels to the scene.

Qualifications and Training

Ambulance care assistants need to be over 18 years of age and to have had a full current UK driving licence for at least one year and often two. Some ambulance services simply require a good standard of education, while others specify GCSEs or equivalent, including English and maths. Selection includes a medical assessment to ascertain that applicants are physically fit with good eyesight. Training takes up to three weeks, covering moving and handling techniques, first aid, basic patient care skills and safe driving techniques.

Technicians must meet the minimum ambulance care assistant requirements, although frequently services will require higher academic qualifications. Some services allow for direct entry technicians and others recruit internally from the ambulance care assistant grade. Technicians spend up to three weeks on an intensive driving course followed by six to nine weeks training in pre-hospital emergency care. This includes regular examinations and assessments. They then work under supervision for up to a year gaining experience completing competency assessments.

Paramedics must have at least one year of experience as a technician and then pass written and practical examinations. Intensive training lasts 10 to 12 weeks. Technicians and paramedics are required to attend regular training and reassessment. Paramedics re-qualify every three years.

Control and Communication staff requirements vary among services; most require a good general standard of education. Control staff can move to ambulance duties providing they meet the entry requirements and successfully complete the selection process.

Personal Qualities and Skills

Ambulance personnel must be honest, show initiative, have good people skills, a caring personality and be prepared to work with all types of people. They have to be well organised and work well as part of a team, though able to make their own decisions when necessary. They must stay calm under pressure and be good communicators. Physical fitness is essential as staff regularly lift patients and equipment.

Control and Communication staff need strong powers of concentration because calls involve assimilating a lot of information quickly and making decisions rapidly. They must be able to take clear notes and operate high technology equipment.

Technicians and paramedics require a high level of technical knowledge, a cool head in emergencies and the manual dexterity to carry out treatment in awkward conditions. Paramedics need to cope with advanced theoretical studies and be able to apply clinical judgement in emergencies.

Starting Salary

An ambulance care assistant working in the NHS earns between £12,200 to just under £17,000. A paramedic earns between £19,200 and £25,000 a year. A fully qualified ambulance technician earns around £19,800 a year. Additional allowances may be paid to staff on standby, and to staff based in London or the South-East.

info

NHS Learning and Development;
08000 150 850; e-mail:
learning@nhscareers.nhs.uk

NHS Careers, PO Box 376,
Bristol BS99 3EY; 0845 606 0655;
www.nhscareers.nhs.uk

Ambulance Service Association,
Friars House, 157–168 Blackfriars Road,
London SE1 8EZ; 020 7928 9620;
www.asa.uk.net

Skills for Health, 1st Floor,
Goldsmiths House, Broad Plain,
Bristol BS2 0JP; 0117 922 1155;
www.skillsforhealth.org.uk

ANIMALS

(*see also* Veterinary Science *and* Zoology)

There is a wide range of occupations that involve working with animals. An obvious prerequisite for anyone wanting to work in this field is to have a love of animals and concern for their welfare.

Animal care worker

Animal care workers feed, groom, clean, exercise and generally care for small animals of many kinds. They may also have to keep records and to deal with members of the public. They work in many different settings including kennels, catteries, animal rescue centres, open farms and animal sanctuaries. They also work as kennel assistants at quarantine centres and as auxiliaries at animal hospitals.

Qualifications and Training

The right attitude and some relevant experience either paid or voluntary, is more important than qualifications. Some organisations may require you to have passed GCSEs, but this is by no means standard. Work with animals is popular, so it is often much easier if you have done some voluntary work; see the Info panel to find out where to volunteer. This demonstrates to employers that you really are committed to this caring work. There are Edexcel/BTEC certificate and diploma courses available in animal care. For these you will need three GCSEs grades A–C and one should be in a science subject.

Personal Qualities and Skills

You must be kind and gentle when handling animals, but you must also be calm and confident. You need to be patient and you can't afford to be squeamish. While being caring is essential, you must be resilient enough not to get too easily upset, in for example animal rescue situations, where you might be dealing with animals that have been badly treated or severely neglected. You need to be practical, you might need record-keeping skills and you should be good at dealing with humans as well as animals.

Starting Salary

Pay is often low in this sector, especially with charitable organisations, which want to minimise staff costs. Your pay is often around minimum wage level, but it can rise to £12,000 to £14,000 with experience and responsibility.

Lantra, Lantra House, Stoneleigh Park, Nr Coventry, Warwickshire CV8 2LG; 0845 707 8007; www.lantra.co.uk

RSPCA, Wilberforce Way, Southwater, Horsham, West Sussex RH13 9RS; www.rspca.org.uk

PDSA, Whitechapel Way, Priorslee, Telford, Shropshire TF2 9PQ; 0800 917 2509; www.pdsa.org.uk

Blue Cross, Shilton Road, Burford, Oxfordshire OX18 4PF; 01993 822651; www.bluecross.org.uk

College of Animal Welfare, London Road, Godmanchester, Cambridgeshire PE29 2LJ; 0870 062 1122; www.caw.ac.uk

Animal Care College, Ascot House, High Street, Ascot, Berkshire SL5 7JG; 0870 730 8433; www.animalcarecollege.co.uk

Volunteering England; www.volunteering.org.uk

Volunteer Scotland; www.volunteerscotland.info

info

Animal groomer

Animal grooming is a growing industry, with more dog and cat owners using the services provided by grooming salons of which there are 2,000 in the UK. Most are small private businesses, and some are part of other establishments, including pet shops, garden centres, boarding and breeding kennels. Some mobile groomers visit animals in their own home.

Each breed has different requirements and there are many types of coat, which all require specialist skills and techniques. The work involves bathing, shampooing, drying, clipping, trimming and brushing a variety of long- and short-coated animals. Specialist procedures include nail clipping, teeth cleaning, ear care and treatments for parasites.

Qualifications and Training

There are two main routes into training: a fee-paying course at a private grooming training centre or learning on the job. Candidates with practical animal-grooming experience may enrol for the City and Guilds Dog Grooming

Certificate 775. This two-part exam, with a written paper and a practical element, tests candidates' skills on three different types of animal. This qualification shows employers that the groomer has had correct training and gives customers confidence that the groomer is competent.

The Advanced Grooming Diploma tests the expertise and skill required of the experienced groomer working in a commercial environment. A good working knowledge of the Kennel Club Breed Standards, styles and trimming techniques is required in order to pass all components. The exam consists of a written paper and seven practical modules, which can be taken over a period of time until all seven are complete, working at a timescale to suit the individual.

Starting Salary

This varies from area to area, and hours and rates of pay are negotiable. A general range is £8,000 to £12,000, but more if you run your own business.

info

British Dog Groomers Association, Bedford Business Centre, 170 Mile Road, Bedford MK42 9TW; 01234 273933; fax: 01234 273550; www.petcare.org.uk; e-mail: info@petcare.org.uk

Lantra Connect, Lantra House, Stoneleigh, Kenilworth, Warwickshire CV8 2LG; 0845 707 8007 (Lantra Connect – Helpline); www.lantra.co.uk; e-mail: connect@lantra.co.uk

Local Job Centre Plus and Careers/ Connexions Centres

Animal technician

Animal technicians are a specialised and distinct group of professionals who are responsible for the care and welfare of animals used in biomedical research. Governments around the world require that new medicines have been extensively tested on animals before allowing human clinical trials. Testing is also undertaken on veterinary medicines and other products which may have an effect on human health. Animal technicians are responsible for caring for the animals, undertaking observations, sampling for the scientific studies, and ensuring that the strict laws controlling their use are followed at all times. Applicants should have a genuine desire to work with animals and must demonstrate concern and respect for their wellbeing.

Qualifications and Training

The minimum entry qualifications are five GCSEs at grade C or above, but some entrants have A levels or a degree. The Institute of Animal Technology offers five levels of qualification, from a basic one-year certificate to a postgraduate MSc. You can get exemption from certain modules of these courses if you can offer sciences at A or degree level. These qualifications can be taken as distance learning modules or at local colleges through day release courses.

Personal Qualities and Skills

You have to be comfortable handling animals and you must be kind, caring and calm when doing so. You also have to accept that you will have to do things that are stressful for animals, so you need to be prepared for this. You must be practical, thorough and meticulous, since you have to record scientific information accurately.

Starting Salary

Salaries for trainees range from £10,000 to £12,000 and from £12,000 to £15,000 for qualified technicians, but there is no national agreed rate for this work. A senior laboratory manager can earn up to £35,000.

Institute of Animal Technology, 5 South Parade, Summertown, Oxford OX2 7JL; www.iat.org.uk

Lantra, Lantra House, Stoneleigh Park, Nr Coventry, Warwickshire CV8 2LG; 0845 707 8007; www.lantra.co.uk

Assistance dog trainer

Assistance dog trainers and instructors train dogs to help people with physical disabilities, hearing or sight impairments, or who are prone to seizures, to live independently. There are four types of assistance dogs. Guide Dogs for the Blind help people to avoid obstacles, find entrances, stairs etc. Disability assistance dogs do such things as pick up a telephone, press an emergency button or load a washing machine. Hearing dogs alert people to sounds such as a doorbell or a telephone. Seizure alert dogs watch for tell-tale signs of an impending seizure, warn their owners and care for them if a seizure does occur. Most trainers are employed by the four relevant charities; they are listed in the Info panel. Trainers work closely with dogs to teach them the skills they need and then they work with the dog and the human with whom it is going to live to teach that person how to use the dog and also how to care for it properly.

Qualifications and Training

You must be at least 18 years old and have a full, clean driving licence. Academic and other requirements vary between the different employer organisations, so you should contact them for details. In general, you will need qualifications which are relevant to your client group, eg know British Sign Language if you are working with hearing impaired people and their assistance dogs. GCSEs grades A–C may be required and some employers prefer one of your subjects to be a science.

Personal Qualities and Skills

You must have great patience and a real understanding of and interest in animal behaviour. You should also get on really well with people, who often need a lot of encouragement and support when they first acquire an assistance dog. You should be practical, well organised and good at thinking up solutions to problems.

Starting Salary

Starting salaries are around £11,000 a year rising to £15,000 with experience. Salaries for trainers working with hearing dogs are a little bit higher.

info

Guide Dogs for the Blind, Head Office, Hillfields, Burghfield Common, Reading, Berks RG7 3YG; 0118 983 5555; www.guidedogs.org.uk

Hearing Dogs for Deaf People, The Grange, Wycombe Road, Saunderton, Bucks HP27 9NS; 01844 348100; www.hearing-dogs.co.uk

Support Dogs, 21 Jessops Riverside, Brightside Lane, Sheffield S9 2RX;

0870 609 3476; www.support-dogs.org.uk

Canine Partners, Mill Lane, Heyshott, Midhurst, West Sussex GU29 0ED; 0845 658 0480; www.c-p-i.org.uk

Dogs for the Disabled, The Frances Hay Centre, Blacklocks Hill, Banbury, Oxfordshire OX17 2BS; 08700 776600; www.dogsforthedisabled.org

Dog handler

Dog handlers work for the Police, the armed services, HM Revenue and Customs, fire and rescue services and private security firms. There are many examples of the kinds of work in which dogs and dog handlers are involved. Police dogs track missing people, help control crowds or guard prisoners. In the army dogs are used to find injured people, guard premises and equipment and even search for landmines. Doing customs work, handlers get their dogs to sniff out drugs, tobacco and food. In the prison service dogs are mainly used for guarding activities. The Fire Service sometimes uses dogs to search for survivors after fires and other disasters. Private security firms mainly use dogs to patrol and guard premises and equipment.

Qualifications and Training

In most organisations you are not taken on as a dog handler. You start like any other recruit and dog handling is a specialist area for which you may then get the opportunity to train. You need to check the entry requirements of the other different career paths, but many will require you to have at least four GCSEs grades A–C, including maths and English. Check the info panel and other career entries in this guide.

Personal Qualities and Skills

It is essential that you love working with dogs, that you are confident and sure of yourself when handling them. The bond that builds up between handler and dog is often very strong and you may have to spend a lot of time working on your own, just with your dog. Depending on the organisation you are working for, you may have to work in stressful or dangerous situations, or in uncomfortable and unpleasant conditions. You also need to be good at communicating with people.

Starting Salary

With a wide range of different employers, the salary range is equally wide. A rough guide would be around £15,000 for new dog handlers and up to £25,000 or more for handlers with experience and other management responsibilities.

---

info

Police service portal; www.police.uk

Security Industry Authority (SIA), PO Box 9, Newcastle upon Tyne NE82 6YX; 0870 243 0100; www.the-sia.org.uk

RAF Careers; 0845 605 5555; www.rafcareers.com

National Search and Rescue; www.nsarda.org.uk

British Army; 08457 300111; www.army.mod.uk

HM Revenue and Customs; www.hmrc.gov

Groom

Grooms look after all aspects of the horse's welfare. Their duties include grooming and strapping, mucking out, feeding, cleaning tack, saddling up, exercising and leading both mounted and dismounted, elementary veterinary care and sick nursing, preparation for and travelling with horses by road, sea and air and care of the horse when at grass. Grooms work in racing stables, hunting establishments, private stables, studs and breeding concerns, riding schools, occasionally (seasonally) with polo ponies and at trekking centres.

Qualifications and Training

No formal qualifications are necessary but it is recommended that grooms take the British Horse Society examinations stages 1, 2 and 3 in Horse Knowledge and Care, which comprise the Grooms Certificate. Alternative options are NVQs in Horse Care, levels 1, 2 and 3.

Training is usually on the job and should be sufficient to prepare students for exams. There are also courses of varying lengths to prepare students for particular exams; however, the fees are often high. Funding may be available for the achievement of British Horse Society qualifications providing that the person is not eligible for any other type of funding.

Personal Qualities and Skills

A love of horses is essential, plus patience and the willingness to work long hours and perform many routine tasks. A heavy goods vehicle driving licence may be an advantage.

Starting Salary

Stable staff generally earn the national minimum wage. In some cases food and accommodation may be free, in others they may be deducted from the wage. The hours may be long. The BHS issues guidelines on salaries for those with BHS qualifications; details are on their website.

info

Association of British Riding Schools (ABRS), Queens Chambers, 38–40 Queen Street, Penzance, Cornwall TR18 4BH; 01736 369440; www.abrs-info.org

British Horseracing Board (BHB), 151 Shaftesbury Avenue, London WC2H 8AL; 020 7152 0000; e-mail: info@careersinracing.com; www.careersinracing.com

British Horse Society, Stoneleigh, Deer Park, Kenilworth, Warwickshire CV8 2XZ; 0870 120 2244; www.bhs.org.uk

British Racing School (BRS), Snailwell Road, Newmarket, Suffolk CB8 7NU; 01638 665103; www.brs.org.uk

Lantra, Lantra House, Stoneleigh Park, Nr Coventry, Warwickshire CV8 2LG; 0845 707 8007; www.lantra.co.uk

Northern Racing College (NRC), The Stables, Rossington Hall, Great North Road, Doncaster, South Yorkshire DN11 0HN; 01302 861000; www.northernracingcollege.co.uk

Thoroughbred Breeders' Association, British Stud Staff Training Scheme, Stanstead House, The Avenue, Newmarket, Suffolk CB8 9AA; 01638 661321; www.thoroughbredbreeders association.co.uk

Kennel work

Kennel staff ensure that the animals in their care have clean accommodation, are fed a regular and nutritious diet, kept clean and well groomed and given sufficient exercise. Where animals are sick or recovering from an operation, the kennel staff must also be able to provide adequate nursing care.

There are a number of different types of kennel – greyhound kennels train dogs for racing, hunt kennels for hunting – and they involve a lot of outdoor work, exercising the dogs and perhaps travelling to meetings. There are quarantine kennels licensed by the Department for the Environment, Food and Rural Affairs (DEFRA) and breeding kennels where duties also include weaning and training puppies, preparing dogs for shows and possibly handling them. Boarding kennels look after animals while their owners are away. Some of the racing and quarantine kennels are large operations situated near racing stadia, airports and ports but others may be smaller, family-run concerns.

Qualifications and Training

No formal qualifications are needed to work in kennels and most employers prefer school leavers to train on the job. The NVQ level 2 in Animal Care and the

National Small Animal Care Certificate are nationally recognised by the industry and provide a good base for further study. Many training organisations and agricultural colleges throughout the country offer this qualification. Entry requirements vary depending on the institution.

Personal Qualities and Skills

Good health, general fitness and stamina are required for this manual, physically demanding, outdoor work. Kennel staff must be unsentimental about animals but at the same time have a genuine concern for their wellbeing; they require patience and a placid but firm nature. A willingness to work long days, weekends and public holidays is also required.

Starting Salary

£150–£200+ a week.

Lantra Connect, Lantra House, Stoneleigh, Kenilworth, Warwickshire CV8 2LG; 0845 707 8007 (Lantra Connect – Helpline); www.lantra.co.uk; e-mail: connect@lantra.co.uk	*Our Dogs*, 5 Oxford Road, Station Approach, Manchester M60 1SX; 0161 228 1984 (weekly magazine featuring job offers and advertisements from kennels. Also publishes *Cats*)
Animal Care College, Ascot House, High Street, Ascot, Berkshire SL5 7JG; 01344 628269; www.animalcarecollege.co.uk; admin@rtc-associates.freeserve.co.uk	Local Job Centre Plus and Careers/ Connexions Centres *Running Your Own Boarding Kennels* (Kogan Page)

info

Jockey

Jockeys are employed by trainers of flat racing and National Hunt (jump) racehorses to ride horses at race meetings. They may ride for one trainer or for several. To become a jockey it is necessary first to work in a racing stable as an apprentice jockey or stablehand.

Only those showing most talent – about 1 in 10 – are chosen to ride in a race. The others remain as stable hands, and may be promoted to Head Lad (this title applies to boys and girls).

Stable hand

Stable hands (formerly known as 'stable lads') do a lot of labouring work, mucking out, fetching straw, filling haynets and sweeping. They must also learn to groom and exercise the horses, and usually become responsible for a certain number of their 'own'. On race days, a stable lad will accompany a horse, groom him, walk him round before the race and lead him into the winner's enclosure if he wins.

Qualifications and Training

No specific educational qualifications are needed to become a jockey. Some experience of riding is useful but serious training is given by the stable. The racing industry has introduced NVQs, levels 1, 2 and 3 in racehorse care and management, and Foundation and Advanced Modern Apprenticeships. Flat-racing apprenticeships start at 16 and last until the age of 24. National Hunt apprenticeships start at 17–18 and last until the age of 25.

There is a nine-week training course available at the British Racing School in Newmarket, funded by racing, and open to school leavers who wish to work in a racing yard. Pupils are taught to ride, look after horses and carry out elementary stable management. The Northern Racing School at Doncaster runs a 10-week residential course for school leavers who wish to work in a racing yard and for those already in the industry who wish to further their training as stable staff. Training is compulsory for all 16- to 19-year-olds employed by the industry.

Personal Qualities and Skills

Apprentice jockeys must be prepared to work long hours in all weather conditions. At 16, flat-racing apprentices should weigh 7–8 stone (44–51 kg), girls 8–9 stone (51–57 kg); National Hunt jockeys may be heavier. Jockeys need strong hands and arms, and must be able to deal with nervous horses in a calm, confident and unemotional way. Jockeys must also be able to work within the strict, rather conservative traditions of the racing world.

Starting Salary

Apprentice jockeys and stable hands over 19 with a year's experience earn about £140 a week. Apprentice and conditional jockeys receive their normal wage plus half the riding fee when racing. Racing jockeys' salaries vary according to their success; there is a rate per ride plus a percentage of the prize money.

info

British Racing School, Snailwell Road, Newmarket, Suffolk CB8 7NU; 01638 665103; www.brs.org.uk; e-mail: careers@brs.org.uk

British Horseracing Board (BHB), 42 Portman Square, London W1H 6EN; 020 7396 0011; www.bhb.co.uk;

e-mail: info@bhb.co.uk; 'Careers in the horseracing industry' can be downloaded from the website

Northern Racing College, The Stables, Rossington Hall, Great North Road, Doncaster DN11 0HN; 01302 861000; www.northernracingcollege.co.uk; info@nrcdonc.demon.co.uk

Riding instructor

Riding instructors teach people, individuals or groups, how to ride horses. They may also accompany riders who hire horses by the hour, and be required to help train horses and look after them, cleaning tack and stables. The work includes teaching in riding schools and clubs and in summer camps, training competition riders and occasionally sitting as a judge or examiner.

Qualifications and Training

To take the British Horse Society's Assistant Instructor certificate, candidates must be members of the society and, if under 18, have four GCSEs, one of which should be English. On completion of Stages 1, 2 and 3, the Preliminary Teaching Test, an approved first aid certificate and 500 hours of teaching experience, they are awarded the Assistant Instructor's certificate.

There are several methods of training: at a riding school, paying fees for instruction, board and lodging – the courses can be as short as three months or as long as a year, depending on the type of course; or as a BHS Apprentice at a BHS approved riding centre, doing stable work while receiving instruction. This takes approximately one year. Pupils pay for their keep. For more information on the BHS apprenticeship scheme, contact the BHS Approvals Office. After being awarded the Assistant Instructor's certificate, candidates may take the Intermediate Instructor's exams after reaching the age of 20. At 22, Intermediate Instructors may go on to take the British Horse Society Instructor's certificate. The Fellowship may be taken from 25 years of age.

Personal Qualities and Skills

Patience and authority, but above all a love of horses, are essential for this work. A riding instructor must enjoy being out of doors and get on well with people, especially children.

Starting Salary

£8,000–£10,000 for an Assistant Instructor as a rough guide; salaries vary depending on whether instruction is being provided, accommodation and stabling for the instructor's own horse and the instructor's age and experience.

British Horse Society, Stoneleigh, Deer Park, Kenilworth, Warwickshire CV8 2XZ; 0870 120 2244; www.bhs.org.uk

Info

RSPCA inspector

Inspectors for the Royal Society for the Prevention of Cruelty to Animals (RSPCA) deal with complaints from the general public about the alleged ill-treatment of animals and also perform more routine tasks. Inspectors have no power to take an animal from its owner unless the owner legally signs it over. They may caution people and, in some circumstances, the organisation will ensure that cases go before the courts. Inspectors also visit boarding kennels, pet shops and riding schools. They can be involved in physical rescues, often working unsociable hours and driving considerable distances.

Qualifications and Training

Applicants require GCSEs or equivalent in English language and a science, a valid driving licence and the ability to swim 50 metres fully clothed. Experience of working with animals is desirable.

About 20 inspectors are recruited each year from over 2,000 applicants. Training lasts six months and covers animal welfare legislation, basic veterinary training, mountain and boat rescue techniques, investigation skills, interview techniques, court work, animal-handling techniques, media training and public speaking. After written examinations, students serve six months' probation before becoming fully qualified. Minimum age for entry is 22.

Personal Qualities and Skills

Inspectors have to be very good at handling animals of all kinds. They must be calm, kind and authoritative. They need excellent interpersonal skills, must be able to be assertive, to deal with both sensitive and potentially confrontational situations. They must be able to speak in public, whether it is in court or in a classroom.

Starting Salary

In the RSPCA the starting salary is just under £16,000 a year. Fully trained inspectors earn from £20,000 to £22,500. An accommodation allowance is included in the salary and there are additional allowances for officers working near London.

info

Volunteering England;
www.volunteering.org.uk

Volunteering Scotland;
www.volunteerscotland.info

RSPCA, Wilberforce Way,
Southwater, Horsham, West Sussex
RH13 9RS; www.rspca.org.uk

SSPCA, Braehead Mains,
603 Queensferry Road, Edinburgh
EH4 6EA; 0131 339 0222;
www.scottishspca.org.uk

Zoo keeper

Keepers look after animals in zoos, mucking out their living quarters, preparing their food, feeding them and engaging in all other aspects of animal husbandry. There is increasing emphasis on education, public relations and research. Keepers work long hours – from 8 am to as late as 7 pm – much of the time outdoors and the work is often physically demanding.

Qualifications and Training

No specific qualifications are needed although an interest in biology or natural sciences is advantageous. On-the-job training is by a correspondence course followed by a City and Guilds qualification. However, many applicants for posts in zoos have done courses in Animal Care or Welfare. These are available at First, National and Higher National Diploma level and there are also related degree courses. Graduates are more likely to enter posts in education and research. Applications for such jobs far exceed the number of places available, and zoos prefer people to enquire only when a vacancy is advertised.

Personal Qualities and Skills

Affection and respect for animals, combined with an unsentimental approach, are essential. Keepers must have practical common sense, an interest in education and conservation and the ability to communicate effectively with the public.

Starting Salary

Salaries range from about £8,000+ to £13,000+.

Association of British Wild Animal Keepers; www.abwak.co.uk (Contact details for members of the Association can be found on the website)

Careers Working with Animals (Kogan Page)

ANTHROPOLOGIST

Anthropologists study the development of human societies, making comparisons between different communities and cultures. This academic discipline is linked with the other social sciences and with evolutionary biology. Much of the work still concerns non-industrial, 'primitive' or rural cultures, but changes brought about by contact with more sophisticated outside influences and pressures from 'modern' societies are an important aspect of study and many anthropologists now undertake research in urban or industrial societies. The career involves a combination of research, teaching and finding out more about the people being studied by going to live with them over a period of time.

Increasingly, anthropologists are finding employment as consultants, for instance in the development, health and humanitarian fields and in such professions as journalism, human resource management, planning, tourism and heritage, museum curatorship and medicine.

Qualifications and Training

A good degree in anthropology. Postgraduate study is usually required.

Personal Qualities and Skills

Those wishing to embark on this career must normally be committed to an academic way of life, although there is growing demand outside universities. Field researchers must be prepared to spend long spells abroad, often in basic conditions. Physical and mental stamina is required, as well as independence and resourcefulness. Anthropologists must be prepared to work on their own. However, as anthropology has diversified, so the ways of working life adopted by anthropologists have become more varied too and they now work in every imaginable setting, from offices and day-care centres to out in the field. Linguistic ability is useful.

Starting Salary

Salaries vary; around £12,000–£14,000 is a rough guide. Salaries may be very different when working on overseas projects.

Royal Anthropological Institute, 50 Fitzroy Street, London W1T 5BT; 020 7387 0455; fax: 020 7383 4235; www.therai.org.uk; e-mail: admin@therai.org.uk

ANTIQUE DEALER

The buying and selling of antiques for profit entails expert knowledge of the field, combined with sound managerial and business sense. Comparatively few people make a living at this trade, and many businesses are family concerns. Dealers frequently specialise in particular types of antiques, and trade among themselves as well as with private buyers and sellers. Dealers may sell from shops, antiques markets, antiques fairs and from home. An increasing number trade on the internet using auction sites such as eBay as well as their own websites.

Qualifications and Training

No specific qualifications are required, although a broad artistic background may be useful. The accepted route into the business is via a job with an established antique dealer, which provides an opportunity to learn the trade.

Personal Qualities and Skills

Above all, you must be genuinely interested in the antiques you are dealing with. You need a keen eye for detail, and the ability to investigate thoroughly. A sound financial head and the ability to get on well with people are also extremely important.

Starting Salary

Most antique dealers are self-employed, so income varies enormously. Some antique dealers employ assistants who earn around £10,000 to £12,000. A dealer running his or her own successful business at the upper end of the market, or with highly specialised expertise, can earn £50,000, but this is unusual.

British Antique Dealers' Association, 20 Rutland Gate, London SW7 1BD; 020 7589 4128; www.bada.org; e-mail: enquiry@ bada.demon.co.uk

Info

ARCHAEOLOGY

Archaeology is the examination of the human past through the study of buried remains and artefacts.

Archaeologist

Archaeology – building up a picture of the past – is both an art and a science. Archaeologists use highly technical and scientific methods of discovery, analysis and identification to reconstruct and study men and women from the past using their material remains. The evidence is collected through fieldwork, including excavations, where clues are sought in objects, their surroundings, the ground itself and the remains of living things. The evidence is then analysed, subjected to experiment, assessed, identified, catalogued, conserved and possibly exhibited. Archaeologists usually specialise in a particular period, technique or geographical area. Opportunities for full-time, permanent positions are limited; consequently competition is fierce for the few jobs available. These are to be found in central and local government, museums and universities, independent units and trusts, as well as a variety of positions in commercial operations. Job availability is closely related to building and development work. Some work includes the opportunity to spend time abroad.

Qualifications and Training

There are several degree courses in archaeology and most people who work as archaeologists will also have a postgraduate qualification and some work experience of volunteering on archaeological digs. There are also postgraduate courses in archaeological conservation.

Personal Qualities and Skills

Archaeologists need to be practical, thorough and very careful and observant. They should be able to work well as part of a team, or as a team leader. They need to have a real passion for and commitment to their work.

Starting Salary

Salaries are relatively low in this work. Many people start as volunteers and salaries of £9,000 to £11,000 are usual. A fieldwork supervisor earns around £14,000 to £15,000 a year.

Archaeological surveying

see Surveying

ARCHITECTURE

Architecture is a profession requiring the practical combination of imaginative design with scientific and technological principles, to produce designs for new buildings and for the extension, or renovation, of those already existing.

Architect

Architects are professional experts in the field of building design and construction. They advise individuals, developers, local authorities and commercial organisations on the design and construction of new buildings and the area around them. Architects are also involved in the restoration and conservation of historic and existing buildings. In its wider definition the professional association for architects, RIBA, says, 'Society looks to architects to define new ways of living and working, to develop innovative ways of using existing buildings and creating new ones.'

Architects create designs based on information supplied by the client on the function of the building, the proposed budget and the site. An architect needs to have an understanding of structure, finance, planning law and design, and in many building projects acts as the coordinator in a team of specialist consultants such as engineers, builders and interior designers.

The architect works to the client's requirements and produces working drawings for the builder. These show dimensions, materials and how everything will be put together. An architect will also negotiate with local authorities and submit the designs to planning officers for approval. On large jobs there will be a team of architects working with engineers and other specialists, and it may take months to prepare all the drawings and schedules. Alternatively, very small jobs take only a few weeks. After the contract documents have been prepared and a builder selected, work begins on the site. The architect visits frequently as the building goes up. This can involve tramping around in boots and a hard hat, climbing up and down ladders as well as taking the chair at site meetings.

Opportunities exist for employment in private practice, with local authorities, in research, teaching, central government and some industrial organisations. Increasingly, interior design and companies working in associated fields employ architects as part of their team. Specialist areas can include domestic, public building and retail architecture. The use of computer-aided design packages plays a significant part in the work of architects.

Qualifications and Training

Candidates should have passes in at least two subjects at A level, or one A level and two AS levels, together with passes in at least five other subjects at GCSE level. Subjects should be drawn from academic fields of study and include maths, English language and a separate science (physics or chemistry), or a double certification in science. Training takes a minimum of seven years, but only five of those are spent at a school of architecture. After a three-year degree course, students spend a year in an architect's office. Students often work abroad during this year or work in other parts of the building industry. Another two years' further study to obtain a diploma or higher degree are followed by a further year of working in an office, ending with a professional practice exam to become registered as an architect with the Architects' Registration Board and a corporate member of the RIBA. This allows the use of the title Architect in business. Part-time training is an alternative offered by a few schools for students already working in an architect's office on a day-release basis. Membership of the Royal Institute of British Architects (RIBA) and Royal Incorporation of Architects, Scotland (RIAS) is open to students while studying and also to those who are fully qualified.

Personal Qualities and Skills

Architects must have artistic ability and be imaginative, but at the same time need to be able to understand and apply technical information. They must adopt a practical approach to their work and be able to communicate their ideas and instructions to a variety of people. Business acumen, a professional approach, discretion and willingness to conform to a strict code of conduct are very important.

Starting Salary

While completing their two years' practical training, architectural students may expect to earn between £12,000 and £16,000; when fully registered this will increase to about £21,000, and thereafter be dependent upon position, experience and employer. £32,000 is the average.

info

Royal Institute of British Architects (RIBA), Public Information Line, 66 Portland Place, London W1B 1AD; 020 7580 5533; fax 020 7255 1541; www.architecture.com; e-mail: info@inst.riba.org (There is a comprehensive careers section on the website.)

Architects' Registration Board (ARB), 8 Weymouth Street, London

W1N 3FB; 020 7580 5861; www.arb.org.uk; e-mail: information@arb.org.uk

Royal Incorporation of Architects in Scotland (RIAS), 15 Rutland Square, Edinburgh EH1 2BE; 0131 229 7545; www.rias.org.uk; e-mail:information@rias.org.uk

Architectural technologist

Architectural technologists work alongside architects and other professionals as part of the building design and construction team. Technologists can negotiate the construction project from inception to completion. Specific, specialist skills could include surveying land and buildings, preparing and undertaking feasibility studies, presenting design solutions, analysing and detailing drawings, and managing and applying computer-aided design (CAD) techniques.

Qualifications and Training

A degree in architectural technology, an HNC/HND in Building Studies (with specific additional units) or an NVQ level 4 in Architectural Technology lead to Associate Membership of the British Institute of Architectural Technologists (BIAT) and the designation ABIAT.

Personal Qualities and Skills

Architectural technologists should be able to work both as part of a team and on their own initiative. Attention to detail is necessary, as is the ability to take account of other professionals' needs. Effective communication skills are necessary when working as part of the team, liaising with clients or tendering for contracts and they should feel comfortable with new technology and innovative concepts.

Starting Salary

Junior technologists, £11,000–£13,000; qualified technologists with three years' experience, £12,500–£14,000; senior technologists with appropriate educational qualifications and 10 years' experience, up to £25,000.

Chartered Institute of Architectural Technologists (CIAT), 397 City Road, London EC1V 1NH; 020 7278 2206; Freephone (UK only) 0800 731 5471; www.biat.org.uk; e-mail: careers@biat.org.uk

Modelmaker

see Modelmaker

ARCHIVIST

In the course of business many organisations and people create or collect archives. These include government agencies, local authorities, universities, hospitals, businesses, charities, professional organisations and families and individuals. Archives may be books or papers, maps or plans, photographs or prints, films or videos, or computer-generated records. Archives are intended to be kept permanently, to preserve the past and allow others to discover it.

It is the job of the archivist to preserve and exploit this archival heritage and the information contained within it. This includes assisting visitors or users, promotional work including exhibitions, presentations or media liaison, as well as the curatorial skills of selecting archives for preservation and interpreting them for archive users.

Qualifications and Training

This is a small profession, requiring a strong academic background. Entrants should have a good degree and an interest in heritage and information management, and good customer service skills. The recognised qualification is a postgraduate Diploma/MA, usually taken as a one-year full-time course at one of five universities in the UK and Ireland.

The Society of Archivists also offers an in-service diploma to graduates who are currently employed in archives or records management. Competition for places on these courses is fierce, and substantial practical paid or voluntary experience is required for applications to be successful. Lists of graduate placements are kept by the Society of Archivists' Training Officer and in addition, many local archives are also prepared to accommodate occasional volunteers interested in a career in archives.

Personal Qualities and Skills

Archivists must be good communicators, able to relate to and encourage a wide variety of people. They must also be ready to accept and exploit the technological advances that will continue to have a profound effect on demands for and use of information. A logical mind is essential for identifying and sorting archives before they can be interpreted or used effectively, and although archivists are not researchers, an understanding of research skills is helpful in all aspects of their work, particularly advising users. Archivists need to be prepared to continue their development after qualification, acquiring management, budgetary and other relevant skills.

Starting Salary

Salaries for new entrants range from £18,000 to £23,000. Business organisations, central government and universities usually offer higher pay than local authorities.

Info

The British Library, 96 Euston Road, London NW1 2DB; 020 7412 7332; www.bl.uk

Business Archives Council, c/o Ms F Maccoll, Rio Tinto plc, 6 St James Square, London SW1Y 4LD; 020 7753 2123; www.businessarchivescouncil.com

Museum, Libraries and Archives Council, 16 Queen Anne's Gate, London SW19 9AA; 020 7272 1444; www.mla.gov.uk

The National Archives, Kew, Richmond, Surrey TW9 4DU; 020 8876 3444; www.nationalarchives.gov.uk

Society of Archivists, Prioryfield House, 20 Canon Street, Taunton TA1 1SW; 01823 327030; www.archives.org.uk

ARMY

The Army is the largest of the three armed services and offers a wide range of career opportunities at basic and officer entry level. As a solider you start as an infantryman, a gunner or a tank operator, and officer training is offered by all the Army's regiments. Army careers include nursing, medicine, dentistry, engineering, information technology, catering, finance and human resources. There are also opportunities for civilians in many of these fields. Visit the Army's online Careers Service for details on the full range of career options. The Army also offers special gap year opportunities, if you want to try the Army life between school and university.

Qualifications and Training

Officers

Officer recruits are normally aged 18–29 and of graduate calibre. The Army recruits graduates from all disciplines to all areas of the Army. All officers are awarded an initial three-year Short Service Commission (SSC) on commissioning from Sandhurst, and this is the minimum length of commitment. An SSC can be extended up to a maximum of eight years. After two years' SSC service, officers can apply to convert to an Intermediate Regular Commission (IRC), which provides up to 16 years' service. After two years' IRC service, officers can apply to convert to a Regular Commission, which provides service up to the age of 55.

Sponsorship

Cadetships and bursaries are available for those studying for a recognised first degree. All successful applicants complete 11 months' officer training at the Royal Military Academy, Sandhurst.

Soldiers and servicewomen

Eligibility is determined by the results achieved on the Army Entrance Test (known as BARB). This assesses an applicant's ability for training by using computer touch-screen question and answer techniques. Entry is from age 16 to 30. Recruits usually enlist on an open engagement by which they agree to serve for 22 years, although it is possible to leave after a minimum of four years' service provided a year's notice is given.

Personal Qualities and Skills

Applicants must be British or Commonwealth citizens, born of British or Commonwealth parents and have been resident in the UK for the past five years. All candidates must be medically fit, intelligent, have the ability to work in a team and show dedication, courage, patriotism and a sense of responsibility.

Starting Salary

The starting salary for recruits is £11,774 a year. Privates earn £13,866 to £18,841 a year. More senior ranks can earn £19,293 to £36,416 a year. On entry, second lieutenants earn £21,301 a year. Lieutenants earn £25,605 to £28,298 a year. Captains earn from £32,000 to £39,000.

Additional allowances are paid to personnel working overseas, and where accommodation is provided some deduction is made from your basic pay.

www.armyjobs.mod.uk	British Army; 08457 300111;
Army Training and Recruitment Agency, Trenchard Lines, Upavon, Wiltshire SN9 6BE; 01980 615041; www.army.mod.uk/atra	www.army.mod.uk
	Welbeck College, Forest Road, Woodhouse, Loughborough, Leics LE12 8WD; www.welbeck.mod.uk

ART AND DESIGN

There are many different careers in art and design and artists work with many different mediums. Popular areas include fashion and textiles, jewellery, furniture, interior design, graphic design, industrial design and photography. Less commercial applications include painting and sculpture.

Artist

Only a very few artists are able to earn a living solely by the sale to clients of original work. Many more work as designers in advertising, industry and publishing, the latter also offering opportunities for illustrators, particularly for covers and jackets of children's books, or teach art in a school or college.

There are limited opportunities for work as a community artist, community arts officer (encouraging art in the community) and artist-in-residence.

Qualifications and Training

For the majority of artists, academic qualifications are necessary. These range from two-year diploma courses for 16-year-olds with some GCSEs or equivalents, to degrees. Many degree courses require the completion of a one-year Foundation course. A portfolio of work is normally required alongside academic qualifications for entry to art-related courses. Art teachers require appropriate teaching qualifications; *see also* Teaching.

Personal Qualities and Skills

The qualities required vary according to the work undertaken. Creativity, talent and imagination are all important, as well as enthusiasm and, in some cases, the ability to work as part of a team and to meet deadlines.

Starting Salary

Teachers' salaries start at over £18,000. Salaries are very unpredictable. Many artists take on casual jobs to support their creative careers.

info

Arts Council, 14 Great Peter Street,
London SW1P 3NQ, 020 7333 0100;
www.artscouncil.org.uk

Design Council, 34 Bow Street,
London WC2E 7DL; 020 7420 5200;
www.designcouncil.org.uk and
www.yourcreativefuture.org.uk;
e-mail: info@designcouncil.org.uk

Creative and Cultural Skills,
4th Floor, Lafone House,
The Leathermarket, Weston Street,
London SE1 3HN; 020 7015 1800;
www.ccskills.org.uk

Graphic designer

A number of different disciplines come under the umbrella heading of graphic design. These can include design studies, film and animation work, typography and lettering, illustration, printing processes, display and exhibition work, technical graphics for engineering, calligraphy, packaging and design for advertising, corporate identity and multimedia. Graphic design incorporates drawing and presentation skills and requires an understanding of colour, lettering and patterns. Many graphic designers work in three dimensions using specialist computer software. A high level of technical skills is therefore expected along with design ability. A rapidly growing area in graphic design is the field of new media, with new opportunities in multimedia, digital imagery and computer-aided design/manufacture.

Qualifications and Training

It is sometimes possible to get work as a graphic designer without formal qualifications, provided you have relevant experience and a really impressive portfolio of your design work – this is a highly competitive field. In practice, most graphic designers have either a degree in graphic design or in another art and design-related subject. To be accepted on many art and design degrees you also need a recognised foundation course. You will need to have or to get training in a number of relevant computer graphics packages, including Quark Xpress, Photoshop, Illustrator, Freehand and Dreamweaver. Local colleges offer courses in many of these, and the Chartered Society of Designers funds a programme of continuing professional development for designers who want to keep their skills and knowledge current.

Personal Qualities and Skills

You must be creative and imaginative with drawing as well as computer graphics skills. You should have some knowledge of printing technology, be able to work to a budget and to deadlines, and be an excellent communicator.

Starting Salary

Starting salaries for newly qualified designers are between £12,000 and £14,000. Experienced designers earn between £19,000 and £26,000. Someone with exceptional talent and a good reputation can earn more than this and many graphic designers are self-employed, working freelance.

Design Trust;
www.thedesigntrust.co.uk

Design Council, 34 Bow Street,
London WC2E 7DL; 020 7420 5200;
www.design-council.org.uk

Creative and Cultural Skills,
4th Floor, Lafone House,
The Leathermarket, Weston Street,
London SE1 3HN; 020 7015 1800;
www.ccskills.org.uk

Chartered Society of Designers;
www.csd.org.uk

info

Illustrator

Illustrators create illustrations for a range of clients using painting and drawing skills. The main area of work is within print media although technical and medical illustrators are also employed in industry and medicine respectively (*see also* Medical Illustration). Illustrators work to a client's brief and produce ideas incorporating design and creative ideas. Increasingly, computer-generated illustrations are also expected in this sector. Many illustrators work in a freelance capacity, and will often require representation through an agent to find work.

Qualification and Training

It may not be necessary to have a qualification to find work as an illustrator, as employment can be found by presenting a good portfolio of work. However, a diploma or MA in Graphic Design or Illustration might provide a good basis for entry into the profession.

Personal Qualities and Skills

Design and artistic skills. Ability to develop good client relationships and to interpret client briefs. Ability to work in a variety of styles. Self-motivation and marketing skills.

Starting Salary

Illustrators tend to be self-employed and are paid per illustration.

Association of Illustrators,
81 Leonard Street, London
EC2A 4QS; 020 7613 4328;
www.theAOI.com

Design Council, 34 Bow Street,
London WC2E 7DL; 020 7420 5200;
www.designcouncil.org.uk and
www.yourcreativefuture.org.uk;
e-mail: info@designcouncil.org.uk

info

Industrial product designer

Trained designers work within industry with engineers who have created products. These range from household goods and furniture to specialised equipment for science, industry and commerce. Designers are concerned with creating products that both look attractive and are efficient and convenient in use. The competition for the sale of new goods, from suitcases or spectacles to cassette players or cars, has resulted in an increased demand for the services of industrial designers.

Qualifications and Training

Employers recruit from those with an HND or degree in a design-related subject; some courses offer specialist modules in industrial design. Entry to such courses is normally via a National Diploma course after GCSEs or a Foundation course at an art college after A levels. Applicants for art and design courses are expected to have a portfolio of their artwork when interviewed.

Personal Qualities and Skills

As well as artistic ability, an understanding of mass-production processes is necessary; the industrial designer should also be able to work as part of a team, to schedule and recognise the needs of the consumer.

Starting Salary

Starting salaries range from £15,000 to £20,000, and experienced designers working for large companies can earn as much as £40,000.

info

Design Business Association (DBA), 32–38 Saffron Hill, London EC1N 8FH; 020 7831 9777; www.dba.org.uk

The Design Council, 34 Bow Street, London WC2E 7DL; 020 7420 5200; www.design-council.org.uk

Institution of Engineering Designers, Courtleigh, Westbury Leigh, Wiltshire BA13 3TA; 01373 822801; www.ied.org.uk

Local Job Centre Plus and Connexions/Careers Centres

Interactive media design

(*see also* Information and Communication Technology)

Interactive media design is a new and highly popular area within art and design. There are now over 500 multimedia courses in the UK. Multimedia design draws on both technical and design skills, and is used in designs for interactive media products such as websites, CD ROMs, interactive TV and computer games. Career opportunities exist in a wide variety of organisations, from corporations with websites to specialist producers of computer games.

Qualifications and Training

Technical and design skills are essential. Many general courses in Art and Design also have a multimedia option, although there are now specialist multimedia and interactive design courses available. The majority of employers expect an HND or degree.

Personal Qualities and Skills

Strong design and IT abilities are essential, as are the ability to work within a team and to understand the requirements of the organisation if employed on a company website. The development of new multimedia products such as computer games and CD ROMs would also require an understanding of business and marketing principles.

Starting Salary

Starting salary approximately £18,000 although experienced designers can achieve £40,000+.

Info

British Computer Society, 1 Sanford Street, Swindon, Wiltshire SN1 1HJ; 01793 417417; www.bcs.org.uk

British Interactive Multimedia Association, 5–6 Clipstone Street, London W1P 7EB; 020 7436 8250; www.bima.co.uk

British Web Design and Marketing Association, PO Box 3227, London NW9 9LX; 020 8204 2474; www.bwdma.com

UK Web Design Association, Fareham Enterprise Centre, Hackett Way, Fareham, Hampshire PO14 1TH; www.ukwda.org

Skillset, Prospect House, 80–120 New Oxford Street, London WG1A 1HB; 020 7520 5757; www.skillset.org

Careers and Jobs in IT (Kogan Page)

Interior designer

Interior designers work for commercial organisations as well as undertaking private commissions. They are responsible for the interiors of buildings (whereas an architect is responsible for its shell). Interior design can cover materials for floors and ceilings, fitments and fittings, and colour schemes, along with electrical and spatial planning. The commercial organisations may be offices, hotels, pubs, stores or banks. Interior designers may work with architects, have their own consultancies, or work in design units within large organisations.

Qualifications and Training

Entry to art school and college via a Foundation course is the same as for an industrial product designer (see page 34). Once at art college, the student may specialise in interior design.

Personal Qualities and Skills

A natural aptitude for art and the ability to work as part of a design team and to present work to customers are necessary.

Starting Salary

£13,000–£20,000 according to experience and ability.

Design Council, 34 Bow Street, London WC2E 7DL; 020 7420 5200;
www.designcouncil.org.uk and www.yourcreativefuture.org.uk;
e-mail: info@designcouncil.org.uk

Signwriter

Signwriters design and paint company names and logos on to shop fronts and
the sides of vans and lorries; they may also paint estate agents' signboards and
a wide variety of other temporary signs and notices. Signwriters increasingly
use a range of materials and techniques, including computer technology, to
create signs. The letters are often formed from plastics, metal or wood and
stuck on to the background.

Some signwriters are in business on their own; others work for commercial
signwriting companies.

Qualifications and Training

There are no formal academic entry requirements for this type of work, but artistic
talent combined with an interest in lettering is important. Some graphic design
courses include typography and signwriting and provide wider training. Some
commercial signwriting firms take on trainees and NVQs in Assembly,
Fabrication and Manufacturing Processes and Signmaking are available at level 2.

Starting Salary

Salaries start at around £12,000, rising to £17,000. The highest salaries are
around £21,000 to £23,000.

British Signwriters and Graphics
Association, 5 Orton Enterprise
Centre, Bakewell Road,
Orton Southgate, Peterborough,
Cambs PE2 6XU; 01733 230033;
www.bsga.co.uk

Creative and Cultural Skills,
4th Floor, Lafone House,
The Leathermarket, Weston Street,
London SE1 3HN; 020 7015 1800;
www.ccskills.org.uk

Art therapist

see Therapy

Arts administration

This is the administration and management of theatres, orchestras, opera houses, ballet companies and arts centres. The Arts Council, responsible for the promotion of art throughout the country, has its own administrative staff. The British Council, responsible for displaying British arts abroad, also employs a small number of staff.

Qualifications and Training

Experience is often more important than formal qualifications, although a good general education is expected; many entrants are graduates. Commercial awareness plus a knowledge of and interest in the arts is essential. Postgraduate courses such as an MA in Arts Administration can be studied part- or full-time.

Personal Qualities and Skills

You have to be good at dealing with the public and also with artists, so a full range of interpersonal skills is important. You must be well organised, a very good administrator and have good ideas about marketing, publicity and fund raising. Basic accounting skills are useful.

Starting Salary

Salaries start at around £11,000 to £12,000 and are often linked to local author-ity pay scales. £18,000 is a typical salary once you have some experience.

Arts Council, 14 Great Peter Street, London SW1P 3NQ; 0845 300 6200; www.artscouncil.org.uk; e-mail: enquiries@artscouncil.org.uk

Scottish Arts Council, 12 Manor Place, Edinburgh EH3 7DD; 0131 226 6051; www.sac.org.uk; e-mail: help.desk@scottisharts.org.uk

Arts Marketing Association, 7a Clifton Court, Clifton Road, Cambridge CB1 7BN; 01223 578078; fax: 01223 245862; www.a-m-a.co.uk; e-mail: info@a-m-a.co.uk

ASTRONOMER

Astronomers study the sun, planets, stars, galaxies and other objects in the sky, analysing the radio, infrared, optical, ultraviolet, X and gamma radiations they emit, to find out how they work. Some of these radiations do not penetrate the earth's atmosphere, so observations by satellite are necessary as well as from the ground. Modern astronomical detectors are usually based on electronic methods and give results which can be analysed by computer.

Qualifications and Training

To become a research astronomer, a good degree in physics or maths is necessary and it is possible to do degrees in astronomy or astrophysics. This is normally followed by postgraduate study and research. Various grants are available to support students undertaking such courses.

Astronomy-related careers at an engineering or technical level are also open to those with skills in applied physics, electronics, computer hardware and software, optics and mechanical engineering.

Personal Qualities and Skills

Astronomers need curiosity and imagination; they must be able to make logical deductions from the available observations. Working long and unusual hours and travelling to remote observatories may also be involved.

Starting Salary

Post-doctoral salaries start at around £18,000; technical salaries after training are around £15,500–£22,000, depending on qualifications.

info

The Library, Royal Astronomical Society, Burlington House, Piccadilly, London W1V 0NL; 020 7734 3307; www.ras.org.uk; e-mail: info@ras.org.uk

Public Information Officer, Royal Observatory Greenwich, National Maritime Museum, London SE10 9NF; 020 8858 4422; www.rog.nmm.ac.uk

AUCTIONEER

(*see also* Land and Property)

The auctioneer's work involves the sale by auction of property of all kinds, including buildings (houses, farms and estates), livestock, and goods such as furniture, antiques, paintings, glass, toys, carpets and china. The work also entails valuations for various purposes, including investment and insurance.

Qualifications and Training

An auctioneer's work involves the valuation of land and property, so surveying or valuation qualifications are necessary. There are two components to qualifying as a Chartered Surveyor or Valuer. First is successful completion of a Royal Institution of Chartered Surveyors (RICS) accredited degree or diploma, followed by enrolment onto the Assessment of Professional Competence (APC). This is two years' practical training while in employment, finishing with an RICS professional assessment interview. One-year full-time and two-year part-time postgraduate conversion courses are also available.

Personal Qualities and Skills

Attention to detail is important for this job, together with a practical attitude and an aptitude for figures. In fine art auctioneering, a certain flair and the ability to distinguish a fake from the genuine article are essential.

Starting Salary

Trainees starting at 18, £8,000–£9,000; graduates with relevant degrees, £11,000–£13,800 rising to £19,000+ or higher in London.

Royal Institution of Chartered Surveyors, 12 Great George Street, London SW1P 3AD; 020 7222 7000; www.rics.org.uk/afa

AUDIOLOGY TECHNICIAN

Audiology technicians carry out tests to assess the presence, nature and extent of a hearing loss, using complex and advanced techniques. They take aural impressions for individual moulded ear inserts, fit and instruct the patients on how to use hearing aids, and review their progress.

Qualifications and Training

Four GCSEs at C grade or equivalent, in English, maths, physics and another science and two A levels, one of which must be a science. Training involves two years of combined theory and practice while in employment, leading to an Edexcel (BTEC) qualification in medical physics and physiological measurement, or NVQ equivalent.

Personal Qualities and Skills

Candidates must be patient, have a clear speaking voice and the ability to get on with people.

Starting Salary

Trainee £8,000+. Once qualified, depending on grade, £15,000–£30,000+.

British Society of Audiology, 80 Brighton Road, Reading RG6 1PS; 0118 966 0622; fax: 0118 935 1915; www.thebsa.org.uk

British Society of Hearing Aid Audiologists, Bridle Croft, Burgh Heath Road, Epsom KT17 4LF; 01372 725348; www.bshaa.co.uk; e-mail: information@bshaa.com

BANKING AND FINANCE

Banking

Banks provide a delivery point for financial services. The most obvious side of banking is the high street branches but other work includes international banking (financing foreign trade and providing an overseas banking service for UK customers); corporate finance (dealing with the requirements of large companies); human resources, recruitment, training and staff development; insurance; computer services; marketing; training; and trust work (when a bank is appointed as executor or joint executor of a will).

The recent reduction in the number of bank branches and the growth in internet and telephone banking is a trend that is expected to continue, with some opportunities being offered in bank call centres, although some are now located abroad.

Commercial

Commercial banks provide financial services to individuals, small businesses and large organisations. They usually have high street branches and provide such services as bank accounts, cash transactions, cheque clearing; credit and debit cards, loans (including mortgages), foreign currency; and advice on insurance, pensions and savings products. Most commercial banks also offer telephone and online banking facilities for their customers. Junior posts involve routine office work and dealing with customers by telephone and in person. With experience the work will involve building links with business, solving complex customer queries and making business decisions. There are also specialist opportunities in IT, human resource management and marketing.

The Bank of England

This is the banker to the government. It is concerned with the financial structure of Great Britain, with other banks in the country and with operating accounts for overseas central banks. The Bank of England is responsible for the printing, issue and withdrawal of British banknotes and it also controls interest rates and raises short-term government finance. The monitoring of economic developments at home and abroad provides information for the Bank, the Treasury and other government departments. It does not offer banking facilities to the general public. Specialists such as economists, statisticians and librarians are recruited in addition to other banking staff.

Investment banks

These are generally financial houses, which started from trading as merchants and have expanded their role to financing the trading and commercial activities of others, especially in the international marketplace. An investment banking group nowadays includes the following services for its clients: corporate finance and advisory work, banking for governments, institutions and companies, investment management and securities trading.

Qualifications and Training

Each bank has different entry points, recruiting school leavers after GCSEs and A levels as well as graduates. Structured training programmes often provide access to qualifications of the Institute of Financial Services in England and Wales or Chartered Institute of Bankers in Scotland (CIOBS). As well as covering traditional areas of banking there are a range of new qualifications such as certificates in Commercial Banking in the Networked World, Capital Markets, and the New Economy and E-Finance.

The Chartered Institute of Bankers in Scotland first-level qualification (the Certificate in Financial Services) requires no previous qualifications for entry. Students completing the certificate can progress to the Associateship and Membership examinations. NVQs level 2–4 in providing financial services are available.

Most banks welcome applications from graduates who have qualified from a range of disciplines such as law, accountancy or business. There are also vacancies for individuals seeking a career in information technology.

Personal Qualities and Skills

Accuracy, integrity, good powers of concentration, attention to detail and a clear mind are essential for success in a banking career. It is important to be able to get on with people and to work as a member of a team.

Info

British Bankers Association (BBA), Pinners Hall, 105–108 Old Broad Street, London EC2N 1EX; 020 7216 8800; www.bba.org.uk

Chartered Institute of Bankers in Scotland (CIOBS), Drumsheugh House, 38b Drumsheugh Gardens, Edinburgh EH3 7SW; 0131 473 7777; www.ciobs.org.uk/

The Financial Services Authority (FSA), 25 The North Colonnade, Canary Wharf, London E14 5HS; 020 7066 1000; www.fsa.gov.uk

Financial Services Skills Council, 51 Gresham Street, London EC2V 7HQ; 020 7216 7366; www.fssc.org.uk

Institute of Financial Services (IFS), IFS House, 4–9 Burgate Lane, Canterbury CT1 2XJ; 01227 762 600; www.ifslearning.com

Starting Salary

Starting salaries in most commercial banks are around £12,000 to £13,000, or £15,000 to £21,000 for graduates. Salaries tend to be higher in investment banking and commence at around £25,000 to £30,000.

Building societies

The traditional function of building societies is to attract savings and investments from the public, and then use these funds to make loans for home ownership. However, more recently most building societies have moved into offering a range of financial services, such as banking, insurance, credit cards, investment, estate agency and unsecured lending, but the savings and loan activities remain the most important. The number of building societies has decreased since deregulation as many have converted to banks and there are now 65 in the UK.

Building society assistants deal with customers' enquiries and are expected to sell some of the society's financial services, as well as being responsible for routine and administrative tasks. With the increase in telephone and internet banking the number of jobs in building society branches has decreased, but some call centre work is available.

Building society managers work with customers on mortgage and loan applications, financial planning queries and with customers facing repayment difficulties. They may be in charge of a single large branch or a number of small branches, where they have responsibility for managing staff and ensuring targets are met.

Qualifications and Training

Assistants need four GCSEs or equivalent including English and maths. Competency-based on-the-job training is common and can include the opportunity to take Chartered Institute of Bankers (CIB) or Chartered Institute of Bankers in Scotland (CIOBS) modules or examinations. Those with CIB/CIOBS Associateship qualifications can move into management. Graduates are also recruited into management training posts; entry can be from any degree discipline and further professional training is available through CIB/CIOBS.

Personal Qualities and Skills

Honesty and discretion are essential as well as good communication, mathematical and IT skills. The ability to market financial products is becoming increasingly important. Managers need negotiating, decision-making and problem-solving skills, in addition to good people management skills.

Starting Salary

Assistants earn from £9,000 to £15,000 depending on qualifications and experience. Graduate trainees start on £16,000–£18,000+.

Building Societies Association, 3 Savile Row, London W1S 3PB; 020 7437 0655; www.bsa.org.uk

Institute of Financial Services, 4–9 Burgate Lane, Canterbury, Kent, CT1 2XJ; 01227 818609; www.ifslearning.com

Chartered Institute of Bankers in Scotland, Drumsheugh House, 38b Drumsheugh Gardens, Edinburgh EH3 7SW; 0131 473 7777; www.ciobs.org.uk

Careers in Banking and Finance (Kogan Page)

Economist

see Economist

Financial adviser

Financial advisers provide advice on all aspects of financial planning to a wide range of clients. They work with individuals and corporate clients and other groups of people such as societies or charities. They can offer advice on such diverse matters as loans, mortgages, pensions, investments and other financial products and services.

Their work involves meeting clients and explaining financial products and services to them clearly and carefully. They have to assess people's different financial circumstances in order to advise on the most suitable products. They conduct in-depth research into different products and liaise closely with banks, building societies, insurance companies, etc – the financial product suppliers. They are often self-employed, so they also have to be good at marketing and promoting themselves and seeking out new clients.

There are approximately 75,000 financial services advisers working in the UK, and almost half class themselves as independent rather than tied advisers. Being independent, however, does not necessarily mean being self-employed. Both tied and independent financial services advisers may work for an organisation or may be self-employed. Many independent advisers work for firms which themselves are known as independent financial advisers.

Tied advisers work for financial services companies, insurance companies, investment firms, banks and building societies. Some are employed by estate agencies, law firms and by retailers that have developed financial services as a part of their business.

Qualifications and Training

You don't have to be a graduate, though degrees in business studies, accountancy or financial services can give you an advantage. Many employers are happy to take people from a wide range of working backgrounds and do not require academic qualifications. You nearly always need a driving licence, and some employers set lower age limits of 21 or older for trainees.

All entrants to the professions have to pass the Financial Planning Certificate examinations parts 1, 2 and 3 or the Certificate for Financial Advisers in order to be licensed by the Financial Services Authority. A lot of the training is provided on-the-job and when you start you often learn by shadowing a more experienced adviser.

Personal Qualities and Skills

You need excellent communication skills, to be able to talk convincingly to corporate clients and sensitively to private individuals. You must be smart, well organised and highly motivated – this is a competitive sector. You need good numeracy and IT skills and the ability to deal with highly complex information.

Starting Salary

Most advisers earn a basic salary, plus commission from the products they sell. Starting salaries for tied advisers are between £10,000 and £15,000; successful advisers earn in excess of £70,000.

An experienced independent financial adviser can expect to earn between £30,000 and £40,000 – based on performance a successful adviser can earn in excess of £100,000.

info

Association of Independent Financial Advisers (AIFA), Austin Friars House, 2–6 Austin Friars, London EC2N 2HD; 020 7628 1287; www.aifa.net

Chartered Insurance Institute, 42–48 High Road, South Woodford, London E18 2JP; 020 8989 8464; www.cii.co.uk; e-mail: customer.serv@cii.co.uk

Institute of Financial Planning, Whitefriars Centre, Lewins Mead, Bristol BS1 2NT; 0117 945 2470; www.financialplanning.org.uk

Institute of Financial Services (IFS), IFS House, 4–9 Burgate Lane, Canterbury, Kent CT1 2XJ; 01227 818609; www.ifslearning.com; e-mail: customerservices@ifslearning.com

The Personal Finance Society, 20 Aldermanbury, London EC2V 7HY; 020 8530 0852; www.thepfs.org; e-mail: customer.serv@thepfs.org

Investment work

Investment Analysts

Investment analysts analyse the financial markets to advise on the best investments for clients. Investment managers rely on their information. There are two main types of investment analyst. First are those who work for stockbrokers and undertake their own analysis to provide information for fund manager clients. The aim is to generate 'buy and sell' orders for the stockbrokers for whom they work. This is known as the 'sell side'. Second, there are those who work for investment management institutions. They provide ideas and information to enable their in-house fund managers to make the best decisions for their clients. This is known as the 'buy side'. The majority of investment analysts work on the 'sell side'.

Fund manager

Investment fund managers invest the funds of other people – private clients and institutions, such as insurance companies, charities, independent schools and specialised research institutions. Managers must keep their clients' interests continually under review, offering advice on how to retain their clients' income and when to change investments. Investment fund managers may be employed by the larger institutions, or work in specialist firms that tend to serve smaller clients.

Qualifications and Training

It is becoming increasingly difficult to enter this profession without a degree. The most favoured subjects include mathematics, accountancy, economics and statistics. Some global companies like applicants to have a Masters in Business Administration.

A basic qualification for all trainees is the Investment Management Certificate (IMC) from the Society of Investment Professionals. This takes around a year to complete, and covers the regulations that investment companies and their staff must adhere to in the UK, plus statistics, maths and economics. Many analysts and managers take the Chartered Financial Analyst (CFA) qualification. This usually takes up to three years to complete.

Personal Qualities and Skills

Analysts and fund managers have to be good communicators face-to-face and on the telephone. You need to be able to work as part of a team, but also to use your own initiative and take decisions. You must be interested in current affairs and be able to make the link between these and their potential impact on financial markets and funds.

Starting Salary

Salaries for trainees range from £15,000 to £27,000, though you would have to be a pretty impressive applicant to start at the top end of this scale. Very high earnings are possible in this field.

Association of Private Client Investment Managers and Stockbrokers (APCIMS), 114 Middlesex Street, London E1 7JH; 020 7247 7080; www.apcims.co.uk

Chartered Financial Analyst (CFA) Institute, 29th Floor, 1 Canada Square,

Canary Wharf, London E14 5DY; 020 7712 1719; www.cfainstitute.org

UK Society of Investment Professionals (UKSIP), 90 Basinghall Street, London EC2V 5AY; 020 7796 3000; www.uksip.org

info

Stockbroker

Stockbrokers buy and sell securities on the Stock Exchange on behalf of investors, who may be individuals but are increasingly institutions, such as banks, insurance companies, pension funds or unit trusts. They also advise clients on shares they hold and suggest good times to sell or buy. Stockbrokers work from their offices using the phone and internet to keep in touch with financial markets and news.

Qualifications and Training

A degree is desirable, but good A levels may be accepted. Before being allowed to trade, all staff must pass the Registered Representative Examination, administered by the Securities Institute. Stockbrokers train on the job, working alongside experienced brokers. Many employers expect their staff to study for the Securities Institute Diploma.

Personal Qualities and Skills

Entrants should be confident, numerate and able to express ideas clearly and concisely. Good interpersonal skills are essential, in order to ensure effective client relationships, as is the ability to work as part of a team.

Starting Salary

Depending on location, starting salaries vary from £16,000 to £25,000. Brokers' salaries depend on the amount of business carried out; top brokers can earn between £100,000 and £250,000.

Association of Private Client Investment Managers and Stockbrokers (APCIMS), 114 Middlesex Street, London E1 7JH; 020 7247 7080;www.apcims.co.uk

Financial Services Skills Council, 51 Gresham Street, London EC2V 7HQ; 020 7216 7366; www.fssc.org.uk

BEAUTY

Beauticians are predominantly, although not exclusively, female. There are a variety of occupations within the beauty sector, ranging from therapists who provide body and face treatment to make-up artists who work in film and television.

Beauty sales consultant

Working in the cosmetics department of a large store, in a luxury hotel, at home and overseas, on an ocean liner or at airports, sales consultants sell and promote their firm's products, answering questions from potential buyers on skin care and make-up. They occasionally give talks at schools and colleges or to women's organisations, and may travel for their companies at home and abroad.

Beauty therapist

(*see also* Hairdresser)

Beauty therapists work in salons, health clubs and private homes and, at the glamorous end of the market, for film, television and fashion magazines. Beauty therapists offer a range of treatments to their clients, such as facials, massage, make-up, manicures, waxing and body toning and tanning treatments. Beauty therapists who visit clients in their own homes have to be good business people, keeping accounts, ordering stock and keeping up to date with the latest developments. The top end of the market is highly competitive, but it is a profession that gives you a lot of flexibility. UK hairdressers and beauty therapists are generally highly thought of.

Qualifications and Training

There are no specific entry requirements, but it is an advantage to have GCSEs in English, maths and a science and some employers may set their own entry standards. There are two ways to train: through a college course leading to a GNVQ Level 3, or through a Modern Apprenticeship, which also leads to GNVQ Level 3. The main difference is that on a Modern Apprenticeship you are based with an employer, though some college work is also included. Many people choose to do the combined hairdressing and beauty therapy Modern Apprenticeship, to give themselves a more flexible qualification. Some private beauty colleges offer training and it is very important that you check what qualifications they award before you pay for one of these courses.

Personal Qualities and Skills

You must be excellent at putting people at ease, as the work leads to a lot of close, physical contact, in massage or body waxing for example. You have to be friendly, reassuring and patient. You need good physical stamina as you are on your feet for a great deal of the time.

Starting Salary

Salaries start at around £9,500, though with experience it is possible to earn more than £20,000. One of the attractions of the job is that you can be self-employed and work the hours you choose.

Hairdressing and Beauty Industry Authority, Oxford House, Sixth Avenue Sky Business Park, Robin Hood Airport, Doncaster DN9 3GG; 08452 306080; www.habia.org.uk

British Association of Beauty Therapy and Cosmetology (BABTAC),

Meteor Court, Barnett Way, Barnwood, Gloucester GL4 3GG; www.babtac.com

Local Job Centre Plus and Connexions/Careers Centres for vacancy information, local colleges for course details

Body artist/tattooist

Body artists/tattooists working in studios or parlours draw designs of words, patterns and pictures on the bodies of customers. This form of body adornment has grown increasingly popular over recent years. The body artist either draws the design freehand or works from a transfer placed on the customer's skin. He or she then follows the outline with an electrically operated needle which delivers permanent ink dyes just under the skin.

Qualifications and Training

No formal qualifications are required, but you will have to persuade a registered tattooist to take you on as an apprentice. It is illegal to tattoo if you are not registered with your local Environmental Health Department. This department should be able to provide you with names of local registered artists and the Tattoo Club of Great Britain can also help you with this. Training takes from one to three years, but it takes at least five years to become really competent.

Personal Qualities and Skills

Body artists/tattooists must have a flair for design and also be very good at working with people. Customers may want a tattoo, but they are often a bit nervous about it. Body artists must be extremely careful about their art work, since the designs are permanent. They must also have scrupulous hygiene and health and safety awareness.

Starting Salary

Trainees earn around £10,000 rising to £16,000 with considerable experience. It is possible to earn more than this if you develop a really good reputation and have obvious talent, or if you work in a highly fashionable studio.

Tattoo Club of Great Britain, 389 Cowley Road, Oxford OX4 2BS; 01865 716877; www.tattoo.co.uk

Make-up artist

Make-up artists prepare and work on make-up and hair styling required for each individual such as artists, singers, dancers, actors and others appearing on television and in film production. Make-up artists also work in other environments such as on cruise liners, in beauty salons in large hotels, stage shows, fashion shows or in the medical profession, where they provide make-up to camouflage client injuries following an accident or surgery.

An experienced make-up artist will work on more versatile projects using elaborate make-up, wigs, materials to change the shape of a face or create scars and wounds for television and film productions. This will require research and design of the make-up required for a production, through to completion ready for filming. It is necessary to be able to liaise closely with producers, directors, costume designers, hairdressers and the performers.

Qualifications and Training

While there are no set entry qualifications many applicants have degrees or HNDs in art and design-related subjects and/or beauty therapy and hairdressing qualifications. There is a wide range of training courses available and Skillset gives useful advice on these. Examples of some relevant qualifications include the BTEC/SQA National Certificate/Diploma in Performing Arts (Make-up), Vocational Training Charitable Trust (VTCT) level 3 Diploma in Theatre and Media Make-up, and International Therapy Examinations Council (ITEC) level 3 Diploma in Fashion, Theatre and Media Make-up. The London College of Fashion offers a foundation degree in make-up artistry. Most people start as make-up assistants while doing one of the courses mentioned above.

Personal Qualities and Skills

You need to have artistic flair and imagination. You must be practical, methodical and patient, but you must also be able to work quickly under pressure. You should be able to get on well with all sorts of people, and be confident and tactful, able to make suggestions and put people at ease. You should be good at working as part of a team.

Starting Salary

As a make-up assistant, you may have to consider working for very low wages or even working voluntarily. Salaries vary enormously, from £10,000 to £40,000. If you work freelance, you are paid for individual contracts.

info

Broadcasting Entertainment Cinematographic and Theatre Union (BECTU), 373–377 Clapham Road, London SW9 9BT; 020 7346 0900; www.bectu.org.uk

FT2 – Film & Television Freelance Training, Third Floor, 18–20 Southwark Street, London SE1 1TJ; 020 7407 0344; www.ft2.org.uk

Greasepaint, 143 Northfield Avenue, Ealing, London W13 9QT; 020 8840 6000; www.greasepaint.co.uk

International Therapy Examination Council, Heathfield Terrace, Chiswick, London W4 4JE; 020 8994 4141; www.itecworld.co.uk

London College of Fashion, 20 John Prince's Street, London W1G 0BJ; 020 7514 7344; www.fashion.arts.ac.uk

The Make-up Centre, Ealing Studios, Building D, Second Floor, Ealing Green, London W5 5EP; 020 8579 9511; www.themake-upcentre.co.uk

Producers Alliance for Cinema and Television (PACT), Proctor House, 1 Proctor Street, Holborn, London WC1V 6DW; 020 7067 4367; www.pact.co.uk

Revelations School of Make-up, Revelations House, Royal Oak Yard, off Little Underbank, Stockport, Manchester SK1 1JZ; 0161 476 5009; www.schoolofmakeup.co.uk

info

Scottish Screen, 249 West George Street, Glasgow G2 4QE; 0141 302 1700; www.scottishscreen.com

Skillset (Sector Skills Council for the Audio Visual Industries), Prospect House, 80–110 New Oxford Street, London WC1A 1HB; 020 7520 5757; www.skillset.org

Vocational Training Charitable Trust, 3rd Floor, Eastleigh House, Upper Market Street, Eastleigh, Hants SO50 9FD; 023 8068 4500; www.vtct.org.uk

BIOLOGY

Those who work in the field of biology are concerned with the structure, processes and functions of living organisms.

Biochemist

Biochemistry is the study of chemical substances and processes in living cells and tissues. Most biochemists work in laboratories although some make their careers in education or industry, in brewing, food technology, forestry, agriculture, dietetics, pharmaceuticals, management and planning.

Many biochemists are employed in hospitals, where they manage and develop the service and carry out research into disease. Pharmaceutical firms also employ biochemists to develop new drugs and study their effects on diseases and patients. Qualified biochemists are also employed in research institutions funded by the Medical Research Council, the National Institute for Medical Research and Biotechnology, and the Biological Sciences Research Council, as well as some funded by charities such as the Imperial Cancer Research Fund (ICRF).

Qualifications and Training

Biochemists entering the professions in universities, hospitals and industry will be graduates, usually with good honours degrees in biochemistry or a related science subject. Laboratory technicians in universities and industry often join with good GCSE passes in mathematics and science subjects, or A levels or equivalent. They will usually study part time for Edexcel (BTEC) higher certificates in appropriate subjects. Biomedical scientists in hospital laboratories can enter with either degrees (usually an accredited BSc in biomedical science) or A levels, following which they will study part time for a degree.

Personal Qualities and Skills

It is important to be able to work independently or as part of a team in any branch of science. Patience, powers of concentration and meticulous attention to detail are also important.

A career in Biomedical Science

About Biomedical Science
Biomedical science is the laboratory investigation of disease enabling diagnosis and treatment. This can range from a simple blood test to complex tissue analysis.

About the Job
Biomedical scientists largely work in hospital pathology laboratories but may also work in research, armed forces and the pharmaceutical industry. All have an understanding of the laboratory investigation of disease and work in a dynamic technological environment.

Professional attributes
- Ability to work methodically and efficiently
- Good problem-solving skills
- Critical analysis and research skills
- Good communication
- Ability to work in a multi-professional team
- Flexible and adaptable

INSTITUTE OF BIOMEDICAL SCIENCE

Education and Training
'Biomedical scientist' is a registered profession title and all practitioners have met the education and training standards defined by the Health Professions Council (**www.hpc-uk.org**), the regulatory body.

Over forty universities in the UK offer approved BSc honours degrees in biomedical science suitable for HPC registration. These have been accredited by the Institute of Biomedical Science (IBMS) and a list is available on the Institute's website **www.ibms.org**

Accredited degrees are based on the core subjects of human anatomy and physiology, biochemistry, genetics and molecular biology, microbiology and immunology. These underpin the biomedical science subjects of:
- Medical Microbiology and Virology
- Haematology and Transfusion Science
- Immunology
- Clinical Chemistry
- Cellular Pathology (Histopathology & Cytopathology)

Practical laboratory training is essential for acquiring the knowledge and skills required of the registered practitioner. This can be provided through a laboratory placement during the degree course or in a post graduate trainee post leading to HPC registration.

Career Prospects
After registration biomedical scientists usually specialise in a single pathology discipline. This may lead to further post graduate and professional qualifications.

The Institute of Biomedical Science
The Institute of Biomedical Science is the professional body that represents biomedical scientists. Further information can be obtained by visiting the website **www.ibms.org**

A Career in *Biomedical Science*

Biomedical scientists are essential members of the healthcare team. It is through their investigations that the diagnosis of disease, evaluation of effectiveness of treatment, and research into causes and cures of disease become possible. Most biomedical scientists specialise, after their basic training, in one discipline.

MEDICAL MICROBIOLOGY is the study of disease causing organisms. The most suitable antibiotics are identified and serum is tested for antibodies to infective agents. Some laboratories undertake food testing to ensure fitness for human consumption and do environmental monitoring. Specialists in **VIROLOGY** detect viruses, such as herpes simplex, influenza and human immunodeficiency virus (HIV).

HAEMATOLOGY is the study of blood, principally to aid diagnosis and treatment of anaemia and leukaemia. Other important areas are the study of abnormalities of blood coagulation (clotting) and the monitoring of treatment of patients taking anticoagulants such as warfarin.

In the **TRANSFUSION SCIENCE** specialism biomedical scientists work in hospital blood banks and the blood transfusion service. They ensure there is enough blood available for transfusions, identify blood groups and test for compatibility of donors' blood with that of patients.

IMMUNOLOGY is the investigation of abnormalities and disturbances of the immune system associated with infectious disease, allergy, malignancy and organ transplants. A variety of analytical methods are used to identify, monitor and aid in the treatment of such conditions.

CLINICAL CHEMISTRY involves the chemical analysis of blood and body fluids. Techniques used include the use of computer controlled analysers, alongside manual techniques employing chromatography, electrophoresis, spectroscopy, electrochemistry, radio tracers, immunoassay and molecular diagnostics.

In a **HISTOPATHOLOGY** laboratory the biomedical scientist processes samples of tissues from surgical operations and autopsies. Tissue sections are cut and stained so that cellular structures and detail can be visualised under a light microscope.

CYTOPATHOLOGY is best known for work in the cervical screening programme but additionally receives cell samples from many other body sites for microscopic examination.

Biomedical scientists work mainly in teams alongside other scientific and medical colleagues. Their work demands practical skills performed with precision and accuracy and the ability to follow instructions and to use complicated equipment where necessary. This is an interesting and rewarding career.

www.ibms.org

Starting Salary

Salaries vary with the type of employment and the responsibility involved. Graduates entering the professions as biochemists start on £12,000–£18,000. Laboratory technicians with good GCSE passes have salaries of £6,000+, and trainee biomedical scientists will start at £11,000+. Additional academic and professional qualifications attained during employment will permit career development and usually lead to positions of greater responsibility with higher salaries.

Institute of Biology, Red Lion Court, London EC4A 3EF; 020 7936 5900; www.iob.org

Institute of Biomedical Science, 12 Coldbath Square, London EC1R 5HL; 020 7713 0214; www.ibms.org

Biochemical Society, 3rd Floor, Eagle House, 16 Procter Street, London WC1V 6NX; 020 7280 4100; www.biochemistry.org

NHS Careers, PO Box 376, Bristol BS99 3EY; 0845 606 0655; www.nhscareers.nhs.uk

Biomedical scientist

Biomedical scientists (including medical laboratory scientific officers in the NHS) investigate specimens of body fluids and tissues, and play an important role in the diagnosis and treatment of diseases. Most are employed in hospital laboratories and pathology departments, but many also work for the blood transfusion service, in public health laboratories, for veterinary establishments, universities, pharmaceutical and other manufacturing companies. There are sometimes opportunities to assist in research and to teach.

Qualifications and Training

The profession has all-graduate entry. A guide to courses can be obtained from the Institute of Biomedical Science. Trainees in the NHS and related bodies have to proceed to state registration and need a degree to do so.

Personal Qualities and Skills

Biomedical scientists must be able to work quickly, accurately and methodically. Complicated and new equipment must be used, so technical as well as scientific ability is needed.

Starting Salary

As a graduate trainee salaries start around £12,000 to £14,000 – there is some regional variation. On registration salaries rise to a range of £17,000 to £24,000.

info

Health Professions Council (HPC), Park House, 184 Kennington Park Road, London SE11 4BU; 020 7582 0866; www.hpc-uk.org

Health Protection Agency, 7th Floor, Holborn Gate, 330 High Holborn,

London WC1V 7PP; 020 7759 2700; www.hpa.org.uk

Institute of Biomedical Science (IBMS), 12 Coldbath Square, London EC1R 5HL; 020 7713 0214; www.ibms.org

Biotechnologist

Biotechnology is the application of living organisms and biological systems to industrial processes. Various aspects of biological science are involved – biochemistry, microbiology and genetics. At present, the main industrial areas in which biotechnologists are employed are fermentation, waste systems management, production of antibiotics, vaccines, hormones, and animal and human food production.

Qualifications and Training

Most new entrants are graduates. Degree entry requirements are a minimum of five GCSEs including maths, plus three A levels or equivalent including biology and chemistry.

Personal Qualities and Skills

A high degree of accuracy, thoroughness, lots of patience and the ability to check and recheck details are needed.

Starting Salary

£20,000 upwards for graduates.

info

Biotechnology and Biological Sciences Research Council, Polaris House, North Star Avenue, Swindon SN2 1UH; 01793 413200; www.bbsrc.ac.uk

SEMTA, 14 Upton Road, Watford, Hertfordshire WD18 0JT; 0808 100 3682; www.semta.org.uk

Royal Academy of Engineering, 29 Great Peter Street, Westminster, London SW1P 3LW; 020 7227 0500; www.raeng.org.uk

Association of The British Pharmaceutical Industry, 12 Whitehall, London SW1A 2DY; 020 7930 3477; www.abpi.org.uk; www.abpi-careers.org.uk

BOOKMAKER

As a bookmaker or in betting shop management, you work with people who are placing bets on everything from horse and greyhound racing results through to whether or not there will be a white Christmas. The majority of betting shops are part of large chains, but there are a few small, independent operators. This sector has done a lot to improve its image and make its outlets more appealing to customers, especially since the advent of online gambling.

Qualifications and Training

There are no formal entry qualifications, except that trainee managers must be over 21. You are likely to face aptitude tests to check your numeracy skills as part of your application. Many trainee managers do have A levels or degrees, but all kinds of background experience are viewed as useful. Training is on the job, usually starting behind the counter. Training covers how to set bets, customer care, numerical skills and security procedures.

Personal Qualities and Skills

You need excellent customer service skills, a lot of common sense, good numerical skills and the ability to manage other people.

Starting Salary

Trainee managers start on between £14,000 and £16,000, while branch managers earn between £17,000 and £24,000.

Association of British Bookmakers Ltd, Regency House, 1–4 Warwick Street, London W1B 5LT; 020 7434 2111; www.abb.uk.com

National Association of Bookmakers, PO Box 242, East Molesey, Surrey KT8 2WE; 01884 841859

People 1st, 2nd Floor, Armstrong House, 38 Market Square, Uxbridge, Middlesex UB8 1LH; 0870 060 2550; www.people1st.org

info

BOOKSELLER

In a bookselling career it is essential to have in-depth product knowledge and the ability to sell. It is important to keep up to date by reading new books and reviews, in order to assist customers and to display the books to advantage. The ability to find information in catalogues and directories, both online and in hard copy, is essential. Managers are responsible for stock ordering and for giving their shops an image that will attract regular customers to help them compete with the discounts offered by supermarkets. A growing number of bookshops sell their products through the internet.

Qualifications and Training

A good general education is essential. Some bookshops require a degree. The industry-recognised qualification, the Diploma in Professional Bookselling, is available through the Booksellers Association of the United Kingdom and Ireland, together with a number of comprehensive training resources. An understanding of e-commerce is an advantage.

Personal Qualities and Skills

A liking for books and people, good general knowledge and an interest in reading and handling books are necessary, as are good health and stamina for a job which involves much standing. An interest in selling and customer care is essential to create a friendly and reassuring atmosphere, where book buyers know that they are being looked after in an efficient manner by professional, knowledgeable staff.

Starting Salary

Starting salaries are usually between £10,000 and £12,000. With experience these can reach around £12,000 to £14,000 a year. Salaries of up to £30,000 can be earned if you are very successful.

info

Skillsmart Retail, 40 Duke Street, London W1A 1AB; 0800 093 5001; www.skillsmartretail.com

Book Careers; www.bookcareers.com

Booksellers Association of the UK and Ireland (BA), Minster House, 272 Vauxhall Bridge Road, London SW1V 1BA; 020 7802 0802; www.booksellers.org

BREWING

Brewing is the complex process of making and packaging beer. Specialist technicians are responsible for the choice of all raw materials – malt, hops, etc, and plant equipment. Brewing technicians and brewing scientists are required to maintain consistently high-quality products. There are opportunities for non-qualified people to work as plant operators.

Qualifications and Training

No formal qualifications are necessary for non-technical jobs in the brewing industry. For technical jobs the main demand is for honours graduates in science and engineering, particularly if they have specialised in brewing, biochemistry or chemical engineering. Specialist degrees in brewing are available at Heriot-Watt University and will provide exemption from the Associate Membership examination of the Institute of Brewing and Distilling, which offers training and internationally recognised qualifications at various levels.

Personal Qualities and Skills

Good health is required for a job that will inevitably involve some night and shift work. The ability to organise and communicate effectively at all levels, and a keen interest in science and engineering, are the hallmarks of successful brewers and brewing scientists.

Starting Salary

Non-technical staff can earn from £13,000 to £15,000 once experienced; graduate trainees start on £15,000–£22,000+.

Brewing Research International (BRi),
Lyttel Hall, Coopers Hill Road,
Nutfield, Surrey RH1 4HY;
01737 822272;
www.brewingresearch.co.uk

Institute of Brewing and Distilling
(IBD), 33 Clarges Street, London
W1J 7EE; 020 7499 8144; www.ibd.
org.uk/igbsite/home/index.asp

Local Job Centre Plus and
Connexions/Careers Centres

Info

BROADCASTING

Broadcast media has several aims – to inform, to entertain, to educate and to increase and retain audiences and to generate profits. The range of programmes is enormous and expanding, but this is a competitive field to enter. Relevant qualifications, training and experience are often essential. Broadcasting companies prefer individuals who are multi-skilled: digital technology and internet-related skills are in demand. It is important to demonstrate enthusiasm through practical involvement in relevant activities such as writing for a local newspaper or website, or working behind the scenes in amateur theatre. Vacancies can be found on broadcasting company websites as well as in a number of national newspapers.

Assistant floor manager and floor assistant

These people carry out a variety of tasks according to each production. They are often in charge of the prompt book.

Audio assistant

Audio assistants work on radio and television programme origination throughout the UK, doing similar jobs to sound operators and studio managers. There is a tendency now in BBC regions for the job to split into these two categories.

Broadcast engineer

Engineers are involved in maintaining and testing the equipment used in studios and in outside broadcasts in radio and television, together with operating and maintaining the transmission chain. They may also be involved in project development and research work. Recently there has been a shortage of skilled broadcast engineers owing to an ageing workforce and staff moving towards new media (internet-based media).

Camera operator

Camera operators work both in studios and on outside broadcasts. They have deep interest in subjects such as photography and lighting. An ability to establish good working relationships with other crew members and the director is necessary.

Costume designer

After gaining the relevant diplomas, costume designers should have theatrical experience. The work involves liaison with producers and make-up staff and responsibility, where necessary, for hiring and adapting costumes. They must have had basic training in pattern-making, cutting and dressmaking, and have gained practical experience in a fashion house or theatrical costumier.

Costume dressmaker

The dressmaker carries out necessary alterations and adaptations on hired or existing costumes, as well as making up new designs.

Director

The director has the responsibility of making the finished programme, and this role also requires good technical knowledge of the media as well as a strong creative ability.

Dresser

Duties involve the maintenance of costumes and the dressing of artists for performances. Requirements are sewing ability, and relevant experience in the theatre, the film industry or as a theatrical costumier.

Film editor/video editor

Film and video editors increasingly work with both formats. The editor must be able to visualise the director's/producer's ideas and make the required creative decisions. Film and video editors have usually had experience in a technical/creative capacity before moving to an editor's position.

Floor manager

Floor managers work in television doing a similar job to the stage manager in the theatre. The broadcasting floor manager's job can be strenuous – actors working on different sets cannot see each other and the floor manager's function is to cue and coordinate them all. The floor manager is also responsible for health and safety in the studio.

Journalist/reporter

(*see also* Journalism)

Journalists work in all forms of media, reporting on current affairs, events and general items of interest. They carry out research and interviews for newspapers, broadcast news programmes and online services. A candidate who is able to script, record and edit his or her own piece digitally would stand a stronger chance of gaining employment. There has been an increase in the number of journalists working for online publications.

Presenter

Presenters work at the front line of radio and television, entertaining or informing the audience. They work on many different types of programme, including current affairs, documentaries, special interest and game shows. They work in all areas of broadcasting: national and regional television and radio, satellite and cable channels. Another version of presenting is the role of Continuity Announcer. They are the people who make announcements between scheduled broadcasts. Presenters and announcers have to do a great deal of preparatory work and liaise closely with their production staff, so it is not simply a matter of presenting a programme.

Producer

The producer has overall responsibility for the project and may recruit all the people involved, including the director, the writer, camera staff and actors. The role requires a good technical knowledge of the media, with financial management and budgeting skills as well as the necessary creative ability.

Producer's assistant

They work for the producer, organising all the administrative work. They retype scripts to incorporate any changes that have been made, ready for the next rehearsal or performance.

Production assistant

The production assistant works as part of the production team. He or she must have good keyboard and organisational skills, be able to deal with a wide range of contacts and work to deadlines. Part of the job involves sitting in the control gallery timing the programme. In addition, PAs may do research for programmes.

Programme assistant

They work in radio and are responsible for the technical and artistic presentation of programmes. They need to be able to operate the equipment and be good at dealing with other people in the team and with the people who are interviewed or who work on the programmes.

Sound operator

They help to set up and operate sound equipment in studios and on outside broadcasts. An understanding of MD recording would be an advantage. They have a deep practical interest in subjects such as hi-fi and sound. The ability to establish good working relationships is necessary.

Studio manager

Studio managers work in radio and are responsible for all issues relating to the artistic and technical operation of a programme. They must know how to interpret the producer's ideas correctly and how to achieve the best sound effects.

Television make-up and hairdressing

(*see also* Beauty)

This is a highly skilled area of work, and competition for any vacancies is keen. It requires a thorough knowledge of period hairstyles and an understanding of the effects of lighting and camera on people's faces. In television, the make-up designer/assistant is responsible for both make-up and hair, whereas in films, the jobs are separate.

Vision mixer

Vision mixers are responsible for recording the images from different cameras under the instruction of the director. They must have strong concentration and the ability to work under pressure.

Qualifications and Training

Many companies offer in-service staff training schemes that are advertised as they occur. Competition for places on these schemes is fierce. The selection boards are impressed by good all-rounders as well as candidates with specialist knowledge.

In technical areas, engineers require, at trainee level, at least English GCSE plus A level maths and physics or a national diploma in electronics. Qualified engineers need to have a degree or HND in electronic engineering. There are a number of degree courses, including foundation degrees in Digital Broadcast Technology.

Technical operators require a good standard of education; at least GCSE grades A–C in English, maths and combined sciences (preferably physics). To improve their chances, candidates often progress their education further. Evidence of in-depth relevant practical involvement, often through amateur interests, always impresses. Many training courses now have an equivalent NVQ or Skillset professional qualification.

Trainee studio managers need to have knowledge of sound equipment together with practical involvement in radio. GCSEs in maths and physics are generally required. Production trainees must have practical experience of work directly related to production, either professionally or in an amateur capacity. No specific qualifications are asked for but applicants must have a wide range of interests.

Journalism training opportunities require applicants to have a demonstrable interest in news and current affairs, with evidence of practical involvement. Training schemes attract a large response and the standard is high.

Secretarial and clerical staff must have a good standard of education. Qualifications for clerical posts vary, depending on the department – for example, in finance an aptitude for figures is essential. Accurate keyboard skills are required for clerk-typist posts. Secretaries must have accurate typing; shorthand is an advantage.

Make-up trainees need to demonstrate involvement in professional or amateur theatre, and must have had formal training in make-up and hairdressing. Applicants should have A levels including art.

Personal Qualities and Skills

The qualities and skills mix required varies from a designer who must be very creative, to a sound engineer who needs excellent technical skills. There are some skills common to everyone working in this field. You have to work well as part of a team, and be capable of working under pressure and keeping calm in the face of problems. Jobs like reporting or presenting require great self-confidence and an ability to work well with a diverse mix of people.

Starting Salary

The salary range is wide, varying with the job you do and the qualifications you need to do it. Some junior jobs are relatively low paid, around £12,000, while assistant producers and editors earn close to £20,000. A lot of this work is paid on short-term contracts, per number of programmes or per individual show, for example.

info

Skillset Careers; 0808 030 0900 for England, Wales and Northern Ireland; 0808 100 8094 for Scotland; www.skillset.org/careers

Skillset, Prospect House, 80–110 New Oxford Street, London WC1A 1HB; www.skillset.org

Radio Academy, 5 Market Place, London W1W 8AE; 020 7255 2010; www.radioacademy.org

Commercial Radio Companies Association, The Radiocentre, 77 Shaftesbury Avenue, London W1D 5DU; 020 7306 2603; www.crca.co.uk

Community Media Association, The Workstation, 15 Paternoster Row, Sheffield S1 2BX; 0114 279 5219; www.commedia.org.uk

Hospital Radio Association; www.hbauk.com

Broadcast Journalism Training Council, 18 Miller's Close, Rippingale, near Bourne, Lincolnshire PE10 0TH; 01778 440025; www.bjtc.org.uk

National Council for the Training of Journalists, The New Granary, Station Road, Newport, Saffron Walden, Essex CB11 3PL; 01799 544014; www.nctj.com

The National Film and Television School, Beaconsfield Studios, Station Road, Beaconsfield, Bucks HP9 1LG; 01494 731425; www.nftsfilm-tv.ac.uk

Equity, Guild House, Upper St Martin's Lane, London WC2H 9EG; 020 7379 6000; www.equity.org.uk

Broadcasting Entertainment Cinematograph and Theatre Union (BECTU), 373–377 Clapham High Road, London SW9 9BT; www.bectu.org.uk

BUSINESS ADMINISTRATION

The term 'business administration' covers all of the roles required to ensure the smooth running of the day-to-day functions of a business regardless of the business purpose. 'Business' refers to any type of organisation in the public, private or voluntary sectors. The jobs range from the Company Secretary's duties (at director level) to the duties of the accounts staff and a variety in between.

Administrative assistant

Administrative assistants undertake a wide variety of routine and clerical tasks in every kind of office and organisation. The same job shares many different job titles, including clerical assistant, clerical worker, office assistant, office junior and administrative support worker. It is very hard to describe a typical job, because you may be working in such different settings and dealing with such different office procedures. You may be the only administrative worker in a very small company, or you could be working in a hospital, a local authority department, a charity or a multinational company. There are some common threads to the work. These include processing paperwork, entering data into computer files, dealing with telephone queries, arranging filing systems, electronic and paper, dealing with incoming post and sending out correspondence, checking and updating records, photocopying and gathering and disseminating information. Some jobs involve considerable responsibility, with the opportunity to supervise, train and manage other members of staff.

Qualifications and Training

Employers usually expect a good standard of general education and often require you to have four or five GCSEs grades A to C including English and maths. A lot of the training is on the job, because you will need to learn about an organisation's particular systems, procedures and structures. Administrative and clerical work can be a very good starting point for other careers in finance, human resources and many other fields. It is common to find people with A levels and degrees starting their careers in administration and clerical support, but this is by no means essential. College courses in administration leading to NVQ levels 1 and 2 awards may improve your chances.

Personal Qualities and Skills

You need good written English skills, including good spelling and grammar. You may need to have good numeracy skills and you should have good basic IT skills. You need to be able to deal with people, cope with problems, but also concentrate on repetitive tasks.

Starting Salary

Salaries vary considerably because this work is available with so many different types of employer. A fairly typical range of starting salaries is £11,000 to £13,500 depending on geographical location and size and type of employer. With experience salaries rise to between £14,000 and £19,000.

Council for Administration, Graphite Square, Vauxhall Walk, London SE11 5EE; 020 7091 9620; www.cfa.uk.com

info

Company Secretary

The Company Secretary plays a major part in the organisation's governance. Duties include ensuring that the company complies with relevant legal and regulatory matters, administration of mergers and acquisitions, drafting contracts, advising the board of directors on company law and procedures and maintaining company records. Other duties can include pensions administration, personnel matters, shareholder issues, property management and finance.

Qualifications and Training

The law recognises the importance of the Company Secretary role, mandatory for every company, by requiring the Company Secretary of a public limited company (plc) to have specific knowledge and experience. Only the Institute of Chartered Secretaries and Administrators (ICSA) qualification specifically addresses the requirements of the role.

The ICSA Qualifying Scheme comprises three programmes: Foundation, Pre-Professional and Professional. Graduates and holders of recognised postgraduate qualifications are eligible for direct access onto the Professional Programme. It consists of core modules in Corporate Governance, Corporate Administration, Corporate Secretaryship, Corporate Financial Management, and top-up modules in Corporate Law, Management Accounting, Financial Accounting and Strategic Management.

Upon completion of the ICSA Qualifying Scheme, candidates become Graduates of the Institute (Grad ICSA). To become a Member, an ICSA Graduate has to demonstrate three years' relevant experience and have two sponsors of professional status to confirm his or her fitness to practise. There are two grades of Membership: Associate and Fellow.

Personal Qualities and Skills

As a Company Secretary you must be prepared to take responsibility and be discrete in handling confidential or sensitive information. You must be able to understand numerical information and other complex documents. You need excellent communication skills, often having to be diplomatic and tactful, and be comfortable dealing with people at all levels within an organisation.

Starting Salary

Salaries for trainees start at between £21,000 and £27,000; larger or London-based organisations pay the highest rates. With a few years experience salaries rise to £20,000 to £30,000.

Graduate Recruitment Manager, Institute of Chartered Secretaries and Administrators (ICSA), 16 Park Crescent, London W1B 1AH; Tel: Graduate Recruitment Manager, on 020 7580 4741; www.icsa.org.uk; e-mail: gradrec@icsa.co.uk

Personal assistant

(*see also* Secretary)

A senior secretary or personal assistant (PA) may work with one or more senior executives. Accurate skills in shorthand, audio typewriting, word processing and information management, and a knowledge of office-based software are desirable. The PA may also act as administrator, information centre, organiser of the manager's day, progress chaser, arranger of travel and meetings, receptionist and communicator (oral and written) internally and externally. A senior secretary or PA assumes responsibility without direct supervision and takes decisions within the scope of assigned authority.

Qualifications and Training

A minimum of GCSEs in maths and English is usually required, but it is not uncommon for people with A levels or degrees to go into this work. Any relevant IT training courses on software packages for managing data or accounts are also useful. Some colleges run full-time and part-time secretarial and administrative courses to GNVQ levels 2 and 3. Courses can also be taken through part-time study whilst working, through the London Chamber of Commerce and Industry Examination Board (LCCIEB), Oxford, Cambridge and RSA Examination Board (OCR) and Pitmans Qualifications (City & Guilds), which offer relevant qualifications that take one to two years to complete. Personal assistant work spans everything from fairly junior jobs in small companies, to extremely responsible roles working with directors of large organisations. The training courses available reflect this, and courses are offered at several different levels.

Personal Qualities and Skills

You must be friendly but discrete and diplomatic. You need to be extremely well organised and calm when you are under pressure or working to deadlines. Knowing when to use your own initiative is also important.

Starting Salary

The starting salaries for personal assistants vary enormously, from around £14,000 to £26,000. This range reflects the different levels of responsibility and experience required for the variety of posts on offer.

Institute of Qualified Professional Secretaries (IQPS), Suite 464, 24–28 St Leonards Road, Windsor, Berks SL4 3BB; 0844 800 0182; www.iqps.org

London Chamber of Commerce and Industry Examinations Board (LCCIEB), 112 Station Road, Sidcup, Kent DA15 7BJ; 0870 720 2909; www.lccieb.com

Oxford and Cambridge and RSA Examinations (OCR), 9 Hills Road, Cambridge CB2 1PB; 01223 553311; www.ocr.org.uk

Pitman Qualifications, City & Guilds, 1 Giltspur Street, London EC1A 9DD; 020 7294 2800; www.pitmanqualifications.com

Info

Receptionist

Receptionists work in hotels, large organisations and private firms, sometimes combining the job with the duties of telephonist. In hotels, they welcome the guests, make bookings and prepare the final accounts. They also deal with reservation correspondence and act as a general information office. In small hotels this can be handled by one person but in most, and especially the larger, hotels, they work in a team headed by the Reception Manager. In large official organisations, such as a town hall or in firms with many staff, receptionists direct visitors to the correct department. In small firms the job is often combined with answering the phone, typing and franking the mail.

Medical receptionists work in a variety of environments. They need, in addition to the standard skills of a receptionist, a full understanding of the principles of medical ethics and confidentiality, knowledge of the NHS and social services, medical terminology and clinical procedures.

Qualifications and Training

Formal educational qualifications are not necessary, but proficiency in English and maths is an advantage. For some posts knowledge of other languages is important. Many further education colleges offer one-year full-time courses and a range of part-time courses in reception skills. A range of qualifications is available, including NVQs at levels 1, 2 and 3 and Modern Apprenticeships.

The AMSPAR (see p. 72) diploma in health service reception is a nationally recognised professional qualification. It can be achieved by examination and is available from a wide network of approved centres throughout the UK.

Personal Qualities and Skills

Receptionists should be friendly, pleasant with a good phone manner and neat appearance. They also need stamina, as they are often expected to work shifts that include evenings and weekends. They should have a real liking for people and a good memory for faces. Computer literacy is also important.

Starting Salary

Outside London salaries can start rather low at £8,500; in London, around £12,000 to £14,000. Hotel receptionists usually start on around £15,000 and some of these posts include accommodation, meals, etc.

info

People 1st, 2nd Floor,
Armstrong House, 38 Market Square,
Uxbridge UB8 1LX; 0870 060 2550;
www.people1st.co.uk

Local Job Centre Plus and
Connexions/Careers Centres

Secretary

Secretaries work in all types of organisations. Sometimes they are assigned to one person, sometimes they provide support services for several people. Most secretaries need to have well-developed ICT skills but there is still a demand for those with shorthand and audio typing. As well as producing documents, secretaries undertake a range of organisational tasks such as arranging travel and meetings. They may also work as receptionists and deal with callers and queries by phone or e-mail. Those in senior positions may make decisions on behalf of managers.

Bilingual secretary

A bilingual secretary is fluent in a second or third language and may work in commerce, overseas or as an EU employee. The work will include composing, reading and translating documents in the foreign language. They may use speaking/listening skills in their languages for telephone work, receiving visitors and interpreting at meetings.

Farm secretary

In addition to normal secretarial work, farm secretaries will be responsible for completing complex forms, keeping records and accounts and calculating wages. A farm secretary may work for one employer, be freelance or be sent out by an agency to smaller farms.

Legal secretary

Accurate skills have always been paramount for legal paperwork, but word processors have made the job easier. Legal secretaries are employed by barristers and solicitors in professional practice and in large commercial organisations.

Medical secretary

Medical secretaries are good administrators, keep records, handle correspondence and filing. They work in hospitals, for individual doctors/consultants and in health centres. Accuracy and confidentiality are essential, as is a thorough knowledge of medical terminology.

Qualifications and Training

There is a range of full- and part-time courses available. Courses usually include word processing, audio, shorthand and office procedures. There are training opportunities for young people leading to NVQ levels 1, 2 and 3 in Administration.

GCSEs are usually required to obtain a place on a full-time secretarial course. A good working knowledge of the English language is essential. Additional qualifications are needed to specialise as a legal, medical or farm secretary. There are a number of postgraduate diploma courses for graduates wishing to train as bilingual secretaries.

Personal Qualities and Skills

Good secretaries are judged by what they do, but qualities such as self-motivation, discretion, tact, loyalty, flexibility, excellent communication skills and smart appearance are expected.

Starting Salary

Varies from £8,000 to £20,000+ depending on experience, location and type of employer. Bilingual and legal secretaries are better paid.

info

Institute of Business Administration and Management, 16 Park Crescent, London W1B 1AH; 020 7580 4741; fax: 020 7323 1132; www.ibam.org; e-mail: info@ibam.org

Institute of Qualified Private Secretaries Ltd (IQPS), First Floor, 6 Bridge Avenue, Maidenhead SL6 1RR; 01628 625007; fax: 01628 624990; www.iqps.org; e-mail: office@iqps.org

Association of Medical Secretaries, Practice Managers, Administrators and Receptionists (AMSPAR), Tavistock House North, Tavistock Square, London WC1H 9LN; 020 7387 6005; www.amspar.co.uk; e-mail: amspar@atlas.co.uk

ILEX Paralegal Training, Kempston Manor, Kempston, Bedford MK42 7AB; 01234 841000; www.ilex.org.uk; e-mail: info@ilex.org.uk

Institute of Para-legal Training, The Mill, Clymping Street, Clymping, Littlehampton, West Sussex BN17 5RN; 01903 714276

Institute of Linguists, Saxon House, 48 Southwark Street, London SE1 1UN; 020 7940 3100; www.iol.org.uk; e-mail: info@iol.org.uk

CALL/CONTACT CENTRE

'Contact centre' is replacing the term 'call centre' as it more accurately describes the activities in places where customer support is provided by e-mail, fax and web chat as well as by telephone. It is an expanding industry with approximately 800,000 people working in over 5,000 contact centres in the UK. The business and organisations behind these vary from local and national government (DVLA, NHS Direct) to charities (Childline, Oxfam) through to highly technical help desk functions (Microsoft, IBM, British Telecom). The work can be sales or advice oriented, and in some centres language skills are essential as calls are taken from all over the world. The areas of growth tend to be in local government and small to medium enterprises, while some larger organisations are relocating their centres abroad.

Management

Call centre management can involve leading a small team of agents or managing a multi-site global operation which employs thousands. Managers need technical expertise and product knowledge as well as people skills. Opportunities to move into management from team leader or agent positions are common as this is a growing industry.

Call centre agents

The work involves dealing with queries and requests for information from the public, often in a very regulated environment with strict adherence to start, finish and break times. The role can be varied, with agents working across a number of departments to resolve the enquiry. Varied working patterns mean the opportunity to work part time or term-time only is common.

Qualifications and training

Keyboard skills, good communication abilities and, for e-mail and web chat, reasonable spelling and grammar. Increasingly the simpler activities in contact centres are becoming automated, leaving the human operator to deal with more complicated queries.

Many employers offer work-based training programmes in product knowledge, language skills, technical know-how and people skills and some offer

Modern Apprenticeships. There are a growing number of Certificate, Diploma and Degree-level courses in Call Centre Management. These are often available through distance or web-based learning.

Personal Qualities and Skills

This work requires you to be calm, friendly and patient, and to possess a sense of humour, a thick skin and a lot of common sense.

Starting Salary

Salaries start at between £10,000 and £11,000 for trainees. Experienced staff earn between £12,000 and £15,000, and supervisors earn between £16,000 and £19,000. Salaries for senior managers range from £20,000 to £60,000. The average is around £30,000.

info

The Call Centre Management Association (CCMA), International House, 174 Three Bridges Road, Crawley, West Sussex RH10 1LE; 01293 538400; www.ccma.org.uk/

CCA – The Professional Body for Customer Contact, 20 Newton Place, Glasgow G3 7PY; 0141 564 9010; www.cca.org.uk

e-skills UK, 1 Castle Lane, London SW1E 6DR; 020 7963 8920; www.e-skills.com

CARDIAC TECHNOLOGIST

Cardiac Clinical Scientific Officers (CCSOs) and cardiac clinical physiologists are members of the medical team responsible for the recording and analysis of different physiological data required to assist in the diagnosis and treatment of known or suspected heart disease. The CCSO is the friendly professional face in this highly technological environment, linking the patient with the diagnostic equipment. The CCSO normally works in a Cardiology Department within a hospital. The variety of procedures carried out varies from hospital to hospital. Some smaller hospitals may include procedures from other disciplines, eg respiratory function tests.

Qualifications and Training

In various parts of the UK the training schemes and courses have undergone significant changes. The profession is moving towards being graduate entry only. Degree courses in clinical physiology leading to State Registration came on stream in 2003, but at the moment there is still some flexibility within the profession. To get onto these courses you need three A levels or their equivalent, maths or physics being the preferred subjects. At present some hospitals are still operating training schemes for people with four GCSEs including maths, English and a science.

Personal Qualities and Skills

You have to be practical and confident with advanced technical equipment, but also extremely good at working closely with people. Your patients may be anxious, uncomfortable or uncertain about the procedures you are using and so will require a lot of reassurance. You also have to be attentive and meticulous in recording and observing information, and good at working as part of a team.

Starting Salary

Salaries range from £11,000 to £15,000 for new entrants. Senior staff earn between £18,000 and £32,000, but there are limited numbers of these senior posts.

The Society for Cardiological Science and Technology (SCST), Suite 4, Sovereign House, 22 Gate Lane, Goldmere, Sutton Coldfield B73 5TT; 0121 354 6512; www.scst.org.uk	Local Job Centre Plus and Connexions/Careers Centres and local hospital cardiology or human resource departments	

CAREERS ADVISER

Careers or Personal Advisers/Careers provide information, advice and guidance to school and college students and to adults in the community. They work both inside and outside education. In England, careers advisers work mainly in the Connexions Service as personal advisers (PAs), helping young people aged 13–19 make choices about employment and further study, and helping them overcome any difficulties they face in this area. The work involves one-to-one interviews with clients, presentations to groups of clients or parents, and marketing work with local and national employers.

Outside England, careers advisers work in Careers Scotland, Careers Wales and the Training and Employment Agency in Northern Ireland. Some careers advisers also work in higher education and are employed by individual universities and colleges.

Qualifications and Training

Most careers advisers have a degree or equivalent qualification. In addition they need to complete a qualification in careers guidance (QCG). This can be done either via a one-year full-time or two-year part-time course, or a work-based training course. Candidates also complete a portfolio of evidence that can be used for NVQ/SVQ level 4 in Advice and Guidance. Details of colleges and universities offering the QCG are listed on the Institute of Career Guidance (ICG) website. This site also lists employers who are registered to offer work-based training. Experience in other careers such as teaching, social work, commerce or industry is an advantage in this profession. Experience of working with young people, in a paid or voluntary capacity, is also beneficial. Everyone working in this field will have to undergo a full Criminal Records Bureau (CRB) check.

To become a Connexions Personal Adviser in England you have to do additional training once you have joined the service. For careers services in Northern Ireland, Scotland and Wales this is not the case.

To work in higher education, you do not necessarily have to have a QCG, though many applicants do. Universities and colleges set their own requirements. There are in-service certificate and diploma courses available in careers education, information and guidance in higher education.

Personal Qualities and Skills

Excellent communication skills are essential. You are dealing with young people, their parents, teachers, employers and other professionals. You have to be well organised, good at disseminating information, able to present material to individuals and groups and have reasonable IT skills. You should be confident, persuasive, assertive and tactful and you must be a good listener.

Starting Salary

Salaries for trainees start at between £18,000 and £20,000 rising to £24,000 once qualified. The whole funding system for Connexions services is due to change in mid-2008 and this may have some impact on salaries and on training.

info

Association of Graduate Careers Advisory Services (AGCAS), Millennium House, 30 Junction Road, Sheffield S11 8XB; 0114 251 5750; www.agcas.org.uk

Connexions, Department for Education and Skills (DfES), Supporting Children and Young People Group, W408, Moorfoot, Sheffield S1 4PQ; 0870 000 2288; www.connexions.gov.uk

Department for Education and Skills (DfES), Sanctuary Buildings, Great Smith Street, London SW1P 3BT; 0870 000 2288; www.dfes.gov.uk

Department for Employment and Learning in Northern Ireland (DELNI), Adelaide House, 39–49 Adelaide Street, Belfast

BT2 8FD; 028 9025 7726; www.delni.gov.uk

The Improvement and Development Agency, Layden House, 76–86 Turnmill Street, London EC1M 5OG; 020 7296 6880; www.idea.gov.uk

Institute of Career Guidance (ICG), Third Floor, Copthall House, 1 New Road, Stourbridge, West Midlands DY8 1PH; 01384 376464; www.icg-uk.org

Learning and Skills Council, Cheylsmore House, Quinton Road, Coventry CV1 2WT; 0845 019 4170; www.lsc.gov.uk

National Assembly for Wales, Cardiff Bay, Cardiff CF99 1NA; 029 2082 5111; www.wales.gov.uk

CARPENTRY

see also Construction

Cabinet maker

You don't need any specific qualifications, but some employers might like you to have GCSEs particularly in maths or a technical subject. If you are aged between 16 and 24, you could train through an apprenticeship. If you are over 24, you need to have some relevant skills, experience or qualifications.

There are several college-based City & Guilds courses in furniture production; these courses are aimed at newcomers and current employees in the industry.

Personal Qualities and Skills

You must be very practical and confident in using machine and hand tools. You should be able to follow a technical drawing, adapt designs and do drawings of your own. You need good numeracy skills and if you become self-employed you also need some business awareness.

Starting Salary

Expect around £10,000 when you start off, rising to £14,000 with three or four years' experience. Cabinet makers who become really skilled and get a good reputation can earn £35,000 plus.

Furniture Furnishing and Interiors National Training Organisation, 67 Wollaton Road, Beeston, Nottingham NG9 2NG; 0115 922 1200; www.ffinto.org

Skills Direct; 0870 850 5262

Construction Skills Certification Scheme; 0870 417 8777; www.cscs.uk.com

CARPET FITTER

Carpet retailers, furniture stores and department stores all employ their own trained personnel who deliver and fit carpets and other floor coverings to customers' homes, shops, offices or hotels. Many fitters are also self-employed.

Qualifications and Training

GCSE English and maths or equivalents are usually required. Training is mainly given on the job, working with an experienced fitter, although in some firms there are possible opportunities for day-release courses leading to the examinations of the National Institute of Carpet and Floorlayers. Short one- to five-day and tailored courses are available through the Flooring Industry Training Association.

Personal Qualities and Skills

Strength and fitness are important in order to handle heavy rolls of carpet. A good head for calculations and an eye for detail (such as matching patterns) are also essential. Generally, too, it is necessary to be able to drive.

Starting Salary

Around national minimum wage rates. A new entrant earns between £10,500 to £12,000, and with experience can earn up to £15,000. Companies employing carpet fitters pay £18,000.

info

National Institute of Carpet and Floorlayers, 4d St Mary's Place, The Lace Market, Nottingham NG1 1PH; 0115 958 3077; fax: 0115 941 2238;

www.nicfltd.org.uk; e-mail: info@nicfltd.org.uk

Local Job Centre Plus and Careers/ Connexions Centres

CARTOGRAPHY

Cartography embraces all aspects of map-making including the making of charts, globes and models of the earth or heavenly bodies.

Cartographers

Cartographers are involved primarily in the initial stages of the collection and editing of material up to the point of actual generation and production of the finished product, which is generally done by cartographic draughtsmen (and women) and assistants.

Most cartographic work is undertaken in government departments such as the Ministry of Defence, the Meteorological Office and the Department for Environment, Food and Rural Affairs. The Ordnance Survey no longer employ cartographic draughtsmen or assistants as their mapping is produced digitally, but they do recruit trainee surveyors.

Vacancies sometimes occur in local authority planning departments and with specialist publishing houses or survey companies. Computers are reducing the need for manual draughtsmen, especially in repetitive work, and the increasing application of Geographical Information Systems (GIS) via a graphics workstation is significantly changing the work of professional cartographers. There is substantial growth in the number of map/chart products becoming available on CD, many of which are designed for interactive use.

Qualifications and Training

Cartographers are increasingly graduates with a relevant undergraduate or postgraduate qualification. Universities offering courses in cartography, GIS, topographic science or surveying and mapping science include Newcastle, Oxford Brookes and East London. Admission requirements vary, but are likely to include geography A level.

Personal Qualities and Skills

Neatness, precision, aesthetic appreciation and a fine attention to detail are important, as are mathematical awareness and an ability to analyse visual judgements on graphic efficiency.

Starting Salary

For a graduate, from £14,000 to £16,000; mapping and charting technicians, from £11,000; and assistants, £8,500+.

info

Association for Geographic Information (AGI), Block C, Fourth Floor, Morelands, 5–23 Old Street, London EC1V 9HL; 020 7253 5211; www.agi.org.uk

British Cartographic Society, BCS Administration, 12 Elworthy Drive, Wellington, Somerset TA21 9AT; www.cartography.org.uk

Countryside Agency, John Dower House, Crescent Place, Cheltenham, Gloucester GL50 3RA; 01242 521381; www.countryside.gov.uk

Defence Geographic and Imagery Intelligence Agency Headquarters (DGIA), Watson Building, Elmwood Avenue, Feltham, Middlesex TW13 7AH; 020 8818 2422

Department for Environment, Food and Rural Affairs (DEFRA), c/o Nobel House, 17 Smith Square, London SW1P 3JR; 0845 933 5577; www.defra.gov.uk

Lantra: The Sector Skills Council for the Environmental and Land-based Sector, Lantra House, Stoneleigh Park, Nr Coventry, Warwickshire CV8 2LG; 024 7669 6996; www.lantra.co.uk

Ordnance Survey (OS), Romsey Road, Southampton SO16 4GU; 0845 605 0505; www.ordnancesurvey.co.uk

Ordnance Survey work

The Ordnance Survey is part of the civil service and responsible to the Department for Communities and Local Government. It produces all kinds of official maps covering the whole of Britain. Large-scale computerised Ordnance Survey mapping is used by local authorities, estate agents, solicitors, architects, civil engineers and government departments, while leisure paper maps are popular with ramblers, riders and cyclists. Other Ordnance Survey maps show historical detail, such as Roman Britain, or statistical data (for example, population density).

Job opportunities may be limited since organisations no longer employ cartographic draughtsmen or assistants as all maps are produced digitally. There are, however, sometimes opportunities for trainee surveyors. These are advertised in the locality of the vacancies. The work includes checking new features such as buildings, hedges, fences and roads and noting any alterations since the map was last printed. These are input on hand-held computers.

Increasingly, Ordnance Survey work involves the use of information technology, ranging from base data for digital atlases and computer games to complex geographical databases. Ordnance Survey's head office is in Southampton and most employees are based there. Field surveyors, however, may be posted virtually anywhere in England, Scotland or Wales.

Qualifications and Training

A good general education and five GCSE passes at grade C or above, including maths, English, geography or information technology and a minimum of 18 months' experience working in a related field. Computer literacy and a driving licence are desirable. Candidates also take an aptitude test.

Personal Qualities and Skills

A willingness to work in an outdoor environment, excellent interpersonal skills and an ability to work with all sections of the community, as well as the confidence, initiative and motivation to work alone or as part of a small team.

Starting Salary

£13,000–£14,000 for trainee surveyors, £18,000–£22,000 with more experience.

Ordnance Survey, Romsey Road, Southampton SO16 4GU; 0845 605 0505; 0845 605 0504 (dedicated Welsh language helpline); www.ordnancesurvey.co.uk

CATERING

see Hospitality and Catering

CHEMISTRY

Chemistry is the basis of a wide range of careers and is the science which deals with the composition, structure and uses of chemicals and substances.

Analysts

Analysts work in industry providing a service for research, development and production departments. They analyse the results of experiments and advise what a newly produced substance may be. An analyst may check the quality of raw materials bought in by a company and examine the quality of the company's own products. Public analysts are employed by local authorities to examine, for example, the state of the water supply; the adequacy of the sewage treatment system; toxic and suspect materials and leachate from landfill sites. They may also be asked to examine food from a suspect restaurant. Public analysts are frequently required to give witness on their findings in courts of law, and should be familiar with the law relating to goods and services.

Chemist

The majority of trained chemists work in the manufacturing industries within organisations producing such materials as foodstuffs, plastics, pharmaceuticals, cosmetics, petroleum, detergents and fertilisers. Large numbers teach in schools, colleges and universities, generally combining teaching with research work; there are also openings with local authorities, the Health Service, the civil service and the nationalised industries, as well as in marketing and sales, information and patents and specialised publishing. Chemistry is essential in many other careers such as medicine or veterinary science.

Qualifications and Training

Most professional chemists and analysts have membership of the Royal Society of Chemistry, for which a degree or equivalent qualification is necessary. Entry requirements for degree courses generally include at least two A levels or equivalent in science subjects, including chemistry and another scientific or mathematical subject. To become a public analyst it is necessary to hold the Mastership in Chemical Analysis (MChemA), a qualification awarded by the Royal Society of Chemistry.

Chemistry technicians usually need three GCSEs or equivalent for entry to a national certificate in science or chemistry – these are generally day-release courses. This can be followed by a higher certificate or degree level qualification.

Personal Qualities and Skills

Chemists usually form part of a team, so an ability to work alongside others is essential. The actual work varies enormously, but generally a chemist also needs an enquiring mind and practical experimental ability and experience. Attention to detail and a sense of responsibility are important.

Starting Salary

For new entrants, starting salaries range from £14,000 to £29,000, this broad range reflecting the different jobs, from trainee technician to research chemist.

info

Analytical Science Network (ASN),
c/o Royal Society of Chemistry,
Burlington House, Piccadilly, London
W1J 0BA; 020 7440 3326;
www.chemsoc.org

Royal Pharmaceutical Society of
Great Britain (RPSGB),

1 Lambeth High Street, London
SE1 7JN; 020 7735 9141;
www.rpsgb.org.uk

Royal Society of Chemistry (RSC),
Burlington House, Piccadilly, London
W1J 0BA; 020 7437 8656;
www.rsc.org

CHILD CARE

This sector covers a range of occupations, but all involve the care of children, especially pre-school children.

Childminder

A registered childminder looks after children and provides a caring environment along with stimulating play and learning activities. Childminders need to be responsible, trustworthy and affectionate. Childminders look after babies and children under five; there is a limit to the number of children of different age groups that can be cared for by a childminder.

A childminder's job needs careful planning and good organisation skills to arrange individual routines for children of different ages to include periods of play, exercise, naps and meals. It is important to keep records of payments, expenses and insurance. It is essential for the children's learning and development to include activities such as painting and drawing, reading stories and singing, playing with natural materials and construction toys in and out doors.

A childminder is expected to provide food for the children, and with babies prepare bottles, feed the babies and change nappies. Older children will require physical care, such as washing hands and going to the toilet. It is important not to discriminate against children from different ethnic groups, religious backgrounds and family types.

Qualifications and Training

All childminders have to be registered and to meet a set of national standards, though these are not based around formal qualifications. Many childminders are parents themselves or have experience in other childcare work. You need to be 18 or over to undertake this work.

In England your Local Authority's Children's Information Service can provide information about how to register and send you an application pack. The Office for Standards in Education (OFSTED) is the registration body for England. You have to be interviewed and your home is also inspected. If you are approved, you must take a registered training course. The Council for Awards in Children's Care and Education (CACHE) and the National Childminding Association have developed NVQ level 3 certificate and diploma courses in home-based childcare.

In Scotland you should contact the Care Commission, in Wales the Care Standards Inspectorate, and in Northern Ireland your local Health and Social Care Services Trust.

Personal Qualities and Skills

Of course you have to really enjoy working with children and to be prepared to share your home with them. You should have an open-minded attitude about different ways of bringing up children and you should be quite comfortable with both you and your home being scrutinised. You have to be extremely responsible, sensitive and patient. You need to be practical, with a sense of humour, and keep calm if problems arise. You have to be able to communicate well with parents as well as with their children. You need to be imaginative, sympathetic and sensible. You need to be very alert, especially on matters of health and safety.

Starting Salary

Salaries are between £10,000 and £18,000. What you earn depends on how many children you care for and for how many hours. Childminders are self-employed and can set their own fees, but these will tend to be in line with what everyone else is charging.

Council for Awards in Children's Care and Education (CACHE), Beaufort House, Grosvenor Road, St Albans, Herts AL1 3AW; 01727 847636; www.cache.org.uk

Office for Standards in Education (OFSTED), Alexandra House, 33 Kingsway, London WC2B 6SE; 0845 640 4045; www.ofsted.gov.uk

Northern Ireland Childminding Association, 16/18 Mill Street, Newtownards, Co Down BT23 4LU; 028 9181 1015; www.nicma.org

National Childminding Association, Royal Court, 81 Tweedy Road, Bromley, Kent BR1 1TG; 0845 880 0044; www.ncma.org.uk

Children's Workforce Development Council, 3rd Floor, Friends Provident House, 13–14 South Parade, Leeds LS1 5QS; 0113 244 6311; www.cwdcouncil.org.uk

Childcare Link; 08000 960296; www.childcarelink.gov.uk

Scottish Childminding Association, Suite 2, 37 Melville Terrace, Stirling FK8 2ND; 01786 445377; www.childminding.org

Care Commission Scotland; 0845 603 0890; www.carecommission.com

Care Standards Inspectorate for Wales; 01443 848 450; www.csiw.wales.gov.uk

Info

Nursery nurse

A nursery nurse works with babies and children under eight in the public, private and voluntary sectors. This can include schools, nurseries and hospitals. In schools, nursery nurses work in nursery, reception and infant classes alongside the teacher, providing and supervising educational and play activities. They may also be involved in providing out of school care at after-school clubs and on holiday schemes. Nursery nurses in hospitals can work in maternity and special care units, and on children's wards. Day nurseries, both private and local authority, employ nursery nurses to care for children under five whose parents are unable to care for them during the day. Nursery nurses can also be employed in clinics, residential homes, the community, family centres and private homes as nannies.

Qualifications and Training

The Council for Awards in Children's Care and Education (CACHE) level 3 Diploma in Child Care and Education (previously known as the NNEB) is a prerequisite for many jobs and can be done as a two-year full-time course or part time up to five years. There are no minimum entry requirements, but many colleges ask for GCSEs at C or above, including English. The BTEC National Diploma in early years, a two-year course, requires four GCSEs at grade C or above. Modern Apprenticeships are available; apprentices are trained by their employers and work towards NVQ level 3 in early years care and education.

Nursery nurses in Scotland must register with the Scottish Child Care and Education Board; this requires completion of a one-year programme of SQA National Certificate units plus the one-year HNC in child care and education or a programme of SVQ level 3 units in early years and education.

Personal Qualities and Skills

A genuine love of children is essential, with the ability to work with patience, tolerance, imagination and energy. Good motivation skills and a sense of fun are important.

Starting Salary

£9,000–£11,000 as a nursery assistant, £11,000–£15,000 as a nursery nurse/officer, £17,000+ as a manager. Nannies working for private families can earn from £250 to £600 a week depending on location and experience. Large businesses that operate nurseries for their employees pay salaries higher than these.

Council for Awards in Children's Care and Education (CACHE), Beaufort House, Grosvenor Road, St Albans, Herts AL1 3AW; 01727 847636; www.cache.org.uk; e-mail: info@cache.org.uk

Professional Association of Nursery Nurses, 2 St James' Court, Friar Gate, Derby DE1 1BT; 01332 372337; www.pat.org.uk; e-mail: pann@pat.org.uk

Scottish Childcare and Education Board, 01294 470380 (9.00 am to 12.30 pm weekdays)

National Day Nurseries Association (NDNA), Oak House, Woodvale Road, Brighouse, West Yorkshire HD6 4AB; 0870 774 4244; www.ndna.org.uk

www.skillsforcare.org.uk; 0113 245 1716

Local Job Centre Plus and Connexions/Careers Centres

info

Play worker

Play workers work with school-age children in many different settings, including breakfast clubs, after-school clubs, holiday play schemes, adventure playgrounds and play centres. What play workers actually do varies according to the age of the children they are working with and the ethos of the organisation which employs them. What all play work has in common is an emphasis on giving children and young people choices on how to use their leisure time and ideas on how to enjoy and be exposed to a wide range of activities. Play workers help children socialise and try out new activities. Play workers organise a wide range of activities including games, drama, sports, creative art, outings, story telling and quiet time.

Play workers interact with children of different ages, abilities and backgrounds and they have to be able to engage effectively with all these children. Play workers also have to liaise with parents, keep records, come up with new ideas and take responsibility for health and safety.

Some play workers are based in hospitals working with children who are sick or recovering from surgery. These play workers have to find activities that are suitable for each individual child's mental and physical condition. Play can have a significant effect on how well children recover or are able to cope with their illnesses, so hospital play work is highly specialised.

Qualifications and Training

While no formal academic qualifications are required, some voluntary work with children will give you a real advantage. Local Authority Children's Information Services often run short courses on working with children. These only last one to three weeks; they are not a qualification, but an opportunity for you to get some idea about whether work with children would suit you. Current regulations mean than anyone working in play will now have to gain a formal qualification. Part-time accepted courses are run by the Council for Awards in Children's Care and Education (CACHE).

Personal Qualities and Skills

Of course you must really enjoy working with children. You must be resilient, imaginative and patient. You should have good practical skills and be acutely aware of health and safety issues. You must be a good communicator: you will often be talking to parents as well as children. You need to be well organised, as you may have to do some paperwork.

Starting Salary

Many people start as volunteers and the hours are not normal 9 to 5: they may be pre-school, or school holidays only. Pro rata play worker salaries are between £10,000 and £11,000. With management and planning responsibility you can earn £14,000 to £15,000.

info

Council for Awards in Children's Care and Education (CACHE), Beaufort House, Grosvenor Road, St Albans, Herts AL1 3AW; 01727 847636; www.cache.org.uk

DFES Children's Workforce Qualifications; eypquals.cwdcouncil.org.uk

Skills Active, Castlewood House, 77–91 New Oxford Street, London WC1A 1PX; advice line: 08000 933300; www.skillsactive.com

Childcare Link; 08000 960296; www.childcarelink.gov.uk

National Association of Hospital Play Staff, Fladgate, Forty Green, Beaconsfield, Bucks HP9 1XS; www.nahps.org.uk

CHIROPODIST (OR PODIATRIST)

Chiropodists are also known as podiatrists; the profession is in the process of changing its name. They are concerned with the health of feet. Those working in the NHS deal with problems caused by diabetes or arthritis and may work with those suffering from sports injuries. Ailments such as corns, bunions and malformed nails are more likely to be dealt with by those in private practice.

Chiropodists perform minor operations under local anaesthetic. They may work in the NHS in hospitals, clinics or health centres, or in private practice or large organisations. Many undertake postgraduate training to specialise in areas such as sports medicine, biomechanics and podiatric surgery.

Qualifications and Training

Degrees in chiropody or podiatry are run at many institutions throughout the UK, and the only route into the profession is via one of these degrees. You then apply to the Health Professions Council for State Registration and are able to work either in the NHS or in private practice. The need for private practitioners to have an approved degree course is the result of a recent change in regulations. To get onto a degree course you need five GCSEs, including maths,

English and a science. Other qualifications and experience, such as nursing, may give you some exemptions from parts of the course.

Personal Qualities and Skills

You must be calm, caring and reassuring, as well as practical, careful and patient. In the NHS you are likely to be part of a team, but you might also be visiting people in their own homes, so you must be able to work on your own and use your initiative. In private practice, you may need business skills too.

Starting Salary

In the NHS starting salaries are just over £18,000 and rise to £35,000 in senior management posts. In private practice you can earn more; the range is £25,000 to £50,000.

Department of Health (DH),
Quarry House, Quarry Hill, Leeds
LS2 7UE; 0113 254 5000;
www.dh.gov.uk

Health Professions Council (HPC),
Park House, 184 Kennington Park Road,
London SE11 4BU;
020 7582 0866; www.hpc-uk.org

Institute of Chiropodists and
Podiatrists, 27 Wright Street,
Southport, Merseyside PR9 0TL;
01704 546141;
www.inst-chiropodist.org.uk/

Society of Chiropodists and
Podiatrists (SCP), 1 Fellmonger's Path,
Tower Bridge Road, London SE1 3LY;
020 7234 8620; www.scpod.org

info

CIVIL AVIATION

The civil aviation sector relates to all the occupations within the world of civil aircraft flying, including passenger and goods transportation.

Aeronautical engineer

(*see also* Engineering)

Air traffic engineers are responsible for the efficient operation of the wide range of sophisticated telecommunications, electronic systems and specialist equipment needed in air traffic control centres, airports and other specialist centres. This involves the installation, calibration and maintenance of radar, air-to-ground communication systems, navigational and landing aids, computer data and processing equipment and visual display units. Opportunities may exist for engineers to look after day-to-day maintenance and, at graduate level, for field management, installation and development work.

Air cabin crew

Flight attendants (air cabin crew) look after the safety, comfort and welfare of passengers. Before a flight they check stocks of equipment, welcome passengers on board and go through safety routines. During the flight they will serve ready-cooked meals and drinks, sell duty-free goods and deal with any problems passengers have. Flight reports are prepared by senior stewards, who also attend to first-class passengers and supervise junior staff.

Aircraft maintenance engineer

(*see also* Engineering)

Aircraft maintenance engineers make sure that aircraft are airworthy. They maintain, service and overhaul the aircraft, their engines and equipment, working to very high standards set by the Civil Aviation Authority (CAA). Every part of every job is checked and certified. Engineers usually specialise in either mechanics or avionics, and work on major overhaul or in 'turnarounds' – the work carried out after each flight. Apart from working with the airlines, other opportunities are found with firms that specialise in aircraft maintenance. There are also a few openings for professional engineers in works management, production, planning and research and development.

Air traffic control

The safe and efficient movement of all aircraft through British air space and airports is the responsibility of National Air Traffic Service (NATS) air traffic control officers and assistants. With the aid of sophisticated radio, radar and computer systems and with visual checks on visibility and weather conditions made from the control tower, they ensure that aircraft are kept a safe distance apart and that pilots are well advised as to their position and prevailing conditions, give clearance to land and directions to loading bays. Air traffic controllers mainly work for NATS, although there may be limited opportunities with other employers, such as local authorities or aircraft manufacturers. All must hold a CAA licence stipulating the service they are qualified to give and where they can operate. Some of the more routine tasks, such as checking flight plans, updating weather information, logging aircraft movements and keeping runways clear, are carried out by the air traffic control assistants. Prospects for promotion to officer level are good, but air traffic control staff are employed to work at any location within the country.

Airline customer service agent

Airline customer service agents work for individual airlines, handling companies, and airports and terminals. They deal with passengers from the moment they check in to when they board their flights. They are responsible for checking in luggage as well as customers. Customer service agents have to ensure that unaccompanied children or other passengers with special needs are safely escorted to their flights and they are also expected to calm nervous passengers before they board their planes.

Pilot

Commercial pilots in the UK fly fixed-wing aircraft and helicopters. Before take-off the pilot must prepare a flight plan, study the weather, make sure that the craft is airworthy, check that the cargo and fuel are safely loaded and work out estimated arrival times. Little time is spent actually flying the aeroplane manually. The pilot spends most of the time carefully monitoring sophisticated computer-controlled automatic flying, navigational and communications systems. Pilots keep in touch with air traffic control and must be prepared to deal with sudden changes in weather and other conditions. Pilots work irregular hours but their actual flying time is strictly controlled.

Most UK pilots are employed by one of the major carriers of passengers and goods and when flying large aircraft they are part of a team. Opportunities for pilots of small aircraft and helicopters are to be found in flying executive jets, in the field of air taxiing (especially in the North Sea), conducting aerial surveys, or as test pilots or flying instructors.

Qualifications and Training
Air cabin crew
Airlines usually train their own cabin crews at special centres on courses lasting four to six weeks. Applicants should be over 18, have a good level of general education to GCSE standard, preferably including English and maths, and have conversational fluency in at least one European language. Experience in a customer care setting can be helpful.

Aeronautical engineer/Aircraft maintenance engineer
Entry to aircraft maintenance engineering is via craft, technician or student apprenticeships; entry qualifications depend upon the type of apprenticeship. The apprenticeships take the form of on-the-job training and part-time study at local colleges to prepare for aeronautical engineering/aircraft maintenance engineering qualifications offered by City & Guilds and Edexcel (BTEC)/ SQA or the CAA. Qualified aircraft engineers (including those from the armed forces) have to meet certain practical experience requirements before they can take examinations to become licensed aircraft maintenance engineers. There are some full-time courses in aeronautical engineering and aircraft maintenance, usually lasting two and a half years.

Air traffic control officer
Entrants for the NATS scheme must be eligible for work within the UK, have security clearance, be aged between 18 and 29 and pass a medical. The training lasts just under 18 months and includes practice at Bournemouth Airport. This is followed by an extensive period of practical training at a designated site.

Air traffic engineer

NATS runs a training scheme for graduate electrical/electronic engineers lasting a minimum of 15 months. The training is approved by the Institution of Engineering and Technology and will lead after approximately three years to chartered engineering status.

Airline customer service agent

There are no standard entry requirements, but individual airlines and handling companies set their own requirements. They normally ask for a good standard of education and may require you to have GCSEs grades A–C in English. A foreign language qualification can also be useful, as can previous experience in customer service work. You will need to live reasonably near an airport and you may well need your own transport because shift work could make reliance on public transport difficult. You will have to undergo security checks and many companies also ask you to have a medical examination.

Pilot

UK pilots are required to hold a licence issued by the Joint Aviation Authorities (JAA) which represent the civil aviation departments of a group of European states that have collaborated to set common safety standards called Joint Aviation Requirements. Licence holders can work as pilots in any of the JAA member states. Full details of licensing requirements and organisations providing approved courses can be obtained from the CAA (see info box). Training to be a commercial pilot costs £50,000–£60,000 and may be integrated (*ab initio*) or modular. Helicopter courses tend to be more expensive. Most applicants wishing to undertake integrated courses are sponsored privately or by an airline. Such sponsorship is highly competitive and difficult to obtain. Trainees are generally expected to contribute to training costs either while training or by repaying some of the fees once in employment. An alternative entry route is via a short service flying commission with either the RAF or Royal Navy. All pilots are expected to attend retraining and refresher courses throughout their careers.

Entry requirements for sponsored pilot training vary between airlines, but most ask for a minimum of two/three A levels or equivalent, including maths and physics. Many airlines recruit graduates up to the age of 26. Eyesight must be of a very high standard. Normal colour vision and an excellent level of health and fitness are essential.

Personal Qualities and Skills

Air cabin crew

Air cabin crew must be reassuring and approachable, smart, have lots of energy and stamina and have the confidence and the ability to act quickly and decisively in a firm but polite and tactful manner.

Aeronautical engineer/Aircraft maintenance engineer

Maintenance engineering requires a combination of practical interest, mechanical aptitude, accuracy and manual dexterity. Engineers must be willing to adapt and to retrain. Very high standards and a responsible attitude are also most important.

Air traffic control officer

The work is stressful; officers need to be able to assimilate and interpret a great deal of information and instantly act upon it. They must be able to react quickly if conditions suddenly change, be healthy, reliable and emotionally well balanced; good eyesight and colour vision are also important.

Air traffic engineer

Normal colour vision, great care, accuracy and a basic understanding of the practical applications of electricity and magnetism are required.

Airline customer service agent

You need excellent customer service skills. Delays and changes to flights mean customers are often stressed, anxious or angry. You need to keep calm and follow procedures quickly, but without cutting corners. You must be smart, tidy and presentable and reasonably physically fit.

Pilot

Pilots must be very well balanced, physically fit, have stamina, be mentally and physically alert and ready to respond quickly to changing conditions. They must be unflappable, confident, self-assured leaders with considerable technical skill.

Starting Salary

The range is wide, relating to the variety of different careers. Air cabin crews and customer service agents start on fairly low pay – £10,000 to £13,000. Air traffic controllers start on between £20,000 and £21,000, and pilots start on around £33,000, but can earn much more. There are other benefits. Air cabin crew receive extra payments for the hours they spend flying, air traffic controllers get an accommodation allowance, and individual airlines offer various travel and other discounts to their employees.

Info

Civil Aviation Authority (CAA), CAA House, 45–59 Kingsway, London WC2B 6TE; 020 7379 7311; www.caa.co.uk

Institution of Engineering and Technology (IET), Savoy Place, London WC2R 0BL; 020 7240 1871; www.iee.org

National Air Traffic Services (NATS), Recruitment and Selection, Mailbox 15B, LACC, Sopwith Way, Swanwick, Hampshire SO31 7AY; 01489 612157; www.nats.co.uk

The British Air Line Pilots Association (BALPA), 81 New Road, Harlington, Hayes, Middlesex UB3 5BG; 020 8476 4000; www.balpa.org/

British Women Pilots Association (BWPA), Brooklands Museum, Brooklands Road, Weybridge, Surrey KT13 0QN; www.bwpa.demon.co.uk

Royal Aeronautical Society, 22 Hamilton Place, London W1J 8BQ; 020 7670 3200; www.raes.org.uk

Go Skills: The Sector Skills Council for Passenger Transport, Concorde House, Trinity Park, Solihull, West Midlands B37 7UQ; 0121 635 5520; www.goskills.org

SEMTA: the Sector Skills Council for Science, Engineering and Manufacturing Technologies, Head Office, 14 Upton Road, Watford WD18 0JT; 01923 238441; www.semta.org.uk

Individual airlines

CIVIL SERVICE

The Civil Service is one of the UK's largest employers and it employs staff in a diverse range of occupations and professions. The Civil Service is made up of more than 170 departments and agencies all carrying out the work of government, from advising ministers on policies to dealing with daily enquiries about planning issues, benefits payments or education. While each department carries out its own recruiting and sets entrance requirements for specific jobs, there is an overall structure across most departments. This structure means you can decide at which level you would like to enter and what sort of work appeals to you.

Work falls broadly into three groups: corporate services, which are concerned with finance, IT, human resources and communications; operation services, which is the day-to-day delivery of services through government offices. This type of work includes all the face-to-face dealing with the public. Finally, there is policy delivery, which is concerned with developing and implementing policies, working very closely with the government.

Administrative officers and administrative assistants

Administrative officers and administrative assistants carry out the daily clerical and customer contact functions in every department and agency. Their work may involve dealing directly with the public, such as answering telephone enquiries, gathering information, processing documents, keeping records and entering data into computer systems.

Junior managers/executive officers

Junior manager is the next step up the ladder after administrative officer. Junior managers are responsible for running small teams who carry out day-to-day functions for every department and agency. Tasks and responsibilities include motivating and training members of the team, carrying out annual appraisals and preparing and presenting reports on work progress to senior managers. They also have to deal with problems. If, for example, a client is unhappy with the service he or she has received, this will be referred to the junior manager in the first instance.

Fast Stream development programme trainees

The Civil Service offers a fast track accelerated training programme for recruits who want to get into senior management. Fast Stream entrants can be placed within many central government departments; there is a special training route for anyone who wants to join the Diplomatic Service; and a further pathway called the European Fast Stream. This places trainees in departments where there is a strong focus on European issues.

There are also some specific professional areas that have their own Fast Stream programmes. These include Fast Stream Economists, Fast Stream Statisticians and Fast Stream Technology in Business pathways. Government Communications Headquarters at Cheltenham also has its own Fast Stream training scheme.

Some government departments have graduate recruitment schemes that are not part of the Fast Stream Programme. These include HM Revenue and Customs, Defence Engineering and Science Group, The Highways Agency and HM Treasury.

Qualifications and Training

At whatever level you enter a great deal of your training will be on the job. All civil servants have to be either UK nationals or members of the Commonwealth or an EU country. For some posts, only UK nationals are acceptable.

Each department or agency sets its own entry requirements, but there are some common guidelines.

To become an administrative assistant or an administrative officer you do not need any formal qualifications. In practice, you often need five GCSEs grades A–C. Many applicants have A levels or are graduates. Many junior manager/ executive officer posts ask that you have two A levels.

Fast Stream graduate trainees need a good honours degree, a First or a 2.1, to be considered for the programme. Fast Stream Economists must have a 2.1 in economics. Fast Stream Statisticians must have at least a 2.2 in a numerate discipline. Fast Stream Technology in Business trainees must have a 2.1 in a business, engineering, technical, mathematical or scientific discipline.

Applicants to the Diplomatic Service must either have a degree or several years' work experience. They must pass a medical, undergo rigorous security checks and be prepared to work anywhere in the world. The Diplomatic Service also participates in the Graduate Fast Stream Programme.

For posts at all levels, departments often set aptitude tests of various kinds, which are designed to measure the kinds of skills applicants will need to do the job effectively. There is strong competition for Fast Stream posts in all areas.

For undergraduates considering a career in the Civil Service, there are a number of work experience and vacation work opportunities available. See the Civil Service recruitment website.

Because the Civil Service has a structured route to development and promotion, it is possible to move into higher level jobs through experience and performance if you do not meet the initial selection criteria.

Personal Qualities and Skills

Of course there is some variation in these according to the type of work you are involved in and the level of responsibility you have. All civil servants should have an interest in delivering high quality services and information to the government, the members of the general public and to other organisations. Civil servants need to be flexible, able to cope with change, good at working under pressure and good at communicating in both written and spoken English. Beyond this, there are specific skills which you will need to help you perform your own role effectively.

Professional occupations

There are also many opportunities in the Civil Service for people with a wide range of vocational and professional skills. There are posts for accountants, actuaries, architects, engineers, chemists, physicists, biologists, vets, lawyers, surveyors, IT specialists and many more. For many of these posts applicants need to have relevant professional and vocational qualifications in particular areas such as science, engineering, law or finance. See the Civil Service recruitment website for more details.

Starting Salary

Salaries for administrative assistants range from £12,000 to £13,500. For administrative officers the range is £14,000 to £17,000. Junior managers earn between £14,000 and £22,000. Fast Stream salaries start at around £24,000 and

info

Government Skills SSC Secretariat, c/o Cabinet Office, Admiralty Arch, The Mall, London SW1A 1WH; 020 7276 1611; www.government-skills.gov.uk

Civil Service Careers (check website for contact details of specific departments); www.careers.civil-service.gov.uk

Civil Service Fast Stream, Application Helpdesk, Parity House, Fleet Mill, Minley Road, Fleet, Hants GU51 2RD; 01252 776923; www.faststream.gov.uk

Defence Engineering and Science Group (DESG), Central MOD, PO Box 2443, Bath BA1 5AB; 01225 449106; www.desg.mod.uk

Department of Trade and Industry (DTI), Response Centre, 1 Victoria Street, London SW1H 0ET; 020 7215 5000; www.dti.gov.uk

Foreign and Commonwealth Office (FCO), King Charles Street, London SW1A 2AH; 020 7008 1500; www.fco.gov.uk

Government Skills SSC Secretariat, c/o Cabinet Office, Admiralty Arch, The Mall, London SW1A 1WH; 020 7276 1611; www.government-skills.gov.uk

Government Communications HQ, The Recruitment Office, Room A2c, Hubble Road, Cheltenham, Glos GL51 0EX; 01242 709095; e-mail: recruitment@gchq.gsi.gov.uk

HM Revenue & Customs (HMRC) (see website for departmental contact information); www.hmrc.gov.uk

HM Treasury, Allington Towers, 19 Allington Street, London SW1E 5EB; 020 7270 1524; www.hm-treasury.gov.uk

Home Office, Direct Communications Unit, 2 Marsham Street, London SW1P 4DF; 020 7035 4848; www.homeoffice.gov.uk

Ministry of Defence (MOD), Main Building, Whitehall, London SW1A 2HB; 020 7218 9000; www.mod.uk

Scottish Executive, St Andrew's House, Regent Road, Edinburgh EH1 3DG; 0131 556 8400; www.scotland.gov.uk

Many administrative assistant, administrative officer and junior manager posts are advertised in the local press and through Jobcentre Plus.

are around £36,000 at the end of a four to five year training period. Many posts attract performance-related pay bonuses and there are higher salaries for people working in London or Brussels.

CLOTHING INDUSTRY

(*see also* Fashion)

The clothing industry is diverse and complex, with products ranging from off-the-peg garments that are turned out in thousands, to exclusive *haute couture* designs from top fashion houses. There are job opportunities in large factories, small workrooms, with large wholesaling firms, in small family businesses and on production lines. The largest sections of the industry are men's and boys' outerwear, women's and girls' outerwear, children's clothing, bespoke tailoring (made to measure) and dressmaking. More specialised areas such as millinery and glove making are relatively small. Skilled workers are generally in great demand in most areas.

The main craft jobs are pattern cutting and grading, lay making (positioning the pattern to make the most economical use of the cloth), cutting, marking or fixing (putting the different pieces of an individual garment together and marking the stitch lines), hand sewing and pressing. There are also opportunities for semi-skilled workers and operators, particularly machinists. Much of this work can be repetitive. Production lines are arranged so each machinist sews only one part of a garment. However, opportunities exist to move into more skilled work later, such as sample machining. Technology is changing the clothing industry with more advanced sewing machines, computer-controlled pattern laying and die cutting of bulk quantities. The industry needs skilled operatives and mechanics to work with, maintain and care for these increasingly sophisticated machines.

The clothing industry also employs people in its commercial sections – marketing and sales, or purchasing and supply – where there are often close links with the major textile and fibre companies. As more and more companies outsource their production overseas, the need for additional garment technologists has become apparent. This involves overseas travel and the use of a wide range of technical skills.

Qualifications and Training

Formal educational qualifications are not always needed to train for the craft skills. These are traditionally learnt by courses leading to City & Guilds and Edexcel (BTEC) examinations. The Foundation Modern Apprenticeship scheme which leads to NVQ level 2 qualifications and the Advanced Modern Apprenticeship scheme which leads to NVQ level 3 awards are available. Machinists are generally trained on the job by the employing company.

An alternative route to learn is via further and higher education. Courses are run at many colleges and universities across the UK leading to National Diplomas, Higher National Diplomas or degrees in a variety of clothing-related disciplines.

Personal Qualities and Skills

These vary according to the particular sector of the industry concerned. It is generally advantageous to have deft hands and high standards of neatness and precision. In factories, a willingness to be part of a team is needed, while in bespoke tailoring a candidate should have a pleasant manner and be able to put potential customers at their ease.

Starting Salary

Depends upon individual employers. Graduates generally start on £14,000. Many factory floor jobs are paid at minimum wage level.

Pattern cutter/grader

Pattern cutters make the patterns that enable a designer's sketch to be made into a garment. Pattern graders work from a pattern representing a basic size and create the patterns needed for a range of sizes. Jobs vary from company to company. The two ways of making patterns are by flat pattern cutting, when the cutter works from the designer's sketches or working drawings and makes a pattern for each part of a garment, or by modelling onto a stand, when the cutter works from the designer's drawings and drapes and pins fabric on to a dummy and fits it in accordance with the drawings. Computers are increasingly used to help in designing garments, creating patterns and for pattern grading.

Pattern cutter/spreader

The cutter or spreader checks that the cloth is smooth and free of wrinkles and flaws and that patterns or other features will match when it is sewn together. The laying-up process is done manually by two people or by machine. Once it is ready, the fabric can be cut using a number of methods. Hand cutting is done using shears, an electric knife or a vertical band knife. Die-cutting is done by machine. Computer-controlled cutting is also being introduced, with machines capable of cutting up to 250 inches per minute, depending on the depth of the lay. In laser cutting computer images are used to operate the cutter with great accuracy.

Qualifications and Training

Pattern cutter/grader

An Advanced Modern Apprenticeship in Apparel Manufacturing Technology leading to an NVQ level 3 in one of four routes (pattern cutting and grading, sample technician, garment technologist, hand craft garment making) is available. This is a work-based route providing an alternative to further and higher education.

Pattern cutter/spreader

Training is largely given on the job. Some employers offer the NVQ level 2 qualification for cutters or the Foundation Modern Apprenticeship route.

Personal Qualities and Skills

Pattern cutters/graders should have an interest in fashion and an appreciation of what their designers are aiming for. Numerical ability is essential for measurement and calculation. Some technical drawing skills and an aptitude for working on computers are also useful.

Spreaders/cutters need to be physically fit. They must have good eyesight and perfect colour vision. Some numerical ability is required.

Starting Salary

For a pattern cutter/grader, earnings vary tremendously, from £10,000 to £20,000, depending on qualifications and experience. Experienced cutters/spreaders are paid according to their skill and the level of responsibility in their job.

The British Apparel & Textile Confederation (BATC), 5 Portland Place, London W1N 3AA; 020 7636 7788; www.batc.co.uk

Skillfast, Sector Skills Council for Apparel, Footwear, Textiles and Allied Businesses, Richmond House, Lawnswood Business Park, Redvers Close, Leeds LS16 6RD; 0113 2399 800; www.skillfast-uk.org

info

COASTGUARD

HM Coastguard coordinates maritime search and rescue for the UK. Its area of responsibility, which covers approximately 10,500 miles of coastline and a million square miles of sea, is divided into four Search and Rescue Regions. Each is headed by a Regional Inspector, and within each Region are Maritime Rescue Coordination Centres and Sub Centres from which searches and rescues are coordinated.

At these centres, a constant watch is kept on international distress frequencies, satellite, radio and telephone communications, all of which are responded to immediately. HM Coastguard can call upon a wide range of facilities for search and rescue, including lifeboats, helicopters, tugs and local rescue organisations for rescues at sea. On-shore rescues from cliffs and mud are carried out by teams of Auxiliary Coastguards.

Qualifications and Training

Most entrants start as watch assistants. For this you need good basic literacy, numeracy and IT skills, and a strong interest in maritime affairs. Watch Officers need good GCSEs grades A–C in English and maths, or their equivalent. For applicants without formal qualifications, The Maritime and Coastguard Agency can set competency tests. Watch Officers must also have extensive experience of the sea. Many Watch Officers have been in the Royal Navy or the Merchant Navy, or had other firsthand experience of the sea. Auxiliary coastguards must be aged 16 or over. Posts are open to UK nationals and to EU and Commonwealth citizens. Applicants must be physically fit, with good hearing and eyesight.

All recruits attend a training course at the Maritime and Coastguard Agency's Training Centre in Dorset, after which training is a combination of classroom and practical-based assignments.

Personal Qualities and Skills

As a coastguard you will have to take important decisions quickly and calmly. You need a clear speaking voice and the ability to work with modern communications equipment. You should have good leadership skills and work well as part of a team.

Starting Salary

Salaries for watch assistants start at around £12,000, rising to £15,000. Watch Officers earn from £20,000 to £22,000.

Maritime and Coastguard Agency, Human Resources Recruitment Team, Bay 3/19 Spring Place, 105 Commercial Road, Southampton SO15 1EG; 023 8032 9308; www.mcga.gov.uk

COLOUR SCIENCE AND TECHNOLOGY

Colour technologists are concerned with producing dyes and pigments that have a wide range of applications, including the textile, paint, rubber, plastics, paper, leather and foodstuffs industries. They must ensure that exact colours can be produced at an economic price and in the right quantities whenever they are needed. They are often involved in research and development projects. Technologists are also employed in sales, management, buying, development and research, quality control, customer liaison and technical services departments (depending on the industry involved and the expertise needed).

Textile technologists may work in the design, manufacture and operation of textile machinery, and in the design, production, coloration, finishing and manufacture of fibres, yarns and fabrics of all types.

Qualifications and Training

Two, preferably three, A levels or equivalents, one of which must be chemistry or a subject including chemistry, are required for entry to a degree course in colour chemistry or textile chemistry. Minimum entry requirements for part-time technician courses leading to the Edexcel (BTEC)/SQA certificate and higher certificate in textile coloration (textile dyeing) are GCSE or equivalent in maths, an appropriate science and English.

For textile technologists, the basic professional qualification is the Associateship and Chartered Textile Technologist (CText ATI) of the Textile Institute, awarded on the fulfilment of the academic and industrial/professional experience requirements. The professional qualification for a specialist in colour technology is the Associateship and Chartered Colourist of the Society of Dyers and Colourists (CCol ASDC) or the Licentiateship of the Society of Dyers and Colourists (LSDC).

Personal Qualities and Skills

Good colour vision is essential, as is scientific or technical ability and the ability to work as part of a team.

Starting Salary

£15,000+ with a degree; £9,000+ for a textile technologist.

Society of Dyers and Colourists, PO Box 244, Perkin House, 82 Grattan Road, Bradford, West Yorkshire BD1 2JB; 01274 725138; www.sdc.org.uk; e-mail: education@sdc.org.uk

info

COMPLEMENTARY MEDICINE

The field of complementary medicine and treatments is growing, with new therapies and treatments being added continuously. Therefore the list of occupations shown here is not exhaustive, but gives a cross-section of the more established ones.

Acupuncturist

Acupuncture is a system of treatment which involves the insertion of fine needles into one or more points of the body to restore the overall health of the person and help alleviate symptoms from which they may be suffering. Acupuncture can also be used for relieving pain, and in China is used to anaesthetise patients during operations. It has been practised in China and other Far Eastern countries for thousands of years and is a growing profession in the UK. Many health professionals, for example nurses and physiotherapists, train as acupuncturists.

Qualifications and Training

The training of acupuncturists is monitored by the British Acupuncture Accreditation Board (BAAB), an independent body which is allied to the British Acupuncture Council (BAcC). Training standards are detailed in the BAcC's Guidelines for Acupuncture Education and graduates of accredited or candidate colleges have automatic right of membership of the Council. Details of accredited, three-year full-time courses or their part-time equivalents are available from the Council.

Personal Qualities and Skills

Acupuncturists need the necessary practitioner skills, including a knowledge of Western medicine appropriate to the practice of acupuncture. They must also be able to put patients at their ease and to gain their confidence.

Starting Salary

Salaries vary depending on location, number of patients and amount charged. After qualifying, most acupuncturists will be self-employed and may practise from home, in a clinic, or occasionally within the NHS.

British Acupuncture Council, 63 Jeddo Road, London W12 9HQ; 020 8735 0400; www.acupuncture.org.uk

Institute for Complementary Medicine, PO Box 194, London

SE16 7QZ; 020 7237 5165; www.i-c-m.org.uk

British Medical Acupuncture Society (BMAS); www.medical-acupuncture.co.uk

Aromatherapist

Aromatherapists use the organic essential oils from aromatic plants to treat a whole range of physical and emotional symptoms. Based on discussing a client's symptoms, lifestyle, diet, overall state of health, etc, the aromatherapist prescribes a combination of essential oils to treat the person. This is done either by massage, or by giving a client oils to use in their baths, on their pillows, or to scent their rooms. While aromatherapists may work in beauty salons they are also employed by healthcare organisations and often work closely with GPs, nurses and other healthcare professionals.

Qualifications and Training

There are no specific academic qualifications but certificate and diploma courses are run at a number of state and private colleges. Some courses do set particular entry requirements such as a GCSE in biology and they may also set admissions tests. The length of courses varies from a weekend to an evening a week over one or two years. The longer courses offer a much greater depth of study.

Personal Qualities and Skills

Aromatherapists must be very good at putting people at ease. They must be caring, patient and good listeners. They must be comfortable with close physical contact with other people.

Starting Salary

Many aromatherapists are self-employed and charge between £20 and £40 an hour. Aromatherapists who are employed earn from £15,000 to £20,000 a year, though some earn much more than this.

Institute for Complementary Medicine, PO Box 194, London SE16 7QZ; 020 7237 5165; www.i-c-m.org.uk

Aromatherapy Consortium, PO Box 6522, Desborough, Kettering, Northants NN14 2YX; 0870 774 3477; www.aromatherapy-regulation.org.uk

International Federation of Aromatherapists (IFAS), 61–63 Churchfield Road, London W3 6AY; 020 8992 9605; www.ifaroma.org

Chiropractor

Chiropractic is a healthcare profession concerned with, but not limited to, the diagnosis, treatment and prevention of structural and functional disorders affecting the musculo-skeletal system. Common complaints include low back and leg pain, headaches and neck and arm pain, as well as sports injuries. Working in a primary contact profession, a qualified chiropractor may be approached directly, without a medical referral, by patients seeking help.

Chiropractors are trained to utilise a wide variety of diagnostic techniques, including X-ray. Manual manipulation (adjustment) of spinal and extremity joints as well as soft-tissue structures is the most common treatment method employed. They will also offer advice on nutrition, rehabilitative exercises and modifications to activities of daily living. There is an increasing demand for chiropractic services and employment prospects are good both in the UK and in Europe.

Qualifications and Training

Chiropractors are subject to statutory regulation by the General Chiropractic Council (GCC). It is illegal for anyone to describe themselves as a chiropractor if they are not registered with the GCC. Recognised courses are provided by the Anglo-European College of Chiropractic, McTimoney College of Chiropractic and the Universities of Glamorgan and Surrey. Entry requirements vary but normally include two science A levels or equivalent. Fees for courses vary considerably because some colleges are private.

Personal Qualities and Skills

Manual dexterity and practical skills as well as a sound theoretical knowledge of the body are necessary. An ability to communicate with patients and inspire confidence is important.

Starting Salary

Salaries vary according to number of patients and how well established the practice is. Patients are usually charged per session at £20 to £60 per hour. A new entrant earns up to £15,000 per year. With experience it is possible to earn £30,000; a large practice will pay an experienced person up to £40,000.

info

General Chiropractic Council,
44 Wicklow Street, London
WC1X 9HL; 020 7713 5155;
www.gcc-uk.org;
e-mail: enquiries@gcc-uk.org

British Chiropractic Association,
Blagrave House, 17 Blagrave Street,
Reading, Berkshire RG1 1QB;
0118 950 5950; fax: 0118 958 8946;
www.chiropractic-uk.co.uk; e-mail:
enquiries@chiropractic-uk.co.uk

Anglo-European College of
Chiropractic, 13–15 Parkwood Road,
Bournemouth, Dorset BH5 2DF;
01202 436200; fax: 01202 436312;
www.aecc.ac.uk

McTimoney College of Chiropractic,
Kimber House, 1 Kimber Road,
Abingdon, Oxfordshire OX14 1BZ;
01235 523336;
www.mctimoney-college.ac.uk;
e-mail: chiropractic@mctimoney-
college.ac.uk

University of Glamorgan, Chiropractic
Field, School of Applied Sciences,
Pontypridd, Glamorgan, CF37 1DL;
01443 482287; www.glam.ac.uk

University of Surrey, European
Institute of Health and Medical
Sciences, Duke of Kent Building,
Stag Hill, Guildford, Surrey GU2 7TE;
01483 686700; www.eihms.surrey.ac.uk

Homeopath

Homeopathy is a system of healing which assists the natural tendency of the body to heal itself. There are three main principles of homeopathy. First is treating like with like – what produces the symptoms of a disease may also cure it; the patient is treated by a small amount of the substance causing the symptoms and the natural defences are stimulated. Second, the lower the dose the better the result. Third, the remedy should be unique to the particular patient at a particular time. Homeopathic remedies may be used to treat almost any reversible illness in adults, children or animals.

Many newly qualified homeopaths set up in partnership in a clinic with other homeopaths and some now work with GPs in fundholding practices. Homeopathic patients may come privately or be referred by GPs. Medical homeopaths (doctors who have trained in homeopathy) work as GPs, private practitioners or in one of the NHS homeopathic hospitals.

Qualifications and Training

Medical doctors who have been qualified for a minimum of two and a half years may take a postgraduate course at one of the five teaching centres accredited by the Faculty of Homeopathy.

Non-medically qualified candidates have a choice of institutions and courses. Several organisations register homeopaths as professionally competent. The largest, the Society of Homeopaths, is involved in developing professional education and is currently establishing a formal procedure for accrediting courses in homeopathy. There is a database of recognised courses on its website.

Personal Qualities and Skills

Homeopaths must have an interest in people, an ability to consider and interpret information and be good listeners and communicators.

Starting Salary

Because most of the work is paid for on an hourly basis, salaries range from between £5,000 and £30,000 pro rata. Homeopaths charge between £30 and £100 per hour, depending on their experience, their location and their clientele. £35 to £50 an hour is the most usual rate.

Alliance of Registered Homeopaths, Millbrook, Millbrook Hill, Nutley, East Sussex TN22 3PJ; 08700 736339; www.a-r-h.org

British Homeopathic Association incorporating the Homeopathic Trust, Hahnemann House, 29 Park Street West, Luton LU1 3BE; Tel: 0870 444 3950;

www.trusthomeopathy.org/trust/ tru_over.html

Faculty of Homeopathy, Hahnemann House, 29 Park Street West, Luton LU1 3BE; 0870 444 3950; www.trusthomeopathy.org/faculty/ fac_over.html

Massage therapist

Massage is the scientific manipulation of soft tissues for a therapeutic effect, such as encouraging relaxation, relieving musculo-skeletal aches and pains or promoting healing. Massage therapists work in a range of settings such as health centres, hospitals, in professional sport, beauty clinics or as freelancers. The growth in alternative therapies has increased the demand and acceptance of massage therapy.

Qualifications and Training

There is a wide range of massage courses available and most specialise in specific types of massage, although there are some general massage courses too. Every mode of delivery is available from part and full time, to distance learning, weekend and block courses. There are also some postgraduate courses in sports therapy, electrotherapy and manual lymphatic drainage. NVQs are available at levels 2 to 5 in a range of institutions and further education colleges.

Personal Qualities and Skills

Massage therapists must be physically strong, have good interpersonal skills and the ability to make people feel comfortable. They must also be good listeners and maintain excellent personal hygiene as the work involves close physical contact with clients.

Starting Salary

Varied, depending on employer. Freelancers charge £15–£30 an hour.

info

Northern Institute of Massage,
14–16 St Mary's Place, Bury,
Lancashire BL9 0DZ; 0161 797 1800;
www.nim56.co.uk;
e-mail: information@nim56.co.uk

London School of Sports Massage,
28 Station Parade, Willesden Green,
London NW2 4NX; 020 8452 8855;
www.lssm.com;
e-mail: admin@lssm.com

Naturopath

Naturopaths work in private practice since naturopathy is not offered by the NHS. They believe in treating the whole patient and in encouraging the body to cure itself, so do not generally give drugs which, they consider, often treat the symptoms without dealing with the actual cause of a problem. A naturopath uses treatments designed to correct total body chemistry; diet is seen as a major factor and patients are encouraged to eat more natural food. Hydrotherapy is often used to stimulate the blood to a specific area of the body or to draw it away from another (by applying cold packs to combat throbbing headaches, for example).

Naturopaths also need to be skilled in psychology since they recognise that physiological complaints may frequently be caused by psychological problems. Any remedies used tend to be nutritional, herbal or homeopathic, and naturopaths may also be trained in acupuncture or other systems of alternative or complementary medicine. In the UK, naturopathy is closely linked to osteopathy, and many naturopaths are qualified osteopaths using these skills in treating their patients.

Qualifications and Training

Two graduate courses are offered by the British College of Osteopathic Medicine in London: a BSc (Honours) degree in Osteopathic Medicine combined with a Naturopathic Diploma and a BSc (Honours) degree in Naturopathic Medicine.

The usual minimum entry requirements are three good A levels or equivalent, one of which should be chemistry. Mature students may be considered on an individual basis, taking into account their academic and life experiences.

Personal Qualities and Skills

Professional skills must be combined with a sympathetic and caring manner.

Starting Salary

Salaries vary depending on hours worked, number of patients and fee scales. Fees range from £25 to £100 an hour.

British College of Osteopathic
Medicine, Lief House,
120–122 Finchley Road, London
NW3 5HR; 020 7435 6464;
fax: 020 7431 3630; www.bcno.ac.uk;
e-mail: info@bcom.ac.uk

General Council and Register of
Naturopaths, Goswell House,
2 Goswell Road, Street, Somerset
BA16 0JG; 08707 456984; fax: 08707
456985; www.naturopathy.org.uk;
e-mail: admin@naturopathy.org.uk

info

Osteopath

Osteopathy is a system of diagnosis and treatment where the main emphasis is on conditions affecting the musculo-skeletal system. Osteopaths use predominantly gentle manual and manipulative methods of treatment to restore and maintain proper body function. They work in private practice and are increasingly being asked to work as part of mainstream medicine. All osteopaths are required to register with the General Osteopathic Council (GOsC).

Qualifications and Training

Entry requirements are one of the following: a minimum of two A levels in biology and chemistry; a science access or foundation course; mature students with professional qualifications of a similar level to studying at undergraduate level, or equivalent qualifications from European and overseas applicants. Courses include the study of anatomy, physiology and biochemistry, together with a clinical course in the principles, diagnoses and techniques of osteopathy. Extensive hands-on clinical experience with patients is a key feature of any course. Studying for a degree at the British School of Osteopathy leads to a Bachelor degree in osteopathy (BOst).

Personal Qualities and Skills

Osteopaths require good manual dexterity plus a genuine desire to help and care for people. An ability to get on with and gain the confidence of their patients is also important.

British College of Osteopathic
Medicine, Lief House,
120–122 Finchley Road, London
NW3 5HR; 020 7435 6464;
fax: 020 7431 3630; www.bcom.ac.uk;
e-mail: info@bcom.ac.uk

British School of Osteopathy,
275 Borough High Street,
London SE1 1JE; 020 7407 0222;
www.bso.ac.uk;
e-mail: admissions@bso.ac.uk

General Osteopathic Council,
Osteopathy House,
176 Tower Bridge Road, London
SE1 3LU; 020 7357 6655;
fax: 020 7357 0011;
www.osteopathy.org.uk

*Working in Complementary and
Alternative Medicine* (Kogan Page)

info

Starting Salary

Within the first five years of practice new graduates can earn approximately £25,000–£30,000.

Reflexology

A reflexologist applies pressure to the feet, or to the hands, to stimulate the reflexes, which acts as a treatment to release tensions in the body, improving circulation and stimulating the body's own natural healing processes. A usual session conducted with a client involves applying pressure to the hands and feet, to clear blockages and improve circulation, easing tension and restoring the body's natural balance to all organs and parts of the body.

Qualifications and Training

Reflexology courses are available at colleges of further or higher education and private centres throughout the UK. The number of hours of study required by courses varies between 60 and 200. Most courses are private and there is a fee, but grants may be available.

Personal Qualities and Skills

A reflexologist helps people and is sensitive and sympathetic to the client's needs and condition. It is essential to have good communication skills, including listening and understanding. The work involves solving problems. Reflexologists must be logical thinkers able to offer a solution to health problems and understand when to refer patients to suitable medical practitioners.

Starting Salary

Most reflexologists are self-employed and incomes vary considerably. Each session is charged on an hourly rate, usually ranging from £20 to £60 an hour. A new entrant can earn £12,000 a year and with experience this could increase to £15,000. Working in a large practice reflexologists could earn £25,000.

Reflexology Forum, PO Box 2367, South Croydon, Surrey CR2 7ZE; 0800 037 0130; e-mail: reflexologyforum@aol.com

Prince of Wales's Foundation for Integrated Health, 12 Chillingworth Road, London N7 8QL; 020 7619 6140; www.fimed.org

Reiki healer

Reiki healing is a form of energy-based healing founded in Japan. Reiki healers endeavour to guide energies through the bodies of their clients, attempting to activate natural healing processes within the body. There are many systems of

Reiki, but they all aim to help physical, emotional, mental or spiritual problems. Reiki is used to treat pain, stress and tiredness and it aims to induce calm and increase clients' energy levels. It is sometimes used in conjunction with traditional and other complementary therapies.

During a Reiki session, the client lies fully clothed on a bed or sits in a chair while the healer places his or her hands in a sequence of positions over the client's body. The whole body is treated rather than specific symptoms or areas. Treatment can take between one and two hours. Reiki is non-diagnostic, non-interventionist, non-manipulative and no pressure is applied.

Qualifications and Training

There are no specific academic entry requirements, though many Reiki healers will have qualifications in other aspects of healthcare, counselling, or complementary therapies. You should have experience of working with people and you also need to undergo some Reiki healing yourself, to experience how it operates. Training is through one-to-one sessions with a Reiki master or teacher.

Training courses in Reiki are also offered at a number of colleges at introductory and advanced level. It is possible to gain a certificate or diploma awarded by an exam body such as the VTCT (Vocational Training Charitable Trust) or the OCN (Open College Network).

Personal Qualities and Skills

You must have very good interpersonal skills. You need to be able to put people at ease, reassure them and listen to them. You need to have an open mind and a positive attitude about how Reiki healing works. You must be physically fit. If you are self-employed you need some business awareness, and financial and marketing skills.

Starting Salary

Most Reiki healers are self-employed, charging for each individual healing session. Fees range from £20 to £70 an hour. What you can charge varies according to your geographical location and your level of experience.

The Reiki Federation, PO Box 1785, Andover, Hants SP11 0WB; 0870 850 2209; www.reikifed.co.uk

Reiki Association, 2 Spa Terrace, Fenay Bridge, Huddersfield HD8 0BD; www.reikiassociation.co.uk

COMPUTING

see Information and Communication Technology

CONSERVATION

Conservation falls broadly into two categories: environmental, and heritage and arts. They are each concerned with protecting and preserving – the former, the world in which we live and the latter, our cultural history.

Environmental conservation

see Environment

Conservation/restoration art and heritage

Conservators and restorers look after historic buildings, paintings, pieces of sculpture, ancient books, historic tapestries, carvings, pieces of furniture and other objects. Conservators examine items for any signs of damage or deterioration. They do their best to ensure that objects are looked after properly, and protected and preserved in the most effective ways possible. Finally, they may take steps to restore them to something as close as possible to their original condition.

Conservators have to understand the effect of the environment on different materials, and to ensure that objects are not stored or displayed in harmful conditions. They have to be aware of and be able to control light, humidity temperature and sources of pollution. They employ many different scientific techniques and they make photographic records of their work.

Qualifications and Training

Most conservators have a degree. You need either a degree in art followed by a specialist postgraduate qualification in conservation, or a degree in a specific area of art, eg, ceramics and glass, or textiles. The Institute of Conservation lists relevant courses on its website. Highly skilled and experienced craftsmen and women who do not have a degree may also be able to get into conservation work if they can demonstrate their practical skills and knowledge of working with specific materials.

Personal Qualities and Skills

Conservators must have a blend of interests in artistic, scientific and technical matters. They have to pay close attention to detail and be prepared to work patiently and extremely carefully. They also need to be good communicators, being able to explain their requirements and concerns convincingly.

Starting Salary

New entrants earn between £16,000 and £17,000. This rises to around £20,000 after two or three years' experience. Senior conservators can earn between £25,000 and £35,000. If you develop a really good reputation and are able to work on prestigious pieces, you may earn more than this.

Institute of Conservation, 3rd Floor, Downstream Building, 1 London Bridge, London SE1 9BG; 020 7785 3807; www.icon.org.uk

Museums, Libraries and Archives Council, Victoria House, Southampton Row, London WC1B 4EA; 020 7273 1444; www.mla.gov.uk

Museums Association, 24 Calvin Street, London E1 6NW; www.museumsassociation.org

Guild of Master Craftsmen, 166 High Street, Lewes, East Sussex BN7 1XU; 01273 478449; www.thegmcgroup.com/theguild

Creative and Cultural Skills, 11 Southwark Street, London SE1 1RQ; 0800 093 0444; www.ccskills.org.uk

info

CONSTRUCTION

The construction industry is the overarching sector for any occupation that is involved in the building and decorating of new and existing buildings. Building work involves the construction and maintenance of any structure. It is allied to civil and structural engineering, building and environmental engineering, municipal engineering, and highway and transportation engineering. There is a huge range of career options within the industry for graduates, technicians and at craft level.

Trades available include carpenters and joiners (*see also* Carpentry), form-work erectors, wood machinists, mastic asphalters, bricklayers, painters and decorators (*see also* Interior Decorator), crane drivers and mechanical equipment operators, electricians, refrigeration fitters, thermal insulators, plumbers and gas fitters, plasterers, glaziers, scaffolders, paviours, steel erectors, stone-masons, roofers, floor, ceiling and wall tilers, coiling fixers, heating and ventilation specialists. Each craftsperson is responsible for a specific part of the job but also works as part of a team whose collective responsibility is to produce high-quality work. The Construction Industry Training Board (CITB) predicts that the sector will need some 76,000 new recruits every year until 2006, to replace those leaving, and to fill new vacancies. Nearly 60 per cent of the new recruits needed are for trade occupations.

Building control surveyor

Building control is undertaken by local authorities and Approved Inspectors. The main activities involve the examination and assessment of plans, site visits to inspect work, and liaison with designers, builders and other professionals within the construction team, and the fire authorities to ensure that new building construction and alterations to existing buildings conform to building regulations. A broad knowledge of the many areas of building work and skills in dealing with people need to be developed.

Imagine what you could do.

There are hundreds of different careers in construction.

How will you make your mark? Visit bconstructive.co.uk

Qualifications and Training

There are two components to qualifying as a Chartered Building Control Surveyor: successful completion of a Royal Institution of Chartered Surveyors (RICS) approved degree or diploma, followed by enrolment onto the Assessment of Professional Competence (APC) which is two years' practical training while in employment, concluding with an RICS professional assessment interview. Postgraduate conversion courses are also available.

Personal Qualities and Skills

You have to be a good communicator, able to talk to property owners and builders, and you have to be firm and assertive when explaining, for example, why some work has to be redone. You have to have good technical knowledge and be able to convey this to other people. Maturity and common sense are vital.

Starting Salary

Salaries begin at around £15,000 to £19,000, sometimes more for mature applicants with a lot of relevant industry experience.

info

Association of Building Engineers (ABE), Lutyens House, Billing Brook Road, Northampton NN3 8NW; 0845 177 3411; www.abe.org.uk/siteman/index.asp?orgid=791

Construction Industry Training Board, CITB – Construction Skills,

Bircham Newton, Kings Lynn, Norfolk PE31 6RH; 01485 577577; www.citb.org.uk

Royal Institution of Chartered Surveyors (RICS), RICS Contact Centre, Surveyor Court, Westwood Way, Coventry CV4 8JE; 0870 333 1600; www.rics.org

Contract manager

The contract manager is the person responsible for the overall control of a building project. This means coordinating the subcontractors and specialist firms, the technical staff and the machine operatives and making sure that the whole project is completed within the specified time limit and to budget.

Clerk of works

The clerk of works undertakes independent inspection of the works in progress to ensure that they conform to the specification so that the client obtains value for money.

CONSTRUCTION TRADES

There are many different construction trades: carpenters, painters and decorators, electricians, plasterers, plumbers and roofers. While they each have their own specialist knowledge and technical skills, much of the training and qualification route is similar for all of these trades. Have a look at the Qualifications and Training section at the end of this entry to see how to qualify and what kind of training to expect.

Carpenter

There are several different jobs covered by the general term carpenter – what they all have in common is that carpenters work with wood. They use wood to make doors, window frames, skirting boards, floorboards, cupboards and all the other woodwork you can think of in any domestic, public or commercial building. Some of the different roles include bench joiners, who prepare doors and window frames in a workshop ready for other workers to install them in properties; carpenters and joiners who work on site or inside or outside buildings, fitting cupboards, doors, window frames, etc; and wood machinists who prepare floorboards and skirting boards in the workshop ready for the carpenter and joiner to fix in place and finish.

Demolition work

Demolishing a building properly and safely is one of the most highly skilled areas in construction.

Demolition operative

Demolition operatives use heavy machinery to bring down walls, buildings and other structures. They have to be acutely aware of safety, calculating exactly how a building will collapse. They are also involved in clearance of the site once the building has been razed to the ground.

Scaffolder

Scaffolders build scaffolding that might be used in demolition, but more significantly in construction. They build scaffolding from steel tubes and wooden platforms, and it is essential they build scaffolding that is safe for other construction workers to stand on and work from.

Graduate profile

Balfour Beatty is the UK's largest construction, engineering and services group with an impressive £5 billion annual revenue and over 27,000 employees in 24 countries. We deliver complex (often unprecedented) projects on time, within budget and to our customers' satisfaction – and with the greatest respect for safety, the environment and the communities we work in.

Phillip joined Balfour Beatty Civil Engineering in 2001. He has an MEng in Civil Engineering from Queen Mary and Westfield College, University of London.

"The last major project that I worked on was the M25 widening scheme, for junctions 12 to 15. I was fortunate to be employed in the team assembled to construct structures to facilitate the flow of traffic into and out of the new Heathrow Terminal 5 complex.

I am extremely proud to have engineered the construction of two new three-span road bridges, designed to minimise associated maintenance works.

Since leaving the M25 project I have been working as a Temporary Works Design Engineer on a design secondment. In this role I design temporary schemes to facilitate construction of permanent structures. However, I still feel attached to the M25 project.

I often travel to the west of England, sometimes taking a detour to drive past the bridges that I helped to construct. Seeing the structures brings back memories – names and faces, good days and bad days. I feel proud to have been involved."

To find out more about Phillip go to
www.balfourbeatty.com/graduates/phillip.htm

To read more about Balfour Beatty go to page 114

Steeplejack

Steeplejacks work not just on steeples, but on any high structures, chimneys, clocks, etc. They have not only to work at a great height, using special safety equipment, but also have to have a good working knowledge of many different trades because they are likely to have to carry out repairs to and with many different materials: glass, wood, paint, plaster, mortar, etc.

Interior and finishing trades

Once a basic structure has been completed by bricklayers, carpenters, roofers, etc, there is still a great deal of work needed to make the building comfortable to live or work in and useful for the purpose for which it has been built. Ceiling fixers, floor layers, glaziers, painters and decorators, plasterers and plumbers are examples of some of the interior and finishing trades on offer.

Ceiling fixer

Ceiling fixers and dry liners install ceilings, especially in large modern buildings with large expanses of high ceiling. They build structures to fit large sheets of plasterboard to, and cover the whole thing with a very thin layer of plaster.

Electrician

This is a major construction industry career with many different options and pathways. You can see full details on page 146.

Glazier

Glaziers work with glass, installing glass windows, doors and glass partitions. They have to be skilled in cutting and fixing glass, from basic double-glazing to more ornate glass effects.

Painter and decorator

No building looks complete until the important finishing touches of painting, wood staining and papering have been applied. Interior decorators work inside and outside all kinds of buildings, from private houses to large warehouses, shops and offices.

Plasterer

This is a highly skilled occupation, as plasterers have to line walls or ceilings with a layer of even, smooth and attractive plaster to act as a basis for painting, wallpaper or other finishes. They have to work quickly, achieving the desired finish before the plaster dries out. Some plasterers go on to develop skills in ornamental and decorative plasterwork.

Plumber

Plumbers install and maintain all the necessary pipes, valves, tanks, boilers, etc that keep water and heating systems flowing through any building. They install and maintain drainage systems and repair flashing on roofs.

Roofers

Roofs come in many different shapes and sizes and are made from many different materials. It is the job of roofers to fix roofs onto buildings and to ensure that these roofs are safe and weatherproof. Within roofing there are several different specialist trades: felt roofing tiling and slating, lead roofing and many more. You may choose to work mainly with one of these materials, and become a specialist, or you may decide to work with all the different types of roofing material.

Trowel trades

If you work with brick or stone you will learn one of these trades. Of the many construction occupations available, these offer you the chance to be creative as well as using practical skills.

Bricklayer

Bricklayers build the external and internal walls of all kinds of buildings, from private houses to large hospitals, hotels and offices. They build garden walls and lay patios. They work mainly with ready-prepared bricks, building them up in layers, working to produce smooth and weatherproof results.

Stonemason

Stonemasons have employed their skills for hundreds of years, using natural stone as their basic building material. Today stonemasons work both restoring historic buildings and building modern structures. This is highly skilled work and a flair for design as well as practical ability is very important.

Building Products

Large companies include: Hanson, Marley-Eternit, Tarmac and Bison.

Three major sub sectors:

Clay building products are used in the construction of domestic, commercial and businesses premises and include the manufacture of bricks, roof tiles, sewage pipes and rain wall cladding systems, paving blocks for driveways and decorative terracotta ware.

Precast concrete building products range from small decorative screening blocks used for walling, to large pre-stressed concrete beams used to support bridges, they are fundamental to the construction industry and transportation infrastructure. They include paving slabs, concrete flooring, drainage culverts, sewage pipes, building blocks, preformed stairways, roadway lighting stanchions and roadside curbs.

Refractory products are heat-resistant materials which can withstand extreme temperatures.

Jobs available in the sector are Sales people, Warehouse operator, Concrete Casting Operatives, Machine operators, Plant operators, Brick throwers, Masonry specialists, Computer operators, Floor managers, Masonry managers, Technical managers – particularly project engineers. New recruits are encouraged and full training with qualifications is provided by most Employers. For more information regarding jobs, training, careers in Building Products visit our careers website on: **www.prospect4u.co.uk**

Glass Industry

Eight main sub-sectors:

- Flat glass – windows, doors, stained glass and shower screens
- Fibreglass – insulation, boat building, reinforcement for rubber and fibre optics
- Scientific and special glass – laboratory glassware and spectacles
- Glass tableware – drinks glasses, ornaments and paperweights
- Glass containers – food jars and containers, vases and perfume bottles
- Automotive glass – windscreens and security glass
- Fenestration and installation – the positioning and installation of windows in domestic and commercial buildings
- Glazing structures – the use of glass for partitions, walls and roofs (e.g. modern offices and conservatories)

Flat glass, which includes automotive glass, has grown at the rate of 5% per year for the past twenty years.

Big companies include, Pilkington's, Guardian, St.Gobain, Rockware Glass, Quinns, Anglian Home Improvements, Everest, Bowater Zenith. Jobs range from working on a manufacturing and processing line, specialised sectors – glass blowing, working in the field installing windows, doors and conservatories, surveying, sales and marketing, IT, accountancy and many more. For more detailed information on jobs, skills, qualifications and career paths, visit Proskills website on: **www.prospect4u.co.uk**

Extractives and Mineral Processing

The Extractives and Mineral Processing sector comprises: the extraction and processing of aggregates, slate, dimensional stone, gypsum, china clay and ball clay, silica and industrial sands), materials for cement manufacture, the processing of blast furnace/steel slag, the production and laying of asphalt, the production of ready mixed mortar and concrete and ancillary operations of these activities and the mining industry.

As is evident from this list, the sector comprises of a wide variety of industries, companies and occupations, ranging from Multi-national cement manufacturers to micro-employers specialising in engraving of decorative stone.

The eight major companies in the Extractives and Mineral Processing industry are:

- Quarrying
  - ⋆ Aggregate Industries
  - ⋆ Hanson
  - ⋆ Cemex
  - ⋆ Lafarge
  - ⋆ Tarmac
- Kaolin and Ball Clay
  - ⋆ Imerys
  - ⋆ WBB Minerals
- Coal Mining
  - ⋆ UK Coal

Whoever you are and whatever you enjoy doing, you'll find that there's a job for you in the quarrying industry. Be part of a multi-million pound industry that affects all our lives all the time. The career opportunities are endless and range from environmental management, to engineering, and marketing. Reducing the impact of quarrying on the environment is a key objective for the industry. Job roles range from restoration managers and landscape architects to environmental management advisors. Help sell the £3 billion worth of products that we all use everyday. We're looking for internal and external sales representatives, plus communications experts. For more information on jobs, careers and skills visit Proskills UK web site at: **www.prospect4u.co.uk**

Supervisory roles

With so many different workers involved in building projects, both large and small, it is very important that there are people to take overall responsibility for employing workers, purchasing materials, health and safety, and day-to-day management.

Site technician

Site technicians get involved with the general running and safety of the site. Your role would include hiring and buying materials and machinery, and organising people and equipment. It would be your responsibility to ensure budgets and plans are followed, and that everything meets technical requirements.

To become a site technician, you will need to have a strong knowledge of building methods and materials, and health and safety requirements, which you will have to teach workers on your site. You will need good communication and organisational skills, have a high level of competence in computing, and work well as part of a team.

There are no specific academic entry requirements to train as a site technician, although it is helpful to have GCSE/Standard Grade passes in science, maths and technology for the measurements and planning.

Site manager

Many site technicians become site managers, taking on more responsibility for larger projects and being in charge of everything that happens on the site.

Construction project manager

Construction project managers have overall responsibility for the planning, management, coordination and financial control of a construction project. It is their responsibility to see that the clients' wishes are adhered to and that the project is completed on time within the agreed budget.

Qualifications and Training

You do not need any formal qualifications to enter the building trades described above. For most trades it is a definite advantage to have GCSEs in maths, English and technology. There are several routes to entry and each route has its own specific entry requirements. Generally, training courses that do not require any formal educational qualifications lead to what are called craft level awards, and training that requires you to have four GCSEs leads to technician level awards. Many of the routes below offer both of these options. Most training takes between three and four years.

Foundation Certificates (FCs) are available at some schools and colleges in England and Wales and are really taster courses, to help you decide whether construction is for you. They are a good way of demonstrating your commitment if you are applying for further courses or traineeships in construction.

The Construction Apprenticeship Scheme (CAS) takes three to four years to complete, and you are based with an employer, earning a wage, but also receiving some structured training at your workplace and through college. At the end of your apprenticeship, if you are on a craft level scheme you will get a Construction Award (CA), and if you are on a technical level scheme you will get a National Certificate.

National Certificates (NCs) and National Diplomas (NDs) are technical qualifications available in many construction trades. You can study part-time or full-time for these awards. There are no formal entry requirements for these.

Higher National Certificates (HNCs) and Higher National Diplomas (HNDs) are one step up from NCs and NDs. You can either go from the basic level to the higher-level course or, if you have A levels, you can go straight onto a higher-level course.

National Vocational Qualifications (NVQs) are another way to combine practical on-site work and study at college, usually through day or block release. Most construction NVQs are based with employers, but there are some full-time college courses leading to this qualification. There are no formal exams with NVQs: your on-site and college work is assessed throughout the course. For most NVQ construction courses you need four GCSEs grades A to C, and these should include English, maths and technology.

Construction Awards are available at three levels: Foundation, Intermediate and Advanced, and are available in many construction occupations. They are college-based courses that you can study full time, or part time while working for an employer. All your assessments are based on what you do at college.

Construction project managers and site managers often have a degree in construction, civil engineering or quantity surveying.

There are increasing numbers of short, privately run training courses in some trades, particularly plumbing, painting and decorating and plastering, but others too. These are aimed at mature applicants wishing to change career. They can be extremely expensive and it is important that you check exactly what accreditation and qualifications they lead to.

If you are trying to sift through this rather bewildering set of options, start by considering whether you want to be mainly employed as you train or mainly based at college. It is also true that not every route is always available for every trade, and employment opportunities vary in different geographical areas. The CITB-ConstructionSkills website is a very helpful and thorough starting point to help you compare trades and look at routes to qualification.

Personal Qualities and Skills

While a variety of trades have been described and each has its special requirements, there are many skills and qualities that are important for all these occupations. You need to have a special interest in and feel for the particular material you are working with – wood, metal, plaster, stone, etc. You must be good at measuring and calculating, working out how much material you will need, and measuring exactly to ensure that something fits.

For all jobs you must be physically fit, though some work, such as bricklaying, is especially demanding. You may have to climb up and down scaffolding, work outside in unpleasant weather, or work in cramped spaces such as somebody's loft.

You need to get on with people. You often work as part of a team, and if you progress to supervisory or management roles you have to be organised and be good at motivating other people. If you are working in private houses, you must be polite, pleasant and trustworthy, and good at coming up with solutions to problems. If you become self-employed you must develop good business and financial skills.

Starting Salary

Salaries for apprentices throughout the construction industry are agreed annually. First-year apprentices earn around £7,500, second-year apprentices earn just under £10,000. Third-year apprentices earn around £12,000, more if they have achieved GNVQ level 3, and on completion of apprenticeships salaries rise to around £17,000. With experience, all trades can earn between £18,000 and £22,000. There is considerable regional variation in salaries. There may also be opportunities to earn overtime payments, or bonuses on very busy projects. Many people with experience in one of the construction trades choose to become self-employed.

Salaries for management posts range from £19,000 to £32,000.

info

CITB – Construction Skills, The Sector Skills Council for Construction, Bircham Newton, Kings Lynn, Norfolk PE31 6RH; 01485 577577; www.CITB-ConstructionSkills.org.uk

Summit Skills, Vega House, Opal Drive, Fox Milne, Milton Keynes MK15 0DF; 01908 303960; www.summitskills.org.uk

www.bconstructive.co.uk/apprenticeships

www.apprenticeships.org.uk (England)

www.modernapprenticeships.com (Scotland)

www.elwa.org.uk (Wales)

Local Job Centre Plus and Connexions/Careers Centres

CRAFTS

There are many occupations which can come under the banner of a 'Craft' and listed below is a selection.

Cabinet maker

see Carpentry

Florist

The florist's job involves designing and creating flower arrangements and displays such as table decorations, bouquets, sprays and wreaths, as well as selling cut flowers and plants. Some florists buy from flower markets; others have stock delivered from wholesalers, local nurseries or overseas producers. The work can include providing office displays, making arrangements for banquets, functions and receptions and decorating hotels and public buildings. Florists generally work a 40-hour week, including Saturdays.

Qualifications and Training

Edexcel (BTEC) qualifications are offered by a number of colleges at First Diploma, National Diploma and HND level. The Society of Floristry offers two professional qualifications – the Intermediate Certificate (ICSF) and the National Diploma (NDSF); these are for experienced florists. NVQs in floristry are available at levels 2 and 3.

Personal Qualities and Skills

Imagination and creative flair, colour sense, organisational ability, an ability to work to deadlines, a friendly manner, patience and dexterity are necessary. Good health and stamina are essential because the work can be physically demanding.

Starting Salary

Rates of pay vary according to size and location of the business and according to the individual's own skills and qualifications, experience and seniority. Salaries are similar to those in other retail work. Part-time work may be available.

Jewellery trade

Design

Jewellery designers craft a wide variety of items either by hand or using methods of large-scale production. These may be very expensive, traditionally styled pieces using gold or platinum, cheaper costume jewellery using synthetic stones and base metals, or fashion accessories made from beads, plastic or wood.

Although there are a few openings for designers of expensive jewellery, the more costly costume jewellery and mass-produced jewellery, there is more scope for original designers on either a freelance or artist/craftsperson basis, making fashionable ranges with semi-precious stones.

Manufacture

The jewellery, silverware and allied industries encompass a vast range of specialist skills. Apart from mounting and silversmithing, other skills needed to support these occupations include gem setting, engraving (hand and machine), enamelling, chasing, engine turning, spinning, electro-plating and polishing.

Qualifications and Training

To work in a jeweller's shop you do not need any formal qualifications, but some employers do expect you to have GCSEs in maths and English. Training is usually with a more experienced jeweller and you can take NVQs levels 2 and 3 in retail sales and retail operations.

You can study for a Professional Jewellers' Diploma with the National Association of Goldsmiths (NAG). This covers introductions to precious metals, gem stones and to hallmarks (the marks which certify a precious metal's quality). This is a distance learning course which lasts about 18 months. NAG also runs a Professional Jewellers' Management Diploma designed for shop managers or people who would like to become shop managers. There are several independent training courses available for jewellers; the Jewellery and Allied Industries Training Council (JAITC) holds details of these (see the info panel for contact details).

In the jewellery manufacturing trades there are a number of apprenticeships available.

Most jewellery designers have a degree in three-dimensional design and have specialised in jewellery design within that course.

Personal Qualities and Skills

For retail jewellery work, you have to have good communication and customer care skills and a real interest in the products you are selling. You should have an eye for detail and an awareness of colour and fashion. You need good numeracy skills and you should be highly dextrous, easily able to handle small and expensive items carefully. Anyone working in jewellery manufacture must be practical and careful, with an interest in scientific and technical processes as well as artistic effect.

Jewellery designers have to be artistic, imaginative, with a good understanding of the properties of different metals, gems and other materials. They also need to be good at promoting their products and have a sound understanding of business.

info

Creative and Cultural Skills,
4th Floor, Lafone House,
The Leathermarket, Weston Street,
London SE1 3HN; 020 7015 1800;
www.ccskills.org.uk

Design Council, 34 Bow Street,
London WC2E 7DL; 020 7420 5200;
www.design-council.org.uk

Goldsmiths Company,
Goldsmiths Hall, Foster Lane, London
EC2V 6BN; 020 7606 7010;
www.thegoldsmiths.co.uk

Goldsmiths Company Directory;
www.whoswhoingoldandsilver.com

National Association of Goldsmiths,
78A Luke Street, London EC2A 4XG;
020 7613 4445;
www.jewellers-online.org

Skillsmart Retail, 40 Duke Street,
London W1A 1AB; 0800 093 5001;
www.skillsmartretail.com

Jewellery and Allied Industries
Training Council (JAITC),
British Jewellers' Association,
10 Vyse Street, Birmingham B18 6LT;
www.jaitc.org.uk

SEMTA, 14 Upton Road, Watford,
Hertfordshire WD18 0JT;
0808 100 3682; www.semta.org.uk

Starting Salary

Starting salaries in jewellers' shops are between £10,000 and £12,000. Store managers earn between £15,000 and £22,000. Some own and run their own businesses and this may mean they can earn more. In manufacturing, salaries range from £13,000 to £18,000 depending on your level of skill and experience.

Jewellery designers earn between £15,000 and £20,000. Some designers with real flair and an eye to the changing world of fashion can earn far more than this, especially if they are designing jewellery for the rich and famous.

Pottery

Employees in the pottery industry make ordinary domestic china, earthenware, vases and ornaments, fine bone china, ceramic tiles, sanitary ware, industrial and electrical porcelain and huge insulators used in distributing electricity. Although the industry is mechanised, there is still a predominant demand for skilled workers: hand painters, fettlers and spongers, casting, lithographing, binding and lining, to name a few. Some potters work individually, hand throwing or casting their own pieces and selling them personally or through a shop or gallery.

Qualifications and Training

No formal educational requirements are needed for the industry and training is mainly on the job. Craftsmen potters sometimes become apprenticed to master potters, and Foundation and Advanced Modern Apprenticeships are now available. Vocational or degree courses are also available at some art schools.

Personal Qualities and Skills

Potters need a good eye for shape and design, a steady hand and a delicate touch. Potters working for themselves must also be inventive and have business skills and marketing ability.

Starting Salary

Industry employees start at £80+ a week. Craftspeople set their own rates, and if they are selling their work through a gallery, must pay the owner a percentage.

Association for Ceramic Training and Development, St James House, Webberley Lane, Longton, Stoke-on-Trent ST3 1RJ; 01782 597016; www.actd.co.uk

Crafts Council, 44a Pentonville Road, London N1 9BY; 020 7278 7700; www.craftscouncil.org.uk

Craft Potters' Association, 21 Carnaby Street, London W1V 1PH; 020 7437 6781

Saddler

Saddles are still made by hand, by craftspeople of considerable experience. They usually work in one of the many small companies that specialise in saddlery, making harnesses and other leather goods such as satchels and wallets. Saddlers' shops stock all these items and may also stock suitcases and sports goods and offer a repair service.

Qualifications and Training

The Society of Master Saddlers administers a four-year apprenticeship indenture scheme leading to certification by the Worshipful Company of Saddlers. Saddlery courses of varying lengths are available at the Capel Manor College at Enfield, Middlesex, Walsall College of Arts and Technology, Cambridge Saddlery Courses in Bury St Edmunds, Suffolk, Cumbria School of Saddlery in Penrith, Cumbria and the Saddlery Training Centre in Salisbury, Wiltshire. Cordwainers at Capel Manor College offers two courses in saddlery: a diploma in saddlery studies and an HND in saddlery technology. Both courses cover many aspects of running a small business and both last for two years.

The Society of Master Saddlers administers the National Saddlery Skills Assessment Scheme by which those making saddles, bridles and harnesses may have their skills assessed and gain qualifications in each specialist area at levels 1, 2 and 3. The City & Guilds National Skill Assessment and Qualification Scheme for the Saddlery Trade is also available. These qualifications are recognised within the trade.

info

Cordwainers College at Capel Manor, Bullsmoor Lane, Enfield, Middlesex EN1 4RQ; 020 8366 4442; www.capel.ac.uk

Walsall College of Arts and Technology, Leather Department, Shelley Campus, Scarborough Road, Walsall WS1 1XN; 01922 720889; www.walcat.ac.uk

Cambridge and District Saddlery Courses (INT) Ltd, 31 St John Street, Bury St Edmunds, Suffolk IP33 1SN; 01284 700640; www.racenetservices.com/businesslinks/careers/saddlerycourses.htm

Cumbria School of Saddlery, Unit 9, Redhills Business Park, Penrith, Cumbria CA11 0DL; 01768 899919; www.saddlerycourses.com

Saddlery Training Centre, 14–17 The Malverns, Cherry Orchard Lane, Salisbury, Wiltshire SP2 7JG; 01722 341144; fax: 01722 349669; www.saddlerytraining.com; e-mail: sales@saddlerytraining.com

Society of Master Saddlers, Green Lane Farm, Stonham, Stowmarket, Suffolk IP14 5DS; 01449 711642; www.mastersaddlers.co.uk; e-mail: enquiries@mastersaddlers.co.uk

Worshipful Company of Saddlers, Saddlers' Hall, 40 Gutter Lane, London EC2V 6BR; 020 7726 8663; www.saddlersco.co.uk; e-mail: clerk@saddlersco.co.uk

Personal Qualities and Skills

Painstaking attention to detail and pride in craftsmanship are needed. Owners of saddlers' shops often have a strong interest in horses too.

Starting Salary

£125–£400+ per week with experience.

Thatcher

Thatchers are self-employed craftspeople who roof, re-roof or repair thatched buildings with long straw, combed wheat straw, reed and other materials. The materials and methods they use have to preserve the building in its original form. A thatched roof gives good insulation against heat and cold and lasts 20 to 50 years. A roof is thatched by taking off the old thatch and then pegging down layers of new straw or reed.

Qualifications and Training

Academic qualifications are not essential. Thatching can be learnt on the job as an apprentice to a Master Thatcher. Training takes four to five years. The Countryside Agency runs a training scheme for people of all ages, leading to NVQ level 2 in thatching.

Personal Qualities and Skills

Thatchers need to be robust, good with their hands and not mind bad weather or heights. They also need common sense, the ability to make decisions and deal with customers.

Starting Salary

Salaries start at between £13,000 and £16,000 rising to £22,000 with two or three years' experience. In some regions it is possible to earn more than this because there is a high demand for thatches.

New Entrants Training Scheme, Herefordshire College of Technology, Folly Lane, Hereford HR1 1LS; 01432 365314; www.hereford-tech.ac.uk

Thatching Information Service, Thatcher's Rest, Levens Green, Great Munden, Nr Ware, Hertfordshire SG11 1HD; 01920 438710

National Society of Master Thatchers, c/o The Secretary, 15 High Street, Steventon, Abingdon, Oxfordshire OX13 5RZ

CUSTOMS AND EXCISE

There is far more to this work than high profile drugs or arms seizures. Customs and excise officers carry out three main types of work. They check passengers, luggage, freight and mail at ports and airports, ensuring that people are not carrying illegal goods or items upon which appropriate tax has not been paid. They visit distilleries and oil refineries ensuring that appropriate excise duty has been paid on these items. They visit and inspect businesses to ensure that their VAT records are correct and up to date.

Qualifications and Training

There are several entry levels for this work. To start on Band 2 you must have two GCSEs grades A to C. To start on Band 3/4 you must have five GCSEs grades A to C. You can start as a junior manager (Band 5) and you will need five GCSEs grades A to C and two A levels or their equivalent. At all levels one of the GCSEs must be English language. Many successful Band 5 applicants are graduates. All the above levels are recruited directly by HM Customs and Revenue. If you apply for Fast Stream entry, you apply to Central Civil Service Recruitment then, if you join HM Customs and Revenue you become a customs officer straight away. For the Fast Stream you must have a good honours degree, either a 1st or an upper 2nd. Most of the training is on-the-job and includes appropriate short courses and sometimes opportunities to take professional qualifications.

Personal Qualities and Skills

You must be able to get on with people, being polite, tactful and able to question and listen carefully. You should be honest and fair and be able to analyse complex information. For much of the work on the excise and VAT side you must have good numeracy skills.

Starting Salary

On Bands 2 to 4 starting salaries range from £12,000 to £18,000. Junior managers (Band 5) start on salaries of £18,500 to £22,500 a year. There are additional allowances for working in and around London and for working antisocial hours. Performance-related pay has also been introduced.

info

HM Revenue and Customs;
www.hmrc.gov.uk

Civil Service Fast Stream;
www.faststream.gov.uk

Skills for Justice, Riverside House,
Don Road, Sheffield S9 2TJ;
0114 261 1499;
www.skillsforjustice.com

DENTISTRY

All professionals in dentistry in the UK must be registered with the General Dental Council. This includes dentists, dental hygienists, dental therapists, dental nurses and dental technicians.

Dentist

Dentists aim to prevent tooth decay and gum disease and to identify and treat such diseases. This involves filling, crowning and extracting teeth, scaling and cleaning teeth and gums. They design and fit dentures and plates and take corrective measures for teeth growing abnormally. They are also involved with the rectification of fractured jaws and surgery of the mouth. Much of the dentist's work today is highly technical and requires a lot of manual dexterity. There is growing emphasis on preventive work, and the dentist is expected to counsel and educate.

Opportunities exist both in the UK and abroad. In general dental practice dentists work on contract to the NHS, but growing numbers work in private clinics. Some work in hospitals, community services, school services or the armed forces. There are also opportunities for dentists to work in university dental teaching and research.

Specialist areas of dentistry include paediatric dentistry and oral and maxillo-facial surgery. A number of large companies also provide dental treatment facilities for staff at work and there are some openings within occupational dentistry. The armed services also provide short service commissions or permanent careers for medical and dental staff.

Dentists need to have confidence and the ability to reassure patients as many are apprehensive about dental treatment. Team work is important as working closely with the surgery assistant and any specialists the practice employs is essential.

Qualifications and Training

To qualify, a dentist must have a degree in dental surgery. All dentists must be registered on the Dentists' Register, which is maintained by the General Dental

Council. Competition for degree course entry is stiff, requiring good A level grades in physics, chemistry and biology. Entry requirements vary: some schools have pre-dental courses for students who have not studied science A levels. All applicants are expected to have spent time work-shadowing a dentist.

The undergraduate course lasts at least five years. It incorporates a sound academic education combined with theoretical and practical training in all aspects of dental practice.

In the armed forces, dental cadetships leading to a commission are open to candidates who have completed part of their training at a dental school.

Personal Qualities and Skills

Manual and visual dexterity combined with medical knowledge and clinical skills are essential. Candidates should be equable, sympathetic and have an agreeable nature and an ability to communicate. Good administrative and managerial skills and the ability to work in a team are important.

Starting Salary

General dental practitioners and orthodontists earn the fees that they receive from patients or the NHS; these start from £25,500. Salaries for senior posts are over £50,000.

Dental hygienist

Dental hygienists clean, polish and scale teeth and in some cases prepare patients for oral operations. Through lectures and practical experience they also endeavour to educate children and adults on the importance of proper dental care. Dental hygienists work to the written prescription of a dentist.

Qualifications and Training

Applicants for the Diploma in Dental Hygiene must be over 18 with five GCSE passes, including biology and English. They also need two years' experience as a dental nurse or two A levels or equivalent. Manchester University offers a three-year BSc in oral health science. Graduates work as oral health therapists which combines the skills of a hygienist and therapist.

Personal Qualities and Skills

Manual and visual dexterity. Candidates should have an ability to communicate in order to educate patients in good dental hygiene practice. The ability to work in a team is important.

Starting Salary

Dental hygienists earn £13,500+.

Dental nurse

Dental nurses prepare the surgery and get the appropriate instruments ready. During treatment, they assist the dentist by passing instruments, mixing materials, taking notes from the dentist's dictation for records and making sure the patient is comfortable at all times. Once the patient has left, the dental nurse tidies the surgery and sterilises all the instruments. Sometimes, particularly in general practice, dental nurses also help with reception work – making appointments, taking payments, dealing with the paper work, meeting and reassuring patients.

Qualifications and Training

Many dentists like to train their own assistants and expect applicants to be educated to GCSE standard. In 2004 it became necessary for dental nurses to have obtained NVQ level 3 in oral healthcare or passed the National Certificate of the Examining Board for Dental Nurses. Preparation for this exam can be obtained either at evening or day-release classes or via full-time attendance on a course lasting between one and two years. A certificate is awarded on passing the exam and completing 24 months' practical experience. Courses are offered by colleges of further education and dental hospitals. Courses offered by dental hospitals usually require four GCSE passes, including English and biology.

Personal Qualities and Skills

Candidates should be equable, sympathetic and have an agreeable nature and an ability to communicate. Good administrative and managerial skills and the ability to work in a team are important.

Starting Salary

Salaries for dental nurses vary greatly depending on the type of practice and its location. Some employers pay around the national minimum wage; others pay more and include additional benefits. Average salaries are between £9,000 and £12,000.

Dental technician

Dental technicians design and fabricate a wide variety of different materials and equipment to make crowns, dentures, metal plates, bridges, orthodontic braces and other appliances prescribed by a dentist.

Qualifications and Training

The usual entry requirements for courses are five GCSEs or equivalents (English, maths, physics and chemistry). The Edexcel (BTEC) diploma in dental technology is a full-time three-year course but can also be studied part time.

Personal Qualities and Skills

Good technical skills and the ability to work in a team.

Starting Salary

Dental technicians earn £7,500–£9,000 while training, rising to £10,000–£18,000 when qualified.

Dental therapist

Dental therapists work in local authority clinics and hospitals assisting dentists by carrying out simpler forms of treatment such as fillings and the extraction of first teeth. They also give guidance on general dental care. Dental therapists must always work to the written prescription of a dentist.

Qualifications and Training

To become a dental therapist you must take either a diploma in dental therapy or a degree in oral health sciences including modules on dental therapy and hygiene. The British Association of Dental Therapists (BADT) can provide details of relevant dental schools; diplomas last two years, degree courses three years.

   To get onto either course you need five GCSEs grades A–C, including human biology, plus two A levels. If you are already a qualified and experienced dental nurse, you may be able to do a course without meeting the usual academic requirements.

Personal Qualities and Skills

You must be very good at working with people, able to reassure, be calm, encourage and teach. You should have an interest in science and healthcare and you should also be practical, with good manual dexterity and good eyesight. You must be physically fit and resilient.

Starting Salary

Salaries range from £15,000 to £22,000. With experience, and working in private practice, you can earn considerably more than this.

Orthodontist

Orthodontists work in a specialist branch of dentistry that is concerned with the development and management of irregularities of teeth, jaws and face. The treatment is aimed at correcting dental and jaw abnormalities. Orthodontists generally (although not always) see patients for an initial assessment between the ages of 7 and 10.

Qualifications and Training

To become an orthodontist, a qualification as a dentist is required in order to gain entry to a specialised orthodontic course, which lasts three years full time and usually includes some research work, resulting in an MSc.

Personal Qualities and Skills

As with dentists, manual and visual dexterity combined with medical knowledge and clinical skills are important qualities for orthodontists. Candidates should be equable, sympathetic and have an agreeable nature and an ability to communicate. The ability to work in a team is important.

Starting Salary

Orthodontists earn the fees that they receive from patients or the NHS; these start from £24,500. Salaries for senior posts are over £50,000.

British Association of Dental Nurses, 11 Pharos Street, Fleetwood, Lancashire FY7 6BG; 01253 778631; www.badn.org.uk; e-mail: admin@badn.org.uk

British Dental Association, 64 Wimpole Street, London W1G 8YS; 020 7935 0875; www.bda-dentistry.org.uk

National Examining Board for Dental Nurses, 110 London Road, Fleetwood F17 6EU; 01253 778417

British Dental Hygienists' Association, 13 The Ridge, Yatton, Bristol

BS19 4DQ; 01934 876389; www.bdha.org.uk

Dental Technicians' Education and Training Advisory Board (DTETAB), 64 Wimpole St, London W1M 8AL

General Dental Council, 37 Wimpole Street, London W1G 8DQ; 020 7887 3800; www.gdc-uk.org

British Orthodontic Society, BOS Office, 291 Gray's Inn Road, London WC1X 8QJ; 020 7837 2193; www.bos.org.uk

DIETITIAN

A dietitian is an authority on diet and the application of the principles of nutrition. Dietitians working in hospitals collaborate with medical staff, other healthcare professionals and catering staff in planning the correct balance of foods for all the patients, depending on their general state of health and medical requirements. Dietitians are also employed by local health authorities to work with general practitioners, in health centres and clinics dealing with infant welfare and antenatal treatment. Some dietitians may now be employed directly by fundholding GPs. They are also called upon to educate other healthcare professionals in nutrition. Other opportunities for dietitians exist in education, research, the food industry and the media. Increasingly, dietitians work in a freelance capacity.

Qualifications and Training

To become a state registered dietitian and practise in the National Health Service you must either do a four-year degree course or a two-year postgraduate course following on from a degree in another relevant subject, such as food science, medicine or nursing. Both of these include practical placements as well as academic study and some courses are developing part-time routes.

You must have three A level passes grades A to C in sciences for most degree courses; chemistry is the one most courses insist on. Advanced level GNVQ or BTEC National Diploma courses in health and science-based subjects are often accepted as alternatives to A levels. For most degree and postgraduate courses the NHS pays your fees and you can also apply for NHS grants to help support you while you are studying and training.

Personal Qualities and Skills

The complex nutritional and scientific knowledge you acquire is only useful if you can communicate it really effectively to your clients. People are often unhappy, unwilling or uncertain about how to change their diets, so you need to be able to explain scientific ideas in layman's terms; you need to be positive, encouraging and realistic and have an interest in the aesthetic as well as the nutritional properties of food. You should be able to work as part of a healthcare team, but be happy working one-to-one with patients.

Starting Salary

Salaries start at around £18,000 to £19,500, with higher salaries when qualified. Senior dietitians can become consultants earning close to £40,000.

info

British Dietetic Association (BDA), Charles House, 148/9 Charles Street, Queensway, Birmingham B3 3HT; 0121 200 8080; www.bda.uk.com

NHS Careers, PO Box 376, Bristol BS99 3EY; 0845 606 0655; www.nhscareers.nhs.uk

Health Professions Council (HPC), Park House, 184 Kennington Park Road, London SE11 4BU; 020 7582 0866; www.hpc-uk.org

DISC JOCKEY

Disc jockeys provide music and entertainment at a range of venues such as clubs, private parties and radio stations. They use a variety of high-tech equipment for mixing, pitch control and cross-fading, and may also be responsible for lighting and multimedia effects.

Qualifications and Training

A strong interest and enjoyment of different music styles is essential, and it is useful to have an interest in technology and electronics. Some DJs specialise in specific music genres such as soul, funk, hip-hop and pop. Most are self-taught and usually begin their career by volunteering their services at clubs, radio stations or to friends. It is useful to send a tape demonstrating DJ skills when asking for work.

Personal Qualities and Skills

DJs must have a lively personality, a sense of fun and natural creativity. They need to have a good knowledge of and genuine interest in music and be able to interact effectively with an audience.

Starting Salary

Sometimes you have to start off doing unpaid work. Very often you are paid by the session, anything from £50 to £300, most sessions lasting a few hours. Really experienced club and radio DJs with an established reputation can earn up to £1,000 per session.

Skillset, Prospect House, 80–110 New Oxford Street, London WC1A 1HB; 08080 300 900 for England, Wales and Northern Ireland; www.skillset.org

Radio Academy, 5 Market Place, London W1W 8AE; 020 7255 2010; www.radioacademy.org

Hospital Broadcasting Association; www.hbauk.com

Community Media Association, The Workstation, 15 Paternoster Row, Sheffield S1 2BX; 0114 279 5219; www.commedia.org.uk

Commercial Radio Companies Association, The Radiocentre, 77 Shaftesbury Avenue London W1D 5DU; 020 7306 2603; www.crca.co.uk

Info

DIVING

Diver

Professional divers are mainly employed by commercial diving contractors in the North Sea, ports and docks. There are also opportunities in the armed services and police forces. The growth of diving as a popular sport has created a number of positions for instructors worldwide. Currently there are many more qualified divers looking for work than there is work available.

Qualifications and Training

Diving is potentially hazardous and it is essential for anyone who wishes to become a commercial diver to attend and satisfactorily complete a course of training at a diver training school which has been approved by the UK Health and Safety Executive (HSE). This leads to certificates of competence relevant to offshore and inland/inshore commercial diving. All commercial offshore divers need to hold a current first aid certificate. In addition, other skills are required, including welding, cutting and using underwater tools.

The Royal Navy and police forces train their own personnel. In the case of the latter, pupils must have a minimum of two years' experience as a constable.

BSAC or other sport diving qualifications do not qualify divers for commercial diving.

Personal Qualities and Skills

Divers must be sound swimmers and physically fit; all professional divers have to pass a full commercial diving medical, which complies with HSE Diving Operations at Work regulations. They must be able to tolerate hard exercise, extreme conditions and recognise and work within their own personal limits. They must be very responsible and willing and able to work as part of a team. Initiative and the ability to sell their own skills to a potential employer are essential.

Starting Salary

There is no uniform pay rate for divers who work inland/inshore; it varies from £50–£120 per day. Divers who work in the UK sector of the North Sea on oil- or gas-related activities are paid around £160 per day, which rises to about £260 once they have spent 300 days offshore as members of a diving team and have completed 150 'approved' dives. Sport diving instructors work largely for travel and enjoyment and pay can be low.

info

Health and Safety Executive, Magdalen House, Trinity Road, Bootle, Merseyside L20 3QZ; 0870 154 5500; www.hse.gov.uk

International Marine Contractors Association, Carlyle House, 235 Vauxhall Bridge Road, London SW1V 1EJ; www.imca-int.com/careers; e-mail: imca@imca-int.com

Fort Bovisand Underwater Centre, Plymouth, Devon PL9 0AB; 01752 408021; www.fortbovisand.com; e-mail: dive@fortbovisand.com

Society for Underwater Technology, 80 Coleman Street, London EC2R 5BJ; 020 7382 2601; www.sut.org.uk

Underwater Centre, Fort William, Inverness-shire, Highland PH33 6LZ; 01397 703768

British Sub Aqua Club, Telford's Quay, South Pier Road, Ellesmere Port, Cheshire CH65 4FL; 0151 350 6200; fax: 0151 350 6215; www.bsac.org

Local police forces

Royal Navy Careers Offices; Royal Navy Careers enquiries; 0845 607 5555; www.royal-navy.mod.uk

ROV pilot technician

Remotely operated vehicles (ROVs) were introduced into the military and offshore fields in the late 1970s and early 1980s and now offer a career path for well-educated technical staff. ROVs are operated by the Royal Navy, offshore companies, environmental agencies, police and salvage companies. These underwater robots carry out the work of a diver at depths where diving is impossible.

Qualifications and Training

Employers normally require ROV personnel to have a good background in electronics or hydraulics. Experience with pneumatics, plant maintenance or electrical engineering is also of interest. Candidates who do not have formal qualifications (academic, trade or in the services) in one of these areas are unlikely to be considered. Training courses are available at a number of schools which allow newcomers to the industry to learn the basics; however, none of these courses is formally required and they will not normally be accepted as a basis for employment unless the person has the right sort of background and qualifications. Details of courses are available from the International Marine Contractors Association website.

Personal Qualities and Skills

Initiative and ability to work in small close-knit teams and a willingness to work outside the UK are essential. To work offshore in any capacity it is necessary to undergo and pass a special medical examination.

Starting Salary

Starting salaries are £18,000+, rising to £28,000+.

International Marine Contractors Association, Carlyle House, 235 Vauxhall Bridge Road, London SW1V 1EJ; 020 7931 8171; fax: 020 7931 8935;

www.imca-int.com;
e-mail: imca@imca-int.com

Local Royal Navy Careers Information Offices

Info

DOMESTIC APPLIANCE SERVICE ENGINEER

Domestic appliance service engineers service and repair all kinds of household goods including washing machines, fridges, televisions, DVD players – in fact all kinds of electrical and gas appliances. Service engineers work for retailers, for manufacturers, for servicing companies and some are self-employed. As well as replacing worn or damaged parts in appliances, they may offer routine servicing, checking that everything is running smoothly and removing dust, limescale or other debris from appliances. They also advise customers on the best way to care for their appliances.

Qualifications and Training

While no formal qualifications are necessary, in practice most organisations will expect you to have qualifications and background experience in at least two of the following areas: electrics, electronics, gas fitting, mechanics, plumbing or refrigeration. There are several relevant Edexcel BTEC and City & Guilds courses at levels 2 and 3. Look for courses with units in consumer goods or specialist options on TV, video and PC repair and maintenance. People aged 16 to 24 who are interested in this work could consider apprenticeships in electrics, gas fitting or plumbing. Training is usually provided by the employer and consists of new trainees assisting and learning from a more experienced engineer until they are able to take on more complex jobs or work on their own.

Personal Qualities and Skills

As well as good practical skills and knowledge of a wide range of appliances, you must have good problem-solving ability and you must be good at dealing with people. You must be polite and friendly to customers, good at explaining problems, and able to listen to their concerns.

Starting Salary

Salaries start at between £12,000 and £14,500. With a few years' experience this rises to £10,000 to £20,000. Anyone with highly specialised skills such as gas servicing, may earn more than this.

info

SEMTA, 14 Upton Road, Watford, Hertfordshire WD18 0JT; 0808 100 3682; www.semta.org.uk

Domestic Appliance Service Association, 69 The Maltings, Stanstead Abbotts, Hertfordshire SG12 8HG; www.dasa.org.uk

CORGI (The Council for Registered Gas Installers), 1 Elmwood, Chineham Business Park, Crockford Lane, Basingstoke, Hants RG24 8WG; 0870 401 2300; www.corgi-gas-safety.com

DOMESTIC SERVICE

The term 'domestic service' applies to those occupations such as housekeeper, maids, cooks, butlers, footmen and valets. Duties may involve the general running of a household, announcing guests, serving drinks and supervising other staff preparing food, waiting at the table, cleaning and/or looking after the employer's clothes. Some jobs can be done on a temporary basis and agencies exist to provide domestic staff for special occasions.

Qualifications and Training

While no formal qualifications are needed, catering qualifications are often extremely useful and even some management qualifications could be useful for some positions. Sometimes private training courses are an option, but check carefully what you would have to spend and what you would get for your money.

Personal Qualities and Skills

Of course you have to be very good at dealing with people, tactful, patient and sometimes quite thick-skinned. You also have to be friendly and comfortable meeting people. You need to be discrete and honest, well organised and calm. You may need a variety of practical skills associated with domestic work such as cooking, cleaning and general household tasks. Good references and personal recommendations are important in this sector.

Starting Salary

What you are paid varies according to whether food, accommodation, a car, or other benefits come with the job. For many daily or part-time domestic jobs such as cleaning and ironing you get the minimum wage. If you are aged 22 or above, this is currently £5.35 an hour. If you are aged 18 to 21 it is £4.45.

Local Job Centre Plus and Careers/ Connexions Centres	*The Lady*, 39–40 Bedford Street, Strand, London WC2E 9EN; 020 7379 4717; www.lady.co.uk (job advertisements)	

Butler

A butler is employed to organise the domestic arrangements of the employer. This may include supervising other domestic staff, serving meals and refreshments, answering the telephone and door as well as organising social events, room settings for functions and having responsibility for the wine cellar, china and cutlery.

Butlers are employed in a range of settings: private households, five-star hotels, castles and palaces and yachts all around the world.

Qualifications and Training

No formal qualifications are required, although many butlers undertake professional training.

Personal Qualities and Skills

Butlers need to be courteous, discreet and to be motivated to provide a high standard of service to the employer.

Starting Salary

Salaries for a fully trained and experienced butler can start at £30,000+ and accommodation may also be provided.

Guild of Professional English Butlers, PO Box 32380, London SW17 9WJ; 02392 637919; www.guildofbutlers.com	Butler Bureau; www.butlerbureau.com International Guild of Professional Butlers; www.butlersguild.com	

DRESSER

see Broadcasting.

DRESSMAKER

see Fashion

DRIVING

Although many jobs require the ability to drive a vehicle, the occupations in this section refer to those which require professional driving skills.

Chauffeur/Chauffeuse

Chauffeurs are skilled car drivers who are employed either by one person or by companies or organisations where senior personnel need personal transport on hand at all times. Private chauffeurs may live in accommodation provided and have various other duties. Apart from the actual driving, the job will also involve making sure the cars are well maintained and clean. Some chauffeurs have a security role and may also act as bodyguards.

Qualifications and Training

No formal academic qualifications are required, but you must have several years' driving experience and a full, clean UK driving licence. Some employers like you to have an advanced driving certificate from the Institute of Advanced Motorists. For some posts you will need a foreign language and perhaps other skills such as car maintenance or gardening, if your time spent actually chauffeuring is likely to be fairly limited. Many chauffeurs have worked as taxi drivers or have been in the police force or armed services.

Personal Qualities and Skills

You must have excellent driving skills, and be careful, confident and sensible. You need to be polite, smart and tactful and able to respect people's privacy and use your discretion. You must be flexible, calm and reasonably physically fit.

Starting Salary

Starting salaries are between £10,000 and £16,000. With experience these rise to around £25,000. Some posts bring other benefits such as accommodation or a lot of foreign travel.

Institute of Advanced Motorists, IAM House, 510 Chiswick High Road, London W4 5RG; 020 8996 9600; www.iam.org.uk

GoSkills, Concorde House, Trinity Park, Solihull, Birmingham

B37 7UQ; 0121 635 5520; www.goskills.org

British Chauffeurs Guild Ltd, 13 Stonecot Hill, Sutton, Surrey SM3 9HB; 020 8544 9777; www.britishchauffeursguild.co.uk

Courier

Couriers deliver and collect parcels, generally in larger towns and cities. Around 10,000 couriers work in Central London. Mostly the delivery or collection is in the same city, sometimes in a different one and very occasionally in another country. Most couriers use a motorbike, which they may be required to buy. Couriers carrying packages abroad travel by air.

Qualifications and Training

Couriers don't need formal qualifications, but good literacy skills are important. You must be aged 17 or over and have a driving licence appropriate to the vehicle you are to drive, eg motorcycle, car or van. A basic knowledge of motor vehicle maintenance can be valuable and motorcycle couriers usually have to provide their own vehicle, plus its road tax and insurance. Once you are employed you can work towards NVQs levels 2 and 3 in Carry and Deliver Goods. Units include road safety and customer care.

Personal Qualities and Skills

Good, safe driving skills and an ability to deal with people are both important. You are often under a great deal of pressure to be quick, so you must be able to cope with this and not compromise safety. Sometimes knowledge of foreign languages can be useful.

Starting Salary

Couriers start on between £10,000 and £12,000 a year and with experience they can earn £14,000 to £20,000. Remember that out of these earnings, you may have to pay for fuel, insurance and the maintenance of your vehicle. Many couriers are self-employed. Some employers pay bonuses for good attendance, reliability and punctuality. Remember that most work is likely to be in large cities.

Skills for Logistics, 14 Warren Yard, Warren Farm Office Village, Stratford Road, Milton Keynes MK12 5NW; 0870 242 7314; www.skillsforlogistics.org

Driving examiner

Driving examiners must ensure that candidates are competent to drive without endangering other road users and demonstrate due consideration for other drivers and pedestrians. The examiner directs learner drivers over an approved route and asks them to carry out various exercises. While doing this, the examiner must take notes without distracting the candidate's concentration and must make a fair assessment of the learner's ability.

Qualifications and Training

Driving examiners are required to complete a strict selection process, followed by four weeks' training. They must have detailed knowledge of the *Highway Code* and road and traffic safety problems, some mechanical understanding, have held positions of responsibility and dealt with the public. Driving examiners must be over 25 and have had extensive experience of a variety of different vehicle types. Vacancies are advertised both locally and nationally by the Driving Standards Agency. Selection is dependent upon passing a special driving test and interview. For those who are successful, there are continuous checks by a supervising examiner to ensure the maintenance of a high standard.

Personal Qualities and Skills

Examiners should be fair, sympathetic, friendly, clearly spoken and have a calm, unflappable nature. The ability to work to a strict timetable is important.

Starting Salary

Varies depending on hours worked. Examiners generally have annualised hours contracts and minimum working hours are guaranteed on entry into employment.

info

Private Hire, Hackney Carriage and Chauffeur Industry Training Organisation, 14 Widdrington Terrace, North Shields NE29 0BZ; 0191 258 1955

GoSkills, Concorde House, Trinity Park, Solihull, Birmingham B37 7UQ, 0121 635 5520; www.goskills.org

Driving instructor

Driving instructors teach clients how to drive in preparation for all categories of the Driving Standards Agency's theory and practical driving tests. Instructors can also provide post-test training for the Pass Plus scheme as well as prepare clients for advanced driving tests, such as the DIAmond Advanced Motorists test.

The industry is now very much structured to self-employment, with instructors either having their own business or existing as an independent operation within a franchise agreement.

Qualifications and Training

In order to be allowed by law to accept payment for teaching people to drive, car driving instructors must be either registered or licensed by the Registrar of Approved Driving Instructors (ADIs) at the Driving Standards Agency. This requires them to have passed the three-part qualifying test within the space of two years. The ADI exam consists of a written test, a practical driving test and a practical test of the ability to instruct. Training is available from any of the establishments listed in the Official Register of Driving Instructor Training (ORDIT), which is included in the starter pack (see info box below). ORDIT establishments are regularly required to satisfy the inspection criteria under the voluntary scheme of minimum required standards set up and agreed by the Driver Training Industry and the Driving Standards Agency.

Personal Qualities and Skills

Driving instructors must have a calm and friendly nature, be very alert and quick to react, should be clearly spoken and able to express themselves well. Patience, confidence and tact are also important characteristics, as is the willingness to abide by a professional Code of Practice.

Starting Salary

Typical earnings, after business or franchise fees, will vary widely depending on tuition hours worked and operating costs.

Driving Instructors Association, Safety House, Beddington Farm Road, Croydon CR0 4XZ; 020 8665 5151; fax: 020 8665 5565; www.driving.org

Driving Standards Agency, Stanley House, 56 Talbot Street, Nottingham NG1 5GU; 0115 901 2500; fax: 0115 901 2940; www.dsa.gov.uk

Your Road to Becoming an Approved Driving Instructor, AD114 starter

pack, including application forms, for £3.00, from DSA

www.driving-instructor-training.co.uk

Local driving schools, Job Centre Plus and Careers/Connexions centres

The Driving Instructor's Handbook (Kogan Page)

Practical Teaching Skills for Driving Instructors (Kogan Page)

Lorry driver

This work ranges from driving conventional flat-bodied lorries that can carry a variety of loads to driving lorries designed for one purpose, such as car and animal transporters and milk tankers. Drivers often take a load from A to B and then carry one back from B to A in the UK or across Europe. As well as driving, lorry drivers may have to help with the loading and unloading of goods. Drivers of potentially dangerous products must know how to handle them safely and certification is required.

Qualifications and Training

There are no formal academic entry requirements for driving work, but you must be able to read maps, handle documents and deal with people, as well as enjoy driving and already have a normal full, clean, driving licence. To drive vehicles of 7.5 tonnes you need a class C licence and you cannot normally apply for this until you are aged 21. To drive an articulated vehicle you need a C + E licence, which you cannot normally obtain until you are 25. Skills for Logistics, the Sector Skills Council for the Freight and Logistics Industry, has developed a range of specific qualifications. You can take NVQ level 2 in carrying and delivering goods and in goods vehicle driving. These NVQs are employment based, with some college or off-site training. You can also serve apprenticeships in goods vehicle driving. The Young Drivers Scheme (YDS), operated by Skills for Logistics, allows you to obtain a full C class driving licence at age 18 and a C + E licence at age 21.

For older entrants it is difficult to get your training funded by an employer, so you may have to consider paying for this yourself; it costs more than £2,000.

Personal Qualities and Skills

You must be a good driver with a thorough understanding of road safety, and the patience to tolerate long drives and heavy traffic. You must be happy spending many hours on your own, but also be able to work with warehouse employees and customers and remain pleasant and friendly.

Starting Salary

A newly qualified driver earns between £11,000 and £12,000; the pay is less than this while you are on the Young Drivers Scheme. Experienced drivers can earn a lot more than this, especially if they are working antisocial hours.

info

Skills for Logistics: The Sector Skills
Council for Freight and Logistics,
14 Warren Yard,
Warren Farm Office Village,
Milton Keynes MK12 5NW;
0870 242 7314;
www.skillsforlogistics.org

Local Job Centre Plus offices

The LGV Learner Driver's Guide
(Kogan Page)

Professional LGV Driver's Handbook
(Kogan Page)

Passenger transport

About 65 per cent of personnel working in passenger transport on the roads are drivers. Many work on routes within one town or city, but some are employed by coach companies taking passengers from one town to another, across the country, or on international journeys. Other staff are employed as engineers, administrators, or managers.

Engineering work includes vehicle maintenance and repair in mechanical work, electrical and electronic systems and body structures, as well as technical research and design. Increasingly, companies are looking for employees with multiple skills or the willingness to undertake training in other occupational areas.

Administration covers route planning, traffic surveys, publicity, fare scales, computer operation, legal work and financial management.

Qualifications and Training

Modern Apprenticeships are available for engineers; some formal qualifications may be required depending on the scheme offered. NVQs are available at levels 1 to 5, which provide a career pathway within the industry. Semi-skilled engineers and engineers from other occupational areas are often recruited and in-service training is provided.

There are Induction and Foundation programmes (five modules) for coach drivers. Passenger-carrying vehicle (PCV) licence driver training is provided by all major companies. This may be supported by NVQs at levels 2 and 3 in road passenger transport. Formal qualifications are not required.

School leavers and graduates are eligible for training in administration and management. In-service training is an integral part of all careers with the major bus and coach companies.

Personal Qualities and Skills

The work of bus drivers means dealing constantly with the general public, and a friendly attitude is important. Tact and good humour are essential, as well as a liking for the elderly and for young people, who form the majority of the bus-travelling public. Drivers need to be willing to work early and late shifts.

For engineering occupations, a sound mechanical ability and aptitude are preferred. A variety of skills are required within administration; information on these occupations can be obtained from individual companies.

Starting Salary

Salaries vary and applicants should enquire of the individual companies. The average for a driver is £14,500.

Local bus and coach companies	GoSkills, Concorde House, Trinity Park, Solihull B37 7UQ; 0121 635 5520; www.goskills.org.uk

Taxi driver

A 'taxi' is a traditional hackney carriage (like the black London taxis). The hackney carriage driver is allowed to 'ply for hire' – drive around the streets looking for passengers – and can be flagged down by a 'fare' (passenger). They may also operate from taxi ranks (known as 'standing for hire') in the streets. A private hire vehicle, on the other hand, has to be booked over the telephone or in person at the office from which it operates. Drivers therefore spend a good proportion of their time waiting around for passengers. Hours for both types of driver are generally long and unsocial (since there is a good deal of evening or night work, as well as weekend and public holiday work). Drivers may be owner-drivers or work for a company.

Qualifications and Training

Taxi drivers must be at least 21 years of age to be granted a licence, although in practice, because of insurance requirements, most are over 25. A valid Group A driving licence and relevant driving experience are also necessary. Hackney carriage drivers are legally bound to take the shortest or quickest route to a passenger's destination. Trainee drivers usually have to pass special tests, known as 'knowledge tests', to prove that they know their way about sufficiently well. These tests are generally oral, the most demanding being the Knowledge of London Test, which is required before drivers may operate in the capital. This usually takes some 18 months to two years to complete. Specialised training schools exist and there are also special training schemes for the disabled and for people who have been in the forces. In London, too, an additional driving test must be passed before a licence is granted.

Personal Qualities and Skills

Driving in traffic demands a calm, unflappable personality, with lots of patience. Drivers also need to have a good memory. In addition, a taxi driver must be 'of good character', as a licence will not be granted to anyone who has committed certain offences.

Starting Salary

Almost all taxi drivers are self-employed and have to pay tax and National Insurance out of their earnings. Owner-drivers generally earn more than drivers employed by a company (who are often on a fixed rate), although they must also finance the repairs and servicing costs incurred by their own vehicles. Average earnings are around £14,000.

| Local taxi companies | Licensed Taxi Drivers Association, 9–11 Woodfield Road, London W9 2BA; 020 7286 1046 |

ECONOMIST

Economists study the use, organisation and distribution of the world's resources. The field of investigation is very wide, but may include the study of such topics as the reasons for balance of payments crises, the effects of different forms of taxation, international trade or business economics. Economics is not a precise science; it is only possible to forecast the degrees of probability of a particular economic model having certain results. The Government Economic Service (GES) is the largest employer of professional economists in the UK, with nearly 600 people working in 30 government departments and agencies. Economists also work in industry, teaching and research, banking and stock-broking, journalism, international organisations and independent consultancies.

Their primary task is to give advice on the probable consequences of a course of action: for example, they might advise a company on the effects of a rise in the price of its products. Economists are also concerned with collecting data, preparing reports, and, to an increasing extent, with building complex mathematical models.

Qualifications and Training

A good honours degree in economics, or in one of the specialised branches of the subject, is needed. In addition, many economists take a postgraduate qualification. Some degree courses are mathematically biased, and for these an A level pass in maths is essential. For most other courses, GCSEs in maths or English are required and A levels in arts subjects, such as history and modern languages, are useful.

Government Economic Service (GES), HM Treasury, 1 Horse Guards Road, London SW1A 2HQ; 020 7270 4835; www.ges.gov.uk

Royal Statistical Society (RSS), 12 Errol Street, London EC1Y 8LX; 020 7638 8998; www.rss.org.uk

Society of Business Economists, Dean House, Vernham Dean, Andover, Hants SP11 0JZ; 01264 737552; www.sbe.co.uk

Personal Qualities and Skills

An analytical mind, numeracy and the ability to express oneself clearly, both verbally and in writing, are required.

Starting Salary

New entrants to the profession earn between £22,000 and £27,000. After three to five years' experience salaries rise to between £35,000 and £45,000. Many packages include other benefits such as private health insurance.

ELECTRICIAN

Electricians work in domestic houses, factories and commercial buildings and on road systems, railways and vehicles. They install, service and repair every kind of electrical system, from wiring to individual pieces of equipment.

Auto electrician

see Motor Industry

Highway electrician

These electricians install, maintain and replace the electrical and electronic systems that operate street lighting and road traffic management systems. They work from high, mobile platforms.

Installation electrician

Installation electricians install, inspect and test wiring systems in every kind of building. They either strip out old wiring systems and replace them, or work with other members of the construction team on new buildings, installing new wiring systems.

Instrumentation electrician

Instrumentation electricians work mainly in the manufacturing industry, installing and maintaining the electrical and electronic systems that run the manufacturing process, whether this is a conveyor belt to fill bottles of drink, build cars, or pack frozen vegetables. They are involved in measuring how efficiently electrical and electronic operations are working.

Maintenance electrician

Maintenance electricians work mainly in manufacturing, maintaining and testing electrical and electronic equipment.

Panel building electrician

Panel building electricians work from diagrams putting together complex electrical and electronic control panels. An office building could have a central panel that controls heating and air conditioning, and this is an example of the kind of panel that these electricians build.

Repair and rewind electrician

When components in pumps, compressors or transformers go wrong, it is the repair and rewind electrician who analyses what the problem is and either repairs or replaces various components. They work both in industry and in domestic properties, repairing goods such as washing machines and fridges.

Service electrician

The dividing line between repair and servicing is not always distinct. Service engineers check equipment and make minor adjustments, to minimise the risk of things going wrong. These electricians also work in industry and private homes.

Theatre electrician

Away from the world of manufacturing or faulty TV sets, theatre electricians maintain and repair all the systems that operate lighting, sound and other specialist theatrical equipment. They need to be extremely good all-rounders.

Qualifications and Training

To qualify as an electrician you must achieve an electrotechnical NVQ level 3. There are various routes to achieving this, but the most common, provided you are between the ages of 16 and 24, is to do a three to four year apprenticeship. These are mainly employer-based, but include some college work and practical and written assessments. Though it is not always essential, many employers require you to have GCSEs grades A to C in English, maths, technology and a science subject. If you are not eligible for an apprenticeship you can do college-based City & Guilds courses at GNVQ levels 2 and 3.

Electrotechnical NVQ level 3 offers several different pathways, including electrical installation, electrical maintenance, electrical instrumentation and associated equipment, installing highway electrical systems, electrical panel building and electrical machine rewind and repair. A great deal of training takes place on the job.

Recent changes to the Building Regulations have meant that many types of household electrical work must be approved either by a buildings inspector or by an electrician who has acquired an appropriate certificate. Electricians can take part in a short scheme to allow them to self-certify their work.

Personal Qualities and Skills

You must have good practical and technical skills and be able to follow technical drawings and diagrams. You should be reasonably fit, and for some jobs you need to be able to cope with heights or working in confined spaces. You should have good colour vision. You need to be able to work on your own, or as part of a team, and you must have good communication skills, and be able to talk to people without using a lot of technical jargon.

Starting Salary

Apprentices earn from £11,000 to £15,000 and salaries for qualified electricians range from £16,000 to £19,000. There is a lot of scope for self-employment with this work.

info

Engineering Training Council,
10 Maltravers Street, London
WC2R 3ER; 020 7240 7891;
www.engc.org.uk

Summit Skills, Vega House,
Opal Drive, Fox Milne, Milton Keynes
MK15 0DF; 01908 303969;
www.summitskills.org.uk

SEMTA, 14 Upton Road, Watford,
Hertfordshire WD18 0JT;
01923 238441; www.semta.orf.uk

ENGINEERING

The British engineering industry is a major wealth producer, and almost every other industry depends upon engineering in some way. Engineering provides a challenging career for men and women, with employment offered by industry, universities and colleges, consulting engineers, contractors, local authorities and the armed forces. The Engineering Council gives a simple definition of engineering, saying that it involves 'the application of science and maths to the solving of practical problems and the making of useful things'. The variety of specialisations are covered by over 20 professional institutions. A selection is described below.

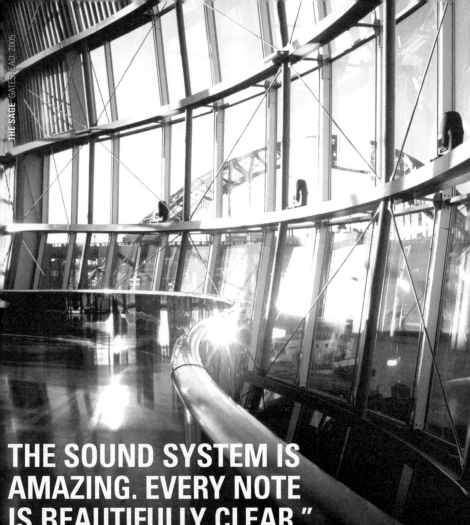

THE SOUND SYSTEM IS AMAZING. EVERY NOTE IS BEAUTIFULLY CLEAR."

CAROLINE HILL CELLIST

CREATE A LASTING IMPRESSION

The Sage Gateshead certainly makes
an impression on the musicians who use
its state-of-the-art acoustic solutions,
performance halls and music school.
It's not just a local icon, but in the same
class as the best orchestral venues in
the world. To find out how you could
leave your mark, go to our website

Balfour Beatty

www.balfourbeatty.com

Company profile

Balfour Beatty is the UK's largest construction, engineering and services group with an impressive £5 billion annual revenue and over 27,000 employees in 24 countries.

The sheer size and scale of our portfolio offers our people an endless stream of challenges and opportunities. Our projects include schools, hospitals, road and rail networks – very often, they'll be the things that are vital to our society – ranging in value from half a million to half a billion!

"We like people who like a challenge and we can offer some exciting high profile projects to work on," says Group Training and Development Manager Jeff Keer. "There is a wide range of opportunities across the group, from major civil engineering, building and rail projects to working in one of our specialist businesses in foundations, utilities, highways management and power transmission." Opportunities include:

- Apprenticeships in electrical, mechanical or plumbing services engineering, construction trades and highways maintenance.
- Traineeships in civil and railway engineering, electrical/mechanical services engineering and building.
- Trainee quantity surveyors and contract administrators.
- Part time degree study in construction, engineering and quantity surveying disciplines.
- Undergraduate placements available to those studying full time built environment degrees which could lead to final year sponsorship. Increasingly the company is also sponsoring students from the first year, usually via direct links with some universities but also through the ICE Quest scheme and CITB's Inspire scholarships.
- Graduate schemes in engineering (civil, electrical, mechanical, building services), construction-related disciplines and quantity surveying. We also recruit graduates from other disciplines who either undertake conversion courses leading to quantity surveying or construction management roles or join as management trainees in areas such as facilities management, HR and finance.
- Experienced hire positions for engineers, construction managers, quantity surveyors and business related professionals etc.

For further information about joining Balfour Beatty please visit
www.balfourbeatty.com

Aerospace engineering

Aerospace engineering is one of the most technically advanced areas of engineering. It is both exciting and rewarding, involving leading-edge technology, variety, skill and innovation. This diversity means that career opportunities can be found across the entire global aerospace spectrum, from research, design, manufacture and maintenance, through to operation and support. However, the dramatic downturn in the aerospace industry in 2001 significantly reduced opportunities, and it may be some time before the good employment prospects once offered by the industry return.

Agricultural engineering

The main areas in which agricultural engineers are involved are: design and production of agricultural machinery; planning, design and construction of farm buildings and associated equipment; field engineering – irrigation, drainage and land resource planning and service engineering, involving the sale, servicing, repairing and installation of farm machinery. They are also involved in forestry engineering, amenity and ecological engineering, and precision farming using satellite positioning systems.

Automotive engineering

In the vehicle manufacturing industry engineers may be employed in design, development, production, operations management and maintenance activities. In motor vehicle servicing, the work tends to be at craft level, with some engineers using their technical base to develop into motor vehicle engineering management. Currently, NVQs in Vehicle Mechanical and Electronic Systems Maintenance and Repair are offered at levels 2 and 3.

Biochemical engineering

This involves the application of engineering principles to industrial processing. Biochemical engineers are involved in the research, design, construction and operation of plant used for the processing of biochemicals such as those used in effluent treatment, fermentation and the production of drugs.

Biomedical engineering

Biomedical engineers, also referred to as clinical engineers or bioengineers, work on the research, design, development and maintenance of technology and equipment used to meet patients' clinical needs both during and after medical treatment. They work in the fields of instrumentation, rehabilitation and biomaterials. They build and test prototypes, run clinical trials and evaluate the performance of equipment and materials. Examples of their work include new heart valves, replacement joints and new types of hearing device.

Building services engineering

(*see also* Construction)

Building services engineers are concerned with heating and ventilation, refrigeration, lighting, air conditioning, electrical services, internal water supply, waste disposal, fire protection, lifts, and acoustic and communication systems. The work involves the planning and design of engineering systems, and supervision of contracts, working in collaboration with architects, surveyors, structural engineers and builders.

Chemical engineering

Chemical engineers are concerned with large-scale processes, not always in the chemical industry. The term 'process engineering' is often used to describe their work, as they are more interested in the physical factors involved in a process than in the chemical reaction itself. Chemical engineers are employed in the oil, chemical, pharmaceutical, food, brewing and process industries.

Civil engineering

Civil engineering plays an important part in everyday life. Civil engineers devise, plan and manage development in vital areas – the design and construction of state-of-the-art roads, dams, harbours, railroad systems, bridges and airports. Civil engineers also play an important part in the provision of electricity and water supplies, and in managing traffic and transport. Every project is unique and involves the expertise of a team of people who plan, design, build and maintain these essential assets.

Control engineering

This is a multidisciplinary field involving electrical and electronic engineering, maths, computer science, instrument and mechanical engineering. Specialisation in control engineering often follows the study of another branch of engineering.

Electrical and electronic engineering

The technology of electrical engineering deals with heavy current, while electronic engineering deals with light current. Applications of heavy current include electrical machinery of all kinds, generating stations and distribution systems. Light current is used for such products as transistors, microprocessors and telecommunications equipment. The two fields are often interdependent and training is closely related. Electronics is a rapidly developing field and offers excellent opportunities, as do the allied disciplines of computer and software engineering.

Energy engineering

This branch of engineering is concerned with the use, production, distribution, conversion and conservation of energy, with due regard to the environment. Energy engineers are employed across the whole spectrum of industry, as energy management and control are essential elements in containing costs, reducing pollution and addressing environmental concerns. The majority of openings are in major fuel industries (including renewables), consultancy and research.

Fire engineering

This involves the application of engineering principles to the assessment, prevention and inhibition of fire risk within buildings, manufacturing plant and industrial processes. The various stages include the use of mathematical principles in the assessment of fire risk, the application of scientific principles to fire safety practices and the use of management techniques for the inhibition and prevention of the onset and spread of fire.

Fire engineers are employed in the fire services, architectural and building design, project management, insurance assessment, industrial processing, the aircraft industry, environmental health and any area of safety where the possibility of fire or combustion represents a hazard.

Gas engineering

Gas engineering involves specialisation in the use, transmission and distribution of gas (natural or manufactured), or in the production of gas, or in related fields such as exploration.

Instrument engineering

Instrument engineers are concerned with the measurement of pressure, temperature, and so on, designing, installing and maintaining instrument systems. *See also* Control engineering.

advertisement feature

Manufacturing systems engineering

This branch of engineering deals with the skills required to operate new manufacturing systems: computerised production, computer-controlled assembly, robotic systems and flexible manufacturing systems.

Marine engineering

This discipline is related to offshore engineering under the general title of 'maritime engineering', which involves engineering systems and equipment in a maritime environment. Both marine and offshore engineers are involved in design, research, consultancy, survey, manufacture, installation and maintenance activities, the former with vessels of all sizes and types, the latter with offshore platforms, sub-sea installations and under-sea vehicles. Employment opportunities exist within firms offering design and research activities, engine- and shipbuilding firms, classification societies, government bodies, the Merchant Navy and the Royal Navy.

Materials engineering

Materials engineers work in a diverse range of industries, working on the research and development of new materials to advance technologies; innovating and modifying materials to improve the performance and efficiency of existing products; and investigating the failure of products or structures. They work with all types of materials including plastics, metals, alloys, glass, ceramics and composites. Some of the industries they work in include telecommunications, power generation, sport and medicine. Materials engineers have developed materials used in modern tennis rackets, replacement hip joints and internet broadband connections; these are just a few examples. Most materials engineers have a degree in materials engineering or materials science, or a degree in applied physics or chemistry.

Mechanical engineering

Mechanical engineering is the biggest branch of the engineering industry. It involves the skills of designing, developing, producing, installing and operating machinery and mechanical products of many types. The field is enormous in scope, and most engineers specialise in a particular area. Other branches of engineering, such as electrical and civil engineering, overlap with mechanical engineering to a certain extent.

Mechanical engineers are employed in almost every sector of industry. Some of the largest areas of employment are machine tools, railway engineering, aerospace and the automobile industry.

Put simply, this is an industry in which your contribution can have a huge impact. The issue of energy is one that's crucial to everybody's future. So when I was looking for a career I was impressed by BP's commitment to being a force for good. I couldn't think of a better place to use my talents.

Graduate careers

BP offers graduates an amazing breadth of opportunity and experience. We face enormous challenges for the future – but fantastic opportunities too. To help us, we need committed and talented people: people who will in time become the scientists and engineers, finance and business professionals who will lead us in the future. That's why we invest so much in you today. We seek the best and the brightest from all over the world, and when we find you we make sure you are supported, stimulated and challenged.

As well as on-job learning, structured courses and personal study, you'll build an international network of expert friends and talented colleagues. You'll find a wealth of memorable experiences in each of the three different placements you take on. And you'll earn more than a generous salary – you'll be earning valuable professional qualifications too.

To find out more and to apply, please visit www.bp.com/careers
We are open for applications all year round.
For information on our company, please visit www.bp.com

BP is an equal opportunities employer

Don't just think about your own future

How do you create more energy for the world without compromising the resources of the planet? Some might say you can't square this circle. We believe you can. Here at BP, our values are simple: to be performance driven, innovative, progressive and green. It takes momentum, ambition, energy and grit, but we aim to live up to these values in everything we do. By having the brightest and the best people on board, and going beyond conventional ways of thinking and working, we will.

A world of opportunity
We are not an average global, blue-chip company. We were voted 'Graduate employer of the year' at the 2005 Target Awards, and short-listed again in 2006. We offer a huge variety of challenging placements either in your home country or, in some cases, further afield.

Non-technical graduates can work in marketing, procurement, operations, trading, finance, business analysis, digital business, project evaluation, mergers and acquisitions and HR.

At the same time, technical graduates can gain cutting-edge experience in positions focused on geoscience, and many areas of engineering including: chemical, instrument, control and electrical, mechanical, petroleum and drilling.

What we look for
We're looking for people willing to learn and ready to make a difference. Single subject excellence is not enough – in addition to mobility and a 2:1, first, Masters, PhD, or equivalent above-average upper quartile performance record, you'll need influencing, analytical and business skills. Those entering technical roles will need to show an acute understanding of their discipline.

The rewards
Outstanding and comprehensive training, support and career progression are a given. In addition benefits include:
- Highly competitive salary
- Settling-in and relocation allowances
- Bonuses
- Pension
- Share scheme
- Flexible working hours

To find out more and to apply, please visit **www.bp.com/careers**

bp

beyond petroleum

Mining engineering

In Britain, most mining engineers are employed by companies in mining areas, working for consultants who monitor mining activity and subsidence. They need some knowledge of related disciplines such as mechanical, electrical and civil engineering, and to understand geology and surveying in relation to mining. The majority of openings in metal mining are overseas.

Nuclear engineering

Nuclear engineering involves the applications of nuclear energy and associated research and development. The work of designing and constructing nuclear reactors and the management of nuclear power stations through waste management and storage and decommissioning of plant is carried out by nuclear engineers.

Offshore engineering

Offshore engineers are concerned with the construction and operation of drilling platforms and wellheads, and other engineering problems related to the exploitation of offshore oil and gas.

Operations engineering

Operations engineers are concerned with specifying, evaluation, acquisition, commissioning, inspection, maintenance, asset management and disposal of facilities, systems, vehicles and equipment. Career opportunities exist at craft and technician level in the servicing and maintenance of a wide variety of industries, of which transport is the largest. Chartered and incorporated engineers may be engaged in asset or fleet engineering management, requiring multidisciplinary engineering, commercial and legal knowledge and encompassing health and safety, reliability, environmental and economic factors, or in specialised inspection roles. Many technicians build on their practical skills by further career development to aspire to these more senior positions.

Petroleum engineering

Petroleum engineers are concerned with exploration and drilling for oil. They obtain and interpret information – for example, the quantities and quality of oil discovered.

Production engineering

Production engineers develop and improve manufacturing techniques. They are responsible for designing production systems to ensure that products can be manufactured to the specified design, in the right quantities, at the right price and by the required date. Their work overlaps with production management.

Recording engineering

Recording engineering is a specialised branch of electronic/radio engineering. Recording engineers are mainly employed by broadcasting authorities and recording studios, and vacancies are limited. *See also* Broadcasting.

Structural engineering

Structural engineers are concerned with the design and maintenance of the framework and fabric of large structures such as bridges, motorways and office blocks.

Transport engineering

Transportation (or traffic) engineers are concerned with managing the best use of roads and related facilities, and work mainly with road traffic. Transportation planners, who are not necessarily engineers, are concerned with the provision of all types of transport. The current priority is to provide an integrated transport system.

Water engineering

Water engineers mostly work for water companies and river authorities, ensuring the supply of fresh water, and dealing with the reclamation and disposal of water which has been used.

Qualifications and Training

Professional qualifications are important throughout the industry. The Engineering Council sets standards for the registration of Chartered Engineers (CEng), Incorporated Engineers (IEng) and Engineering Technicians (EngTech) in all disciplines. There are five main categories of employment in the engineering industry, as follows:

Chartered engineers

Chartered engineers are concerned primarily with the progress of technology through innovation, creativity and change. They develop and apply new technologies; promote advanced designs and design methods; introduce new and more efficient production techniques and marketing and construction concepts; and pioneer new engineering services and management methods. They may be involved with the management and direction of high-risk and resource-intensive projects. Professional judgement is a key feature of their role, allied to the assumption of responsibility for the direction of important tasks, including the profitable management of industrial and commercial enterprises. Entry to a career as a chartered engineer is via a four-year MEng degree accredited by one of the engineering institutions, followed by a period of initial professional development combining training and professional experience. Some disciplines specify a Professional Qualification Scheme – details are available from the engineering institutions. For those not holding an MEng, alternative routes are available. These include an honours degree followed by a Matching Section equivalent to one year of further learning and the Mature Candidate Routes offered by most engineering institutions.

Incorporated engineers

Incorporated engineers (IEng) are specialists in the development and application of today's technology, managing and maintaining applications of current and developing technology at the highest efficiency. With their detailed knowledge and understanding of current engineering applications, they have the skills and know-how to make things happen and often have key operational management roles. They have a detailed understanding of a recognised field of technology, and exercise independent judgement and management in that field. They add substantial value to any organisation where technology is a core activity or supports the business. Entry to a career as an incorporated engineer is via a degree accredited by one of the engineering institutions. Initial professional development, combining training and professional experience, is also required. For those who do not hold a degree, alternative routes include an HND plus a Matching Section equivalent to a further year of learning and the Mature Candidate Routes offered by most engineering institutions.

Engineering technicians

Engineering technicians (EngTech) are creative and skilled engineering practitioners, often with responsibility for operational engineering and other staff. They apply knowledge and proven techniques and procedures to the solution of practical problems in a wide variety of contexts. They carry a measure of supervisory and technical responsibility. They make a key contribution to a range of functions, including design, development, manufacture, commissioning, operation and maintenance of products, equipment, processes and services. Engineering technicians require a National Certificate/Diploma or equivalent qualification, combined with initial professional development. This may be achieved through an Advanced Modern Apprenticeship or similar training scheme.

Craft workers

Craft workers specialise in a particular practical skill, such as tool-making or welding. They must be able to interpret engineering drawings, and to work with a minimum of supervision. Entry is normally at 16 or 17, to an apprenticeship lasting three to four years. GCSEs in maths, science and English are an advantage, although not absolutely essential. On-the-job training, together with day or block release, leads to NVQs awarded by the City & Guilds and the Engineering Industry Training Board. With very good exam results, transfer to Technician courses is possible.

Operators

Operators are employed in a wide range of jobs, and make up about a third of the engineering industry's labour force. Their work is often simple and routine, but in some cases they may require some skill or skills similar to those of craft workers.

No specific academic requirements are needed, but aptitude in English and arithmetic and knowledge of metalwork or technical drawing are useful. Operators may work towards NVQs at an appropriate level.

Aeronautical engineer

There are four main routes to registration as an incorporated engineer in aeronautical engineering: the standard route, registration for licence holders, the mature candidate route and the mature servicemen's route. Details are available from the Royal Aeronautical Society (address below).

Personal Qualities and Skills

Graduate and chartered engineers need academic ability, an imaginative and problem-solving approach, and social and communication skills. Incorporated engineers and engineering technicians should have reasoning ability, numeracy and the ability to communicate. Craft workers, as well as manual dexterity, need basic mathematical ability, patience and self-discipline. Operators should show reliability, patience and the ability to work with others.

Starting Salary

Salaries for graduate entrants to engineering vary quite widely because of the broad range of disciplines included. Starting salaries in the region of £19,000 cover most branches of engineering, and these rise to £25,000 to £45,000 with experience. Some engineers become senior project managers and this will take salaries higher. Technician level jobs attract salaries of between £15,000 and £26,000.

info

Institute of Engineering Technology, Savoy Place, London WC2R 0BL; 020 7240 1871; www.theiet.org

Engineering Council, 10 Maltravers Street, London WC2R 3ER; 020 7240 7891; www.engtech.co.uk

Engineering Training Council in Northern Ireland, Interpoint, 20–24 York Street, Belfast BT15 1AQ; 028 9032 9878; www.etcni.org.uk

Automotive Skills, 93 Newman Street, London W1T 3DT; 0800 093 1777; www.automotiveskills.org.uk

Cogent, Minerva House, Bruntland Road, Portlethen, Aberdeen AB12 4QL; 01224 787800; www.cogent-ssc.com

SEMTA, 14 Upton Road, Watford, Hertfordshire WD18 0JT; 0808 100 3682; www.semta.org.uk

Summit Skills, Vega House, Opal Drive, Fox Milne, Milton Keynes MK15 0DF; 01908 303969; www.summitskills.org.uk

UK Standards for Professional Engineering Competence (UK-SPEC); www.uk-spec.org.uk

Women into Science and Engineering, 22 Old Queen Street, London SW1H 9HP; 020 7227 8421; www.wisecampaign.org.uk

The Women's Engineering Society (WES), Michael Faraday House, Six Hills Way, Stevenage, Herts SG1 2AY; 01438 765506; www.wes.org.uk

Auto Industry, DTI Automotive Regional Unit, 5 St Philips Place, Birmingham B3 2PW; 0121 352 5231; www.autoindustry.co.uk

Institute of Agricultural Engineers, Barton Road, Silsoe, Bedfordshire MK45 4FH; 01525 861096; www.iagre.org

Institution of Chemical Engineers (IChemE), Davis Building, 165–189 Railway Terrace, Rugby CV21 3HQ; 01788 578214; www.icheme.org

Chartered Institute of Building Services Engineers, 222 Balham High Road, Balham, London SW12 9BS; 020 8675 5211; www.cibse.org

Institution of Civil Engineers (ICE), 1 Great George Street, Westminster, London SW1P 3AA; 020 7222 7722; www.ice.org.uk

British Computer Society (BCS) (relevant for electronics engineers), 1st Floor, Block D, North Star House, North Star Avenue, Swindon SN2 1FA; 0845 300 4417; www.bcs.org

Energy Institute, 61 New Cavendish Street, London W1G 7AR; www.energyinst.org.uk

Institute of Materials, Minerals and Mining (IOM3), 1 Carlton House Terrace, London SW1Y 5DB; 020 7451 7300; www.iom3.org

Institution of Mechanical Engineers (IMechE), 1 Birdcage Walk, Westminster, London SW1H 9JJ; 020 7222 7899; www.imeche.org.uk

Institution of Nanotechnology, 6 The Alpha Centre, University of Stirling Innovation Park, Stirling FK9 4NF; 01786 447520; www.nano.org.uk

Institution of Nuclear Engineers, Allan House, 1 Penerley Road, London SE6 2LQ; www.inuce.org.uk

Institute of Physics, 76 Portland Place, London W1B 1NT; 020 7470 4800; www.iop.org

Institute of Physics and Engineering, Fairmount House, 230 Tadcaster Road, York YO24 1ES; 01904 610821; www.ipem.ac.uk

NHS Careers, PO Box 376, Bristol BS99 3EY; 0845 606 0655; www.nhscareers.nhs.uk

Royal Aeronautical Society, 4 Hamilton Place, London W1J 7BQ; 020 7670 4300; www.aerosociety.com

info

Corus Graduate Recruitment – Leading by Example

Have you thought about working for a company that places real commitment on work life balance, has an excellent graduate package, or is truly dedicated to ongoing training and development? The good news is Corus can answer a definite yes to all three of these questions. Due to the nature of what we do we actively seek to recruit various types of Engineers and Physical Science/Metallurgy students. We also offer careers in nine other areas including Finance, Purchasing and Commercial. Of the approximate 140 graduates we recruit annually, the skills and knowledge mix is vast – whatever your degree discipline we can accommodate you.

What can Corus offer you?

Corus will provide opportunity to learn, develop, gain experience and broaden horizons. Corus has the scope to provide challenging and dynamic individually tailored careers giving real work projects from the outset.

The Corus Way

A new initiative has recently been introduced that is said to be a new way of thinking and working known as The Corus Way. Integral to this is the mindset of creating value through cooperating, sharing, learning and striving to improve continuously. This will take with it new and exciting times for graduates. Efforts of Corus employees in 2005 resulted in £10.3bn turnover, re entry into the FTSE 100 and entry into the Times Top 100 graduate employers.

What we do?

The Sky Plaza (Hong Kong), Ashburton Grove (new Arsenal stadium), Terminal 3 Charles de Gaul Airport (Paris), Delhi metro (India) and new Bank of America Building (New York) all have Corus expertise in common. Corus also has major contracts with Airbus, Landrover, Bughatti, and Bosch to name just a few. Other projects we have involvement in include; elimination of hexavalent chromium in consumer goods that causes white rust, a "Munchbox" – a safe, hygenic lunchbox for children and steel barriers at Westminister for security critical situations.

Corus People

To maintain and continue to achieve these results we look for people with certain qualities. These include; drive, ideas, flexibility, team players and communication skills. We need passionate people, determined to make Corus a success.

More information is available online (www.corusgroupcareers.com), by phone (**01926 488025**) or email (**recruitment@corusgroup.com**).

Fast facts

- Number of graduate and placement vacancies per year = 120 graduate, 100 placement
- Work locations = UK wide
- Degree disciplines and class required = preferably a 2:1/1st class hons
- Jobs available = Finance, Commercial, Engineering, Logistics, Purchasing, HR, Research Development & Technology, Manufacturing, Product & Market Development, Metallurgy & Process Technology
- Salary and benefits = competitive salary with bonus, interest-free loan, 35 days holiday
- Application procedure = Fill in our 5 minute registration form online at **www.corusgroupcareers.com**
- Deadline = Please refer to website.

Corus Graduate Recruitment

Leading by example

We are currently involved in projects such as Ashburton Grove (the new Arsenal stadium), the Fusionpolis landmark in Singapore, Delhi metro in India and new Bank of America Building in New York.

To help us maintain our position as a world class company, we recruit into 10 different areas, varying from Engineering to Commercial and Supplies Management to RD&T to Finance – to name but a few. To take the company forward successfully, we need people who have drive, enthusiasm, ideas, commitment, flexibility, imagination and resilience.

In return we offer renowned placement and graduate programmes tailored to your individual and function needs with opportunities to learn, develop, gain experience and make your mark.

All applications are online. To find out more about how Corus can meet your aspirations, and to register your interest in a graduate career or undergraduate placement, please visit our website.

Benefits include competitive salary, bonus scheme, 35 days holiday, employee share-save schemes and interest-free loan.

Corus **Value in steel**

For more information, contact:
T: 01926 488025
www.corusgroupcareers.com

ENVIRONMENT

Occupations in the environment sector are concerned with the protection and preservation of the natural world in which we live.

Energy conservation officer

An energy conservation officer works to improve the energy efficiency of domestic properties, commercial premises and public buildings. This is achieved by applying both practical solutions to energy saving and raising the profile of energy conservation and renewable energy options within an organisation or community. New legislation has meant that all kinds of organisations have to give this issue greater consideration. The major employers in this field are local authorities and organisations such as health trusts and educational institutions. Some large private companies may also employ energy conservation officers.

Qualifications and Training

You need a degree in environmental science, surveying, construction, or business studies to get into this work. Most of the training is on-the-job and there is often the need to do short updating courses, because technology and legislation are changing rapidly in this area.

Personal Qualities and Skills

You must be good at dealing with people and explaining complex information. You need to be confident and persuasive. You have to have a good understanding of energy markets and good organisational skills. You often have to work on your own and suggest solutions to problems.

Starting Salary

Salaries start at around £16,000 to £20,000. This is becoming an area of increasing interest to organisations and this may be reflected in increased salaries in the near future.

info

Association for the Conservation of Energy, Westgate House, Prebend Street, London N1 8PT; 020 7359 8000; www.ukace.org/

Building Research Establishment (BRE), Garston, Watford WD25 9XX; 01923 664000; www.bre.co.uk

Centre for Alternative Technology, Machynlleth, Powys, Wales SY20 9AZ; 01654 705950; www.cat.org.uk

Department for Environment, Food and Rural Affairs (DEFRA), Nobel House, 17 Smith Square, London SW1P 3JR; 0845 933 5577; www.defra.gov.uk/

ENVIRONMENTAL CONSERVATION

Environmental conservation covers a range of activities from recycling waste to habitat management. It does not just involve green issues but is about making the best use of scientific knowledge to produce solutions for a sustainable environment. Conservation includes the protection of rural and urban landscapes, plants and animals and countryside recreation. This includes protection and management of rivers, coastal zones and waterways, together with their fisheries and fish stocks.

There are opportunities in a range of organisations from government departments to the voluntary sector. Competition for jobs is high but there can be a lack of applicants with experience, which often needs to be gained through voluntary work. A large proportion of those working for conservation organisations do so on a voluntary, casual or part-time basis. It is estimated that 47,000 paid employees work in this sector alongside 200,000 volunteers. The majority of those in permanent jobs have higher education qualifications. Many of the permanent jobs are with government agencies, which include the following.

Countryside conservation officer

Countryside conservation offers are involved in the protection and appropriate development of all types of countryside and rural environment. Their work is varied. They may be involved in implementing schemes to protect or improve landscape, or they may advise on the environmental impact of proposed developments. They may put into practice schemes to protect particular plants, birds, insects and animals, or in creating new habitats for these plants and animals. The work may also involve educating the public about how to use the countryside appropriately and negotiating with other land users, or preparing reports for planning committees and other formal bodies. Conservation officers are employed by local government, government agencies, charitable trusts such as the National Trust and the Woodland Trust and environmental consultancies.

Qualifications and Training

For most jobs you need a degree, preferably in a subject such as ecology, geography or environmental conservation. This is a very competitive field so you also need some good practical skills. The majority of people who get full-time paid work of this sort have done some voluntary work first for one of the countryside organisations. Check the info panel for the major countryside organisations in the UK. Once you are employed there are plenty of courses you can do to increase your knowledge and skills in specific areas, eg woodland, birdlife, or coastal erosion.

Personal Qualities and Skills

These vary according to your particular responsibilities and tasks, but a love of the countryside is always essential. Interest in geography, botany and zoology may be important. You should be good at keeping records and measuring scientific data of various kinds. You should be prepared to work outside, but also be able to communicate effectively at meetings or in an educative role.

Starting Salary

Starting salaries range from £14,000 to £16,000, rising to £22,000 to £30,000 with experience.

Countryside ranger/warden

Countryside rangers are responsible for the day-to-day management of areas of countryside such as common land, heaths, woodland or wetlands. They undertake practical work such as tree planting or carrying out field surveys to determine how prevalent particular species are in a specified area. Rangers patrol sites making sure that footpaths, bridges and gates are in good order. They can also provide advice and help to members of the public, keeping an overall eye on safety. They may also have responsibility for managing budgets and for organising exhibitions, or conducting educational tours of sites.

Qualifications and Training

You do not need any formal qualifications to do this work, but you will almost certainly have to do some voluntary work. Some conservation organisations offer a range of short training course to volunteers in subjects such as species identification, hedge layering, coppicing and risk management. You can also do

info

Natural England, 1 East Parade, Sheffield S1 2ET; 0114 241 8920; www.naturalengland.org.uk

Lantra, Lantra House, Stoneleigh Park, Nr Coventry, Warwickshire CV8 2LG; 0845 707 8007; www.lantra.co.uk

Countryside Management Association, Writtle College, Lordship Road, Writtle, Chelmsford, Essex CM1 3RR; 01245 424116; www.countrysidemanagement.org.uk

Institute of Ecology and Environmental Management (IEEM), 45 Southgate Street, Winchester, Hampshire SO23 9EH; 01962 868626; www.ieem.org.uk

LG Careers (Local Government), www.lgcareers.com

Groundwork UK, www.groundwork.org.uk

Field Studies Council, Montford Bridge, Preston Montford, Shrewsbury, Shropshire SY4 1HW; 0845 345 4071; www.field-studies-council.org

Conservation Volunteers Northern Ireland, Beech House, 159 Ravenhill Road, Belfast BT6 0BP; 028 9064 5169; www.cvni.org.uk

British Trust for Conservation Volunteers (BTCV), Sedum House, Mallard Way, Potteric Carr, Doncaster DN4 8DB; 01302 388888; www.btcv.org.uk

National Trust, PO Box 39, Warrington WA5 7WD; 0870 458 4000; www.nationaltrust.org.uk

National Trust for Scotland, Wemyss House, 28 Charlotte Square, Edinburgh EH2 4ET; 0131 243 9300; www.nts.org.uk

City & Guilds courses in environmental conservation, for which you do not need any formal qualifications.

Personal Qualities and Skills

As well as a passion for the countryside you should be very practical and confident in using tools and equipment. You need good communication skills and for many posts you also have to have reasonable office and IT skills.

Starting Salary

Starting salaries vary considerably according to the type of organisation you are employed by. Local authority salaries for rangers are around £17,000.

Recycling officer

Recycling officers work mainly for local councils, planning and developing policies to help local people recycle as much waste material as they can. Recycling officers organise schemes to recycle glass, paper, cans and plastic. They may also organise and manage schemes to encourage residents to make compost, either on their own properties or at central points set up by the local authority. Reducing waste is an important and very topical area of local authority work, so the significance of this area of work has increased. Recycling officers are also involved in organising publicity about recycling. They often attend meetings of both formal bodies such as parish councils, and informal societies such as gardening clubs.

Qualifications and Training

While there are no formal academic entry requirements, most successful applicants have either a degree or a Higher National Diploma. The most useful subjects include environmental science, earth studies, geography, or any science subject. If you don't have a degree, then plenty of useful paid or voluntary work on recycling projects strengthens your application. If you can offer relevant NVQs at levels 2 and 3 this also helps. NVQs at levels 2 and 3 are available in recycling operations, waste management and environmental conservation. Much of the training is on the job. You are likely to need to do frequent short updating courses, because technology and knowledge are changing rapidly in this field.

Personal Qualities and Skills

You must be a good communicator, able to present written information and oral reports. You should be well organised, good at prioritising, and you need reasonable IT skills. Being able to manage teams of people is very important.

Starting Salary

New entrants start on between £18,000 and £20,000. With experience and considerable management responsibility this rises to £25,000 to £30,000.

info

Waste and Resource Action Plan (WRAP), The Old Academy, 21 Horse Fair, Banbury, Oxon OX16 0AH; 0808 100 2040; www.wrap.org.uk

LG Careers (Local Government); www.lgcareers.com

Chartered Institution of Wastes Management, 9 Saxon Court, St Peter's Gardens, Marefair, Northampton NN1 1SX; 01604 620426; www.ciwm.co.uk

Waste Management Industry Training and Advisory Board, Peterbridge House, 3 The Lakes, Northampton NN4 7HE; 01604 231950; www.wamitab.org.uk

Energy and Utility Skills, Friars Gate Two, 1011 Stratford Road, Shirley, Solihull B90 4BN; 0845 077 9922; www.euskills.co.uk

ENVIRONMENTAL HEALTH

Environmental health workers' aim is to protect the public from environmental health risks.

Environmental health officer

Environmental health officers are enforcers, educators and advisers, and are employed in both the public and private sectors. Their responsibilities include pollution control, including noise control, environmental protection, the inspection of food and food premises, health and safety in workplaces and in the leisure industry, and the control of housing standards, particularly in the private rented sector. Much of their time is spent out of the office, dealing with the public and visiting premises of all types.

Qualifications and Training

Training in England, Wales and Northern Ireland involves a four-year sandwich course leading to a degree in environmental health, or a two-year postgraduate sandwich course, for those with a good honours degree in a natural science. The course must be accredited by the Chartered Institute of Environmental Health (CIEH). Degree entry qualifications vary between institutions.

In Scotland, candidates for the professional qualification (Diploma in Environmental Health, awarded by REHIS) must hold a BSc honours degree in environmental health from the University of Strathclyde or Edinburgh. Currently only the University of Strathclyde offers a course for new entrants. Applicants for this four-year degree course need four H grade passes in maths, chemistry, biology or physics and one other subject. Details of current requirements should be checked with the university as there can be flexibility for mature students. Before being awarded the diploma, candidates must have undergone a minimum of 48 weeks' training with a local authority and have passed professional exams.

Personal Qualities and Skills

You have to be a very good communicator, firm and assertive, when carrying out inspections, but also encouraging and helpful, trying to work towards constructive solutions to problems. You have to be well organised, thorough and observant and able to work on your own as well as being part of a team.

Starting Salary

On qualifying, salaries range from £20,000 to £30,000. There is a shortage of employees in this work at present.

Chartered Institute of Environmental Health, Chadwick Court, 15 Hatfields, London SE1 8DJ; 020 7928 6006; www.cieh.org.uk; e-mail: education@cieh.org

Royal Environmental Health Institute of Scotland, 3 Manor Place, Edinburgh EH3 7DH; 0131 225 5444; www.rehis.org; e-mail: rehis@rehis.org.uk

Health and Safety Adviser

see Health and Safety Adviser

Pest controller

Pest controllers control not only mice, rats, cockroaches and ants that may be damaging foodstuffs in a factory, hotel, or private home, but also rabbits, moles, birds and foxes that attack farmers' crops. They work for local authorities and private firms. Service staff are employed to lay traps and set poison. There are also opportunities for graduates in research and management.

Qualifications and Training

Qualifications in pest control are usually preferred, although at assistant level full training is provided on the job, including day or block release to achieve a recognised qualification, such as British Pest Control Association courses. The British Pest Control Association and the Royal Society for the Promotion of Health have merged their basic pest control qualification – BPC Diploma Part 1 and RSPH Certificate in Pest Control. The examination was assessed and piloted between Autumn 2003 and Spring 2004. As part of this partnership other BPCA examinations, including the advanced level certificate (BPC Diploma Part 2), the fumigation certification scheme and the newly introduced Certificate for Surveyors – Pest Control (CSPC) will ultimately be brought under the joint BPCA/RSPH umbrella.

Personal Qualities and Skills

This is not a job for the squeamish and the work demands a mature outlook, an ability to get on with many kinds of people, to work in varying conditions and to work alone. The ability to drive is important.

Starting Salary

Salaries range from £9,000 to £19,000+ for graduates.

EVENTS ORGANISATION

Many organisations and businesses hold both internal and public events. The role of conference and events organisers is one of project management, ensuring that the event runs smoothly and efficiently.

Conference organiser

In many companies, conference organisation is combined with other promotional or administrative duties. Large organisations and industrial concerns may have their own conference departments with staff responsible for coordinating the necessary arrangements for regular sales conferences, staff conferences, product launches and special events. These will employ staff specialising in the organisation of meetings and events. Other firms employ professional conference organisers.

Conference organisers select and book the most suitable venue, organise the invitations and where necessary, accommodation for participants. They also deal with the relevant paperwork, catering and reception facilities, any specialist equipment necessary (such as video, microphones, projectors and closed-circuit television), media coverage and a host of minor details. Some firms of professional organisers have a small core staff and employ temporary freelancers.

Conference centres and hotels specialising in conference facilities have their own staff who are responsible for arrangements for conferences already booked and for advertising and encouraging further bookings.

Party/wedding organiser

Some private individuals, families or groups of friends, with special events like weddings, large parties, or other special occasions to plan, turn to professional organisers to coordinate and arrange everything. In many ways the skills are similar to those of a conference organiser, but you may be working to strict budgetary limits and you have to be sensitive and helpful when dealing with people who want occasions to be extra special. There are no specific qualifications or training for this work, but a real flair for organising, dealing with people and working well under pressure are all important. This is a recent career opening and most people who do it are self-employed, charging for individual events.

Qualifications and Training

There are no formal educational requirements, but NVQs are available. Useful experience could include sales and marketing, knowledge of hotel and venue operations, and language skills, as well as secretarial duties. Computer literacy is important.

Personal Qualities and Skills

A flair for organisation and forward planning is needed, as are tact, discretion and the ability to talk to all kinds of people and anticipate their various demands. In addition, some conference organisers should be prepared to work abroad.

Starting Salary

Large firms offer £15,000–£17,000. Salaries for freelancers vary according to the type and amount of work undertaken.

Association for Conferences and Events, ACE International, Riverside House, High Street, Huntingdon, Cambridgeshire PE18 6SG; 01480 457595;

www.martex.co.uk/ace; e-mail: ace@martex.co.uk

How to Organise Effective Conferences and Meetings (Kogan Page)

Events organiser

Events organisers generally work for a place visited by the public such as a national park or a stately home. They may also be appointed on a temporary basis to cover a festival lasting one or two weeks.

They are responsible for organising long-standing events such as a series of waymarked walks, and activities such as a music festival or summer holiday entertainment for children. If appropriate, the organiser will be in contact with the local education department to encourage school visits. Those working for a large concern will coordinate their work with other members of staff such as information and press officers.

Qualifications and Training

Events organisers do not necessarily need formal qualifications but a background in marketing and experience at promoting events and campaigns is useful. A knowledge of simple financial planning is looked for, plus experience in preparing material for print. The ability to drive is essential.

Personal Qualities and Skills

Events officers should be energetic, sociable and adaptable, able to talk to a variety of people, and have organisational skills and the ability to think up new ideas.

Starting Salary

£12,500+.

Association for Conferences and Events, ACE International, Riverside House, High Street, Huntingdon, Cambridgeshire PE18 6SG; 01480 457595;

www.martex.co.uk/ace; e-mail: ace@martex.co.uk

Jobs are advertised in the Monday edition of the *Guardian*; www.jobs.guardian.co.uk

Exhibition organiser

Exhibition organisers usually work for specialist companies. They plan and coordinate exhibitions, negotiating with all those concerned – managers of the exhibition, exhibitors, stand suppliers, designers and caterers. With overseas exhibitions, government departments are often involved.

Qualifications and Training

Training is usually on the job, and graduates or those with HNDs in business or marketing are preferred. CAM or Institute of Marketing qualifications are also useful. Several universities and colleges offer degree or HND courses in events management. NVQs at levels 2–4 are available but have no industry recognition so there has been little take-up.

Personal Qualities and Skills

Applicants should be good at dealing with people and at administration, with the ability to have a large amount of information at their fingertips. Physical and mental stamina are essential.

Starting Salary

£12,000–£16,000.

Association of Exhibition Organisers, 113 High Street, Berkhamsted, Hertfordshire HP4 2DJ; 01442 873331; fax: 01442 875551; www.aeo.org.uk; e-mail: info@aeo.org.uk

Chartered Institute of Marketing, Moor Hall, Cookham, Maidenhead, Berkshire SL6 9QH; 01628 427500; www.cim.co.uk

FARMING

(*see also* Agriculture)

In recent years, economic conditions and animal health crises have had significant effects on jobs in this sector. Incomes have fallen and opportunities become more limited. There is increasing mechanisation and a tendency towards greater specialisation and larger farms. Mixed farms are now in a minority, and most farmers choose to specialise in one or two areas of production. The most common of these are milk, cereals, poultry, sheep, pigs or beef. In order to survive, many farmers have to consider other activities such as leisure and recreation, niche markets, or crops for energy and raw materials. To make a farm profitable, the modern farmer needs a thorough working knowledge of the type of farming to be undertaken, an understanding of general agricultural science, and years of practical experience as well as an aptitude for farming and farm management.

Opportunities are few, land and equipment are expensive. Land prices have made the chances of a beginner becoming a tenant farmer almost impossible. Most of those who go into farming come from farming families.

Farm manager

Farm managers are employed by the landowner and are responsible for all aspects of the day-to-day working of the farm. They must plan ahead, organise the staff and work schedules, decide which crops to plant or which animals to rear, and keep a check on buildings and machinery. In addition, they must deal with the office work and accounts.

Farm worker

Specialisation and large-scale farming have led to a fall in demand for the farm worker who can turn his or her hand to anything. There is now a need for highly skilled personnel, and new entrants should aim at becoming skilled in a special area such as animal husbandry, mechanics or food, flower or fruit production.

Qualifications and Training

There is a range of qualifications related to farming, including degrees in agriculture or agricultural science, and National Diplomas in general agriculture. Various NVQ awards are available at different levels, such as crop and livestock production, levels 1, 2 and 3.

Personal Qualities and Skills

Being prepared to work outside in all conditions and to accept antisocial hours at very busy times of year is essential. Farm managers have to be able to work alone, but also to supervise other employees, have good financial and business sense and be practical and resourceful.

Starting Salary

Many farm workers start on salaries close to the minimum wage. Wages in the agricultural industry are reviewed and set every year by the Agricultural Wages Board, which sets out clear hourly rates for different levels of work. Typical earnings for new entrants to farming are between £10,500 and £12,000. Experienced workers can earn up to £18,000. Accommodation is sometimes provided as part of your income package. Farm managers start on around £21,000. On large farms and with experience, this can rise to £30,000.

info

Lantra Connect, Lantra House, Stoneleigh Park, Kenilworth, Warwickshire CV8 2LG; 0845 707 8007 (Lantra Connect – Helpline); www.lantra.co.uk; e-mail: connect@lantra.co.uk

Royal Agricultural Society of England, National Agricultural Centre, Stoneleigh Park, Warwickshire CV8 2LZ; 02476 696969; www.rase.org.uk

Department for Environment, Food and Rural Affairs, general enquiries: Library Enquiry Desk, DEFRA, Room 320, Nobel House, 17 Smith Square, London SW1P 3JR; 0845 933 5577; www.defra.gov.uk

Agricultural Wages Board, Nobel House, 17 Smith Square, London SW1P 3JR; Agricultural Wages Helpline: 0845 000 0134; www.defra.gov.uk/farm/agwages/agwages.htm

FASHION

(*see also* Clothing Industry)

Clothing is one of the UK's largest manufacturing industries and employs over 145,000 individuals. The fashion industry covers all aspects of clothing and accessories for men, women and children, and falls into three main sectors: *haute couture* houses, where original model garments are made for individual customers; wholesale *couture*, where trends set by the *haute couture* houses are closely followed, and limited numbers of model garments in stock sizes are made for retail; and wholesale manufacture, which occupies the largest sector

Fashioning the Future at London College of Fashion

The 2006/2007 academic year marks the centenary of London College of Fashion.

With an international reputation for fashion education the College is renowned for offering creative development with a strong vocational slant, balancing academic excellence with professional skills.

Our reputation stems from a set of core principles attached to the values of the capital's evolving fashion trades. In 1906 our direct descendent, the Shoreditch Technical Institute Girls Trade School, was founded for the training of young women in the practices of dressmaking and garment cutting.

Today, whether you want to study for a qualification or a short course to develop your career, start your own business or just fulfil a passion, London College of Fashion offers a wide range of opportunities to work around your requirements and commitments.

Worldwide Links

At London College of Fashion we believe that fashion is an international language. This outlook is reflected in the high number of international students welcomed to the College – from over seventy countries. The cross-cultural mix of students is one of the defining characteristics of the College community. Additionally, our students are supported into placements during their courses at top companies around the world. These include *Adidas Germany; Nike Netherlands; Marc Jacobs USA; Zac Posen New York; Mango Spain; Capelli New York; Maxmara Italy; Kumfs NZ New Zealand*.

Equipment and Resources

The College boasts industry standard equipment, including the Gerber CAD/CAM suite for garment design and pattern cutting. Specialist workshops include 2D and 3D design studios, bespoke craft rooms, make-up and beauty salons, cosmetic science laboratories, photography suite (with studios and darkroom) and broadcast suite (with the latest video/audio editing and recording equipment).

All students have access to modern well-equipped computer suites and open access workshops including word processing, spreadsheet, database, desk top publishing, design and photo manipulation applications plus access to the Internet, University intranet and email facilities.

"I chose to study at the London College of Fashion because it is widely regarded as one of the most respected fashion colleges in the world and, being based in the heart of London, a melting pot of creativity and inspiration.

"I began with very little fashion experience but with a lot of hard work, passion, persistence and with the help of dedicated technicians and tutors, graduated in 2004. The most enjoyable and rewarding time of my study was working on my final collection. I learnt more in those few months than I did in my previous years and won best Menswear at the Profile Fashion show 2004 at Graduate Fashion Week.

"Since graduating I've been lucky enough to work with the Scissor Sisters on a number of occasions for performances and photo shoots. I am now a member of Christopher Bailey's design team for Burberry Prorsum, which I would never have dreamed possible when starting my studies. I am now looking forward to a long, successful career in the fashion industry and would like to thank everyone at LCF for their help in preparing me and sending me off in the right direction."

Russell Delaney
BA (Hons) Fashion Design Technology (Menswear)

Subject Strengths

Full and part time courses are offered, at Foundation, Diploma, Undergraduate and Postgraduate degree levels, together with professional Short Courses and Study Abroad semester and summer school programmes (for international students wishing to study at the College).

Key areas include:
Make-up, beauty and hair styling
Fashion photography and media
Business start-ups
Cosmetic Science
Fashion marketing, management, buying and merchandising
Fashion Journalism and Fashion Promotion
Product design and development for the fashion industry
CAD/CAM and computer skills
Fashion design
Pattern cutting
Garment production
Footwear and accessories
Millinery
Textiles, embroidery and knit
Costume design and production

For more information about London College of Fashion go to
www.fashion.arts.ac.uk

of the fashion industry. Here, the latest trends are adapted to styles that are attractive to the main market, and mass produced at acceptable prices.

Designer

Designers do more than produce stylish sketches. Their work will, depending on the size and organisation of the particular establishment, include a wide variety of tasks. The work of the *haute couture* designer is both highly creative and intricate. Unfortunately, there is little scope for young designers or assistants as many houses are designer owned; they are nevertheless an excellent training ground for future designers willing to work as sketchers, stylists, fitters, hands etc. In wholesale couture, designers produce original garments, but they generally follow the instructions of an employer as far as style and cost are concerned.

The wholesale manufacture designer must be able to predict future trends, combine this with the firm's own 'brand image', match it to available fabrics and produce a garment that can be produced economically and will appeal to its particular section of the market. When sketches have been drawn, it is necessary to produce working drawings and translate these into flat patterns, so sample garments can be made to show to retail buyers and garment costs in fabric and manufacturing time estimated.

Qualifications and Training

While it is possible to become a designer without a degree or HND, this is now rather difficult. Preferred subjects include fashion, textiles, knitwear, graphic design and art and design. You need to have built up a good portfolio of your work when you start applying for jobs. There is very little formal training, except in areas like computer aided design (CAD) and marketing.

Personal Qualities and Skills

As well as an interest in fashion you have to have an eye for colour and a feel for fabrics. You must be able to work under pressure, as part of a busy team. Skill in drawing either manually or with CAD is important. You have to develop market awareness and have the confidence to promote your own work.

.info

The Chartered Society of Designers (CSD), 5 Bermondsey Exchange, 179–181 Bermondsey Street, London SE1 3UW; 020 7357 8088; www.csd.org.uk

Crafts Council, 44a Pentonville Road, Islington, London N1 9BY; 020 7278 7700; www.craftscouncil.org.uk

The Design Council, 34 Bow Street, London WC2E 7DL; 020 7420 5200; www.design-council.org.uk

Skillfast UK: The Sector Skills Council for Apparel, Footwear, Textiles and Related Businesses, Richmond House, Lawnswood Business Park, Redvers Close, Leeds LS16 6RD; 0113 239 9600; www.skillfast-uk.org

Starting Salary

Salaries start at around £15,000 to £18,000 – often more in London – and the majority of openings are London based. It is quite common to be self-employed doing this work and you can earn £30,000 to £50,000 if you are successful.

Dressmaker

Opportunities for dressmakers occur in *couture* houses which make specially designed costumes for a particular collection or customer, in wholesale fashion houses making mass-produced garments, and in theatres both making and adapting costumes. Dressmakers may also be employed by large stores to carry out alterations, or they may be self-employed making clothes either from home or from a workshop. Teachers of dressmaking are employed in schools, colleges and by adult education centres.

Qualifications and Training

No formal qualifications are necessary; but City & Guilds qualifications and NVQs are available. Some degrees and HNDs in clothing design or fashion have a dressmaking option.

Personal Qualities and Skills

Dressmakers need to combine artistic and practical skills with an ability to follow instructions and to recognise problems as they arise and make the necessary adaptations. They may have to deal with temperamental designers and their customers.

Starting Salary

Dependent on experience, practical ability and specialisations. Trainees can earn £10,000–£12,000. Experienced dressmakers can earn up to £50,000 in London.

Skillfast UK: The Sector Skills Council for Apparel, Footwear, Textiles and Related Businesses, Richmond House, Lawnswood Business Park,	Redvers Close, Leeds LS16 6RD; 0113 239 9600; www.skillfast-uk.org
	Local Job Centre Plus and Connexions/Careers Centres

Leather production

Leather is produced from skins and hides to make shoes, bags, gloves, clothes, upholstery and saddlery. Modern leather production is based on up-to-date science (particularly chemistry) and technology with a responsible regard for environmental factors. There is a worldwide shortage of well-qualified leather technologists.

Qualifications and Training

Vocational qualifications are available for operatives and craftspeople through part-time, full-time and open-learning courses. Technicians require a good general education and GCSEs should include maths, science and English. Recognised qualifications include NVQs in leather production, BSc in leather technology and MSc in leather technology. Entry to a specific course is dependent on the entry requirements of the institution.

Personal Qualities and Skills

Operatives and craftspeople must be physically fit and possess stamina. Technologists must have a practical, responsible approach to their work and be prepared to travel abroad if required.

Starting Salary

Salaries start at around £10,000 for leather craft workers. Experienced craftsmen and women are often self-employed and set their own fees.

The Society of Master Saddlers, Green Lane Farm, Stonham, Stowmarket, Suffolk IP14 5DS; 01449 711642; www.mastersaddlers.co.uk

Milliner

Individual 'model' hats are designed by a milliner and made up by workers in a small retail workroom or factory attached to a boutique or fashion house. Hats for the wholesale trade are mass produced by machine, though some may be hand finished. The designs used are bought from model milliners and passed on to copyists, who work out how the hat can be adapted to machine production.

Qualifications and Training

Training as a junior in a retail workroom or factory may be supplemented by evening classes. Academic qualifications are not necessary, except for designing millinery, when a full fashion training is required. Some fashion courses include modules on hat making.

Personal Qualities and Skills

Making hats in a retail millinery workroom needs manual skill and patience – a hat may take up to three days to complete. Senior posts in wholesale production require an understanding of technology. Designers and copyists should have fashion sense and artistic creativity.

Starting Salary

Salaries start at between £8,500 and £11,500, and rise to £12,000 to £17,000 with experience. If you become well known and have famous clients, you may earn a salary that exceeds these figures, but there are only a few such opportunities.

British Hat Guild, PO Box 48664, London NW8 6WS; 07932 678003; www.britishhatguild.co.uk

Skillfast UK: The Sector Skills Council for Apparel, Footwear, Textiles and Related Businesses, Richmond House, Lawnswood Business Park, Redvers Close, Leeds LS16 6RD; 0113 239 9600; www.skillfast-uk.org

Model

Models work as 'live' or photographic models, generally showing clothes or accessories. Photographic and advertising models rely on an agent to get them work and handle the fees. Competition is intense and very few models get to the top of the profession.

Fashion models are employed full-time by couturiers, wholesalers or fashion stores as 'live' models. They have the garments draped and pinned on them during the design stages, and show them to the public. Live models must be tall, at least 1.72 m (5 ft 8 in). Photographic modelling involves posing in garments chosen to be illustrated in magazines, newspapers, catalogues or on advertising posters. This work is often out of season for the type of garments being modelled and some of the work is done abroad. Expenses include the provision of accessories, a good basic wardrobe and hairdressing.

Qualifications and Training

Private model schools run training courses for live and photographic modelling. Reputable schools will only take entrants whom they think will succeed, and will introduce them to agencies at the end of the training period. The London College of Fashion, a non-commercial college, offers a one-year full-time course leading to a certificate in fashion modelling. Students should have three GCSEs grades A–C or equivalent.

Personal Qualities and Skills

A model must be able to work hard, be punctual and reliable, get on well with people, and have a great deal of common sense. Competition is intense and only those who can interpret what the stylist and photographer want will get to the top. A female model should be at least 1.72 m (5 ft 8 in) tall and have body statistics of about 86–61–86 cm (34–24–34 in). A male model should be at least 1.83 m (6 ft) tall. Models should have clear skin, good hands, nails and teeth, healthy hair and attractive features.

Starting Salary

Salaries vary from £50 a day to £500+ for top models. Agencies can charge fees of 20 per cent.

info

Association of Model Agents,
122 Brompton Road, London
SW3 1JD; 020 7584 6466
(send sae for information)

London College of Fashion,
20 John Princes Street, London
W1M 0BJ; 020 7514 7400;
www.input.demon.co.uk/careers-
modelling.html

Alba Model Information,
31 The High Street, Durrington,
Salisbury, Wiltshire SP4 8AE;
0871 717 7170 (calls from a UK
landline cost 10p per minute);
www.albamodel.info;
www.albamodelinformation.com

FILM PRODUCTION

Opportunities to work in film production arise in television, film companies and advertising. Most people who work in this area are self-employed freelancers. Film production involves both studio and location work. Jobs within film production are much sought after, vacancies are few and competition is consequently fierce. Individuals who are serious about working in this area will need to develop personal marketing skills in addition to their creative craft skills.

Animation

Animation involves the design, creation and operation of animated production and effects. Much of the work is done using computer animation techniques, although there are still opportunities for traditional 'cell' animation.

Announcers

Announcers work to detailed and carefully timed scripts, communicating information to the viewer from a soundproof 'behind the scenes' office. They sometimes write or adapt their own material and need to be able to work on their own.

Archivists/librarians

(*see also* Archivist)

Archivists and librarians collect, collate, preserve and make available collections of recorded visual, sound, written and other materials for use by various productions. Archives are valuable business resources, and some archivists are now involved in selling and marketing materials.

Art and Design

(*see also* Art and Design)

The art and design function is to create a visual effect to meet the needs of the production, creating manual or computer-generated graphics.

Camerawork

Workers in this area operate and assist with still, film and video cameras to record images as directed, using different techniques.

Costume/wardrobe

The wardrobe department interprets the production requirements in terms of costumes and accessories to ensure historical accuracy and an accurate portrayal of the style and ethos of the period.

Direction

The director is responsible for achieving the creative, visual and auditory effect of a production and, equally importantly, motivating a team.

Engineering

Engineers provide a design, maintenance and installation service to the production site and equipment. Research specialists are usually employed by the equipment manufacturers or design consultancies.

Film, video and audio tape editing

Raw tape or film is shaped to interpret the requirements of the director, either by physical cutting (film) or by selecting sequences and re-recording onto a master tape using sophisticated computer equipment.

IT specialists

IT specialists support many aspects of broadcasting, film and video, either within the companies or as consultants, providing and maintaining relevant systems and software.

Journalists

(*see also* Journalism)

Journalists generate and report on local, national or international stories, and research relevant background information. Bi-media (radio and television) contracts are increasing. Some journalists present their own work.

Laboratory

Lab technicians develop and process film, duplicate and check video tapes, ensuring high technical quality.

Lighting

Lighting specialists ensure that the stage or set is correctly lit to meet the needs of the production.

Make-up and hairdressing

(*see also* Beauty *and* Hair)

Make-up and hairdressing professionals interpret the requirements of the production and research to ensure accurate representation of the historical or design concept. They maintain a continuity of approach throughout the production in studio or on location.

Management

Management directs and coordinates the different elements of the industry to ensure their efficient function – ranging from commissioning a production to negotiating international rights. Specialists work in a full range of business areas.

Marketing and sales

Marketing and sales staff work in an international marketplace to raise revenue for broadcasters or film makers. Airtime is sold, sponsorship and co-production rights are negotiated and spin-off products, such as books, toys and videos, are developed.

Modelmaker

see Modelmaker

Producers

Producers perform a variety of management and operational roles to bring together the many elements of a production, either in a studio or on location. Often responsible both for the initial concept and raising the essential finance, they are the team leaders.

Production assistants

Production assistants provide high-quality administrative and secretarial support to the producer and director at every stage of production, coordinating all activities and preparing schedules and scripts.

Production managers

Production managers organise all essential support facilities for the team, from accommodation and transport to on-set catering. They will also roster crews and arrange payments.

Production operatives

Production operatives perform the operational duties of the production such as vision mixing and autocue operations.

Researchers

Researchers support the producer, helping to turn ideas into reality – providing and following up ideas, contacting and interviewing people, acquiring relevant factual material, and writing briefings for presenters.

Runners/gofers

This job is the traditional entry-level job for the industry. Bright, highly moti-vated – often highly qualified – people act as general assistants, taking messages, making deliveries, being indispensable, and learning the basics of the commercial business.

Setcraft/props

People working in this area construct the scenery, sets and backdrops to meet the production brief, reflecting both historical accuracy and required design and style. They also maintain sets during a production, and operate any mechanical features as directed. Props (hired or made) are used to dress the set.

Sound

Sound craftspeople interpret the requirements of a production in terms of sound collection. During post-production they may be involved in recording, editing and dubbing, using a range of sophisticated equipment.

Special effects

Special effects designers create and operate effects for a production, within technical limitations and budget, and operate the necessary machines.

Support staff

Many people working in film, video, television and radio fulfil essential support roles, including administration, catering, driving and cleaning.

Transmission

Technicians and engineers work to exhibit the production in a high-quality form, which can involve projecting images or operating transmission equipment linking electronic signals from the studios to a transmitter.

Writers

(*see also* Writer)

Writers work to produce or edit scripts for a variety of radio, television, video or film productions.

Qualifications and Training

New-entrant training is offered by Film and Television Freelance Training (FT2); competition for places is fierce. Their new entrant technical training programme covers art department assistant, props assistant, camera assistant, grips, assistant editor, sound assistant, production/continuity assistant and make-up/hair assistant. They also offer a set crafts apprenticeship training scheme for fibrous plasterers, carpenters and painters.

Skillset, the National Training Organisation for Broadcast, Film, Video and Multimedia, offers NVQs levels 2–4 in areas such as camera, costume, editing, production, make-up and hair. These are available to those employed in the industry.

The National Film and Television School offers a two-year MA in film and television in 10 professional disciplines: directing (animation, documentary or fiction), screenwriting, producing, cinematography, screen design, editing, screen sound and screen music. Students specialise in one of these. NFTS courses are not for complete beginners and although many of the applicants for the 60 places available are graduates, relevant knowledge and practical experience are essential and treated as equivalent to academic study. Other institutions offering film-related courses can be found on the UCAS website.

Personal Qualities and Skills

In film work it is important to combine artistic ability with technical expertise, to pay attention to detail, to have patience, good powers of concentration and an interest in colour and design. An even-tempered, logical and visually imaginative approach is necessary. It is important to keep in touch with what is happening in the industry, and to be able to create a network of friends and contacts. Absolute reliability is essential, especially at the start of a career.

Broadcasting Entertainment Cinematographic and Theatre Union (BECTU) (for information about rates of pay), 373–377 Clapham Road, London SW9 9BT; www.bectu.org.uk

e-skills UK – The Sector Skills Council for IT and Telecoms, 1 Castle Lane, London SW1E 6DR; 020 7963 8920; www.e-skills.com

Skillset, Prospect House, 80–110 New Oxford Street, London WC1A 1HB; www.skillset.org

British Film Institute (BFI), 21 Stephen Street, London W1T 1LN; 020 7255 1444; www.bfi.org.uk

British Interactive Media Association (BIMA), Briarlea House, Southend Road, South Green, Billericay, Essex CM11 2PR; www.bima.co.uk

European Multimedia Forum, 55 rue Hector Denis, B-1050 Brussels; 32 2219 0305; www.e-multimedia.org

FT2 Film and Television Freelance Training, 4th Floor, Warwick House, Warwick Street, London W1R 5RA; www.ft2.org.uk

The National Film and Television School, Beaconsfield Studios, Station Road, Beaconsfield, Bucks HP9 1LG; 01494 731425; www.nftsfilm-tv.ac.uk

Producers Alliance for Cinema and Television (PACT), Procter House, 1 Procter Street, Holborn, London WC1V 6DW; 020 7067 4367; www.pact.co.uk

Society of British Theatre Designers, Fourth Floor, 55 Farringdon Road, London EC1M 3JB; 020 7242 9200; www.theatredesign.org.uk

UK Film Council, 10 Little Portland Street, London W1W 7JG; 020 7861 7861; www.ukfilmcouncil.org.uk

Careers and Jobs in the Media (Kogan Page)

Info

Starting Salary

With so many different jobs in this industry, here are just a few salary examples to give a flavour of the range of possible earnings. Runners are paid between £10,000 and £11,000, but the experience is extremely useful. Trainee production assistants earn between £10,000 and £14,000. Experienced production staff earn between £18,000 and £25,000. Technicians earn between £14,000 and £26,000. Directors' salaries are not necessarily high, if they are working for small companies on low budget productions.

Many staff work freelance and are paid on a daily basis or a fee per contract. BECTU sets rates in the industry. Your own fee negotiating skills are often important in this field.

FIRE SERVICE

Firefighters save and rescue life and property in emergencies. Fighting fires is only one aspect of their work; other emergencies they deal with are tanker spillages, car, train and aeroplane crashes, flooding, building collapse, and explosions where people and animals may have to be rescued. Some firefighters specialise in particular areas such as training or communications. The Fire Service also promotes fire safety through education programmes, and advice on fire protection and prevention for existing properties and new buildings. In addition it enforces legal regulations to reduce risks of injury by fire, such as the provision of secure escape routes.

The Fire Service is administered by local authorities in the UK. Recruitment is undertaken by each local brigade which is responsible for its own recruitment procedures. The Ministry of Defence, Army, Royal Air Force, Royal Navy and the British Airports Authority all have their own brigades.

Qualifications and Training

No formal qualifications are necessary, but GCSEs in maths, English and science are useful. You must be aged 18 or over to train as a firefighter and you must pass a rigorous medical, including eyesight and hearing tests. You also have to pass a physical fitness test, and individual fire brigades set a range of aptitude tests. The training is on-the-job, with frequent courses on new risks, better procedures, etc.

Personal Qualities and Skills

As a firefighter you have to be calm and courageous, prepared to go into dangerous situations, but sensible enough to tackle things calmly. You must be good at reassuring frightened or injured people and you must be good at working as part of a team. You may also be involved in teaching about fire prevention and safety, so you must enjoy dealing with people.

Starting Salary

Salaries for trainee firefighters start at around £20,000. On achieving full competence, the rate for a firefighter is between £26,500 and £27,000. Firefighters working in London earn an additional £4,500.

info

The Chief Fire Officers Association, 10–11 Pebble Close, Amington, Tamworth B77 4RD; 01827 302300; www.cfoa.org.uk/

Fire Brigades Union (FBU), Bradley House, 68 Coombe Road, Kingston upon Thames, Surrey KT2 7AE; 020 8541 1765; www.fbu.org.uk/

Fire Service College, Moreton in Marsh, Gloucestershire GL56 0RH; 01608 650831; www.fireservicecollege.ac.uk/

Institution of Fire Engineers (IFE), London Road, Moreton in Marsh, Gloucestershire GL56 0RH; 01608 812580; www.ife.org.uk/

The London Fire & Emergency Planning Authority (LFEPA), 8 Albert Embankment, London SE1 7SD; 020 7587 2000; www.london-fire.gov.uk/lfepa/lfepa.asp

How to Pass the Firefighter Selection Process (Kogan Page)

FISH FARMER

In Britain around 500 fish farms produce fish, mainly rainbow trout and Atlantic salmon, for consumption and sport. Pacific oysters, mussels and scallops are also farmed. This is a growing activity and although most farms are owner-run, there are opportunities for farm managers and workers. Scientists also work in the industry, testing new methods for improving conditions, stocks and disease control. Bailiffs are employed to look after the general welfare of the fish from hatchery to harvesting. As more food manufacturers move into fish farming, there is a need for marketing staff.

Qualifications and Training

NVQs in fish husbandry at level 2 and in aquaculture at levels 2 and 3 are available. Certificates, diploma and degree courses in fish farming and agriculture are offered by universities and specialist colleges. The Institute of Fisheries Management (IFM) organises correspondence courses leading to Certificates in Fisheries Management and in Fish Farming, and runs a Diploma in Fisheries Management.

No formal qualifications are required to become a bailiff, although correspondence courses are available from the IFM. Graduate and postgraduate biologists are employed on the scientific side and specialist degrees are available, as are courses dealing with the sporting aspect of fish farming.

Personal Qualities and Skills

Physical fitness, a willingness to work outside, in remote areas and in all conditions, plus an ability to think ahead and act independently are necessary.

Starting Salary

£12,000+ for technicians, £14,000+ for bailiffs, £16,000–£19,000+ for scientists, and £18,000–£22,000 for managers.

info

British Trout Association,
The Rural Centre, West Mains,
Ingliston EH28 8NZ; 0131 472 4080;
www.britishtrout.co.uk;
e-mail: mail@britishtrout.co.uk

Institute of Fisheries Management
(IFM), 22 Rushworth Avenue,
West Bridgford, Nottingham NG2 7LF;
0115 982 2317; fax: 0115 945 5722;
www.ifm.org.uk;
e-mail: admin@ifm.org.uk

Lantra Connect, Lantra House,
Stoneleigh, Kenilworth, Warwickshire
CV8 2LG; 0845 707 8007
(Lantra Connect – Helpline);
www.lantra.co.uk;
e-mail: connect@lantra.co.uk

Vacancies are generally advertised in
local newspapers and in the specialist
magazines such as *Fish Farmer* and
Fish Farming International.

FISHER

Fishers perform many tasks: they cast out and haul in the nets when they are full; gut, clean and stow away the catch; mend nets; maintain the tackle and wash down the decks. Fishers may work on deep-sea trawlers in the North Sea or on 'factory' stern vessels which prepare and deep-freeze the catches of cod, haddock, plaice, halibut and sole at sea. Fishing boats operate close to shore as well as in distant fishing grounds such as Greenland, the North Atlantic and Norway. Crews may stay at sea for weeks at a time. While fishing is actually taking place, all hands must work for stretches of up to 18 hours. On the older ships all work is done on the decks but the more modern factory ships process the catch below decks. Catering staff, engineers and radio operators are also employed on these large vessels.

Fishers on drifters carry out similar tasks but these boats follow fish around the coast and land a catch every day. Small seine-net boats with a crew of only four stay at sea for two weeks. Inshore fishing boats are usually family concerns using a variety of different methods to catch white fish, herring, cod, haddock, whiting, shrimps, lobster and crab.

Although the fishing industry is in decline, there are still employment opportunities at the five main ports of Grimsby, Hull, Lowestoft, Fleetwood and Aberdeen.

Qualifications and Training

No formal education qualifications are necessary for a career in fishing, but to go to sea fishers must undertake training in basic sea survival, firefighting and first aid. Colleges generally require applicants to have spent time at sea before entry on to a pre-seagoing course. Courses are available at colleges in Hull, Fleetwood, Grimsby, Lowestoft and Aberdeen. Further training is gained in employment. NVQs in marine vessel operations are available, as is an Advanced Modern Apprenticeship in sea fishing.

Personal Qualities and Skills

Physical fitness, stamina and courage are essential for fishers, who may have to withstand terrible Arctic conditions and long periods of very hard work. They must also be good sailors, able to turn their hand to any task, react quickly to emergencies, and be able to work in a team.

Starting Salary

Fishers all take a share of the catch; the more they catch, the more they earn.

Job Centre Plus and Careers/ Connexions Centres in port towns	Sea Fish Industry Authority, Seafish House, St Andrew's Dock, Hull HU3 4QE; 01482 327837; www.seafish.org

info

FLORISTRY

see Crafts

FOOD SCIENCE AND TECHNOLOGY

Food scientists study the properties and behaviour of foods from raw materials through processing to the final product, using a variety of scientific disciplines, notably chemistry and biology, but also physics and nutrition. Food technologists use food science and other technological know-how to turn raw materials into finished products for the consumer in an industry that is becoming increasingly sophisticated.

The majority of those qualifying in food science or technology will readily find employment in a variety of positions in the food industry, which covers not only the manufacture of food but its ingredients, food packaging and the manufacture of food-processing machinery. Positions exist in production, quality assurance or in product or process development. The growth of 'own label' products has led to additional opportunities in the food retailing sector, where technologists are responsible for developing new products, identifying suppliers, and ensuring the quality of the product from manufacture, through distribution to the store and, ultimately, to the consumer's table. Those keen to secure a career in research will find opportunities in government service, in research associations, as well as commercial organisations and the universities. There are additional opportunities in environmental health, education, consultancy, public health laboratories and in technical publishing and journalism.

Qualifications and Training

Food science and technology qualifications may be gained via NVQs (levels 1–4), Edexcel (BTEC)/SQA national certificates and diplomas, HNC, HND and degree courses. There is also the opportunity to train while in a job. Qualifications at all levels can be taken as full-time and sandwich courses. There are also a few part-time courses. For minimum entry requirements, contact colleges directly.

Membership of the Institute of Food Science and Technology depends upon satisfying both academic qualifications (minimum HND) and having several years' experience at a responsible level for higher grades.

Personal Qualities and Skills

Food scientists and technologists require a sound theoretical knowledge and scientific ability, a practical approach, an ability to communicate with people and a willingness to work as part of a team.

Starting Salary

Graduate food technologists earn between £16,000 and £20,000. If you have five to ten years' experience and management responsibility, salaries range from £25,000 to £50,000.

info

Food and Drink Federation,
6 Catherine Street, London WC2B 5JJ;
020 7836 2460; www.fdf.org.uk

Food Standards Agency,
Aviation House, 125 Kingsway,
London WC2B 6NH; 020 7276 8000;
www.foodstandards.gov.uk

Improve – The Food and Drink Sector
Skills Council, Ground Floor,
Providence House, 2 Innovation Close,
Heslington, York YO10 5ZF;
0845 644 0448; www.improveltd.co.uk

Institute of Food Science and
Technology (IFST), 5 Cambridge Court,
210 Shepherd's Bush Road, London
W6 7NJ; 020 7603 6316; www.ifst.org

FORENSIC SCIENTIST

The Forensic Science Service (FSS), an agency of the Home Office, employs scientists for both research and operational forensic science. Forensic scientists examine and try to identify, by means of analytical chemistry, molecular biology and microscopic analysis, samples of materials such as clothing, hair, blood, glass, paint and handwriting, in order to provide evidence to expose criminals, the location of a crime, the weapons used, and other relevant details.

Qualifications and Training

This is a highly competitive graduate entry profession. The most relevant degrees are biology, chemistry, biochemistry, crop and soil science, materials science, pharmacology and physiology. While there are many undergraduate degrees in forensic science, not all of these qualify you as a forensic scientist. You should check individual course details very carefully. Most forensic scientists also have relevant postgraduate qualifications and some laboratory work experience. Most training is on the job, but you are also likely to have to attend several short courses to improve your knowledge and skills.

Personal Qualities and Skills

You must have an enquiring and logical mind. You should be patient and able to pay attention to really small details. You should have good scientific skills and knowledge and you must be persistent. Excellent written and oral communication skills are also vital.

Starting Salary

Trainees start on between £18,000 and £20,000. If you have an MSc or a PhD, the starting salary may be a little higher.

Info

Defence Science and Technology Laboratory (DSTL), Porton Down, Salisbury, Wiltshire SP4 0JQ; 01980 613121; www.dstl.gov.uk/about_us/index.htm

Forensic Alliance, Headquarters and Culham Laboratory, F5 Culham Science Centre, Abingdon, Oxfordshire OX14 3ED; 01235 551800; www.forensicalliance.com

Forensic Science Northern Ireland (FSNI), 151 Belfast Rd, Carrickfergus, County Antrim BT38 8PL; 028 9036 1888; www.fsni.gov.uk/

Forensic Science Service (FSS), Trident Court, 2920 Solihull Parkway, Birmingham B37 7YN; 0121 329 5200; www.forensic.gov.uk

Forensic Science Society, Clarke House, 18a Mount Parade, Harrogate, North Yorkshire HG1 1BX; 01423 506068; www.forensic-science-society.org.uk

Home Office, Direct Communications Unit, 2 Marsham Street, London SW1P 4DF; 0870 000 1585; www.homeoffice.gov.uk

LGC, Queens Road, Teddington, Middlesex TW11 0LY; 020 8943 7000; www.lgc.co.uk/

SEMTA: The Sector Skills Council for Science, Engineering and Manufacturing Technologies, Head Office, 14 Upton Road, Watford WD18 0JT; 01923 238441; www.semta.org

FORESTRY

Trees, woodlands and forests cover some 13 per cent of the land area of Britain. The job of the forester is to manage this resource to achieve multiple objectives, balancing competing factors. Forests and woodlands give society many things: they create employment, give space for recreation ranging from rallying to solitary strolls in ancient woodlands while providing a home for a vast array of plants, birds and animals and producing timber for construction, paper and a multitude of other uses.

Forestry needs people with a vast range of skills and abilities ranging from manual workers who tend and manage forests by planting, fencing and felling, to machine operators who drive very sophisticated machines that fell and extract timber from woodlands. These operations are managed by supervisors and foresters who plan and oversee forests and woodlands. Their work is very varied and includes tasks such as managing habitats for bio-diversity, planning the felling and planting of forests along with the management of staff and supervision of large contracts.

Qualifications and Training

Forest workers must have nationally recognised chainsaw and pesticide application qualifications, such as those provided by the National Proficiency Tests Council (NPTC). A number of training schemes are available leading to NVQs in forestry at levels 1–3.

Foresters normally start their career with a degree or HND in forestry and then progress their career with membership of their professional body, the Institute of Chartered Foresters. Entry to courses normally requires a period of work experience in forestry as well as the relevant academic qualifications.

Personal Qualities and Skills

Forestry work requires a good standard of physical fitness, a willingness to work outside, all year round, in all weathers and in remote areas. A driving licence is usually essential. Foresters and managers should be able to organise others and be prepared to do varying amounts of office work.

info

Forestry Commission, Personnel Division, 231 Corstorphine Road, Edinburgh EH12 7AT; 0131 334 0303; www.forestry.gov.uk; e-mail: enquiries@forestry.gsi.gov.uk

Institute of Chartered Foresters, 7a St Colme Street, Edinburgh EH3 6AA; 0131 225 2705; www.charteredforesters.org; e-mail: membership@charteredforesters.org

Royal Forestry Society of England, Wales and Northern Ireland, 102 High Street, Tring, Hertfordshire HP23 4AF; 01442 822028; www.rfs.org.uk; e-mail: rfshq@rfs.org.uk

Arboricultural Association, Ampfield House, Ampfield, Nr Romsey, Hampshire SO51 9PA; 01794 368717; fax: 01794 368978; www.trees.org.uk; e-mail: treehouse@dialpipex.com

Royal Scottish Forestry Society, Hagg-on-Esk, Canonbie, Dumfriesshire DG14 0XE; 01387 371518; fax: 01387 371418; www.rsfs.org; e-mail: rsfs@ednet.co.uk

National Proficiency Tests Council, Avenue 'J' , National Agricultural Centre, Stoneleigh, Warwickshire CV8 2LG; 02476 696553; www.nptc.org.uk; e-mail: information@nptc.org.uk

Lantra Connect, Lantra House, Stoneleigh, Kenilworth, Warwickshire CV8 2LG; 0845 707 8007 (Lantra Connect – Helpline); www.lantra.co.uk; e-mail: connect@lantra.co.uk

Forestry Contracting Association, Dalfling, Blairdaff, Inverurie, Aberdeenshire AB51 5LA; 01467 651368; www.fcauk.com

Starting Salary

Trainee forest workers earn about £100 a week at 16, rising to £150–£180 at 18. Forestry machine operators are normally paid on piece work but can earn in excess of £20,000. Graduate foresters are likely to start on around £15,000 which could rise to around £24,000. If further management responsibilities are taken on this could rise considerably.

FOUNDRY WORK

Foundry work is craft-based. The industry provides for a wide range of industries, metal-cast components such as propellers, turbines, crankshafts, all types of machinery, and domestic items such as fireplaces.

Craftspeople are employed in foundry work as pattern, mould and model makers and to maintain the equipment. The introduction of computerised processes means foundries also employ machine operators with a range of different skills. Technical engineering staff are concerned with estimating, inspection and laboratory work. There are many opportunities for operatives in foundry work as die casters, dressers, finishers, moulders, coremakers and in metal melting.

There are also limited openings for foundry technologists, metallurgists, chemists and engineers in research and development. Graduate trainees are recruited to production and administrative management posts.

Qualifications and Training

Craftspeople and operatives do not require formal qualifications. Foundation and Advanced Modern Apprenticeships are available and training is work based, leading to NVQs levels 1–3. Technicians study on a day-release or full-time basis for the Higher National Certificate/Diploma, in cast metals technology, mechanical or electrical engineering. Management trainees need HNDs or degrees in a relevant subject.

Personal Qualities and Skills

Workers in the foundry industry must be fit and strong as the work is heavy. They should have good eyesight and be skilful in the use of tools. They must be willing to work in noisy conditions and to work shifts.

Institute of Cast Metal Engineers, National Metalforming Centre, 47 Birmingham Road, West Bromwich, West Midlands B70 6PY; 0121 601 6979; fax: 0121 601 6981; www.icme.org.uk; e-mail: info@icme.org.uk

Local Job Centre Plus and Careers/ Connexions Centres

Cast Metals Federation, National Metalforming Centre, 47 Birmingham Road, West Bromwich B70 6PY; 0121 601 6390; www.castmetalsfederation.com; e-mail: admin@cmfed.co.uk

SEMTA, 14 Upton Road, Watford, Herts WD18 0JT; 0808 100 3682; www.semta.org.uk

Starting Salary

Operatives earn £10,000–£12,500; craftsmen, once trained, earn £15,000+; technicians start at around £14,000.

FUNDRAISING

Fundraising managers work mainly for charities, but sometimes for pressure groups, community projects and other organisations. They are responsible for overseeing all those activities that help their organisations to generate income. Their varied activities include working with advertisers and marketing specialists to decide how to target a particular audience; working with businesses to obtain corporate funding such as the sponsoring of a project; and organising special fundraising events. They are also responsible for managing trading through charity shops or mail order catalogues; keeping in touch with donors; and organising and supervising the work of volunteers. The particular mix of tasks varies greatly. Large charities may employ fundraising managers who specialise in just one of the above areas. Working for a small charity, you may have to turn your hand to anything and everything.

Qualifications and Training

While there may be no specific entry qualifications, many fundraisers are graduates with degrees in business studies or marketing. This work is now highly competitive and organisations have to consider who will really be able to help them generate income. A background in advertising, public relations, finance or marketing is ideal. Having done some voluntary work for your chosen charity, or for something similar, can also strengthen your application.

The Institute of Fundraising offers a part-time foundation course in the basics of fundraising, for people who have just embarked on this career. They also offer a certificate in fundraising management, which is equivalent to GNVQ level 4. A great deal of training is informal and on-the-job.

Personal Qualities and Skills

A full range of excellent interpersonal skills is essential. You must be persuasive, good at negotiating and able to speak confidently to groups of people. You need good business sense, IT skills and numeracy, and the knack of spotting an imaginative solution or coming up with an appealing idea.

Starting Salary

Fundraising managers earn between £17,000 and £25,000. With experience and working for a large organisation it is possible to earn far more than this. Some

Institute of Fundraising, Park Place, 12 Lawn Lane, London SW8 1UD; 020 7840 1000; www.institute-of-fundraising.org.uk

Working for a Charity, NCVO, Regent's Wharf, 8 All Saints Street, London NW1 2DP; 020 7250 2512; www.workingforacharity.org.uk

vacancies with small organisations or community groups will be less well paid and many may be part time with pro rata pay for hours worked.

FUNERAL DIRECTOR

Funeral directors collect the deceased from hospital or their residence and prepare them for burial or cremation, which may include embalming. Most funeral premises include private viewing rooms for family visitations. The funeral director often makes all the funeral arrangements on behalf of the family, such as the date, time and place of any ceremony and interment or cremation. The funeral director places the relevant notice of death and acknowledgement of thanks for sympathy in newspapers, pays all the fees, arranges flowers, transports the coffin and mourners to and from church, and will act as a collection point for flowers, or donations in lieu, if desired.

Funeral directors may be employed by large firms such as cooperative societies, or by small family-run concerns. In remote rural areas, a local carpenter or other craftsperson may also work as a funeral director.

Qualifications and Training

Those wishing to obtain the Diploma in Funeral Directing must register with the National Association of Funeral Directors (NAFD) and will also have student membership of the British Institute of Funeral Directors (BIFD). Full details of the diploma course are forwarded to each student. Every student must follow the foundation module – there are no exceptions.

A satisfactory standard must be reached in the foundation module before proceeding to the diploma. A student will be required to have 24 months' experience and have arranged 25 funerals before the diploma is awarded. NVQs levels 2 and 3 in Funeral Services are available for those employed within the profession.

Personal Qualities and Skills

Tact, sympathy and a reassuring, helpful nature are essential to funeral directors when they are advising the bereaved. They also need to combine administrative ability with technical expertise in the varied preparations of funeral arrangements. On-call and out-of-hours work is an integral part of the job and an ability to adapt to irregular hours is essential.

British Institute of Embalmers, Anubis House, 21c Station Road, Knowle, Solihull, West Midlands B93 0HL; 01564 778991; www.bioe.co.uk; e-mail: enquiry@bioe.org.uk

National Association of Funeral Directors, 618 Warwick Road, Solihull, West Midlands B91 1AA; 0845 230 1343; www.nafd.org.uk; e-mail: info@nafd.org.uk

Institute of Burial and Cremation Administration, 107 Parlaunt Road, Langley, Slough, Berks SL3 8BE; 01753 771518; fax: 01753 770518

Starting Salary

Salaries vary greatly depending on size of firm, many of which are family concerns. Average earnings are between £15,000 and £21,000.

FURNITURE AND FURNISHING

Furniture manufacture

Furniture manufacturing and repair companies exist in all parts of the country. The industry maintains much of its craft base, with skilled people carrying out many of the tasks needed to create a piece of furniture. Within larger factories some of this has been mechanised, making use of computerised production methods. At the other end of the scale many small designers/makers bring together the designs, materials, machinery and knowledge of today coupled with the skills from a previous age.

Modern furniture is made from timber, textiles, steel, glass, plastics, stone and a range of polymers. Skilled frame makers provide frames to be filled, sprung and covered by upholsterers. The machining part is increasingly done by use of IT-driven processes, but other work is still done by hand.

There are opportunities to work on a freelance or self-employed basis, or for one of the many manufacturing units which specialise in particular items, or materials, or in certain types of furniture such as school, office or domestic furniture. In the design of furniture, carpets, fabrics, curtaining and wall coverings, opportunities exist to work freelance, in studios and in the retail trade. There are also a number of openings for teachers; craft, design and technology teachers are in short supply.

Qualifications and Training

Craft training is generally gained through a three- to four-year Modern Apprenticeship including NVQs at level 3. Other training is available, from beginner-level courses (City & Guilds/OCN Craft Certificates) through more advanced knowledge-based programmes (City & Guilds Progression Awards) to HND/Cs, foundation and full degrees. Entry to many of these courses is dependent on practical ability, although some courses do have specific academic requirements.

Personal Qualities and Skills

Furniture craftspeople must be neat, accurate and able to follow drawings exactly. They must be interested in practical work which requires great precision, have care and patience, and sufficient strength to lift heavy furniture. Good eyesight is an advantage. Designers are required to work as part of a team to a busy schedule and present their work well; a sound knowledge of how furniture is made is valuable.

Starting Salary

Apprentices earn from £10,000, salaries going up during each year of training. Experienced furniture craftsmen and women can earn between £17,000 and £25,000. Furniture designers earn from £18,000 to £28,000.

Crafts Council, 44a Pentonville Road, Islington, London N1 9BY; 020 7278 7700; www.craftscouncil.org.uk

The Design Council, 34 Bow Street, London WC2E 7DL; 020 7420 5200; www.design-council.org.uk

Furnishing and Interiors National Training Organisation, 67 Wollaton Road, Beeston, Nottingham NG9 2NG; 0115 922 1200; www.ffinto.org

info

Upholstery

The upholstery industry in the UK has a long tradition of supplying and repairing seating. While competition from cheap imports is fierce, the UK's reputation for quality has helped sustain the industry. Companies range from small businesses supplying a local market to large undertakings making suites for the major retailers. The job may entail anything from providing modern chairs and sofas for large hotel chains to the restoration of antique furniture in private homes or museums.

There are three main roles within the sector: the cutter, the sewer and the upholsterer. Often within smaller companies all three roles are carried out by all staff but with some specialisation. Upholsterers measure up, prepare and fit the fabric components in all kinds of furniture. It is highly skilled work and includes not only the visible top coverings (which can vary from velvet to leather), but also the preparation and supports below, such as padding, stuffing, springing or webbing.

Qualifications and Training

Craft training is generally gained through a three- to four-year Modern Apprenticeship including NVQs at level 3. Other training is available, from beginner-level courses (City & Guilds/OCN Craft Certificates) through more advanced knowledge-based programmes (City & Guilds Progression Awards) to HNDs, foundation and full degrees.

Personal Qualities and Skills

Upholsterers need to have nimble fingers, good eyesight and infinite patience, and must enjoy working on individual projects.

Starting Salary

Salary rates vary but pay is generally good, with apprentices at 16 earning £70+ a week. By 19 many are earning in excess of £300 a week. Qualified and experienced staff can earn a lot more. Individual craftspeople working for themselves set their own rates.

info

Furniture, Furnishings and Interiors National Training Organisation, 67 Wollaton Road, Beeston, Nottingham NG9 2NG; 0115 922 1200; fax: 0115 922 3833; www.ffinto.org; e-mail: info@ffinto.org

G

GARDENING

Gardening, also known as amenity horticulture, involves not only planting and caring for flowers, trees and shrubs, but also the routine jobs of cleaning out flower beds, sweeping leaves and, in the winter, shovelling snow.

Gardener

(*see also* Landscape Architecture)

Gardeners may be employed by local authorities to care for parks, school and hospital grounds, work for a garden centre or landscape contractor, or be self-employed. Heritage gardening is a growth area and involves working for organisations such as the National Trust, English Heritage, and other private gardens.

Qualifications and Training

It is desirable but not always necessary to have formal qualifications to become a gardener. Training is given on the job, often as part of an apprenticeship; NVQ levels 1–3 are available. Full-time training courses in horticulture are available at colleges throughout the country, from first diploma level. The Royal Horticultural Society offers a limited number of opportunities for practical training and plantsmanship at its gardens at Wisley, Rosemoor and Hyde Hall.

info

Local Job Centre Plus and Careers/ Connexions Centres

Agricultural Wages Helpline; 0845 000 0134; www.defra.gov.uk/farm/agwages/ agwages.htm

Institute of Horticulture, 14–15 Belgrave Square, London SW1X 8PS; 020 7245 6943; www.horticulture.org.uk; e-mail: ioh@horticulture.org.uk

Royal Horticultural Society, 80 Vincent Square, London SW1P 2PE; 020 7834 4333; www.rhs.org.uk; e-mail: info@rhs.org.uk

Writtle College, Chelmsford CM1 3RR; 01245 424200; www.growing-careers.com

Careers Working Outdoors (Kogan Page)

Voluntary Internships for four or more weeks are available for those studying horticulture at college, and at a number of schools work experience placements are available for secondary pupils.

Personal Qualities and Skills

You must have a real interest in the plants you work with, whether they are commercial fruit and vegetables or ornamental flowers and shrubs. You should be very practical and happy to work in all weathers and you must be patient – some of your work takes a long time to come to fruition. For some gardening jobs you need an eye for design and colour. You should be comfortable working on your own, but able to talk to people about their gardens, their crops and their ideas.

Starting Salary

Salaries in commercial horticulture are set by the Agricultural Wages Board, which has just introduced a six-tier grading system for pay. Basic trainees get £5.05 an hour, standard workers get £5.58 an hour, lead workers get £5.91 an hour, craft workers get £6.58 an hour, supervisors get £6.98 an hour and managers get £7.53 an hour. Very many gardeners are self-employed and the hourly rate they can charge varies with different geographical location; they can earn up to £25,000, but earnings in winter may be very sparse.

GAS SERVICE ENGINEER

Gas service engineers, also known as gas service technicians or gas service fitters, work in people's homes and on business premises, installing, servicing and repairing appliances and systems such as cookers, boilers and central heating systems. They test controls and safety devices to ensure that they are working and they locate and repair gas leaks. Often they specialise either in installation, servicing or repair, but some gas service engineers will work in all three areas.

Qualifications and Training

The usual route to qualification is through a technician-level apprenticeship lasting between three and four years. You need four GCSEs grades A to C including English, maths and science, and you must have perfect colour vision. Most apprentices start at age 16, but you can start up to the age of 24. Successful completion of the apprenticeship also leads to an NVQ level 3 award.

To work as a gas fitter, installer or service engineer, you must register with the Council for Registered Gas Installers, which will check your qualifications and ascertain that you have had suitable training and work experience before allowing you to register.

Personal Qualities and Skills

You must be practical, able to handle tools and instruments, and you must be able to apply technical knowledge to practical problems. You have to be able to work on your own or as part of a team, and it is important that you are polite and friendly and enjoy meeting and dealing with people. Having an acute awareness of safety issues is essential.

Starting Salary

Trainees earn between £10,000 and £12,000, newly qualified technicians earn between £14,000 and £16,500. With several years' experience you can earn up to £24,000.

British Gas Recruitment, The Harrow Way, Basingstoke, Hants RG22 4AR; www.britishgasacademy.co.uk

Energy and Utility Skills, Friars Gate Two, 1011 Stratford Road, Shirley, Solihull B90 4BN; 0845 077 9922; www.euskills.co.uk

The Council for Registered Gas Installers (CORGI),
1 Elmwood, Chineham Business Park, Crockford Lane, Basingstoke, Hants RG24 8WG; 0870 401 2300; www.corgi-gas-safety.com

---

GEOLOGIST

Geoscience is essential to the understanding of the natural resources contained in earth and rocks, oil, water, minerals and precious metals. Geologists also contribute to an understanding of the earth's history and the scientific study of natural phenomena like volcanoes and earthquakes. Since geoscience encompasses so many different areas of expertise, there are many specialist occupations within this field.

Geologists study the earth's crust, its materials, their origin, formation and composition. The work involves examining rocks and mineral deposits; some deposits (for example, coal) are assessed for their value. Specimens of rock, soil, water, fossils and minerals are collected for laboratory analysis and preserved for future reference. Geology includes not only fieldwork but much laboratory work, testing and analysing, often using computers. Geologists work mainly for oil, mining, quarrying or engineering firms and government establishments, and are becoming increasingly involved in environmental issues.

Closely allied to the work of the geologist is that of the geophysicist (*see* Oil/Gas Rig Work), geochemist and hydrogeologist, who use field and laboratory-based techniques to better understand the earth's physical and chemical properties and its underground water supplies. Hence, most of their work is related to the resources and the environment.

Qualifications and Training

The common route for entry into a professional geoscience career is a first degree (BSc/BA) in one of the geosciences. Such a degree also forms the basic qualification for Fellowship of the Geological Society of London, and for becoming a Chartered Geologist.

Personal Qualities and Skills

Geologists must be fit, as they are often required to work in difficult climatic conditions or even underground. They must be able to work both as team members and as team organisers when required. Relevant foreign languages are useful.

Starting Salary

£15,500+ to £23,000+; higher abroad.

info

For careers information:
British Geological Survey,
BGS Personnel,
British Geological Survey, Keyworth,
Nottingham NG12 5GG;
0115 936 3209; 0115 936 3537;

www.bgs.ac.uk;
e-mail: enquiries@bgs.ac.uk

Geological Society, Burlington House,
Piccadilly, London W1J 0BG;
020 7434 9944; www.geolsoc.org.uk;
e-mail: enquiries@geolsoc.org.uk

HAIR

Hairdresser

Hairdressers offer a variety of services involving hair, such as cutting, styling, perming and colouring. Salons or individual stylists may specialise in male or female hairdressing, or a niche market such as specialist colouring, Afro-Caribbean or ethnic hairstyles. Hairdressers may also be responsible for answering the telephone, making appointments, serving drinks to clients, cleaning and stock control. They work in salons, hotels, airports, cruise liners, hospitals and prisons. Some hairdressers work as freelancers. There are over 170,000 hairdressers in the UK.

Qualifications and Training

Most trainees combine on-the-job training with part-time study at a college or training centre towards an NVQ in hairdressing at levels 1, 2 and 3. Salons may offer a three-year apprenticeship which includes training alongside experienced stylists and day release at college. Some colleges also offer full-time NVQs and full- or part-time BTEC courses in design, fashion styling for hair and make-up. Full-time courses usually last for two years and include work experience in a college and external salon. Colleges may also offer the National Diploma of Hairdressing, awarded by the Guild of Hairdressers.

After training, hairdressers are expected to work for at least a year as an improver before being considered experienced. Hairdressers who want to enter salon management, become self-employed or teach hairdressing may need further qualifications in business studies or teaching. It may become necessary for all hairdressers to be state registered with the Hairdressing Council at some time in the future.

Personal Qualities and Skills

Hairdressers should have a genuine interest in people, a natural friendliness, the ability to stay calm under pressure, creative ability and an eye for detail. A presentable personal appearance is also essential. Hairdressers must not have skin conditions that can be affected by chemicals.

Searching for something more?

In this increasingly image conscious world, the opportunities available in the hair, beauty, spa and nail industries are endless and there have never been so many exciting possibilities at the cutting edge of the fashion, style and grooming business. TV and celebrity culture have helped catapult these industries to the forefront of the fashion agenda and you need to be a very special type of person to work in them.

You will need to have a unique combination of skills and will require a great deal of training, however, successful people can take their pick from many jobs – preparing supermodels, working on magazines and photo shoots, or tending to the rich and famous. What's more, with the UK grooming business rightly regarded as the best in the world, there is ample opportunity to travel internationally and show off your skills abroad. You can work as a self-employed freelancer, in salons, spas, health farms, holiday resorts, on film and TV sets or even in the theatre. Some airlines offer in-flight hair and beauty treatments, and most cruise liners will have a hair and beauty salon on board.

Many people in hair and beauty also go on to work in sales, marketing, public relations and photography, whilst others choose to concentrate on the business aspects of running a salon rather than performing treatments. You can even go into education, working as a trainer or lecturer in a salon or training centre to pass on your knowledge and skills.

But before you can do any of the above, you have to learn the skills and knowledge to make clients happy and want to come back for more and one of the best ways to discover this is through an Apprenticeship.

Apprenticeships give you the skills and techniques that employers need and that will give you the grounding for a successful career and Habia can help you with this. Career leaflets are available for Apprenticeships in hair, beauty, nails and barbering in England, Northern Ireland, Scotland and Wales for students and careers advisors by contacting Habia on **0845 2 306080**, email us at **careers@habia.org** or go to **www.habia.org** and click on **Careers**.

habia.
standards · information · solutions

Beverly C
Mary Cole
Pooja Imbert

If you're looking for an exciting, demanding and rewarding career – hair, beauty, nails and spa are full of opportunities.

If you are interested in a career in hair, beauty, nails or spa, or if you just want more information, contact Habia on 0845 2 306080, email us at careers@habia.org or go to www.habia.org.

Detailed career information and diagrams explaining all the options, qualifications and job routes available to you can be downloaded by going to **www.habia.org and clicking on Careers.**

(habia is a not for profit organisation)

Hair: Phil Smith at Toni & Guy, Photography: Malcolm Willison, Make up: Cheryl Phelps-Gardiner, Styling: Roberta Resta

www.habia.org

Starting Salary

Trainees earn between £10,000 and £12,000. Qualified stylists can earn £16,000 to £20,000. At very fashionable salons, earnings may be higher and these may be further increased by tips. Many hairdressers work for themselves, either based in their own homes or visiting their clients' homes.

Hairdressing Council, 12 David Street, 45 High Street, South Norwood, London SE25 6HJ; 020 8771 6205; www.haircouncil.org.uk; e-mail: registrar@haircouncil.org.uk

Hairdressing and Beauty Industry Authority (HABIA), Fraser House, Nether Hall Road, Doncaster DN1 2PH; 01302 380000; www.habia.org.uk; e-mail: enquiries@habia.org.uk

National Hairdressers Federation, One Abbey Court, Fraser Road, Priory Business Park, Bedford MK44 3WH; 0845 345 6500; www.nhfuk.com; e-mail: nhf@tgis.co.uk

Guild of Hairdressers, Unit 1E, Redbrook Business Park, Wilthorpe Road, Barnsley S75 1JN; 01226 786555; fax: 01226 208300

Careers in Hairdressing and Beauty (Kogan Page)

Trichologist

Trichologists treat hair and scalp disorders, the most common being hair loss. Electrical and heat treatments, massage and special lotions and ointments are used. Trichologists practise on their own behalf; some of their patients are referred to them from doctors, but trichology is not available on the NHS.

Qualifications and Training

Basic academic qualifications are necessary. Training may be by a three-year pupillage with a practising trichologist. The necessary theoretical instruction is available at technical colleges, evening classes or by correspondence. It is also necessary to have some practical experience of working in a recognised clinic.

Personal Qualities and Skills

Trichologists must understand the necessary biological principles and have a knowledge of nutrition, plus an interest in helping people. They must have high standards of personal hygiene.

Starting Salary

This is dependent upon number of patients, hours worked and fees charged.

Institute of Trichologists, 0870 607 0602; www.trichologists.org.uk

HEALTH AND SAFETY

Health and safety adviser

Health and safety advisers work for every kind or organisation, from multinationals and government agencies to small businesses. Advisers work in partnership with employers, employees, directors and trade unions, and are responsible for ensuring that all safety legislation is adhered to and that suitable policies and practices are put in place. They help organisations minimise safety risks and they are often involved in staff training.

Health and safety inspector

Health and safety inspectors work to assess and improve every kind of work practice and the health and safety applications attached to it. In the UK one person is killed every day at work, and inspectors working for the Health and Safety Executive (HSE), which is a government agency, are constantly working to try to reduce this statistic. Inspectors check work premises, from building sites to farms and factories, and they have legal powers to demand changes. They are also called in to investigate when accidents do occur.

Qualifications and Training

It is possible to become an adviser without a degree, if you have plenty of work experience in management, engineering, science or health, but there is a move towards making this a graduate entry profession. Degrees in occupational health, engineering, health science and management are the most favoured, and these each have their own entry requirements. Graduates or HND holders of any subject can become health and safety inspectors, but again there is a preference for subjects such as engineering, environmental health or physics.

Personal Qualities and Skills

To be an adviser or an inspector you have to be an excellent and persuasive communicator and negotiator. You must be good at understanding and interpreting legal or technical documents and prepared to keep abreast of changes in legislation. You must be keenly observant, spotting potential problems, but also able to suggest solutions. You must be able to write reports and have the confidence to talk to large groups of people. To be an inspector you must be practical enough to use measurement equipment of various kinds and you need numerical skills to make calculations.

Starting Salary

As an adviser at the start of your career you can expect between £20,000 and £26,000 depending on whether you have had useful work experience as well as offering a relevant qualification. At a senior level salaries rise to around £40,000. Trainee inspectors with the Health and Safety Executive start on £20,000.

info

British Safety Council, National Safety Centre, 70 Chancellor's Road, London W6 9RS; 020 8741 1231; www.britishsafetycouncil.co.uk

Department for Environment, Food and Rural Affairs (DEFRA), Nobel House, 17 Smith Square, London SW1P 3JR; 0845 933 5577; www.defra.gov.uk/

The Health and Safety Executive (HSE), Magdalen House, Trinity Road, Bootle, Merseyside L20 3QZ; 0845 345 0055; www.hse.gov.uk/

Institution of Occupational Safety and Health (IOSH), Membership Department, The Grange, Highfield Drive, Wigston, Leics LE18 1NN; 0116 257 3100; www.iosh.co.uk

National Examination Board for Occupational Safety and Health (NEBOSH), Dominus Way, Meridian Business Park, Leicester LE19 1QW; 0116 263 4700; www.nebosh.org.uk

Royal Society for the Prevention of Accidents (ROSPA), Head Office, Edgbaston Park, 353 Bristol Road, Edgbaston, Birmingham B5 7ST; 0121 248 2000; www.rospa.com/index

HEALTH SERVICE (NON-MEDICAL)

There are plenty of non-medical jobs and career paths open to people in health-care. Some of these services are provided by the National Health Service (NHS), others such as catering, cleaning or laundry are often provided by companies that are contracted to do this work on behalf of the NHS.

Catering staff

Cooks, housekeepers and kitchen assistants working either for the NHS or for catering companies provide a range of hospital meals. They have to cater for special diets and try to provide a range of tempting food. Working within a tight budget is a key skill in this work.

Clerical staff

The NHS employs large numbers of clerks, secretaries, telephonists, reception-ists and other administrative workers. Some of this work involves patient contact, eg receptionists at clinics, or ward clerks. Other work is more behind the scenes, ordering supplies, booking appointments and updating records.

Domestic services staff

Domestic services staff are either employed by the NHS or by private compa-nies that have contracts to clean health service premises and also laundering all the sheets, pillow cases, towels, etc.

Estates staff

Hospitals, clinics and other NHS premises need building services engineers to ensure that lighting, heating, air conditioning and other environmental management systems work at all times. Architects and surveyors are needed to design new premises or plan refurbishment of existing older properties.

Information science and technology

Computer systems of many kinds are important for keeping records, monitoring care and sharing information. All kinds of IT staff are employed, from data input clerks to systems development.

Managers

This is a very broad term. The NHS employs managers in finance, human resources, strategic planning, performance monitoring and the day-to-day running of every kind of health service establishment.

Porters and messengers

Porters move patients and equipment from one part of a hospital or other healthcare centre to another. Messengers take important messages from one department to another. Even in these days of electronic communications urgent messages are delivered by messengers.

Scientists

Scientists are employed in research and development; laboratory technicians work in hospital laboratories, testing blood and other tissue samples. Technicians and scientists apply specific techniques to implement various health screening programmes.

Sterile services staff

Sterile services staff clean and sterilize all medical equipment. Some of this equipment is highly technical, so disinfecting it and preparing it for use is a painstaking and complex task. Applicants for this work usually need GCSEs in English, maths and a science.

Qualifications and Training

These vary considerably for different jobs. It is worth consulting specific career areas such as Accountancy, Biomedical Engineering, Hospitality, Human Resource Management, Information Technology and Secretarial work. For some work, such as being a porter or a kitchen assistant, you may not need any formal academic qualifications. For most management posts you need either a degree or professional qualifications in a relevant area such as accountancy or management studies. Posts in science, engineering or information technology will require relevant qualifications from GCSE to postgraduate level.

Personal Qualities and Skills

The common thread for all these jobs is a genuine commitment to working within and for healthcare and wanting to deliver a good service to patients. For any work involving patient contact, being sensitive and caring is important. All jobs require you to be a good communicator and to be able to work very well as part of a team. Particular jobs require specific practical skills such as cooking, IT skills or being good with technical equipment.

Starting Salary

Porters, messengers, kitchen assistants and staff working in domestic service may earn close to the minimum wage. For technical jobs the salary range is £13,000 to £23,000. Managers earn from £18,000 to £40,000 depending on levels of both experience and responsibility.

info

NHS Careers, PO Box 376, Bristol BS99 3EY; 0845 606 0655; www.nhscareers.nhs.uk

NHS Education for Scotland, Careers Information Service, 66 Rose Street,

Edinburgh EH2 2NN; 0131 225 4365; www.nes.scot.nhs.uk

NHS Learning and Development Service; 08000 150 850; e-mail: learning@nhscareers.nhs.uk

HEALTH VISITOR

see Nursing, Health Visiting and Midwifery

HEALTHCARE ASSISTANT

see Nursing, Health Visiting and Midwifery

HORTICULTURE

Horticulture is the science of growing fruits, vegetable and flowers and there are a variety of occupations to choose from in this sector.

Advisory work

The adviser provides a link between research workers and the grower, to pass on the results of experimental work. The commercial and consultancy firms and producer organisations provide opportunities for advisers. A degree plus practical experience is necessary.

Amenity horticulture

(*see also* Landscape Architecture)

Landscape architects, parks directors, landscape gardeners and groundspeople maintain public and private gardens and parks, sport and recreational facilities, industrial and residential areas, and landscape and plant roadsides. Employers may be local authority public parks and recreation departments, commercial landscaping, contract garden maintenance firms, or owners of major gardens.

Arboriculturist

(*see also* Forestry)

Arboriculturists care for and maintain trees and are mainly employed by local authorities, although there are some opportunities in private firms. The term 'tree surgeon' is often used for a commercial arboriculturist.

Commercial horticulture

Commercial horticulturists grow crops, such as vegetables, on open land, and tomatoes, lettuce and cucumbers in glasshouses. Both orchard and soft fruits account for over one-fifth of the value of all horticultural production. Commercial horticulture also covers the growing of flowers and ornamental plants, including chrysanthemums, roses and carnations under glass, and for the gardening market, nurseries, landscaping and seeds.

Market gardening

Crops grown in market gardens are vegetables, salad crops – such as lettuces and tomatoes – and flowers and ornamental plants. The work consists of preparing the soil, and working by hand on such jobs as transplanting young plants, thinning growing plants, and grading, washing and packing the produce after harvesting so that it can be sold.

Research

Horticultural scientists work on pests and diseases and general research to produce better and healthier plants, in industrial and government organisations and in universities and colleges. There is a wide range of prospects for graduates.

Teaching

Opportunities for teaching in horticulture occur in universities, colleges and schools. A degree or diploma is required.

Qualifications and Training

There are openings in horticulture for people from a variety of educational backgrounds. No GCSEs are required for part- or full-time initial training courses, although beginners should be competent in biology, chemistry and maths. Applicants may work towards NVQs levels 1 to 4.

Those with five GCSEs, including science and maths plus one A level pass or equivalent, and one year's experience can study for the Higher National Diploma, specialising in commercial or amenity horticulture. Two A levels or equivalent are necessary to study for a degree in horticulture.

The Royal Horticultural Society offers a limited number of opportunities for practical training and plantsmanship at its gardens at Wisley, Rosemoor and Hyde Hall. Committed gardeners aged between the ages of 19 and 35 can apply for the two-year Wisley Diploma in Practical Horticulture and the one-year certificate course. Students receive £10,300 per year and accommodation.

Voluntary Internships for four or more weeks are available for those studying horticulture at college, and at a number of schools work experience placements are available for secondary pupils.

Personal Qualities and Skills

A real enthusiasm for plants and an interest in how to provide the ideal conditions for growing them is essential. You have to be prepared to work in all weathers, to be patient when awaiting the results of your work, and you should be observant – quick to note changes or potential problems. Good commercial and marketing awareness is often useful. You should be able to work as part of a team, as well as feeling comfortable working on your own.

Starting Salary

Salaries in commercial horticulture are set by the Agricultural Wages Board, which has recently introduced a six-tier grading system for pay. Basic trainees get £5.05 an hour, standard workers get £5.58 an hour, lead workers get £5.91

an hour, craft workers get £6.58 an hour, supervisors get £6.98 an hour and managers get £7.53 an hour. There are sometimes different rates for seasonal work and some of this work may also include accommodation and food.

Institute of Horticulture, 14–15 Belgrave Square, London SW1X 8PS; 020 7245 6943; www.horticulture.org.uk; e-mail: ioh@horticulture.org.uk

Royal Horticultural Society, 80 Vincent Square, London SW1P 2PE; 020 7834 4333; www.rhs.org.uk; e-mail: info@rhs.org.uk

Lantra Connect, Lantra House, Stoneleigh Park, Kenilworth, Warwickshire CV8 2LG; 0845 707 8007 (Lantra Connect – Helpline); www.lantra.co.uk; e-mail: connect@lantra.co.uk

Royal Agricultural Society of England, National Agricultural Centre, Stoneleigh Park, Warwickshire CV8 2LZ; 01476 696969; www.rase.org.uk

Department for Environment, Food and Rural Affairs: general enquiries: Library Enquiry Desk, DEFRA, Room 320, Nobel House, 17 Smith Square, London SW1P 3JR; 0845 933 5577; www.defra.gov.uk

Agricultural Wages Board, Nobel House, 17 Smith Square, London SW1P 3JR; Agricultural Wages Helpline: 0845 000 0134; www.defra.gov.uk/farm/agwages/ agwages.htm

Local Job Centre Plus and Careers/ Connexions Centres

'Come into Horticulture' and 'Education and Training Courses in Horticulture' (available free from the Institute of Horticulture).

Info

HOSPITALITY AND CATERING

There is a wide variety of job opportunities in this category at all levels, from managers and supervisors to craft workers. Sometimes the dividing lines are not clear-cut, and it is quite usual for individuals to move up from one to another.

Chef/cook

In addition to creating and supervising the preparation of all kinds of different dishes, a head chef/cook has to be trained in the management of a kitchen, being responsible for the staff and the organisation of their workload, planning the menus, budgeting, ordering and approving the necessary ingredients and maintaining high standards of efficiency and hygiene. Chefs are employed in hotels, restaurants, industrial organisations (such as offices or factories), institutions (such as hospitals, schools and universities or colleges) and in the armed forces. In large establishments the chef de cuisine is in overall charge while there may be a number of chefs de partie (in charge of their part of the kitchen) and a number of commis chefs (still learning the trade).

Qualifications and Training

No formal qualifications are necessary, but depending on what training route your employer wishes to put you through, you may need four GCSEs including English and maths. If you want to study full or part time at college before you start training with an employer, you can study for BTEC National Certificates and Diplomas in hospitality and catering; you need four GCSEs grades A to C to get a place on one of these courses. You can study for NVQ courses to levels 1, 2 and 3, either full time before you start work or part time while you are training in a kitchen. There are also apprenticeships (leading to NVQ level 2) and Advanced Apprenticeships (leading to NVQ level 3) available in food preparation and cookery. These last 12 and 24 months respectively. There are also some GNVQ level 4 courses available in kitchen and larder, confectionery and patisserie.

If you have five GCSEs and two A levels, there are several foundation degree courses available in food preparation, including professional cookery, professional patisserie, culinary arts, culinary creativity and hospitality.

Personal Qualities and Skills

You must have a real interest in food, and understand how to be imaginative and creative producing appetising food. You must be able to work under pressure, and be part of, or ultimately lead, a team. You must have a sense of what things cost and you must be well organised and able to cope with several tasks at the same time.

Starting Salary

As a junior chef you can earn between £10,000 and £12,000. A chef in charge of a section of a kitchen earns around £19,000.

Food service assistants

Waiters and waitresses, as well as serving, may cook special dishes at table or specialise in particular skills such as wine-waiting. As well as serving food and drink, they have to maintain contact with their customers; unfriendly staff may ruin the reputation of a restaurant. Promotion is to head waiter/waitress.

Hotel housekeeping

Room staff, cleaners and other support staff keep the hotel clean and comfortable. The head housekeeper is in charge of this aspect of hotel life.

Hotel reception

Receptionists receive guests, handle reservations and perform bookkeeping duties, so it is important to be good at figures, able to handle cash and use computers. Languages are an advantage. Working hours are arranged to deal with early and late arrivals and departures, so may entail shift and weekend work.

Kitchen staff

In the kitchen there are opportunities at all levels, from the chef in charge of a select restaurant to the dishwasher in a snack bar. There are also opportunities for freelance work – catering for directors' dining rooms, private parties and business lunches, for instance. It is demanding work, often in 'unsocial hours', when most people are out enjoying themselves. Some cooking can be repetitious (such as take-away menus), some creatively satisfying.

Management

Catering management can cover work in a roadside or motorway restaurant, a luxury restaurant, a hospital meals service, a snack bar, a take-away service, university and college restaurants, the armed forces, outdoor events or contract catering (providing meals and snacks to the management and staff of the contractor, for example a bank or insurance company). The manager in charge is normally responsible for budgeting, menu planning, stock monitoring, seeing that good food is served as and when it is required, often round the clock, keeping customers satisfied and supervising staff.

Large hotels have a general manager, food and beverage manager, personnel and training manager and house manager, and there may also be heads of departments or sections. There are specialised opportunities in the fields of finance, administration, food and beverage operations, accommodation services, sales and marketing product development, public relations, personnel and training.

Accommodation management is concerned with the domestic side of colleges and universities (where managers are sometimes known as bursars), hospitals, local authority day centres and residential homes, for the aged or disabled, for instance. The demanding duties of such managers include responsibility for accommodation and catering, particularly in halls of residence, which may be used as conference centres during the vacation. The work can involve personal contact with the residents (in homes, for instance, where the population is fairly permanent), or be more in the nature of housekeeping, as in hospitals where the patients are constantly changing and are not the direct concern of the domestic staff.

Qualifications and Training

There are two main routes to qualification: attending a college or university as a full-time student, or joining a training programme operated by an employer or an organisation that works with employers to provide training, such as the Hotel and Catering Training Company (HCTC). In the latter case, entrants learn on the job and attend college or a training centre on a short-course or day-release basis. Recruits on the work-based training programme will generally acquire NVQ awards. An increasing number of employers are offering Modern Apprenticeships which provide a route to higher-level technical or supervisory posts and NVQs at level 3.

Full-time courses are available in hospitality-related subjects, including HNDs, foundation degrees and degree courses.

Personal Qualities and Skills

Craft workers usually need physical fitness and stamina as well as high standards of personal hygiene. Skin complaints may disqualify entrants. Managers need to be well motivated with good interpersonal and team skills. All staff have to be prepared to work split shifts and antisocial hours.

Starting Salary

Average wages for qualified hotel and restaurant staff are £14,500. Salaries for managers start around £16,000 but vary depending on the size of the business. Many employees live in hotel accommodation and have food provided.

info

British Hospitality Association,
Queens House,
55–56 Lincoln's Inn Fields, London
WC2A 3BH; 020 7404 7744;
www.bha-online.org.uk

Hotel and Catering Training Company
(HCTC), HCTC Limited, 2nd Floor,
South Wing,
26–28 Hammersmith Grove, London
W6 7HT; 020 8735 9700;
www.hctc.co.uk

Hotel and Catering International
Management Association (HCIMA),
Trinity Court, 34 West Street, Sutton,
Surrey SM1 1SH; 020 8661 4900;
www.hcima.org.uk

People 1st: The Sector Skills Council
for the Hospitality, Leisure, Travel and
Tourism Industries, 2nd Floor,
Armstrong House, 38 Market Square,
Uxbridge, Middlesex UB8 1LH;
0870 060 2550; www.people1st.co.uk

Publican

The licensee of a pub may be a manager who is paid a salary, a lessee or tenant who rents the property from a brewer, a pub company or a free trader who owns the premises. As well as the ever-popular traditional town and country pubs there is now a wide variety of pubs ranging from theme pubs, café bars and steak bars to pubs with gourmet restaurants and full entertainment facilities. Nearly all pubs serve food and an increasing number also offer accommodation.

Qualifications and Training

To hold a licence individuals generally need a National Licensee's Certificate – an entry-level qualification available from the British Institute of Innkeeping (BII), which also offers a number of other relevant qualifications. NVQs, diplomas and degrees are available in hotel, catering and licensed retail management. Brewery companies put their managers through a comprehensive training programme. Licensees could well be running businesses grossing more than half a million pounds a year. They must know how to market their services and devise new ideas to attract customers. They must also have a good knowledge of subjects such as bookkeeping, licensing laws, hygiene, staff motivation, customer care and cellar management.

Personal Qualities and Skills

Publicans should be ambitious and able to take responsibility. They should enjoy working with people, have a customer-care focus and good interpersonal skills.

Starting Salary

Salaries range from £18,500+ with participation in bonus schemes, to £35,500+. Accommodation, lighting and heating are normally provided.

British Beer and Pub Association, Market Towers, 1 Nine Elms Lane, London SW8 5NQ; 020 7627 9191; www.beerandpub.com; e-mail: enquiries@beerandpub.com

01276 684449; fax: 01276 23045; www.bii.org or www.Barzone.co.uk (dedicated website for careers in licensed retailing); e-mail: Careers@bii.org

British Institute of Innkeeping, Wessex House, 80 Park Street, Camberley, Surrey GU15 3PL;

Pubs, Bars and Clubs Handbook, Danny Blyth (Kogan Page)

Info

HOUSING OFFICER/MANAGER

Housing officers work mainly for local authorities and housing associations, but there are also opportunities in voluntary and private housing concerns. The work covers a broad range of areas that will vary by organisation and sector. In catering for the demand for rented accommodation, the housing officer will manage and maintain properties, which includes dealing with rent arrears, reporting repairs, applications, allocations and arranging property exchanges and transfers. Housing officers often work with social and welfare agencies, and need to have a basic understanding of the different welfare benefits.

Qualifications and Training

The basic qualifications needed for professional training in housing are three GCSEs and one A level or equivalent. Students over the age of 21 who do not meet these requirements but have relevant work experience may be considered as exceptional entrants. Contact local colleges to discuss this in more detail.

Those employed in housing follow a day-release or distance-learning course to study for the Chartered Institute of Housing's professional qualification (PQ). NVQs levels 2, 3 and 4 in housing are available, and anyone working in housing is eligible to do these; NVQ level 4 allows candidates to proceed to stage 2 of the Chartered Institute of Housing's PQ.

In addition to the course, candidates also need to do the work-based Test of Professional Practice (TPP), normally completed within two years. The PQ can take three or four years to complete, depending on whether the graduate or non-graduate route is taken.

Graduates or mature entrant candidates are required to study a one-year graduate foundation course followed by a two-year professional diploma. Non-graduates are required to complete an Edexcel (BTEC)/SQA HNC in housing studies followed by a two-year professional diploma. There are also full-time degree courses and full- and part-time postgraduate diplomas. The Test of Professional Practice will still need to be undertaken with these alternative routes.

Personal Qualities and Skills

An interest in improving people's living conditions, good interpersonal skills, effective organisation skills, sensitivity to an individual's needs and flexibility are all important.

Starting Salary

Trainee posts and general enquiries and customer service jobs pay between £10,000 and £13,000. Housing officer/manager posts pay from £16,000 to £23,000 according to experience and the kind of organisation you are working for. Local authorities may pay more than employers in the voluntary sector.

info

Chartered Institute of Housing, Octavia House, Westwood Business Park, Westwood Way, Coventry CV4 8JP; 024 7685 1700; www.cih.org; e-mail: careers@cih.org

Chartered Institute of Housing in Scotland, 6 Palmerston Place, Edinburgh EH12 5AA; 0131 225 4544; www.cih.org/scotland; e-mail: scotland@cih.org

Chartered Institute of Housing Cymru, 4 Purbeck House, Lambourne Crescent, Cardiff Business Park, Llanishen,

Cardiff CF14 5GJ; 029 2076 5760; www.cih.org/home_cymru/; e-mail: cymru@cih.org

Chartered Institute of Housing in Northern Ireland, Carnmoney House, Edgewater Office Park, Dargan Road, Belfast BT3 9JQ; 028 9077 8222; www.cih.org/home_ni/; e-mail: ni@cih.org

Asset Skills, 2 The Courtyard, 48 New North Road, Exeter EX4 4EP; 01392 423 399; www.assetskills.org.uk

HUMAN RESOURCES

The field of human resources (HR) deals with all the functions in a business or organisation that relate to staff issues, such as recruitment, training and development and employment. In some businesses the term 'personnel' is used, although human resources is more commonly used now.

Human resources adviser/manager

The role of an HR professional can vary and is largely dependent on the individual organisation's needs and the value that the organisation's senior managers place on the HR function. It can include working at a strategic level on a range of HR policies, processes and practices in relation to the business needs of the organisation. More commonly, however, HR advisers work on day-to-day issues such as recruitment, contracts of employment, payroll, training, induction, disciplinary and grievance procedures, redundancy programmes, equal opportunities policies and setting up staff support systems. In large organisations, individuals may specialise in one of these areas, but in smaller companies they will deal with all aspects of the job.

Qualifications and Training

A good general education is essential, and most HR professionals will have NVQ at level 3 or above, or a first degree in an appropriate area. A range of appropriate qualifications includes NVQs in training and development, management or administration, and postgraduate qualifications are also increasingly available. The Chartered Institute of Personnel and Development (CIPD) provides a range of professional qualifications.

Personal Qualities and Skills

You must be highly organised with at least basic computer skills and the ability to interpret and produce statistics. You must have excellent 'people' skills since staff at all levels need to be able to approach and trust you. Sometimes you may have to use negotiating and persuading skills. You need to understand the business or organisation you work for at a strategic level.

Starting Salary

Salaries start at between £19,000 and £25,000, but many human resource staff attain senior management positions in their organisations.

Chartered Institute of Personnel and Development (CIPD), 151 The Broadway, London SW19 1JQ; 020 8612 6200; www.cipd.co.uk

Training officer/manager

Training officers work in medium-sized and large firms and organisations, national and local government, emergency services and voluntary organisations. They are responsible for identifying training requirements, designing training programmes, delivering training to individuals or groups and evaluating the success of training.

Qualifications and Training

This is an area of work that people move into after gaining experience in other posts or following general personnel experience. A professional qualification is advisable. The Chartered Institute of Personnel and Development (CIPD) offers a certificate in training practice for those new to the profession or with limited experience. NVQs in training and development at levels 3–5 are available.

Personal Qualities and Skills

You need to be happy and confident presenting to or facilitating groups of people. You need to be a good problem solver able to get people to change their attitudes. You must also be well organised, positive and enthusiastic. Sometimes you will have to be creative and imaginative, developing your own training materials.

Starting Salary

Salaries start at between £18,000 and £22,000, sometimes a little more in London.

info

Chartered Institute of Personnel and Development (CIPD),
151 The Broadway, London SW19 1JQ;
020 8612 6200; www.cipd.co.uk

Department for Education and Skills (DfES), Sanctuary Buildings,
Great Smith Street, London

SW1P 3BT; 0870 000 2288;
www.dfes.gov.uk

Employment National Training Organisation (ENTO), Head Office,
4th Floor, Kimberley House,
47 Vaughan Way, Leicester LE1 4SG;
0116 251 7979; www.ento.co.uk/

Want a successful career in HR?

Get a CIPD qualification!

Having a CIPD qualification is a requirement of practice for most employers. As the leading professional body in the field of personnel, training and development, we offer a range of qualifications designed to help you advance your career.

**To find out more visit
www.cipd.co.uk/membership**

I

ILLUSTRATION

see Art and Design

Medical illustrator

see Medical Illustration

INDEXER

see Publishing

INFORMATION SCIENCE

Information science is the collection, classification, storage and retrieval of information and knowledge, and the main occupations relating to this are outlined below.

Information scientist

Rather like librarians, information scientists organise, manage and develop information systems. Working with IT and paper-based systems, they store, analyse and retrieve information and distribute it to interested clients. They work for many types of organisation and with all kinds of information, including scientific, technical, legal, commercial, financial and economic. As well as cataloguing and indexing information and dealing with enquiries, information scientists often have to analyse statistics or write reports summarising highly technical or specialised information.

Qualifications and Training

This is a graduate profession and unless your degree is in librarianship or information science/management, you also have to do a one-year postgraduate qualification. Competition for places on these courses is fierce, and you need a year's experience in a library or information centre of some kind before you start your course.

Personal Qualities and Skills

You must be able to get on well with people and enjoy dealing with enquiries. It is important for you to have good IT skills: experience of handling databases is particularly useful. You should have a good memory and either a breadth of knowledge or highly specialist knowledge in a particular field such as law or science.

Starting Salary

Salaries start at between £16,000 and £21,000. You may be eligible for funding from the Arts and Humanities Research Council during your postgraduate studies.

ASLIB, The Association for Information Management, Holywell Centre, 1 Phipp Street, London EC2A 4PS; 020 7613 3031; www.aslib.co.uk

Chartered Institute of Library and Information Professionals (CILIP), 7 Ridgmount Street, London WC1E 7AE; 020 7255 0500; www.cilip.org.uk

Institute of Information Scientists, 39–41 North Road, London N7 9DP; 020 7619 0624/0625; www.iis.org.uk

Librarian/information manager

Librarians and information managers anticipate the information needs of their clients, acquire that information by the most efficient means possible on behalf of their clients, and may well analyse it and repackage it for the client. Information may come in the form of a book or journal, or may be extracted from databases in-house, on CD ROM or online. Librarians and information managers need to be able to use the internet themselves and show others how to do so.

Information needs to be organised to make it accessible to users by indexing, cataloguing and classifying. Librarians and information managers promote and exploit the library's collection to the library or information source users and assist them with any enquiries. They work in public libraries and schools, universities and colleges, in government, in the law, in hospitals, business and industry, and also in accountancy, engineering, professional and learned societies and in virtually all areas of economic activity.

Qualifications and Training

Library assistants are usually required to have four to five GCSEs or equivalent, to include English language; training is on the job. Part-time or distance-learning vocational courses leading to City & Guilds and SQA qualifications are available to library assistants in post. NVQs levels 2–4 in information and library services are also available. To qualify as a professional librarian or information officer and gain Chartered Membership of the Library Association, a degree or postgraduate qualification accredited by the association is necessary.

First degree courses, postgraduate diplomas and Master's are jointly accredited by the Library Association and the Institute of Information Scientists. A full list of the courses offered by 17 universities is available through the Library Association website. The Library Association and Institute of Information Scientists have joined together to create a new organisation, the Chartered Institute of Library and Information Professionals.

Personal Qualities and Skills

Librarians and information managers need to be well educated, with an outgoing personality, and able to communicate with people at all levels with clarity, accuracy and tact. They need intellectual curiosity, breadth of knowledge and a logical and methodical approach to seeking out, organising and presenting information. A good memory is also useful. Management skills and an interest in working with computers are important assets.

Starting Salary

Depending on age and experience, library assistants' salaries range from £9,000 to £16,500; newly qualified librarians earn from £11,900 to £16,500, and middle managers from about £17,000 to £27,000. The most senior qualified library managers of large services can earn above £32,000.

info

Chartered Institute of Library and Information Professionals, CILIP, 7 Ridgmount Street, London WC1E 7AE; 020 7255 0500; fax: 020 7255 0501; www.cilip.org.uk; e-mail: info@cilip.org.uk

ASLIB, Association for Information Management, Holywell Centre, 1 Phipp Street, London EC2A 4PS; 020 7613 3031; fax: 020 7583 8401; www.aslib.co.uk

INFORMATION AND COMMUNICATION TECHNOLOGY

Information and communication technology (ICT) has an effect on all aspects of our lives. Almost all businesses and services make use of ICT to reach more customers, offer better services, reduce costs and improve efficiency. In the airline industry, for example, ICT underpins everything from selling and allocating seats to calculating fuel and filing flight plans. In the UK alone, 1 million people work as ICT professionals: 45 per cent in the ICT industry itself, and 55 per cent working in an ICT role in other industries. The e-skills National Training Organisation (NTO) estimates that around 150,000 to 200,000 additional ICT professionals are needed every year. A career in ICT can mean working in any industry – from the media to healthcare, education to financial services. Most jobs need a combination of technical, business and personal skills and can be divided into the categories that follow.

This is such a significant, growing and developing employment sector, that it is only possible to cover some of the major job titles and work areas in the following sections. When looking for work in this field it is important to read job specs and adverts carefully and to avoid a narrow approach to looking for highly specific job titles.

Computer service technician

Technicians are employed by retailers, manufacturers and organisations that make extensive use of computers in their business. Regular upgrading of office systems means a substantial amount of time is spent on installing and checking new systems, the rest being spent on diagnosing and correcting faults.

Computer games developer

Computer games developers design interactive games for PCs and for games consoles. They design new games and develop and update existing ones. Development of games is very much a team effort, where professionals with different areas of expertise, eg, animation, design, graphic and sound engineering all have to work together. The starting point is the original idea or concept, with all these aspects of the technology contributing to a successful finished title. There are now some degree courses available in computer games development.

Database administration

Organisations obtain and store information about their customers, accounts, orders or stock levels on computers. The database manager takes responsibility for maintaining these and for security, access and the legal use of information held.

Hardware engineer

Engineers design, develop and undertake research into computers and the computerised components of cars and appliances. They are involved in manufacture, installation and testing. As well as dealing with engineering issues they need to be aware of safety, efficiency and environmental factors.

Come for the experience.

With competition for the best jobs and graduate schemes so fierce, students are being advised to get ahead of the game – and get some work experience under their belts before looking for employment. Not only will it give you a clear indication of what working in a given industry is like, it also sends out the right signals to potential employers in terms of your commitment to and interest in their field. Along the way you'll also gain new skills and build relationships with influential colleagues. And at the end of a succession of holiday placements, you'll be able to command higher salaries than the people who didn't go down the work-experience route.

Take Chris Brook. Back in 2001, Chris, now aged 23, worked for RM during his summer break from a degree in Aerospace Engineering. Currently a permanent member of staff specialising in programming, Chris's experience of assisting in RM's HR department proved invaluable. He was invited to work in Credit Control for the next three summers in a row. Having liked what he'd seen of the company, he applied for a place on the RM graduate scheme – and was accepted.

"I was able to build up valuable contacts and experience in a field I was interested in," Chris says. 'I wouldn't be where I am today if I hadn't taken a proactive approach to my job search.' RM's Graduate Recruitment Manager, Justina Moores, couldn't agree more. She stresses that while working hard at university is important, you shouldn't lose sight of the reason you're studying in the first place.

'You're at university to get on to the career ladder by making yourself more employable to recruiters. That way, you'll have a better chance of getting the job of your dreams in the future.'

A real role
from day two.

(We'll give you a chance to settle in first.)

We're the UK's leading provider of IT for education, and are well known for our friendly and supportive culture that allows graduates to thrive from the outset. We're not all talk either. Join us as a graduate and on top of the chance to get stuck into some real projects as soon as you arrive, you'll benefit from a starting salary of £22-£25k and excellent rewards, including a laptop and performance-related bonus scheme.

Whatever your role you'll need to combine a broad blend of skills. While those taking on IT-specific roles should be able to demonstrate technical ability, all our graduates will need fantastic communication skills, excellent problem-solving abilities and a strong customer focus, along with the energy, enthusiasm and determination to succeed. Our training and progression opportunities are first-rate too. In fact our CEO, Tim Pearson, was once taking his intrepid first steps as a graduate himself.

As well as our Head Office in Abingdon, Oxfordshire, we have opportunities in our Glasgow office. So if you have a 2:1 or above, at least 240 UCAS points and would like to find out more, visit

www.rmgraduates.com

Help desk advisers

Help desk advisers give advice to customers by telephone, by e-mail and by online diagnosis. They are the first line of support for customers who are experiencing difficulties with hardware and software. They work with their customers to identify faults and suggest solutions. If they cannot help the customer to solve the problem, they may refer them to a second line of support. They work for retailers, manufacturers, broadband providers and in-house for all kinds of large organisations.

IT research and development

Those who work in this sector create new technologies or new products. This could mean researching new approaches to mobile communications, or developing software packages. Job titles in this area include software developer, product tester and technical author.

IT sales and marketing

This covers promoting or selling products, services and IT solutions. You may be assigned to a particular customer or group of customers, or specialise in particular products or services.

IT services

This covers a range of customer-facing roles and could include developing websites, designing and installing IT systems for customers, supporting customers with software or hardware problems, and managing projects. Job titles include software support professional, technical architect and hardware engineer.

Multimedia programmer

Multimedia programmers write computer programs that draw together text, sound, graphics, digital/analogue photographs, 2D/3D modelling, animation, video, information and virtual reality in order to produce a multimedia product. Multimedia products are designed to work with the internet, interactive TV, CD ROMs, information kiosks, DVDs, computer games consoles and WAP mobile phones.

Network engineer

A network is a system of computers and other communication equipment linked to exchange information. This could be used to enable staff to share information through a company intranet or for global communication via the internet. Network engineers advise clients on options and benefits, as well as installing and testing equipment. They also diagnose faults and maintain the hardware, software and cabling systems.

Programmers

These are the people who write software such as operating systems. They may be employed by software manufacturers or in the computer departments of large organisations. As well as creating new programs they can be involved in identifying bugs in existing programs, modifying them, testing new programs and preparing user manuals.

Software engineers

They have a similar role to that of programmers but use this in technical and engineering settings. They may, for example, work on systems for contact centres or air traffic control. Most have a degree in software engineering or a related computer science. Many universities ask for maths A level or equivalent for entry to such courses. As most commercial and manufacturing functions now have established IT systems, the work undertaken by software engineers has shifted emphasis from creating new systems to using existing software and devising appropriate interfaces to integrate it with new products.

Systems analysts

Systems analysts work on delivering the best IT solutions for an organisation's needs. They examine how and where computerised systems would be of benefit, assess the hardware needed and look at the most cost-effective solutions. Systems analysts then work with programmers and supervise software production.

Systems support staff

Systems support staff work for suppliers of software and hardware, internet service providers or the computer departments of large companies. They provide technical support to users, often via the phone or e-mail. The work involves establishing what the problem is, helping the client put things right or deciding to refer the problem to other specialists. It requires detailed product knowledge as well as extreme patience and excellent communication skills. Training is often on the job, with entrants coming from a variety of backgrounds in which they have been able to demonstrate high levels of computer literacy.

Trainers

Software packages are increasingly complex and users require training to get the best out of them. Trainers are employed by software vendors, training consultancies and user companies for their own staff. Trainers need to be familiar with the packages at all levels, and have excellent communication and teaching skills. They may also be required to develop and write materials.

Web designers

(*see also* Art and Design)

Web designers design and plan websites either for their own company or for clients. The complexity of the task varies according to the nature of the site, and can include extensive use of multimedia or implementing secure systems for financial transactions. A considerable amount of time is spent testing sites and checking they are user-friendly. Once the site is working properly, designers upload it to a server and may be responsible for registering it with search engines in terms of both content and design.

Designers need an in-depth knowledge of the internet and must be up to date with technological developments. Many designers work on a freelance basis. The availability of jobs in this area is decreasing as increasingly sophisticated software packages are making web design less of a specialist area.

Qualifications and Training

Many employers set their own entry requirements, but are increasingly asking for academic or vocational qualifications from NVQs to degrees. Applicants for posts may be asked to take aptitude tests to assess their numeracy, logic, accuracy, thinking speed and verbal reasoning. Systems analysts and programmers are generally expected to be graduates. Entry to computer science degrees is normally with 2–3 A levels or equivalent, including maths. Web designers need knowledge of HTML and Java as well as familiarity with web design software such as Dreamweaver and Flash. Technicians and network engineers usually have a related National Diploma or vendor qualifications.

There are a large number of computer-related courses, and entry requirements vary according to the nature of the course. A growing number of foundation degrees with flexible entry requirements are becoming available. Product-specific and professional qualifications are offered by companies such as Microsoft, Cisco and Novell and by professional bodies such as the British Computer Society, the Help Desk Institute and the Institute for the Management of Information Systems.

Employment-based training opportunities include Modern Apprenticeships for school leavers and Graduate Apprenticeships for those from non-IT disciplines. Many companies run their own programmes as well as sending trainees on relevant external courses.

Not sure of your next step?

Instead of contemplating your future, why not take one of Pitman Training's office, IT or business skills courses?

No one has helped more people gain valuable business skills than Pitman Training. And it's nothing like school!

Whether you are a first-time job seeker or looking for a better career direction, a Pitman Training course will really make the difference.

You'll give yourself the opportunity to start earning and learning without delay, gain valuable on-the-job experience and be able to make much more informed decisions about your future job direction.

If you have recently left school or college, you'll find the Pitman Training system a breeze. No stress, no worry, no homework.

You work at your own pace in one of our comfortable premises; you choose your own working hours and are guided by experienced tutors.

You progress through your personalised workbook, one module at a time, learning the right things in the right order, practicing them, and then moving on logically as you master each part of the course. It's a formula that works like magic.

There are 90 Pitman Training Centres throughout the UK and Republic of Ireland offering more than 250 courses covering office, IT and business skills. Among the most popular are Microsoft Word, Microsoft Excel, web design, shorthand, Sage Payroll, IT technical courses and prestigious diplomas.

Your only problem now is choosing – which is where the experienced staff at each Pitman Training Centre can advise you. You can reach your nearest centre by calling **0800 220 454** (or **ROI 1800 532 632**) quoting reference "**2007A-Z**".

Personal Qualities and Skills

The balance of skills that are most important varies between some of the above roles, but excellent problem solving, analytical and technical expertise and the willingness to develop with technological advances are all essential, though to different degrees. Being able to work under pressure, be part of a team and communicate well, especially to less technically trained colleagues, are equally important.

Starting Salary

An industry that encompasses so many jobs offers a wide range of starting salaries, reflecting qualifications, experience and market needs. Database managers start on between £15,000 and £21,000, database support staff around £15,000 to £18.000. Programmers start on between £19,000 and £27,000. Network engineers and systems administrators start on a similar range. Sales jobs often include an element of commission, and some roles offer overtime, shift allowances and extra payment for working at weekends.

e-skills UK, 1 Castle Lane, London SW1E 6DR; 020 7963 8920; fax: 020 7592 9138; www.e-skills.com; e-mail: info@e-skills.com

British Computer Society, 1st Floor, Block D, North Star House, North Star Avenue, Swindon, Wiltshire SN2 1FA; 0845 300 4417; www.bcs.org; e-mail: bcshq@hq.bcs.org.uk

Help Desk Institute, 21 High Street, Green Street Green, Orpington, Kent BR6 6BG; 01689 889100; fax: 01689 889227; www.hdi-europe.com; e-mail: support@hdi-europe.com

Institute of Analysts and Programmers, Charles House, 36 Culmington Road, Ealing, London W13 9NH; 020 8567 2118; www.iap.org.uk; e-mail: dg@iap.org.uk

Institute for the Management of Information Systems, 5 Kingfisher House, New Mill Road, Orpington, Kent BR5 3QG; 0700 002 3456; fax: 0700 002 3023; www.imis.org.uk; e-mail: central@imis.org.uk

British Interactive Media Association, Briarlea House, Southend Road, South Green, Billericay CM11 2PR; www.bima.co.uk

Careers and Jobs in IT (Kogan Page)

INSURANCE

Insurance is a very significant employer in the UK. Many large insurance companies, providing insurance cover for every kind of item, situation and mishap, are based in the UK or have large operations here. There are many different career pathways open to people who have an interest in working with people and with financial information.

Agent

An agent is really a salesperson, working for an insurance company. The agent explains and tries to sell insurance products of all kinds to customers, both private individuals and large and small businesses.

Broker

Insurance brokers are the link between customers and insurance providers. They have a detailed knowledge of insurance products, whether this is life assurance, motor insurance, buildings insurance or any other specific field. They do not work for one insurance company – they work for customers trying to find the most appropriate insurance cover at the best possible price.

Claims administrator

Claims administrators, sometimes known as claims settlers or claims technicians, deal with policy holders who are making claims. Administrators issue forms, explain procedures to customers, gather further information and issue payments where claims are simple. If there is some dispute or the claim is very complex, they may have to refer it to their managers. Claims administrators work for brokers or for insurance companies. They normally specialise in a particular type of insurance, eg motor or household.

Claims inspector

When anyone makes a claim on their insurance, the claims inspector assesses the claim to insure that it is truthful and also to check that the insurance company is liable for payment. Inspectors carry out detailed inspections of damaged goods or property and their work often involves interviewing claimants either in person or by telephone.

Loss adjuster

Loss adjusters carry out very similar work to that of the claims inspector – the key difference is that they are independent. They investigate claims on behalf of insurance companies. They assess the causes of loss or damage, and make sure that the insurance claim is valid and covered by the policy. They can deal with all kinds of insurance claim, including damage by fire, flooding, theft or accident.

Risk surveyor/analyst

Insurance risk surveyors, also known as insurance risk analysts, work for general insurance companies, brokers, or firms of specialist surveyors. Their main role is to advise about risk, based on technical knowledge, experience and good practice. They visit sites such as commercial premises or engineering works and produce detailed reports on any particular risks associated with the site. They can also advise people on how to reduce the impact of these risks.

Technician

Insurance technicians provide all the day-to-day administrative and clerical back-up that keeps the insurance industry going. In fact, they are often referred to as insurance clerks or insurance administrators. The work includes sending out routine correspondence such as policy renewal reminders, entering data onto computer systems or sending out marketing information. Exact tasks and responsibilities vary according to what kind of insurance organisation and for what department they are working.

Underwriter

Underwriters assess the financial risk involved in insuring particular items, premises or projects. They calculate the prices for insurance premiums, aiming to fix on a price which will be profitable for the insurer but also competitive for potential customers.

Qualifications and Training

Insurance claims administrators and technicians usually need four or five GCSEs grades A–C, including English and maths. Exact requirements vary from firm to firm. For brokers and underwriters, different firms set their own entry requirements. These vary from five GCSEs grades A–C to two A levels or a degree in a mathematical subject. Many firms like you to have had some experience in insurance or other financial work. Study for examinations from the Chartered Insurance Institute while working is usual and takes two to five years depending on the level you are working towards.

Brokers are regulated by the Financial Services Authority (FSA) and need to meet the FSA's training and competency standards. Brokers who deal in long-term investments such as pensions and life assurance need an approved qualification from the FSA.

Loss adjusters normally have several years' experience in the insurance industry or in other professional fields such as accountancy, law or surveying.

Personal Qualities and Skills

People working in insurance must have excellent written and spoken English, be able to talk to people and write concise accurate reports. Some roles require good negotiating skills and the ability to deal with sensitive situations. Some degree of numeracy skill is important for all jobs. To be an underwriter, you need to be able to analyse complex statistical information.

Starting Salary

New entrants to the industry start on between £12,000 and £15,000 (more for very large firms or on graduate training schemes). With two to three years' experience salaries rise to between £20,000 and £35,000. Senior managers or loss adjusters with many years experience can earn £50,000 to £70,000.

Financial Services Authority,
25 The North Colonnade,
Canary Wharf, London E14 5HS;
020 7066 1000; www.fsa.gov.uk

Lloyds, One Lime Street, London
EC3M 7HA; 020 7327 1000;
www.lloyds.com

Insurance Careers;
www.insurancecareers.cii.co.uk

Chartered Insurance Institute,
20 Aldermanbury, London EC2V 7HY;
020 8989 8464; www.cii.co.uk

Financial Services Skills Council,
51 Gresham Street, London
EC2V 7HQ; 020 7216 7366;
www.fssc.org.uk

INTERIOR DECORATOR

see Construction

CITB-Construction Skills, Bircham Newton, King's Lynn, Norfolk PE31 6RH;
01485 577577; fax: 01485 577793; www.constructionskills.net

INTERIOR DESIGNER/ INSCAPE DESIGNER

Interior designers work for commercial organisations as well as undertaking private commissions. They are responsible for the interiors of buildings (whereas an architect is responsible for its shell). Interior design can cover materials for floors and ceilings, fitments and fittings, and colour schemes, along with electrical and spatial planning. The commercial organisations may be offices, hotels, pubs, stores or banks. Interior designers may work with architects, have their own consultancies, or work in design units within large organisations.

Qualifications and Training

Most interior designers have a degree in one of the following subjects: fine art, fashion and textile design, product design, interior design or graphic design. It is possible to get into this work without a degree if you have really demonstrable creative flair or a lot of relevant experience. Most training is on-the-job, working closely with more experienced and established designers. It can be valuable to do short courses on photography, desktop publishing and new product knowledge, in order to remain current.

Personal Qualities and Skills

As well as an eye for colour and a feel for fabric, you need considerable technical and product knowledge and technical drawing skills, either on paper or with computer aided design (CAD). You need to be able to work closely with other people and, if you work freelance, you should be confident enough to promote your own work.

Starting Salary

Salaries start at between £16,000 and £21,000, but can go much higher if you have established your reputation. If you work freelance you can charge £30 or more an hour. What you can charge depends upon geographical location and upon personal recommendations of your work.

The Chartered Society of Designers (CSD), 5 Bermondsey Exchange, 179–181 Bermondsey Street, London SE1 3UW; 020 7357 8088; www.csd.org.uk

Crafts Council, 44a Pentonville Road, Islington, London N1 9BY; 020 7278 7700; www.craftscouncil.org.uk

The Design Trust, 9 Burgess Hill, London NW2 2BY; 020 7435 4348; www.thedesigntrust.co.uk

The British Interior Design Association (BIDA), 3/18 Chelsea Harbour Design Centre, Lots Road, London SW10 0XE; www.bida.org

J

JEWELLERY

see Crafts

JOURNALISM

Journalism is the profession that writes and produces material for print, broadcast and digital media. Newspapers, magazines, television, radio and the internet offer myriad opportunities for journalists. Journalists can develop specialist fields or work in a general capacity. They can work as salaried employees or as freelancers, for national or local press.

Editor

The editor of a publication is responsible for its policy, content and the appointment and organisation of staff. An editor will prepare schedules for content and will build up key relationships with external bodies. An editor of a publication will become the spokesperson for the title and will be expected to speak at conferences and to comment publicly on issues of importance. The editor works closely with the different groups within the team including writers, production staff, advertising sales team, marketing and the publisher (*see also* Publishing). The editor will hold regular editorial meetings to discuss current work and to plan forthcoming features. The editor will also oversee the editorial budget. Section editors (newspapers and magazines) specialise in specific areas and run their own teams of journalists and commission articles for their sections. Typical newspaper sections include home affairs, foreign affairs, health, media, education and travel.

Qualifications and Training

Most editors have come from a background in journalism and have worked their way up to the job, and so may have journalism qualifications.

Personal Qualities and Skills

Editors coordinate the editorial team and need to have good leadership and managerial skills. Financial planning is also a key element to the job and being able to manage financial resources is important. The editor's role as a spokesperson for the publication requires confident communication skills and the ability to speak in public and in the media.

Starting Salary

Editors of trade magazines will earn £20,000 rising to £80,000+ for national newspapers.

Info

Association of British Editors, 49 Frederick Road, Birmingham B15 1HN; 0121 455 7949; fax: 0121 454 6187

Newspaper Society, 74–77 Great Russell Street, London WC1B 3DA; 020 7636 7014; fax: 020 7631 5119; www.newspapersoc.org.uk

National Union of Journalists, Headland House, 308–312 Gray's Inn Road, London WC1X 8DP; 020 7278 7916; www.nujtraining.org.uk

Careers and Jobs in the Media (Kogan Page)

Journalist

Reporters find, research and write news articles and features for newspapers, magazines, special-interest periodicals, news agencies, radio, television and the internet (*see* Broadcast Journalist). Most reporters start out on local papers where they cover a mix of stories from weddings to council meetings. Local reporters are generally expected to multi-skill and might be expected to write the local news or features, sub-edit or take photographs. They work irregular hours and must be able to produce accurate, interesting and readable copy quickly, often in noisy offices or even public places. Editors look for trainees with an interest in current affairs and events, an accessible writing style and a good use of grammar, and an understanding of the role of local newspaper within its community. Good time management and being able to work under pressure are also important qualities as journalists have to work to strict deadlines.

Inexperienced journalists are expected to work their way up, starting with more routine jobs. Regional and local newspapers recruit trainee reporters and photographers under a training contract and some newspaper groups run trainee schemes. These schemes are open to school or college leavers who have not taken a specialist university or college course. Applications should be made direct to the editor for traineeships. Direct entrants to these schemes will be expected to attend block release or day release courses and to sit the National Council for the Training of Journalists (NCTJ) National Certificate or a National (Scottish) Vocational Qualification.

National papers generally employ reporters with some experience, and will look to journalists who have had experience on local newspapers. Trade magazine experience, where a knowledge of a specialist area has been developed, is also a route to entry in the national press. Occasionally national newspapers do advertise for trainee recruits but these opportunities are rare.

Trade magazines are also a route into the industry. Many magazines are produced on a monthly or fortnightly basis and specialise in particular subjects. Reporters on trade magazines are able to develop a specialist subject that can then be used to transfer to writing for national newspapers or to develop into a freelance career.

Experienced journalists have the opportunity to become feature writers or columnists for national newspapers. Feature writers suggest subjects for research, and produce longer than average articles dealing with topics not necessarily of current news value but of general interest. Feature writers will have developed an expertise or specialism within the subject they write about, and may have come originally not from a journalistic background but from the specialist area on which they write. Columnists often write about subjects from a personal point of view. Feature writers and columnists tend to be freelance writers working for a number of different newspapers, magazines and publishers, and will also work in broadcast media.

Qualifications and Training

Most journalists begin their career by serving for two or three years on a provincial newspaper. Minimum entry requirements are five GCSEs and two A level passes, but more than 65 per cent of all entrants are now graduates. There are also a number of degree courses in journalism, but many entrants have a degree in other disciplines plus on-the-job or postgraduate training.

Approximately 1,000 school/college leavers undertake NCTJ pre-entry courses each year at some 30 colleges/universities accredited by the NCTJ. Direct entrants must complete a two-year on-the-job training period that includes either a 12-week block release or day release to an approved course.

info

British Association of Journalists, 89 Fleet Street, London EC4Y 1DH; 020 7353 3003; www.bajunion.org.uk

National Council for the Training of Journalists (NCTJ), NCTJ Training Ltd, Latton Bush Centre, Southern Way, Harlow, Essex CM18 7BL; 01279 430009; fax: 01279 430008; www.nctj.com; e-mail: info@nctj.com

National Union of Journalists, Headland House, 308–312 Gray's Inn Road, London WC1X 8DP; 020 7278 7916; www.nujtraining.org.uk

Newspaper Society, 74–77 Great Russell Street, London WC1B 3DA; 020 7636 7014; fax: 020 7631 5119; www.newspapersoc.org.uk

Periodicals Training Council, Periodical Publishers Association, Queens House, 28 Kingsway, London WC2B 6JR; 020 7404 4166; fax: 020 7404 4167; www.ppa.co.uk; e-mail: info@ppa.co.uk

Careers and Jobs in the Media (Kogan Page)

Personal Qualities and Skills

Journalists must possess powers of self-expression, observation, accuracy, patience and tact. They must take pride in their work, be resourceful, willing to travel and to work under pressure and irregular hours; stamina is required, as is confidence, great curiosity and the ability to put people at their ease. It helps to be able to write fast in longhand; word processing and internet research skills are also important.

Starting Salary

Salaries vary greatly. Trainees on a small weekly paper earn about £10,000, more in London. Experienced journalists earn £18,000–£23,000+.

Broadcast journalist

Broadcast journalists work in radio, television and online. Unlike print journalists, almost all broadcast journalists take a postgraduate pre-entry course. Some journalists still make the transition to broadcasting from newspapers but it is increasingly regarded as a specialist branch of the profession in its own right. As in print, broadcast journalists will need to have good communication skills, an enquiring mind, a knowledge of current events and a sense of what makes a news story. The ability to speak clear, standard English is important. Both the BBC and ITN run traineeships for entrants into broadcast journalism.

Experience in radio journalism can be found in hospital, community and college radio. This can be used as evidence of interest and experience when applying to courses – many postgraduate courses will require a recorded news story as part of their application procedure.

Qualifications and Training

Broadcast journalists tend to be graduates or postgraduates in broadcast, bi-media, multimedia TV or online journalism. The Broadcast Journalism Training Council accredits courses that cover radio, television and online journalism. The BBC and ITN courses are fiercely competitive but will cover key aspects of broadcast journalism.

Personal Qualities and Skills

You need a real interest in and good knowledge of current affairs or particular topics such as sport or economics, depending what you are talking about. You have to be able to analyse information and present it in a way that can be clearly understood. Your speaking voice should be clear and authoritative, though regional accents are perfectly acceptable. You should be able to keep calm and think on your feet.

Starting Salary

Starting salaries range from £12,000 to £20,000; this wide range reflects the difference between working for a small local radio station or one of the large news and broadcasting organisations. With experience you can earn up to £45,000.

info

BBC Training; 0870 122 0216;
fax: 0870 122 0145;
www.bbctraining.co.uk;
e-mail: training@bbc.co.uk

BECTU (the independent union for
those working in broadcasting),
373–377 Clapham Road, London
SW9 9BT; 020 7346 0900;
www.bectu.org.uk;
e-mail: info@bectu.org.uk

Broadcast Journalism Training
Council, www.bjtc.org.uk

CSV Training, 237 Pentonville Road,
London N1 9NJ; 020 7278 6601;
www.csv.org.uk/csv/Media;
e-mail: info@csv.org.uk

Skillset (The Sector Skills Council for
the Audio Visual Industries),
Prospect House,
80–110 New Oxford Street, London
WC1A 1HB; 020 7520 5757;
www.skillset.org;
e-mail: info@skillset.org

UK Association of Online Publishers,
Queens House, 28 Kingsway, London
WC2B 6JR; 020 7400 7510;
fax: 020 7404 4167;
www.ukaop.org.uk

Careers and Jobs in the Media
(Kogan Page)

Press photographer

A small number of trainee photographers are recruited into the press each year.
Press photographers work in newspapers, magazines and online, although
many now work in a freelance capacity. Press photographers can specialise in
areas such as sport or fashion. News photographers will work closely with journalists and editors.

Qualifications and Training

Trainee photographers are expected to gain a National or Scottish Vocational
Qualification or national Certificate in Press Photography during work experience. Direct entrants are expected to have two years' relevant experience or
taken an education course in photography.

info

Association of Photographers,
81 Leonard Street, London
EC2A 4QS; 020 7739 6669;
fax: 020 7739 8787;
www.the-aop.org;
e-mail: general@aophoto.co.uk

British Institute of Professional
Photography, Fox Talbot House,
Ware, Herts SG12 9HN;
01920 464011; fax: 01920 487056;
www.bipp.com

Newspaper Society,
74–77 Great Russell Street, London
WC1B 3DA; 020 7636 7014;
fax: 020 7631 5119;
www.newspapersoc.org.uk

National Union of Journalists,
Headland House,
308–312 Gray's Inn Road, London
WC1X 8DP; 020 7278 7916;
www.nujtraining.org.uk

Careers and Jobs in the Media
(Kogan Page)

Personal Qualities and Skills

Press photographers work under pressure and independently. They need good physical health and the ability to work unsocial hours, as well as technical and creative skills.

Starting Salary

£12,000 rising to £40,000+ for experienced photographers.

Sub-editor

Sub-editors are journalists who work for national daily or weekly newspapers, local and regional newspapers and magazines of every kind. They process all the copy that will appear in their publication to ensure that copy is accurate, free of typographical errors and spelling mistakes, makes sense and reads well. Sub-editors take the stories written by journalists and reporters and rewrite copy to make it fit the 'house-style', adhere to word counts and remain within the law. The sub-editor is responsible for putting the story on the page and is often responsible for designing and laying out pages. Sub-editors write headlines, picture captions and summaries.

Qualifications and Training

Many sub-editors will have been trained as journalists and then specialised. The NCTJ runs short courses and distance learning qualifications for sub-editors. The Periodical Publishers Association also runs courses for sub-editors.

Personal Qualities and Skills

Sub-editors must be meticulous in their work. They are required to make quick decisions and to have the confidence to rewrite or cut the work of others. They must be able to work under pressure and to meet deadlines.

Starting Salary

Starting salaries in local or regional press from £12,000 rising to £35,000 for senior sub-editors.

Web content editor

Web content editors research, write, edit, proof and update material on websites. This material includes images as well as text. Just like any magazine or newspaper journalist or editor, web content editors try to ensure that what they produce is appropriate to their target readership. Web content might include local and national news, opinion, information about products and services, factual information or entertainment. Editors work closely with technical staff who develop and design websites. Web content editors also liaise closely with the clients for whom they are writing, editing and updating material.

Qualifications and Training

There is no one route for entry into this work. Many web content editors have worked as journalists. Some have worked in IT or marketing and many have considerable experience in the profession or subject with which they are going to work. Knowledge of desktop publishing and photo imaging packages can greatly increase your employability.

Personal Qualities and Skills

You need excellent writing skills, with a good grasp of English grammar. You should be creative, but not lose sight of the importance of detail and accuracy. You should be able to write to very specific word counts or house styles and you should be able to communicate really well with other members of your team.

Starting Salary

New entrants earn between £18,000 and £23,000. With three or four years' experience, and depending on the size of the organisation you work for, this can rise to between £25,000 and £33,000.

info

National Council for the Training of Journalists, Latton Bush Centre, Southern Way, Harlow, Essex CM18 7BL; 01279 430009; www.nctj.com; e-mail: info@nctj.com

National Union of Journalists, Headland House, 308–312 Gray's Inn Road, London WC1X 8DP; 020 7278 7916; www.nujtraining.org.uk

Periodicals Training Council, Periodical Publishers Association,

Queens House, 28 Kingsway, London WC2B 6JR; 020 7404 4166; fax: 020 7404 4167; www.ppa.co.uk; e-mail: info@ppa.co.uk

Society for Editors and Proofreaders, Riverbank House, 1 Putney Bridge Approach, Fulham, London SW6 3JD; 020 7736 3278; fax: 020 7736 3318; www.sfep.org.uk; e-mail: administration@sfep.org.uk

Careers and Jobs in the Media (Kogan Page)

LABORATORY TECHNICIAN

Assisting with research, helping to diagnose diseases, measuring pollution levels and developing new products – these are some of the tasks laboratory technicians help to undertake. Laboratory assistants ensure that equipment is clean and in working order. They set up experiments and investigations and record data. They may also be involved in stock control, monitoring and ordering chemicals, equipment and other supplies. Laboratory technicians working in education help school and college students to use equipment safely and record results correctly, and they may be involved in demonstrating how to conduct experiments. Laboratory technicians work in education, in medicine, in the pharmaceutical industry, in food science and in research laboratories of every kind.

Qualifications and Training

Most employers expect you to have at least four GCSEs grades A to C including science, maths and English. A BTEC qualification in science or applied science is also an accepted entry qualification. There is a trend towards employers taking on more applicants with A levels and degrees. Most training is on the job, but many employers provide the opportunity for technicians to attain NVQ levels 2, 3 and 4 in laboratory science. Employers also send technicians on regular updating courses on health and safety, risk assessment and on learning to use specific pieces of equipment or computer systems.

Personal Qualities and Skills

As a laboratory assistant you need to have good practical skills, including manual dexterity, and you need to pay great attention to detail, adopting a methodical approach to your work. You should enjoy working in a team, but also be prepared to take on particular responsibility. In education, there is a lot of contact with teachers and students, so you need to be a good communicator.

Starting Salary

Salaries for new technicians range from £13,000 to £16,000; £20,000 to £22,000 for a senior technician. Salaries tend to be higher in the private sector, particularly in the pharmaceutical industry.

info

The Association for Science
Education, College Lane, Hatfield,
Hertfordshire AL10 9AA;
01727 283000; www.ase.org.uk

CLEAPSS School Science Services,
Brunel University, Uxbridge UB8 3PH;
01895 251496; www.cleapss.org.uk

SEMTA: The Sector Skills Council for
Science, 14 Upton Road, Watford,
Hertfordshire WD18 0JT;
01923 238441; www.semta.org.uk

LAND AND PROPERTY

The land and property sector covers a wide range of occupations all to do with
the management, sale and purchase of land and buildings.

Estate agent

Estate agents are responsible for the sale, letting and management of any kind of
property – factories, shops, offices and farms as well as residential property. In
many cases, they also deal with valuation and survey work, and offer other services
such as auctioneering and financial services advice. Large firms provide a wide
range of these services through specialist departments employing qualified professionals, particularly in the area of surveying and valuation. Dedicated sales staff
fulfil the role of property negotiators, and in the majority of smaller firms with just
one or two branches, a combination of these functions will be found.

Qualifications and Training

The principal professional bodies are the National Association of Estate Agents
(NAEA) and the Royal Institution of Chartered Surveyors (RICS). Membership of
RICS is normally attained through graduate entry coupled with a period of accred-
ited practical training. NVQs in Residential Estate Agency and Lettings and
Management are available through the NAEA's National Assessment Centre. The
NAEA also offers examination-based, nationally recognised qualifications in
Residential Sales (CREA), Lettings and Management (CRLM) and Commercial and
Business Transfer (CCBT). These qualifications also provide the route to member-
ship of the Association at the senior level of Fellow.

Professional qualifications are an asset and becoming more sought-after by
employers. However, anyone can set up in business as an estate agent unless
they have been banned from doing so by the Director General of Fair Trading,
are bankrupt or guilty of a range of other criminal offences proscribed under the
1979 Estate Agents Act.

Established firms will very often provide opportunities for unqualified beginners within the field of property negotiation, but at the same time encourage the
attainment of a more formal qualification.

Personal Qualities and Skills

For most people the purchase or sale of a house is the biggest financial transaction they will ever make, and there are bound to be attendant worries and problems. Estate agents must be able to deal with their clients' problems sympathetically, but in a businesslike way. In addition to being numerate and literate, they should possess an outgoing personality, coupled with the energy and enthusiasm to work in a competitive, fast-moving environment where customer care is of paramount importance.

Starting Salary

School leavers with A levels start on £10,000 to £12,000 – graduates or mature entrants on between £14,000 and £20,000. A substantial part of your salary is made up from commission on sales or lettings of property. A basic income is often guaranteed for the first six months of employment, but after this you have to meet specific sales targets to achieve your predicted salary. Performance-related pay is very much the norm in this profession.

National Association of Estate Agents, Arbon House, 21 Jury Street, Warwick CV34 4EH; 01926 496800; fax: 01926 400953; www.naea.co.uk; e-mail: info@naea.co.uk

Asset Skills, 2 The Courtyard, 48 New North Road, Exeter, Devon EX4 4EP; 01392 423399; www.assetskills.org

Royal Institution of Chartered Surveyors, 12 Great George Street, Parliament Square, London SW1P 3AD; 0870 333 1600; www.rics.org/com; e-mail: contactrics@rics.org

Info

Gamekeeper

Gamekeepers work on large country estates for private landlords, management firms and private syndicates who wish to organise a shoot. They rear the game birds and fish, and protect them from poachers and predators. They must ensure that the proper environment for the game is maintained, and on shooting days, organise the beaters.

Qualifications and Training

There are no formal entry qualifications, but gamekeepers must have a driving licence, be good at handling a dog, and suitable to apply for a shotgun licence. There are part-time and full-time City & Guilds and BTEC courses in gamekeeping, and gamekeeping and countryside management. Some of these courses may set specific entry requirements. The training is on the job and most gamekeepers start as an assistant or under keeper.

Personal Qualities and Skills

You have to love being outside in all weathers and have a real interest in nature. You need to be very practical, good with your hands and physically fit. It is important that you are very observant, both of animal and plant life and of safety issues. You are on your own for a great deal of the time, but you must be able to communicate well with other people when shoots or other events are taking place.

Starting Salary

Salaries start at between £13,000 and £16,500. Many jobs include free or subsidised accommodation, and clothing allowances or other benefits.

info

Game Conservancy Trust, Fordingbridge, Hampshire SP6 1EF; 01425 652381; www.gct.org.uk

British Deer Society, Fordingbridge, Hampshire SP6 1EF; 01425 655434; www.bds.org.uk

Lantra, Lantra House, Stoneleigh Park, Coventry, Warwickshire CV8 2LG; 0845 707 8007; www.lantra.co.uk

Home inspector

From June 2007 everyone selling his or her home on the open market in England or Wales will have to produce a special home information pack. As a result of this legislation, a new career for home inspectors has been created. Home inspectors will be trained and qualified to produce energy rating certificates and general home condition reports, which will form essential parts of these home information packs. Home inspectors will visit homes to carry out their inspections and then write up appropriate reports.

Qualifications and Training

The first home inspectors are likely to be people who already have qualifications in surveying or building technology. The Association of Home Inspectors is developing training in six regions: Bath, Cambridge, Huddersfield, Newcastle, Northampton and Southampton, and this will widen access to training. This career is still in its development stage.

Personal Qualities and Skills

Home inspectors must be good at dealing with people, tactful and truthful. They need good practical skills in taking measurements and a real understanding of construction, with the ability to assess the significance of defects and problems. They will have to be able to write clear, concise and truthful reports.

Starting Salary

There is no available salary data as yet, but given that for most people home inspection will be a second career, salaries are likely to be in the region £20,000 to £35,000.

Home Information Careers;
www.hicareers.co.uk

Home Inspection Information Packs;
www.homeinformationpacks.gov.uk

Asset Skills, 2 The Courtyard,
48 New North Road, Exeter, Devon
EX4 4EP; helpline: 0800 056 7160;
www.assetskills.org

Land agent

Land agents work for estate owners and for large institutional owners. Their work overlaps to some extent with that of agricultural surveyors in that they are both concerned with the use and development of land, and may advise owners on agricultural methods, forestry, accountancy, building or improving of farm buildings. In addition the land agent may be responsible for stocking and for employing estate staff, as well as attending to the owner's personal business matters.

Qualifications and Training

Formal qualifications are not always necessary for a land agent who is employed by a private owner. However, it is advisable to become professionally qualified as a surveyor (*see* Surveying).

Personal Qualities and Skills

Necessary requirements include a love of the land and being out of doors, a practical approach and the ability to direct one's own work.

Starting Salary

A school leaver could expect about £8,000, whereas a newly qualified surveyor with professional competence would receive about £15,000–£20,000.

Royal Institution of Chartered Surveyors, 12 Great George Street,
Parliament Square, London SW1P 3AD; 0870 333 1600; www.rics.org.uk

Valuer

(*see also* Auctioneer, Estate Agent, Land Agent, Surveying)

Valuers are employed by a wide variety of firms to assess the worth of goods and property (including land, buildings, fine arts, chattels, machinery and livestock). They may work for building societies, estate agents, insurance companies, property companies or any commercial, financial or industrial organisation that has to know true commercial values for selling, renting, investment or taxation purposes. Some valuers are also surveyors, auctioneers or land agents.

Qualifications and Training

There are two components to qualifying as a Chartered Surveyor or Valuer. First is successful completion of a degree or diploma approved by the Royal Institution of Chartered Surveyors (RICS), followed by enrolment onto the Assessment of Professional Competence (APC). This is two years' practical training while in employment, concluding with an RICS professional assessment interview. Postgraduate conversion courses are also available.

Professional qualifications in rating and valuations are awarded by the Institute of Revenues, Rating and Valuation (IRRV). Courses leading to IRRV examinations are available on day release or block release and by distance learning.

Personal Qualities and Skills

A valuer needs discretion combined with aptitude to understand the various economic factors involved in commerce.

Starting Salary

Trainees £10,000–£13,000 depending on age and qualifications, with higher salaries in London; £13,000–£19,000 when qualified.

Institute of Revenues, Rating and Valuation, 41 Doughty Street, London WC1N 2LF; 020 7831 3505; fax: 020 7831 2048; www.irrv.org.uk

Royal Institution of Chartered Surveyors (RICS), 12 Great George Street, Parliament Square, London SW1P 3AD; 0870 333 1600; www.rics.org/afa

LANDSCAPE ARCHITECTURE

see Gardening

LANDSCAPE ARCHITECT

Landscape Architecture as a profession covers the three divisions of design, management and science.

Landscape designer

Designers are trained in the planning and design of all types of outdoor spaces. They use design techniques based on their knowledge of the functional and aesthetic characteristics of landscape materials, and of the organisation of landscape elements, external spaces and activities. Their work ranges from large-scale landscape planning to the preparation of schemes for the short- and long-term development of individual sites. It also includes preparing detailed designs, specifications, contract drawings and letting and supervising contracts. Some practitioners are also qualified in other disciplines such as planning and architecture, and the landscape designer draws on many fields in order to promote new landscapes, and sustain existing ones.

Landscape manager

Landscape managers employ management techniques in the long-term care and development of new and existing landscapes, and also in determining policy and planning for future landscape management and use. They have particular expertise in the management and maintenance of landscape materials, both hard and soft, based on established principles of construction, horticulture and ecology. In addition, the landscape manager will have a thorough knowledge of budgetary control procedures, property and resource management, especially related to labour requirements and machinery, and the letting and administration of contracts.

Landscape scientist

Landscape scientists have a specific understanding of the principles and process of natural biological and physical systems. They relate their training and experience in subjects such as ecology, conservation, biology, soil science and botany to the solution of practical landscape problems, providing both traditional and innovative input to landscape design, planning and management work. Evaluation of the significance and effects of planning proposals, along with creating new habitats and environments in association with mineral workings, forestry and agriculture, make up a considerable amount of the work of landscape scientists. Smaller-scale ecological and habitat surveys, species assessments, wildlife management plans and the appraisal and preparation of conservation schemes are frequent tasks. Some landscape scientists are involved in research and teaching.

Qualifications and Training

The recognised professional qualification for those working in all aspects of landscape architecture is Member of the Landscape Institute (MLI), which entitles the use of the title Chartered Landscape Architect. There are three divisions: Design, Management and Science. Associate Membership, the first step towards achieving this, is gained after completing an accredited degree. Two years' relevant work is required as an Associate Member before taking the Institute's Professional Practice Examination and progressing to full Professional Membership. A list of accredited courses is available from the Landscape Institute.

Personal Qualities and Skills

Those working in design need creativity, imagination, a practical outlook, interest in the landscape and an enthusiasm for working outdoors. Those in management require good organisational and interpersonal skills, consistent application and a practical outlook. Scientists need enthusiasm for the subject, technical commitment and good communication skills.

Starting Salary

A recent graduate could expect to earn around £22,000. A fully qualified Chartered Member could expect to start on approximately £26,000.

info

British Association of Landscape Industries (BALI), Landscape House, Stoneleigh Park, Warwickshire CV8 2LG; 0870 770 4972; www.bali.co.uk

Landscape Design Trust, Bank Chambers, 1 London Road,

Redhill, Surrey RH1 1LY; 01737 779257; www.landscape.co.uk

The Landscape Institute (LI), 33 Great Portland Street, London W1W 8QG; 020 7299 4500; www.L-i.org.uk

LAW

The legal profession has many occupations within it, but all are based on upholding the laws of the land and dealing with those who contravene the laws. The word 'lawyer' is a blanket term that covers both solicitors and barristers. Solicitors advise clients and operate in the lower courts. Barristers are instructed by solicitors to act for clients, and work in the higher courts. Opportunities for lawyers can be found in the public and private sector as well as within the legal system. The legal profession also offers careers for those who have not trained as lawyers, such as legal clerks and executives.

Advocate/barrister

The services of a barrister are required by solicitors (*see also* Solicitor) who deal with the clients and then 'brief' the barrister. Barristers give specialised advice on the law and plead counsel in the higher court. They may also appear in the lower courts, where they usually begin their careers. Some are employed in the Army Legal Services, giving advice on all aspects of service and civil law that may affect the Army.

CMS Cameron McKenna LLP

The Firm: CMS Cameron McKenna is a leading International Law Firm and an integral part of CMS, the alliance of Major European law firms. We've earned a reputation for outstanding service, acute business awareness, and for being passionate about client relationships.

Key areas of Work: Banking, Corporate, Commercial, Real Estate, Insurance, EP&C.

Office Locations: London, Aberdeen, Edinburgh, Bristol, Bucharest, Budapest, Hong Kong, Moscow, Prague, Sofia, Warsaw.

Development: As soon as you join us, we will devise your personal development plan with you. This will be your blueprint for your career progression with us. And we'll ensure the right support programmes are in place to enable you to perform effectively against that plan. You will be appraised every three months, so you'll always know exactly how you're progressing.

Opportunities and Benefits: We recruit 60 Trainee Solicitors and have 55 vacation scheme placements. When undertaking a Training Contract you will have the opportunity to spend 6 months in one of our other UK or overseas offices or on a client secondment. Employee benefits include an annual bonus scheme, Life assurance, employee confidential careline, 25 days annual leave & flexible holiday allowance, gym subsidy, pension scheme, Private medical insurance and Study assistance.

Our requirements & applications details: In order to apply for a Training Contract you should be a good communicator and a committed team player. You will need to have achieved 320 UCAS points and a 2:1 degree. To apply, you will need to complete an on-line application form through our website. Closing date for Training Contract applications is 31st July 2007.

Contact details:
Address: Mitre House, 160 Aldersgate Street, London, EC1A 4DD
Telephone: 0207 367 3000
Fax: 0207 367 2000
Email: gradrec@cms-cmck.com
Web Address: www.law-now.com

In Scotland, an advocate is the equivalent of a barrister. Advocates may not select their clients. Provided that a reasonable fee is tendered they may not, without good cause, refuse instructions to act in litigation. Advocates also work in the public sector, Crown Prosecution Service, the legal section of a government department or as Parliamentary drafters.

Barristers specialise in arguing a case in court and offer a legal opinion for solicitors when asked to consider a particular question of law. Barristers are instructed by solicitors on behalf of clients and never directly employed by clients.

The majority of barristers work independently through sets of 'chambers' (which are a collective organisation of barristers), and tend to be self-employed. Once established within chambers, barristers can advertise for work.

Qualifications and Training

Full details of qualifications required for admission are available from the General Council of the Bar, but generally students are expected to hold a UK law degree with second-class honours or better, or a non-law degree at the same standard plus a pass in a special one-year course known as the Common Professional Examination/Postgraduate Diploma in Law.

Every intending barrister must join one of the four Inns of Court. Students intending to practise must also attend a one-year full-time vocational course. A list of institutions offering this is available from the Bar Council. This is followed by a one-year pupillage under the personal instruction and guidance of a barrister. Pupillage may involve researching relevant details of a case, setting them out in detail and drafting documents. During the first six months, pupils may attend court but may not accept briefs.

After completing pupillage a barrister has to find a 'seat' in an existing set of barristers' chambers. Some may choose to work as employed barristers and enter the civil service, local government or commerce and industry. About 15 years after being established at the Bar, a barrister may apply for a 'patent' as a Queen's Counsel. Although 'taking silk', as it is known, is usual (but not obligatory) if a barrister wishes to become a High Court Judge, it can have financial penalties and some barristers stay 'juniors' throughout their career at the Bar.

Full details of the qualifications and training required for advocacy in Scotland are available from the Clerk of Faculty. Generally speaking, applicants require a Scottish law degree with second-class honours or better, or a degree in Scottish law together with an Honours degree, second-class or better, from a university in the UK in another subject. In addition, they will have obtained a Diploma in Legal Practice from a Scottish university and served at least 12 months' traineeship in a solicitor's office in Scotland.

Personal Qualities and Skills

As it will be necessary to understand and interpret complex legal wording into clear basic English, barristers must have an excellent command of the English language and a meticulous understanding of the use of words. Barristers must understand and talk knowledgeably about technical matters in order to be able to cross-examine the most expert witness, for example, on complex aspects of technology. It is also useful if barristers present a highly confident and self-assured manner and can put on a 'good performance' in court. Since the work is confidential, a barrister needs to be trustworthy and discreet.

Starting Salary

Barristers' earnings relate to the amount and type of their work, their reputation, and, if they share chambers, the apportionment and value of briefs. Barristers may find it a struggle to make a living at the beginning of their profession, but the rewards for those who succeed can be high.

info

General Council of the Bar,
2/3 Cursitor Street, London EC4A 1NE;
020 7440 4000;
www.barcouncil.org.uk

Details of education and training at
the Bar: www.legaleducation.org.uk

Faculty of Advocates,
Advocates Library, Parliament House,
11 Parliament Square, Edinburgh
EH1 1RF; 0131 226 5071;
www.advocates.org.uk

Barrister's clerk/advocate's clerk

The barrister's clerk is the administrator or manager of the business chambers, deciding which briefs to accept, which of the barristers in the chamber to give them to, and negotiating the fees with the solicitor. The accounts, the barristers' appointment books and the efficient day-to-day running of the office are all part of the job of an experienced clerk.

Qualifications and Training

The minimum qualification is four GCSE pass grades at A, B or C in academic subjects. Training is on the job and juniors can apply through the Institute of Barristers' Clerks to attend a two-year part-time Edexcel (BTEC) national certificate course studying organisation, finance, management, law, marketing and chambers administration. On obtaining the certificate, juniors may apply, after five years' service, for qualified Membership of the Institute of Barristers' Clerks.

The Bar in Scotland is divided into 10 'stables', each of which is served by an advocate's clerk and a deputy clerk employed by Faculty Services Ltd. Training is provided in service. The job of advocate's clerk is very similar to that of barrister's clerk in England and Wales. Their rates of pay are linked to the civil service scale on a level that roughly relates to a comparable post within the courts' administration. The 10 advocate clerks have clerical and secretarial staff to provide them with administrative support.

Personal Qualities and Skills

In order to manage efficient chambers and the barristers who work from them, a barrister's clerk needs good organisational skills, the ability to lead a team as well as be part of a team, and to get on with the general public. A good command of written and spoken English and an appreciation of the necessity for absolute confidentiality at all times are vital to success in this career.

Starting Salary

Starting salaries are in the region of £10,000. Junior clerks with two or three years' experience receive £13,500–£18,000, going up to £28,000 for very experienced juniors. Senior clerks may earn £60,000–£75,000 plus a performance-related bonus. Senior clerks were traditionally paid a fee which was a percentage of the barrister's own earnings. Some are still paid in this way, and the fee is usually around 5 per cent.

The Bar Council, 289–293 High Holborn, London WC1V 7HZ; 020 7242 0082; www.barcouncil.org.uk/

Institute of Barristers' Clerks (IBC), 289–293 High Holborn, London WC1 7HZ; 020 7831 7144; www.barristersclerks.com

Court staff

Court administrative officer

Court administrative officers and court administrative assistants ensure the smooth day-to-day running of the courts. They book cases, allocate cases to courtrooms, prepare lists of the day's cases and send out correspondence. They may also be involved in the collection of fines and providing information to members of the public. More senior administrative officers lead teams of assistants, ensuring that all the tasks listed above are carried out efficiently.

Qualifications and Training

To work as an administrative assistant you require two GCSEs grades A–C and to be an administrative officer you need five GCSEs grades A–C. If you have other useful administrative experience, you may be considered without these formal qualifications.

Personal Qualities and Skills

You must to able to deal calmly and politely with people. You should have good organisational skills and be able to stay calm in a busy environment. You should be able to pay attention to detail and work well as part of a team.

Court clerk

Court clerks are legal advisers who give advice to unpaid (non-stipendiary) magistrates who are trying cases in the magistrate's courts. They are qualified lawyers, but they do not take part in the decision making about judgments and sentencing. As magistrates do not have to be legally qualified, it is the court clerks who ensure that magistrates interpret and apply the law correctly.

Qualifications and Training

Court clerks have to be either qualified solicitors or barristers, who themselves must have either a law degree or an approved postgraduate legal qualification.

Court clerks follow a set training programme and also learn by working with more experienced clerks, finding out about the many different areas of work – road traffic, licensing, fines enforcement, sentencing, etc.

Personal Qualities and Skills

As well as a real interest in and broad knowledge of the law, court clerks must be logical thinkers, capable of undertaking fairly detailed research. They must be discreet, sensitive and calm, but also able to remain detached when dealing with stressful and upsetting situations.

Starting Salary

Court administrative assistants earn between £12,000 and £15,000. Administrative officers earn between £14,000 and £16,000. Section managers and team leaders can earn up to £20,000. Court clerks start on £18,000 to £25,000. Senior court clerks earn up to £30,000.

info

Her Majesty's Court Service,
5th Floor, Clive House, Petty France,
London SW1H 9HD; 0845 456 8770;
www.hmcourts-service.gov.uk

Scottish Court Service,
Hayweight House, 23 Lauriston Street,
Edinburgh, EH3 9DQ; 0131 229 9200;
www.scotcourts.gov.uk

Skills for Justice,
9 & 10 Riverside Court, Don Road,
Sheffield S9 2TJ; 0114 261 1994;
www.skillsforjustice.com

Court reporter

Court reporters attend court sittings and take down a complete report of all the evidence, the summing-up or judgment and, on occasions, the speeches of counsel in the various cases. Formerly, the proceedings were taken down in shorthand; now a palantype or stenograph is used. This is a typewriter-like machine that enables the reporter to achieve 200 words per minute. In addition, computers may be used to prepare transcripts, with all the advantages of on-screen editing and speed of preparation. The work sometimes involves travelling to a number of different courts. The majority of verbatim reporters begin their careers in the courts but can also work for Hansard, producing reports of proceedings in the House of Commons and the House of Lords. Television subtitlers also use the skills of verbatim reporting.

Qualifications and Training

No specific academic qualifications are demanded for court reporters, although GCSE and A level passes can be an advantage. Applicants need to have proven ability in shorthand or steno-typing (usually over 150 words per minute), good typing speeds, and a thorough knowledge of grammar and punctuation. Legal experience can also be an asset. Details of full-time, part-time and distance learning courses are available from the British Institute of Verbatim Reporters.

In Scotland, there are no college courses but training is provided on the job by working alongside an experienced reporter.

Administrative officers need five GCSE passes (grade C or above), one of which must be English. The Scottish Court Service looks for applicants with Highers. Training lasts for two to three years, during which time trainees work and undertake courses run by the Court Service.

Personal Qualities and Skills

Anyone concerned with the courts must be discreet, honest and trustworthy, as most of the work is confidential. Reporters must show a high degree of accuracy.

Starting Salary

Qualified court reporters earn around £13,000. Freelancers can earn £140+ a day.

British Institute of Verbatim Reporters, Cliffords Inn, Fetter Lane, London EC4A 1LD; 020 8907 8249; www.bivr.org.uk

Individual Courts of Law

Northern Ireland Court Service, Windsor House, Bedford Street, Belfast BT2 7LT; 028 9032 8594; www.nics.gov.uk/pubsec/courts/courts.htm

Law Society of Scotland, 26 Drumsheugh Gardens, Edinburgh EH3 7YR; 0131 226 7411; fax: 0131 225 2934; www.lawscot.org.uk; e-mail: legaleduc@lawscot.org.uk

Careers in the Law (Kogan Page)

Legal services commission research assistant

The statutory government advisory body on law reform, the Law Commission, is currently working on projects in a variety of fields including common law, company and commercial law, crime and property law, and on general revision of statute law. The work is carried out in small teams, each under the direction of a Commissioner, consisting of qualified lawyers and research assistants. Law graduates and graduates of other disciplines who have completed the Legal Practice Course or the Bar Vocational Course are recruited annually to work as research assistants. The work offers the opportunity to take part in the creation of new legislative measures, as well as the in-depth development of skills in a particular area of law. Extensive consultation and investigation takes place before proposals are formulated; a sizeable proportion result in legislation. Projects range from major investigations of controversial areas of law to the consideration of a specific problem.

The firm

Jones Day operates as one firm worldwide with 2,200 lawyers in 30 offices. Jones Day in London is a key part of this international 40 partners and 40 trainees. This means that we can offer our lawyers a perfect combination – the intimacy and atmosphere of a medium sized City firm with access to both UK and multi-national clients.

Types of work

Jones Day has five core departments: corporate, lending and structured finance, real estate, litigation and tax. There are specialist groups for competition, construction, environment, planning, insolvency, insurance, employment and pensions.

Who should apply

We look for candidates with either a law or non-law degree, who have strong intellectual and analytical ability and good communication skills and who can demonstrate resourcefulness, drive, dedication and the ability to be a team player.

Training programme

The firm operates a unique, non-rotational system of training which is designed to provide freedom, flexibility and responsibility from the start. Our trainees work across different practice areas simultaneously and are encouraged to assume their own workload, which allows for early responsibility, faster development of potential and the opportunity to compare and contrast different disciplines alongside one another. Because our trainees do not move to a different department every six months they don't miss the end of deals or trials that they have worked on. Work will vary from small cases which trainees may handle alone (under the supervision of a senior lawyer) to matters where they will assist a partner or an associate solicitor. The firm runs a structured training programme with a regular schedule of seminars to support the thorough practical training and regular feedback that trainees receive from the associates and partners they work with.

When to apply

For September 2009/March 2010: Final-year law and non-law students – from November 2006; Penultimate-year law students – from June 2007, after penultimate-year exam results have been received.

Application deadline: 31st August 2007, but apply by 31st July to ensure an early interview date.

Vacation schemes

Christmas – non-law finalists or graduates-apply by 31st October.
Easter – penultimate or final-year non-law students – apply by 31st January
Summer – penultimate or second-year law undergraduates – apply by 31st January.

Placements last for two weeks with an allowance of £400 per week. Students get to see how our non-rotational training system works in practice by taking on real work from a variety of practice areas. They also get to meet a range of lawyers at various social events.

Sponsorship

CPE/GDL and LPC fees paid and £8,000 maintenance p.a.

"I THINK MOST
OF MY FRIENDS
ARE ENVIOUS
THAT I HAVE MY
OWN OFFICE."

BEN

TRAINEE

AT JONES DAY YOU GET YOUR OWN OFFICE
FROM DAY ONE, WITH GREATER RESPONSIBILITY
AND INDEPENDENCE. TO GO BEHIND THE
SCENES OF A MAJOR GLOBAL LAW FIRM, WITH A
DIFFERENT APPROACH TO TRAINING, VISIT
WWW.JONESDAYLON

Qualifications and Training

The minimum academic standard required is a first or high upper second-class (or equivalent) degree achieved in legal studies (based on the law of England and Wales) of at least two years' duration.

Personal Qualities and Skills

You need a genuine interest in, as well as a thorough knowledge of the law and legal issues. You must have excellent research skills, including the use of databases. You must be able to think and write articulately, be good at solving problems and be able to communicate well.

Starting Salary

Starting salaries range from £20,000 to £29,000. The highest salaries include London Weighting and are also paid to entrants with good postgraduate qualifications as well as a high class of degree.

info

Legal Services Commission,
Legal Services Research Centre,
85 Gray's Inn Road, London
WC1X 8TX; 020 7759 0000;
www.legalservices.gov.uk

Asset Skills, 2 The Courtyard,
48 New North Road, Exeter, Devon
EX4 4EP; 01392 423399;
www.assetskills.org

Paralegal

Paralegals work for firms of solicitors, commercial companies and public sector bodies. They are not qualified solicitors or legal executives, but they develop considerable specialist knowledge. They normally specialise in a specific area of the law such as conveyancing, probate or family law. Their work involves researching information, drafting and managing documents, attending client meetings and some general clerical work. Paralegals also have to keep up to date with legal developments in their specialist field.

Qualifications and Training

While there are no specific entry qualifications for paralegals, many hope to become solicitors, barristers or legal executives. This means that many applicants for these posts have law degrees. In any case, some firms ask for four or five GCSEs grades A–C or two A levels. Training is on the job and there are City & Guilds courses leading to a certificate level 2 and diploma level 3 available in paralegal studies. The Institute of Legal Executives (ILEX) also offers part-time and distance learning courses for paralegals.

Personal Qualities and Skills

You must be very well organised, able to manage your own workload and pay attention to detail. You should have good spoken and written English skills and be interested in legal matters.

Starting Salary

Salaries for paralegals are between £14,000 and £22,000. For large city law firms, salaries can be much higher than this and some firms pay substantial annual bonuses.

Institute of Legal Executives, Kempston Manor, Kempston, Bedfordshire MK42 7AB; 01234 841000; www.ilexpp.co.uk

National Association of Licensed Paralegals, 9 Unity Street, Bristol BS1 5HH; 0117 927 7077; www.nationalparalegals.com

Legal executive

A legal executive is a professional lawyer employed in a solicitor's office or in the legal departments of commerce and central and local government. The training and academic requirements in a specified area of law are at the same level as those required of a solicitor. Consequently, with few exceptions, a legal executive is able to carry out tasks that are similar to those undertaken by solicitors. The main areas of specialisation are conveyancing, civil litigation, criminal law, family law and probate. In addition to providing a worthwhile career in its own right, the legal executive qualification provides access to those wishing to qualify as solicitors via the Institute route. In Scotland, the term 'legal executive' is not used, but solicitors engage assistants to do similar work.

Qualifications and Training

The minimum entry requirement is four GCSEs to include English, but A level students and graduates are welcome. As an alternative, the Institute accepts a qualification in vocational legal studies, and has special arrangements for students who are over 21. In the main, training is on a part-time basis so that there is potential for trainees to 'learn while they earn'. For those already working in a legal environment, but with no formal legal qualifications, an NVQ (level 4) in legal practice is available, and the Institute of Legal Executives (ILEX) is the awarding body.

Personal Qualities and Skills

An ability to communicate, both verbally and in writing, with people at all levels, absolute discretion and trustworthiness, together with meticulous attention to detail, are essential.

Simmons & Simmons

Our firm Dynamic and innovative, Simmons & Simmons has a reputation for offering a superior legal service, wherever and whenever it is required. Our lawyers' high quality advice and the positive working atmosphere in our 20 international offices have won admiration and praise from both the legal community and our business clients.

Types of work We offer our clients a full range of legal services across numerous industry sectors. We have a particular focus on the world's fastest growing sectors, that is: Energy & Infrastructure; Financial Institutions; Life Sciences; and Technology. We provide a wide choice of service areas in which our lawyers can specialise. These include Corporate & Commercial; Communications, Outsourcing & Technology; Dispute Resolution; Employment & Benefits; EU & Competition; Financial Markets; IP; Projects; Real Estate; Taxation & Pensions.

Who should apply We look for a strong track record of achievements from our candidates. We are interested to find out about your academic successes but we will also explore your ability to form excellent interpersonal relations and work within a team environment, as well as your levels of motivation, drive and ambition.

Show us evidence of a rich 'life experience' as well as examples of your intellectual capabilities and we will provide you with everything you need to become a successful member of our firm.

Training programme Our training programme is constantly evolving to build the skills you will need to be successful in the fast moving world of international business. We provide experience in a range of areas of law and a balanced approach to gaining the knowledge, expertise and abilities you will need to qualify in the practice area of your choice.

Sponsorship We will cover your full tuition fees at law school and offer a maintenance allowance of up to £7,500.

Internship Our summer internship is one of our primary means of selecting candidates for a career at Simmons & Simmons. It provides us with the chance to test your suitability for a training contract. It is also a unique opportunity for you to get to know our firm, decide if we are the best firm for you and for you to prove your potential during your time with us.

To apply for a training contract, internship or to find out further information on the firm please visit our website
www.simmons-simmons.com/traineelawyers

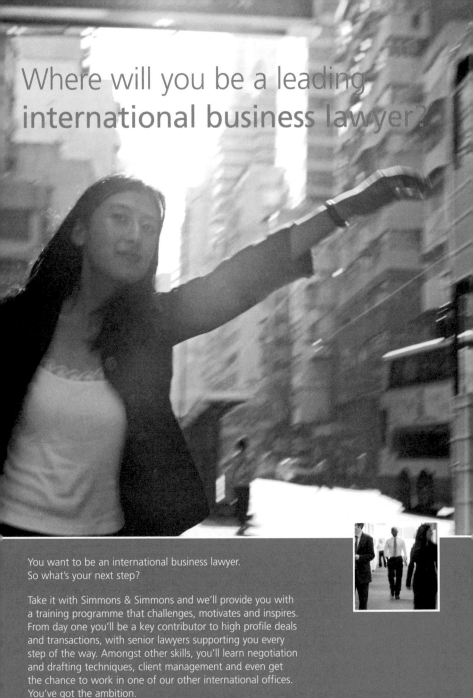

Starting Salary

Varies according to age and qualification, and the type of work undertaken. The average starting salary is around £12,000. Many established legal executives earn £60,000+.

Institute of Legal Executives, Kempston Manor, Kempston, Bedfordshire MK42 7AB; 01234 841000; www.ilex.org.uk; e-mail: info@ilex.org.uk

Notary public

A notary public is an international lawyer, whose main duty it is to prepare and verify legal documents for use abroad. These can be certified translations, powers of attorney and all manner of mercantile documents. There are two types of notaries: general notaries who are usually full-time solicitors with a part-time notarial practice, or scrivener notaries who are full-time notaries with linguistic skills. The latter are usually to be found in central London, the former anywhere in the UK. Although nearly all the work of scrivener notaries is of an international nature, they are competent to advise on certain domestic matters as well.

Qualifications and Training

Qualification as a notary is open to solicitors, barristers and graduates, whose degree need not necessarily be in law. There is a unified system for the initial stage of qualification for both branches of the profession. This consists of a diploma course administered by Cambridge University. A general notary, having obtained this diploma, can then apply for a faculty to practise to the Faculty Office of the Archbishop of Canterbury. A scrivener notary, however, would need to take additional examinations such as those testing knowledge of two languages and the law of the country of one such language, with a require-ment also to spend two years in a scrivener notary's office.

Personal Qualities and Skills

A notary public should be discreet, meticulous and knowledgeable.

Starting Salary

A general notary will receive not only the remuneration earned as a notary but also any income earned as a solicitor. A scrivener notary, on the other hand, will only receive notarial income, and a starting salary upon qualification will be about £30,000.

Info

Notaries Society,
Administration Dept, PO Box 226,
Melton Woodbridge, Suffolk
IP12 1WX; Fax: 01394 383772;
www.thenotariessociety.org.uk;
e-mail:
NotariesSociety@compuserve.com

Society of Scrivener Notaries;
www.scrivener-notaries.org.uk

Worshipful Company of Scriveners,
HQS Wellington, Temple Stairs,
Victoria Embankment, London
WC2R 2PN; 020 7240 0529;
fax: 020 7497 0645;
www.scriveners.org.uk;
e-mail: clerk@scriveners.org.uk

Solicitor

The role of the solicitor is to provide clients with skilled legal representation and advice. The clients can be individual people or companies, or any type of organisation or group. A solicitor may work on all kinds of legal matters, from house purchases to defence of people accused of crimes; from selling a corporation to drafting a complicated will or trust. Solicitors may also represent clients in all courts, but will often brief a barrister (*see* Barrister) to represent the client, and then act as a liaison between them.

Scottish solicitors can appear in all courts and tribunals in Scotland up to and including the Sheriff Court. They can also gain rights of audience enabling them to appear in the higher courts by becoming a solicitor-advocate, or may brief an advocate to represent their clients.

While some solicitors may deal with a variety of legal problems, others specialise in a particular area such as shipping, planning and construction, financial services or social security. Specialisation within the profession is increasing. The majority of solicitors work in private practice, with firms made up of several partners. Many others work as employed solicitors in commerce, industry, local and central government and other organisations.

Solicitors are instructed directly by clients and have a lot of contact with them. They have rights of audience in the magistrates' court and the county court. Unlike barristers, solicitors do not wear wigs but do wear gowns if they appear in county court. Solicitors are governed by a professional body called the Law Society.

Qualifications and Training

England and Wales: the Law Society governs the training of solicitors in England and Wales, which takes place in two stages – the academic and the professional. Most, but not all, entrants to the profession are graduates. Fellows of the Institute of Legal Executives over the age of 25 with five years' qualifying experience do not need to complete the academic stage. Non-law graduates take the Common Professional Examination (CPE) or a Postgraduate Diploma in Law; those with the qualifying law degrees are exempt from this. The next stage, the vocational stage, is taken via the legal practice course, available at a number of colleges or universities. It is a one-year full-time or two-year part-time course. The trainee solicitor then has to undertake a two-year training contract with an authorised firm or organisation. During the course of this, a 20-day professional skills course is undertaken, usually on a modular basis.

Scotland: the Law Society of Scotland governs the training of solicitors in Scotland. It is possible to study for a Bachelor of Laws degree at five Scottish universities: Aberdeen, Dundee, Edinburgh, Glasgow and Strathclyde. Alternatively, it is possible to take the Law Society's own examinations by finding employment as a pre-diploma trainee. After completion of the LLB degree or professional examinations, all graduates who would like to become solicitors must take the diploma in legal practice – a 26-week postgraduate course, which also offers training in office and business skills. After successful completion of the degree and the diploma, those who wish to become solicitors then serve a two-year training contract with a Scottish solicitor. Trainees must undertake a further two-week course of study, keep training records, which will be examined and monitored by the Society, and take a test of professional competence. The trainees can then apply to the Law Society of Scotland for a practising certificate. All Scottish solicitors must hold a Law Society of Scotland practising certificate.

Personal Qualities and Skills

A high level of academic achievement, integrity, good communication skills, patience, discretion, a good command of language and problem-solving skills are all required.

Starting Salary

The range of starting salaries is very wide in this profession. The Law Society suggests that trainees should be paid around £15,000 in the regions and £17,000 in London. In practice, large city firms pay far more than this, somewhere in the region of £25,000 to £35,000. Another factor affecting earning is the field of law in which you practise: commercial law tends to offer higher earnings than family or employment law, for example.

info

Law Society, 113 Chancery Lane, London WC2A 1PL; 020 7242 1222; fax: 020 7831 0344; Legal Education Line: 0870 606 2555; www.lawsociety.org.uk; e-mail: legaled@lawsociety.org.uk

Law Society of Scotland, 26 Drumsheugh Gardens, Edinburgh

EH3 7YR; 0131 226 7411; fax: 0131 225 2934; www.lawscot.org.uk; e-mail: legaleduc@lawscot.org.uk

So... you want to be a lawyer? (Kogan Page)

Careers in the Law (Kogan Page)

LEISURE AND AMENITY MANAGEMENT

People employed in this field may work in leisure centres, Outward Bound centres, theatres and arts centres, historic houses and ancient monuments, country areas offering nature trails, fishing and camping facilities to the public,

"Smart qualifications for active people"

Active IQ is a QCA-approved awarding body operating in the sport, recreation and leisure sector. We aim to provide qualifications that are relevant to industry, enhanced by excellent teaching resources and a friendly efficient support team. We wish to enable approved centres to provide candidates with a high standard of knowledge and skills.

All Active IQ qualifications have been endorsed by SkillsActive (the Sector Skills Council for Active Leisure and Learning) and the Level 2 Certificate in Gym Instructing and the Level 3 Certificate in Personal Training provide access onto REPs.

Mission statement Active IQ, operating within the Active Leisure sector, is committed to providing a comprehensive portfolio of cutting-edge qualifications, with professional support services, suitable for a wide range of individual needs.

Tel: **01225 717257**   Fax: **01225 717258**   Email: **info@activeiq.co.uk**
Active IQ Ltd, Unit 2, Willowside Park, Canal Road, Trowbridge, Wiltshire, BA14 8RH
www.activeiq.co.uk

Active IQ is a Qualifications and Curriculum Authority (QCA)-approved awarding body, operating in the Active Leisure Sector.

Active IQ, is a specialist awarding body with a high level of expertise within the Active Leisure sector and is committed to providing a comprehensive portfolio of cutting-edge qualifications, with professional support services, suitable for a wide range of individual needs.

Active IQ was formerly known as Premier International Qualifications providing qualifications for the health and fitness sub-sector of Active Leisure. Namely;
Level 1 Award in Active Healthy Living
Level 2 Certificate in Instructing Gym
Level 2 Certificate in Instructing Circuit Sessions
Level 2 Award in Teaching Exercise to Children
Level 3 Certificate in Personal Training
Level 3 Certificate in Sports Massage

All Active IQ qualifications have been endorsed by SkillsActive, the Sector Skills Council for Active Leisure and are recognised by the Register of Exercise Professionals (REPs).

On 1st September 2006, the awarding body changes its name to better reflect the current development work taking place which will increase the current suite of qualifications to cover the additional areas of sport, recreation and leisure.

In March 2007, Active IQ will be launching a whole range of new qualifications which support the following job roles in the Active Leisure sector:
- Fitness Instructor
- Advanced Fitness Instructor
- Personal Trainer
- Lifeguard
- Leisure Attendant
- Leisure Receptionist
- Activity Leader
- Duty Manager
- Leisure Manager

There will also be an introduction of "Apprenticeship Packages" – the Apprenticeship scheme offers a stepping stone for young people aged between 16 and 25 to enter into the industry and can lead to some fantastic career opportunities in this exciting and vibrant area of work.

Approved Apprenticeship training providers can find you a placement in a sport, recreation or leisure environment and you will have the opportunity to "earn whilst you learn". During your apprenticeship you will gain valuable qualifications which are specific to the industry.

For more information on approved training providers and Apprenticeship Packages see the Active IQ website **www.activeiq.co.uk**

or even be in charge of bingo or dance halls. Managers, as well as being interested in their particular leisure activity, are responsible for the administrative and financial running of the enterprise. Many in this field are employed in local government, but there are also opportunities in private sports centres, health and fitness clubs and tourist attractions.

Qualifications and Training

The Institute of Leisure and Amenity Management (ILAM) offers five levels of qualification based upon the completion of work-based projects: the ILAM first award for candidates who are new to the industry and who hold junior positions within leisure organisations; the ILAM Certificate in Leisure Operations, for candidates who have a working knowledge of the industry and hold junior supervisory positions; the ILAM Certificate in Leisure Management for candidates with a good understanding of the industry and who hold junior or middle management jobs; the ILAM Diploma in Leisure Management for candidates who have successfully demonstrated their managerial ability at a senior level; and the Advanced Diploma in Leisure Management for those with substantial experience.

HND courses and a range of degree courses, including foundation degrees in leisure studies/recreation management and sports sciences, are available.

Personal Qualities and Skills

A strong interest in the particular area of leisure is necessary, as is the ability to organise, administer and manage people, and be an all-round good communicator.

Starting Salary

Trainee managers start on around £17,000. Experienced managers of large facilities earn between £20,000 and £30,000.

SkillsActive, Castlewood House, 77–91 New Oxford Street, London WC1A 1PX; advice line: 0800 093 3300; www.skillsactive.com

Institute of Leisure and Amenity Management (ILAM), ILAM House, Lower Basildon, Reading, Berks RG8 9NE; 01491 874800; www.ilam.co.uk

Institute of Sport and Recreation Management (ISRM), Sir John Beckwith Centre for Sport, Loughborough University, Loughborough, Leics LE11 3TU; 01509 226474; www.isrm.co.uk

Info

Give your fitness career
the best possible start
with a qualifcation from CYQ

- The UK's leading fitness industry awarding body

- Over 26 qualifications at Levels 1, 2 and 3 including personal training, fitness instructing and exercise referral

- Nationally recognised and government approved

- Approved by REPs

- Over 300 centres across the UK and Worldwide

Get qualified now!

To find you nearest centre or training provider go to **cyq.org.uk**

112 Great Russell Street, London WC1B 3NQ
T 020 7343 1800 F 020 7436 2687 E info@cyq.org.uk W cyq.org.uk
Registered charity no. 213121. Registered in England & Wales no. 119249

Inform, Inspire, Educate

LINGUISTICS, LANGUAGES AND TRANSLATION

Interpreter

Interpreters communicate between people who do not share a common language. They use two main techniques: simultaneous and consecutive interpreting. Conference interpreters usually work using the simultaneous method in a booth with headphones and communicative technology, allowing them to hear the speaker and interpret to their audience.

Very few openings are available for interpreters, even worldwide. Conference interpreters work at international conferences such as the United Nations or the European Commission and at the International Court of Justice, using simultaneous or consecutive interpreting. Some work for international agencies; others are freelance. Demand for conference interpreters in particular languages may fluctuate depending on the political and economic requirements of the day. Interpreters with specialist knowledge, such as engineering or economics, may have the chance to work at conferences on their subject. Interpreters may also work as guides in tourist centres, and to do this they must usually be accredited and trained as guides.

Demand for interpreting in the public services (police, courts, public health and local government) has led to the creation of the National Register of Public Service Interpreters covering a wide range of African, Asian, European and Far Eastern languages. This register is supported by the Home Office and the UK legal agencies. The Institute of Translation and Interpreting (ITI) can also help source qualified public service interpreters from its membership, as can numerous other commercial agencies.

Qualifications and Training

To take a degree course, two A levels or equivalent, including a foreign language, are normally required. At the newer universities and colleges, training in interpreting and translating is offered, combined with regional studies or technological or business studies, aimed at industry, commerce and international organisations. A list of these courses is offered by the Institute of Linguists and the Institute of Translation and Interpreting (ITI). Such degree courses usually involve work or study abroad. The Institute of Linguists Educational Trust also offers the only qualification in public service interpreting – the Diploma in Public Service Interpreting, which is mapped at between NVQ levels 4 and 5.

Personal Qualities and Skills

Fluency in two or more languages should be allied with a natural feeling for words and phrases and a good ear. It is necessary to be able to think quickly, to remain alert for long periods, and to be socially confident. Subject knowledge is essential, especially for simultaneous interpreting, which requires a degree of understanding and anticipation of subject matter and context.

Starting Salary

Starting salaries are between £19,000 and £25,000 – a little less in the civil service and for other public services. Freelance interpreters can earn between £200 and £350 a day.

info

Institute of Linguists, Saxon House, 48 Southwark Street, London SE11 1UN; 020 7940 3100; fax: 020 7940 3101; www.iol.org.uk; e-mail: info@iol.org.uk

Institute of Translation and Interpreting (ITI), Fortuna House, South Fifth Street, Milton Keynes MK9 2EU; 01908 325250; fax: 01908 325259; www.iti.org.uk; e-mail: info@iti.org.uk

Translator

Translators work freelance from home or as staff translators, within a commercial organisation whose main business is not translation, or within a translation agency. Normally, they only translate from another language into their mother tongue. The work translated varies from whole books to business letters and documents. Translators, especially those who specialise in work for publication, must be able to express themselves very well. In areas where the subject matter of the text is specialised, for example computing, maths or mountaineering, expert knowledge is required of the translator. A broad-based general knowledge is always an advantage. Translators may be responsible for finding their own work but may also be registered with a translation company or agency.

Qualifications and Training

Proficiency in a foreign language is obviously necessary, as is the ability to write well in the target language. An understanding of the culture of the relevant countries is important. Increasingly, there is a need to be computer-literate. Most translators have a postgraduate qualification or a diploma in translation. First degree courses in translation are available at a number of universities and diplomas are available via the Institute of Linguists.

Personal Qualities and Skills

Translators must be meticulous, conscientious, creative and persistent. The ability to carry out research as and when necessary, and good interpersonal skills are also required.

Starting Salary

There is a wide range of starting salaries with the lowest being £16,500–£18,000 depending on qualifications and work experience; £75–£120 per 1,000 words depending on language combinations. The rate goes up for translating Chinese characters. Some translators own copyright of their translations and can make money by selling this, or through royalty payments, but these are less common sources of income.

Institute of Linguists, Saxon House, 48 Southwark Street, London SE11 1UN; 020 7940 3100; fax: 020 7940 3101; www.iol.org.uk; e-mail: info@iol.org.uk

Institute of Translation and Interpreting (ITI), Fortuna House,

South Fifth Street, Milton Keynes MK9 2EU; 01908 325250; fax: 01908 325259; www.iti.org.uk; e-mail: info@iti.org.uk

A variety of downloadable documents relating to linguistic careers are available from the ITI website.

info

LITERARY AGENT

Literary agents act as negotiators between authors and publishers, film producers and theatre managements. Initially they read authors' manuscripts and decide whether or not to accept an author as a client. Once accepted, an author may be guided by an agent about ideas for books and changes to existing manuscripts. The agent then finds a publisher or producer for the author's work and negotiates the best possible terms. The agent deals with the publisher on all matters that will affect the client, including the contract, manuscript delivery, follow-up titles, advertising, publicity, paperback, television and film rights, and obtaining payments when due.

Some literary agents also act for foreign publishers attempting to find British publishers who will bring out an English edition of a book already published abroad. Like publishers, agents tend to specialise in areas such as fiction, general non-fiction and specialist publishing.

Qualifications and Training

No particular educational qualifications are necessary. Experience of the book trade is the most important factor, and most literary agents have gained this by working in a publishing house. Foreign languages are an asset, particularly in the international field.

Personal Qualities and Skills

Agents need shrewd literary judgement and a knowledge of worldwide market conditions, negotiating and legal skills, business and financial ability. They must be hard working, persistent, adaptable and sympathetic towards their authors.

Starting Salary

Agencies receive a percentage of the money earned by the author – usually 10–20 per cent. Literary agents working for these companies would receive a salary plus annual bonuses related to the level of commission they bring in.

Association of Authors' Agents; www.agentsassoc.co.uk

The Writers' and Artists' Yearbook, A&C Black (annual publication)

info

LOCAL GOVERNMENT

Local government provides many services, including education, social care, environmental management, leisure management and public protection. Within each of these areas there is a whole range of jobs. Local education authorities employ teachers, educational psychologists and education administrators. Social service departments employ social workers and social care assistants. Building services departments employ architects, surveyors and building trades people. Town planners, recycling officers and cleaning supervisors are employed by local council environment departments. Sports coaches and leisure managers work in local leisure facilities. All of these services are backed up by finance, human resource, information provision and other administrative services. To find out more about many of the professional careers within local government check other relevant entries in this guide and visit the Local Government Careers website.

The administrative back-up and public offices in local government are staffed by administrative assistants, administrative officers, call centre agents, customer services officers, telephonists and typists. Administrative staff also have specialist roles such as managing the electoral register.

Qualifications and Training

Entry requirements depend on which career you opt for. For professions such as accountancy, architecture, social work, town planning or teaching, entrants will have to possess the relevant professional qualifications and training required for that profession. For many professional careers, local government provides support for such training and for further training and career development.

For administrative jobs, entry requirements vary according to job titles and the level of responsibility and skills required. Many councils expect applicants to have four GCSEs grades A–C including English and maths. For some administrative officer posts you may need A levels as well as GCSEs. While many roles do not require you to have a degree, in reality many graduates enter local government careers at all levels.

Personal Qualities and Skills

While every role demands particular knowledge and skill, there are some common threads that are essential for all employees. You must have a genuine interest in and commitment to serving your local community. Most jobs require a good level of communication skills, as many jobs involve direct contact with members of the public. You should be flexible and able to work well as part of a team. You should also be prepared to take on responsibilities. Some jobs require good IT or numeracy skills.

Starting Salary

Pay is determined by what job you do and by the fact that individual councils set their own pay rates. For professions such as accountancy, architecture or law, salaries are likely to be lower than for the same job in the private sector, but still reasonably competitive. A few examples for administrative jobs include administrative assistants, paid between £13,000 and £17,000, administrative officers paid between £15,000 and £20,000, call centre agents earn between £13,000 and £23,000, and committee administrators earn between £18,000 and £23,000.

www.lgcareers.com

Info

LOGISTICS

(*see also* Road Transport)

Logistics is the management of the moving of goods or materials from one place to another.

Freight forwarding

A freight forwarding firm will arrange for the most efficient means of the international transport of goods, and will ensure that all documentation, legal and insurance requirements are met, and customs duties paid. Freight forwarders may be individuals or firms; they may specialise in a particular method of transportation, certain goods or countries. They may arrange for a number of different shipments to be grouped together for more economical transport. Some very large organisations have their own freight forwarding department or a subsidiary company.

Freight forwarders are usually located near ports or airports and in provincial centres. They employ people to deal with a wide range of clerical and administrative tasks such as sales, personnel, timetabling, accounting and computer work.

Qualifications and Training

School leavers can enter the industry through the Modern Apprenticeship route. NVQs are available in International Trade and Services, Distribution and Warehousing Operations and Organising Road Transport. There are several degree courses in international trade, logistics, supply chain management, transport, export studies and overseas business. Large companies may offer graduate training schemes for those with relevant degrees.

The Institute of Freight Forwarders offers an Advanced Certificate in International Trade that can be studied full or part time or by correspondence. The Institute of Logistics and Transport offers a range of professional qualifications from introductory to MSc level which can be studied by distance learning.

Personal Qualities and Skills

People working in freight forwarding need excellent problem-solving and communication skills. Accuracy and clarity are essential, as misunderstandings can cause major problems. IT skills are essential with a growth in internet trading and greater use of technology such as global position satellite systems to plan and manage journeys. Geographical, cultural and religious awareness are also important.

Starting Salary

Clerical salaries are similar to those in other industries. Graduate salaries can be between £17,000 and £25,000, and increase significantly with experience.

info

British International Freight Association, Institute of Freight Forwarders, Redfern House, Browells Lane, Feltham, Middlesex TW13 7EP; 020 8844 2266; fax: 020 8890 5596; www.bifa.org; e-mail: bifa@bifa.org

Chartered Institute of Logistics and Transport, Logistics and Transport Centre, Earlstrees Court, Earlstrees Road, Corby, Northants NN17 4AX; 01536 740100; www.ciltuk.org.uk

Institute of Transport Administration, IoTA House, 7B St Leonards Road, Horsham, West Sussex RH13 6EH; 01403 242412; fax: 01403 242413; www.iota.org.uk

Logistics and Transport Management Careers Guide available for download from www.insidecareers.co.uk

Logistics

When a customer places an order, a chain reaction – the supply chain – is started. The supply chain ensures that the product that has been ordered, whether it is a car for an individual, or a thousand bars of chocolate for a retailer, reaches the customer who placed the order.

Logistics is the management of the supply chain. The professionals working in logistics are responsible for warehouse management, distribution and transport management, inventory (stock) control, information systems, transport, logistics planning and analysis, and supply-chain management.

Qualifications and Training

Entry with GCSEs or A levels is still possible but many new entrants to managerial posts now have a degree or professional qualification. There are several degree courses in international trade, logistics, supply-chain management, export studies and overseas business. Large companies may offer graduate training schemes for those with relevant degrees. The Institute of Freight Forwarders offers an Advanced Certificate in International Trade that can be studied full or part time or by correspondence.

An MSc in logistics or supply-chain management may be an advantage when seeking progression into senior management positions in some organisations. The Institute of Logistics and Transport offers a range of professional qualifications from entry level upwards, which includes a distance-learning MSc offered in conjunction with Aston University.

Personal Qualities and Skills

Logistics can offer early responsibility, so trainee managers should be responsible, able to motivate others and enjoy a challenge. Organisational, numeracy and people management skills are essential. Foreign language skills are an advantage. The ability to use IT packages and electronic communication has become increasingly important with the growing use of the internet. The supply chain is at the centre of many e-commerce developments.

Starting Salaries

Graduate management trainees start between £18,000 and £22,000. Managers' salaries are variable and can reach £60,000, rising as high as £100,000 for directors with board-level responsibility in large organisations.

Chartered Institute of Logistics and Transport (UK), Logistics and Transport Centre, Earlstrees Court, Earlstrees Road, Corby, Northants NN17 4AX; 01536 740100; www.ciltuk.org.uk

GoSkills, Concorde House, Trinity Park, Solihull, Birmingham B37 7UQ; 0121 635 5520; www.goskills.org

Skills for Logistics, 14 Warren Yard, Warren Farm Office Village, Milton Keynes MK12 5NW; 01908 313360; www.skillsforlogistics.org

info

MANAGEMENT CONSULTANT

Management has been defined as the art of getting results through other people, and consultancy as giving professional advice. Management consultants are employed to provide a higher degree of expertise than is available in a particular company; to recommend business solutions and assist in their implementation; to assist in cultural change and to provide expertise to solve specific business issues.

Firms of management consultants specialise, tending to divide their activities into the following areas: organisation, development and policy formation – long-range planning and reorganisation of a company's structure; production management – production control arrangements; marketing, sales and distribution; finance and administration – installation of budgetary control systems; personnel management selection; management of information systems – the provision of software, systems analysis; economic and environmental studies – urban and regional development planning, work for overseas organisations. With the growth in e-commerce many consultancies are providing advice on e-business solutions.

Management coach

This is a relatively new career and management coaches work far more with individuals than with whole organisations or departments. They work mostly with managers at a senior level in all kinds of organisation, helping them to work more efficiently and effectively and working on any problem areas, for example presenting in public, interpreting data, and team leadership.

Qualifications and Training

Management consultancy is a graduate-only profession and preferred degree subjects include business, management, IT, economics and psychology. If you specialise in a particular area of consultancy such as marketing or human resources, a relevant degree is helpful. You should have a 2.1 and an A level points tariff of 320 points. Training is on the job, but many consulting firms provide extensive in-house courses. After about two years in the profession you are likely to have the option either to take a Masters in Business Administration (MBA) or a professional qualification linked to your area of expertise, for example finance, marketing or personnel. Management coaches have often worked as management consultants and developed a special interest in personal coaching and one-to-one work.

Personal Qualities and Skills

You need to be an excellent communicator, one-to-one, with groups and on paper. You should have good IT and numerical skills and the ability to analyse problems and suggest solutions. You should have a broad knowledge of business issues. If you are working as a management coach, you need to be very good at working one-to-one, good at motivating people and accurate in analysing their problems.

Starting Salary

Graduate entrant management consultants' starting salaries range from £20,000 to £35,000. At a senior level you can earn £100,000+ in this work. Management coaches tend to work freelance and may charge £100 per hour, or more.

Chartered Institute of Personnel and Development (CIPD),
151 The Broadway, London SW19 1JQ;
020 8612 6200; www.cipd.co.uk

Chartered Management Institute (CMI), Management House, Cottingham Road, Corby, Northants NN17 1TT; 01536 204222; www.managers.org.uk

Institute of Management Consultancy (IMC), 3rd Floor,
17–18 Hayward's Place, London EC1R 0EQ; 020 7566 5220; www.imc.co.uk

Management Consultancies Association (MCA), 49 Whitehall, London SW1A 2BX; 020 7321 3990; www.mca.org.uk/

MANUFACTURING

Manufacturing encompasses many occupations, all of which are concerned with the large-scale production of goods and packaging.

Factory worker

Factory work is all about the manufacturing of products of every kind: food, furniture, cars, clothing, electronic equipment, etc, in fact, everything that we use. A whole range of jobs support any manufacturing process: administration, research, engineering and marketing, but they are covered elsewhere.

The term 'factory worker' refers to workers who are involved in the production process – and specific tasks and duties vary depending on what is being produced. Workers may operate special machinery for building cars, work on a conveyor belt filling cans of drink, wash and grade raw fruit and vegetables to be processed, assemble complete items by putting components together, or monitor for quality and consistency of any product. The range is really very wide.

Qualifications and Training

For most jobs there are no specific academic requirements, although some employers may like you to have GCSEs in maths, English and technology. Many employers set their own entry tests to measure how well you are likely to perform the tasks you will be expected to do. There are now some GNVQs level 2 available in Performing Manufacturing Operations, and if you are under 24 years old there may be opportunities to do an apprenticeship in electrical, electronic or mechanical engineering.

Personal Qualities and Skills

You need to be good at practical work and quick with your hands. It is important that you don't mind carrying out repetitive tasks and that you can keep your concentration while doing this. You must be able to follow instructions, pay close attention to safety and work well as part of a team.

Starting Salary

Starting salaries range from £11,000 to £15,000, and if you take on some super-visory responsibility they can rise to £20,000. Many jobs include shift work allowances.

info

Local Job Centre Plus and Careers/ Connexions Centres

SEMTA (Science Engineering and Manufacturing Technologies Alliance), 14 Upton Road, Watford, Hertfordshire WD18 0JT; 0808 100 3682; www.semta.org.uk

Improve (Food and Drink Sector Skills Council), 1 Green Street, London W1K 6RG; 020 7355 0830; www.improvefdssc.org

Cogent (Sector Skills Council for the Oil and Gas Extraction, Chemicals Manufacturing and Petroleum Industries), Minerva House, Bruntland Road, Portlethen, Aberdeen AB12 4QL; 01224 787800; www.cogent-ssc.com

Packaging technologist

The purpose of packaging is to protect, preserve, contain and present its contents. It also has a vital function in branding and brand awareness. Opportunities for work exist with manufacturers of raw packaging materials, with companies that produce packaging and companies that have a product to be packed. Many small firms do not have their own packaging adviser/technologist, and hire a consultant when the need arises.

Work opportunities exist in developing materials for packaging purposes, for designing equipment to manufacture or fill packaging, for structural design of parts, for graphic design on packs, for physical and chemical testing and quality assurance.

Qualifications and Training

Packaging modules are available in some first degree courses, and two universities offer the MSc in Packaging Technology. The Diploma in Packaging Technology from the Institute of Packaging is internally recognised as a qualification of excellence. It can be studied in three ways: residential, part time and by distance learning.

Personal Qualities and Skills

Technologists and scientists must be able to look at problems in a practical way and have the ability to communicate their ideas to others both verbally and on paper.

Starting Salary

This varies according to age and qualifications but falls in the region of £15,000 to £20,000.

The Head of Training, Institute of Packaging, Sysonby Lodge, Nottingham Road, Melton Mowbray, Leicestershire LE13 0NU; 01664 500055; fax: 01664 564164 (for details of available training and careers advice); www.iop.co.uk; e-mail: training@iop.co.uk

Brunel University, Department of Design and Systems Engineering, Brunel University, Uxbridge, Middlesex UB8 3PH; 01895 203059; fax: 01895 812556; www.brunel.ac.uk

Info

Sheet-metal worker/plater

Sheet-metal workers/platers are engaged in shaping, cutting and joining together pieces of metal. Sheet-metal workers work with thin metal sheet up to 3 mm thick, using a wide range of hand and power tools. They make such items as aircraft sections and car prototypes. Platers work with metal plates from 3 mm thick upwards. As well as hand and power tools, heavy presses are needed to bend the plate. Products include ship and submarine parts and industrial boilers.

Qualifications and Training

If you are between 16 and 24 years old and want to join a National Apprenticeship Scheme for Engineering Construction (NASEC), you need GCSEs (A–C)/S grades (1–3) in maths, English and a science. If you have engineering drawing, metalwork or other practical subjects as well you may have an advantage. Applicants without the required entry grades may also be considered. These apprenticeships take up to three years and you train on-the-job, working alongside experienced sheet metal workers. This apprenticeship leads to an NVQ level 3 award in engineering production. Older applicants can get into this work without GCSEs, but won't get the opportunity to do a full apprenticeship.

Personal Qualities and Skills

You must have good manual dexterity and be able to concentrate for long periods of time. You should be good at following instructions, but able to work without direct supervision. Normal eyesight is essential and good colour vision is important.

Starting Salary

Salaries range from £12,000 to £16,000, but can go up to £20,000 to £22,000. There are often opportunities for shift work payments.

SEMTA (Science Engineering and Manufacturing Technologies Alliance), 14 Upton Road, Watford, Hertfordshire WD18 0JT; 0808 100 3682; www.semta.org.uk	Local Job Centre Plus and Connexions/ Careers Centres

Toolmaker

Toolmakers work in engineering making a wide range of jigs, used to guide cutting tools and to hold the work in position; fixtures, to hold metal for bending or welding or to hold parts together; press tools in different shapes and sizes for cutting parts; mould tools to make items such as fridge interiors or mobile phone cases and measuring gauges. Toolmakers are often involved in making small quantities of a new product when it is at the design and development stage. Toolmaker machinists make the tools, often specialising in just one kind. Toolmaker fitters work on large structures that are constructed from many parts. They check all the parts, number them and then fit them together.

Qualifications and Training

If you are between 16 and 24 years old and want to do a National Apprenticeship Scheme for Engineering Construction (NASEC) apprenticeship, you need GCSEs (A–C)/S grades in maths, English and a science. If you have engineering drawing, metalwork or other practical subjects as well you may have an advantage. Applicants without the required entry grades may also be considered. These apprenticeships take up to three years and you train on-the-job, working along-side experienced toolmakers. This apprenticeship leads to an NVQ level 3 award in engineering production. Older applicants can do BTEC Certificates in manu-facturing engineering.

Personal Qualities and Skills

You must have good manual dexterity and be able to understand engineering drawings. You should be good at following instructions, but able to work without direct supervision. Normal eyesight is essential and good colour vision is important.

Starting Salary

Salaries range from £12,000 to £16,000, but can go up to £20,000 to £22,000. There are often opportunities for shift work payments.

SEMTA (Science Engineering and Manufacturing Technologies Alliance), 14 Upton Road, Watford, Hertfordshire WD18 0JT; 0808 100 3682; www.semta.org.uk

Local Job Centre Plus and Connexions/Careers Centres

Welder

Welders join pieces of metal together by applying intense heat and melting the edges so that two pieces become one. The sorts of items welded are metal sections of aeroplanes, ships, oil rigs, cars and power turbines. Welders work in light and heavy engineering firms, in foundry work and in shipbuilding. Some plastics are also welded.

Welders work on all types of fabrication from the manufacture of metal-frame chairs, to high-quality, complex applications such as building a submarine.

Qualifications and Training

If you are aged between 16 and 24 you can do an Engineering Apprenticeship. There are no set entry qualifications for this, but many employers do prefer you to have GCSEs in English, maths, technology and a science subject. If you have these GCSEs, this also offers a wider range of further qualifications you can take part time or full time at college. These qualifications are also open to people of any age. There are several different NVQ awards related to welding, including fabrication and welding, performing engineering operations and welding with pipe work.

Personal Qualities and Skills

You must have good practical and technical skills and be able to concentrate for long periods of time. You should be good at following instructions, but able to work without direct supervision. Normal eyesight is essential and good near vision is important.

Starting Salary

Salaries range from £12,000 to £16,000, but can go up to £20,000 to £22,000. There are often opportunities for shift work payments.

info

SEMTA (Science Engineering and
Manufacturing Technologies
Alliance), 14 Upton Road, Watford,
Hertfordshire WD18 0JT;
0808 100 3682; www.semta.org.uk

Local Job Centre Plus and
Connexions/Careers Centres

MARINE SCIENTIST

Marine scientists are drawn from various academic disciplines, mainly biology, geology and oceanography. This is a small but developing profession concerned with a detailed study of plant and animal life in the oceans and along coastlines. Its main purpose, as well as expanding our knowledge and understanding, is to research the food chains and levels of fish stocks in the oceans and to analyse the impact of pollution and other human activity on the ecology of the water. Marine scientists are employed by governments, research organisations, pressure groups and the marine laboratories of private organisations.

Qualifications and Training

Two or three A levels or equivalents in biology, chemistry and maths or another science, plus GCSE level or equivalent in maths and physics are necessary for entry to a first degree course in biology. Some universities offer degrees in marine biology, but it may be advisable to take a broader degree in applied biology first.

Personal Qualities and Skills

Biologists need the same characteristics as all scientists: patience and the willingness to repeat experimental work and measurements to check results, a methodical way of working, good observation and accuracy.

info

Institute of Biology,
20 Queensberry Place, London
SW7 2DZ; 020 7581 8333;
fax: 020 7823 9409; www.iob.org;
e-mail: info@iob.org

Marine Biological Association of UK,
The Laboratory, Citadel Hill, Plymouth
PL1 2PB; 01752 633207;
fax: 01752 633102; www.mba.ac.uk

Scottish Association for Marine
Science, Dunstaffnage Marine
Laboratory, Oban, Argyll, PA37 1QA;

01631 559000; fax: 01631 559001;
www.sams.ac.uk;
e-mail: mail@dml.ac.uk

Southampton Oceanography Centre,
University of Southampton,
European Way, Southampton
SO14 3ZH; 023 8059 6666;
www.soc.soto.ac.uk

Society for Underwater Technology,
80 Coleman Street, London
EC2R 5BJ; 020 7382 2601;
www.sut.org.uk

Starting Salary

New entrants earn between £19,000 and £23,000 – often more with a postgraduate qualification.

MARKETING

Marketing is concerned with undertaking research, identifying consumer needs and demands relative to product or service, price, place and time, organising their production and promoting them to the appropriate customer segment. It includes new product development, packaging, advertising, pricing, sales, distribution and after-sales service. It is often claimed that advertising, PR, market research and the like all come under the umbrella of marketing.

Marketing executive

People usually come into marketing either from sales or from the market research side, or they may have worked for an advertising agency before joining the marketing team of a manufacturing company. Some enter as graduate trainees. There are a growing number of posts in e-marketing.

The responsibilities of a marketing executive vary according to the size of the organisation and the importance marketing takes within the company. In a large firm, for example, the marketing director will have a say in all the company's activities and be involved in product development. Marketing executives will handle products or ranges, and organise advertising, public relations and sales promotion activities for that product.

The increased sophistication of databases has led to the growth of niche marketing known as direct marketing. Information gathered is used, subject to industry codes of practice, to make direct contact between companies and prospective customers. Direct marketing is based on providing relevant, timely products and services and then developing an ongoing relationship with customers and encouraging loyalty. The industry makes use of all communications channels, including mail; telephone; door-drops; fax; field marketing; direct response television, radio and press advertisements and inserts; the internet; mobile phone SMS and interactive television.

Job roles within the industry include creative/copy writing, production, account planning, data planning, and account handling (also known as client service). The most frequently chosen path for people with good marketing qualifications (see below under Qualifications and Training) is account handling. New entrants tend to be graduates, with some work experience in a marketing or sales-led organisation.

Other career opportunities include specialist areas such as field marketing (demonstrations, merchandising; road shows), telemarketing, mailing, e-mail and SMS marketing which can require some technical ability and knowledge.

Qualifications and Training

While there are no specific entry requirements, many people who get into marketing have either a Higher National Diploma or a degree. Any subject is acceptable, but business and marketing subjects are especially useful. If you do not have academic qualifications, then a background in sales or the willingness to work your way up from more junior posts are alternative routes in. Some employers like you to have experience with the types of product or service which you will be marketing. Training is on the job, though large companies may also run in-house courses. There are several organisations that run part-time and distance learning courses relevant to people working in marketing. These are the Chartered Institute of Marketing (CIM), the Institute of Direct Marketing (IDM), the Institute of Export and the Communication Advertising & Marketing Education Foundation (CAM).

Personal Qualities and Skills

You need a broad mix of skills to be successful in marketing. You need to be confident in dealing with people and possess good written communication skills. You need to be numerate, have good IT skills and be able to work under pressure. You should be a good negotiator, able to be persuasive and encouraging. It is helpful if you can think creatively and come up with imaginative solutions to problems.

Starting Salary

Salaries start at between £16,000 and £24,000. There is very strong competition for the best paid jobs with large companies or marketing consultants. A successful marketing executive can earn up to £50,000.

info

Chartered Institute of Marketing (CIM), Moor Hall, Cookham, Maidenhead, Berks SL6 9QH; 01628 427500; www.cim.co.uk

The Communication Advertising and Marketing Education Foundation (CAM), Moor Hall, Cookham, Maidenhead, Berkshire SL6 9QH; 01628 427120; www.camfoundation.com

The Institute of Direct Marketing (IDM), 1 Park Road, Teddington, Middlesex TW11 0AR; 020 8977 5705; www.theidm.co.uk

How to get on in Marketing, Advertising and Public Relations (Kogan Page)

MARKET RESEARCHER

Market research is the collection and analysis of information about markets, organisations and people to support better business decisions. It is used to discover gaps in the market, to ensure customer satisfaction and to plan effective marketing campaigns. In a competitive environment, the more knowledge a business has about its customers, the more likely it is to succeed.

Over the past few decades, market research techniques have developed significantly, making it a more precise science. Methods used depend on the requirements of the business and the budget available, and include interviews with individuals, surveys by telephone, post and via the internet, and increasingly using mobile phone text messaging. These are used to gather quantitative (numerical) data. Qualitative research by face-to-face interviews with individuals or groups is geared to providing insight into why people hold the views they do, and provides greater understanding of customers. Interviewers are known as field workers, and their work, and that of the analysis personnel, is organised by the research executive, who is in overall charge of the project for a marketing executive or client, and is responsible for interpreting the results.

Every year, the Market Research Society (MRS) publishes the *Research Buyer's Guide*, which lists the majority of market research agencies in the UK and outlines the size of each agency, together with their areas of specialisation. The guide also details other organisations that can offer advice on getting started in market research; the online version of the guide is free at www.rbg.org.uk.

Qualifications and Training

Field workers do not need qualifications but must be articulate, persuasive and presentable. Applicants for research and executive positions will be expected to hold a degree. The majority of market research graduates are drawn from disciplines that require strong communication or analytical skills, such as languages, English literature, maths, psychology, geography, history, politics, science and IT. However, graduates with degrees as contrasting as zoology and theatre studies are also welcomed by the industry.

The Market Research Society offers a range of qualifications that are linked to the UK's National Qualifications Framework and are designed to suit a wide range of candidates, from those with no experience to practitioners seeking continuous professional development.

Personal Qualities and Skills

Excellent communication skills and ability to get on with people of all types. Analytical skills, numeracy and data interpretation are important.

Starting Salary

Market research interviewers are paid between £35 and £50 for a six to seven hour day, and for some their pay is linked to target numbers of interviews, or questionnaires completed. Permanent staff who analyse data, plan research strategies and liaise with clients are paid between £16,000 and £20,000 a year.

British Market Research Association (BMRA), Devonshire House, 60 Goswell Road, London EC1M 7AD; 020 7566 3636; www.bmra.org.uk/

The Market Research Society (MRS), 15 Northburgh Street, London EC1V 0JR; 020 7490 4911; www.mrs.org.uk/

The Social Research Association (SRA), PO Box 33660, London N16 6WE; 020 8880 5684; www.sra.org.uk

info

MEAT INDUSTRY

As well as retail and supermarket work as a butcher, or working for large organisations such as hotels, there are other openings in the meat industry. Some wholesale establishments selling pre-packed meat need teams of butchers for boning, cutting and packing the meat, or processing it into pies. Wholesale butchers do not meet the general public but deal with other butchers and retailers. Workers are also needed in abattoirs, to handle and kill the animals, and to inspect and deal with the meat.

Butcher

Career prospects are varied in the meat industry, extending from work in a small retail shop through to supermarkets; from meat buying for large organisations such as hotels and caterers, to the manufacture of meat and poultry products.

Qualifications and Training

A good general education is necessary but there are no formal educational requirements. Training is on the job and courses are available at further education establishments and technical colleges, leading to examinations of the Meat Training Council. NVQs are available at levels 1–4, and higher national diploma/certificate qualifications. Modern Apprenticeships are available. Further training, appropriate to the relevant sector of the industry, in management, meat technology, or small business ownership, may follow an apprenticeship.

Personal Qualities and Skills

Butchers need to be very practical, with good manual dexterity, and not squeamish. They must ensure that they and their work environments are really clean and hygienic and they must enjoy talking to people and giving advice. A good business sense is also useful.

Starting Salary

Trainee butchers earn around £12,000 a year, skilled butchers earn around £16,000 and butcher managers earn £16,000 to £21,000. Some supermarkets offer bonuses and other staff benefit schemes.

info

Meat Training Council, PO Box 141, Winterhill House, Snowdon Drive, Milton Keynes MK6 1YY; 01908 231062; www.meattraining.org.uk

Scottish Meat Training, 8–10 Needless Road, Perth PH2 0JW; 01738 637785; www.foodtraining.net

Improve Ltd, Sector Skills Council for Food and Drink Manufacturing and Processing, Providence House, 2 Innovation Lane, Heslington, York YO10 52F; 0845 644 0448; www.improveltd.co.uk

MEDICAL ILLUSTRATION

A career in medical illustration involves recording medical conditions precisely for the medical profession and related sectors. The profession provides specialist photographic, graphic design, art and video services tailored to patient care, pre/postgraduate medical education, research and medico-legal needs. As a collective body, medical illustrators form an integral part of the clinical healthcare team. Members of the profession include the following.

Graphic designers

(*see also* Art and Design)

They specialise in the design, layout and production of artwork, brochures, scientific posters and other visual material, primarily for patient information or marketing.

Medical artists

Medical artists produce highest quality artwork for publication and medical education purposes.

Medical photographers

They are responsible for recording clinical conditions, working within the studio, clinic, ward and operating theatre environments. Specialised areas include diagnostic services within ophthalmology and planning images for craniofacial surgery.

Medical videographers

Medical videographers produce high-quality programmes for teaching and research purposes.

Qualifications and Training

Many trusts and health authorities now ask for a BSc in Medical Illustration. A prospective candidate may, however, be working towards the BSc, or commit to undertake the BSc upon commencement of employment. Trainees need at least a media qualification to HND level (or equivalent) in photography, video or graphic design.

The Glasgow Caledonian University/Institute of Medical Illustrators (GCU/IMI) BSc in Medical Illustration can be taken as a full-time course or as a three-year distance-learning course. With a first degree in photography, video, graphics, art or media studies, such graduates may apply to undertake the IMI Post Experience Certificate (PEC). Other degree courses available nationally are an MSc in Medical Illustration at the University of Wales College of Medicine and a BSc (Hons) in Biomedical Imaging at the University of Derby.

The Institute of Medical Illustrators is the leading professional body. Members qualify at degree level with the BSc in Medical Illustration, are actively involved in continuing professional development and are registered with the National Board of Registration of Medical Illustrators (NBRMI). They are governed by a Code of Conduct, a Code of Responsible Practice and relevant law, for example the Data Protection Act. These measures cover legal and ethical aspects such as consent, confidentiality and copyright, and are designed to protect both patients and healthcare organisations from the misuse of medical images.

Personal Qualities and Skills

As well as natural artistic ability and an eye for fine detail, you have to have a very good, reassuring manner with people. You also have to be prepared to draw, photograph, etc any part of the human body in any condition of disease, injury or trauma. You have to work quietly and calmly, without getting in anyone's way.

Starting Salary

Trainees start on between £9,000 and £11,500. Once you have completed your training your salary rises to between £12,000 and £22,000.

MEDICINE

Doctor

Doctors work in many healthcare settings in both the NHS and in private clinics and hospitals. For the NHS they work in community medicine, in general practice and in hospitals. In the hospital setting there are many different aspects of health and medicine in which they may specialise. While management structures in the NHS change, these are still likely to remain the distinctive areas of work for doctors. Some doctors may also work in industry, eg pharmaceuticals, in occupational health or in advisory and research roles for public and private organisations.

Community health doctors

Community health doctors work as part of the healthcare team. They are based in community centres and provide a different service to that of the local GP. They will also see patients who do not want to see their own GPs. Community health doctors often work with specific issues such as family planning, child health or asthma management. The work is similar to that of a GP, but without such a large management and administrative caseload. Most community health doctors have already worked as GPs.

General practitioner

Family doctors, or GPs, may form long-standing relationships with their patients. They must be able to diagnose and deal with a broad spectrum of illnesses and disorders, mainly those common within the community, but also to recognise those that are rare. Increasingly, doctors are asked to help their patients to cope with personal and emotional problems. They have to be aware of and take into account physical, psychological and social factors when looking after their patients About 90 per cent of GPs now work together in group practices, allowing some specialisation.

For doctors who work in the community, people are of prime importance. GPs are involved with individuals' problems, whether personal, social, organisational or environmental. General practice is the most personalised of all the health services, based close to patients' homes and with opportunities for long-term relationships between doctor and patient. Within this context, it is the doctor's job to give early treatment and continuing care for the great variety of problems and disorders presented by patients. GPs have to deal with many moral decisions, and much of the work is challenging because of its unpredictability.

General practice differs from all other areas of medicine in that it is not salaried and GPs are technically self-employed. The government sets an average amount that GPs are supposed to earn, and basic pay is based on the number of patients on a GP's list.

Hospital doctor

Hospital doctors treat hospital inpatients and patients who come to the hospital through outpatient clinics. Hospital doctors work in one of 50 different specialist areas within medicine, working to treat illness, disease and infection in one of these areas. The specialisms fall into three main groups: medicine, surgery and psychiatry. During training, they will learn about every aspect of health and with more experience choose a specialist area which interests them. Doctors choosing to work in medical areas can specialise in such fields as cardiology or paediatrics. They prescribe treatments or organise further investigations, and they monitor patients' progress. Surgeons perform operations of many kinds. They can choose to specialise in such areas as orthopaedics, repairing damaged and broken bones. Psychiatrists treat patients with mental illnesses such as anxiety or depression, prescribing drugs, behavioural or talking therapies.

Research and teaching

Research work is carried out in universities, hospitals, public health laboratories, and other research establishments and pharmaceutical manufacturing companies. There are opportunities too for teaching in universities. Teaching may involve very little or no contact with patients, or it may be similar in content to hospital doctors' work. An academic career in medicine either through teaching or research is possible in practically all hospital specialities, general practice and public health medicine.

Qualifications and Training

To become a doctor in the UK you must take a degree in medicine recognised by the General Medical Council (GMC). To be accepted onto a degree course in medicine you must have three A levels, normally an A and 2 Bs including maths and two sciences. In Scotland you need five H grades and two Advanced Science Highers, one of which must be chemistry.

The GMC also approves some six-year degrees in medicine designed for applicants who do not meet the A level science selection criteria. The additional year is a pre-medical course in science. In some cases, an access to higher education course may be accepted. It is important to check carefully with the GMC, to ensure that you embark on an approved course.

During 2006 some UK universities introduced the UK Clinical Aptitude Test (UKCAT) as part of the selection process for students applying for medicine. The test measures behavioural and mental attributes relevant to people working in the field of medicine. Check the UKCAT website to find out about participating universities and how to apply to take the test. It is likely to be introduced at all university medical schools.

All medical degree courses combine a great deal of practical training and clinical experience with academic learning. Having completed your medical degree you then undertake a two-year foundation programme, gaining further experience and consolidating your learning.

Personal Qualities and Skills

All doctors must have excellent interpersonal skills – these qualities have become increasingly important in selecting appropriate students for medical school.

Starting Salary

Junior doctors earn around £35,000. Senior house officers can earn up to £50,000. Consultants earn between £69,000 and £94,000. It is possible, with additional payments and merit awards, for consultants to earn up to £160,000. GPs earn £42,000 to £50,000 and £70,000 to £100,000 when established. Salaries for GPs vary according to the geographical area in which they work and the number and types of services they provide. Consultants working for the NHS can supplement their income by taking on some private patients.

info

Royal College of Surgeons of England, 35–43 Lincoln's Inn Fields, London WC2A 3PE; 020 7405 3474; www.rcseng.ac.uk

NHS Careers, PO Box 376, Bristol BS99 3EY; 0845 606 0655; www.nhscareers.nhs.uk

Royal College of Physicians, 11 St Andrews Place, Regent's Park, London NW1 4LE; 020 7224 1539; www.rcplondon.ac.uk

General Medical Council (GMC), Regent's Place, 350 Euston Road, London NW1 3JN; 0845 357 3456; www.gmc-uk.org

British Medical Association, Tavistock Square, London WC1H 9JP; 020 7387 4499; www.bma.org.uk

UK Clinical Aptitude Test; www.ukcat.ac.uk

MERCHANT NAVY

The 'Merchant Navy' is the collective term for the British shipping industry, which operates worldwide and includes the ferry sector, containership companies, cruise companies, oil, gas and chemical tankers, bulk carriers of ores, grain and coal, and support vessels for the offshore exploration industry.

Communications

Electro-technical officers are responsible for the maintenance and efficient operation of complex electrical, electronic and control systems on board ship.

Deck staff

Deck officers are responsible for controlling the navigation of the ship, communications, cargo handling and ship stability. A deck officer is a step on the way to becoming captain (master). Deck ratings assist in the navigation of the ship, are involved in operating deck machinery such as winches and cranes, and carry out maintenance tasks. There are also some dual officer roles, covering both deck and engineering departments.

Engineering staff

Engineer officers are responsible for the provision and maintenance of all technical services on board, including the propulsion and auxiliary machinery in the engine room. They are responsible for the work of engine-room staff, so managing people is part of the job, as with all ships' officers. An engineer officer is a step on the way to becoming chief engineer officer.

Engineer ratings are involved in routine maintenance, engine operation and repairs.

Hotel and entertainment services on cruise ships and ferries

This includes pursers/receptionists, restaurant and bar staff, chefs, housekeepers, cruise directors, entertainments team, hairdressers, beauticians, photographers and retail staff. Those recruited are qualified and experienced within their own specialism.

Qualifications and Training

Training for careers at sea is provided by shipping companies or group training organisations. It usually consists of programmes of learning and experience based on a sandwich pattern of alternating periods at college and at sea, leading to nationally recognised qualifications and professional maritime certificates of competency. There are four main entry routes, each with deck and engineering options. Each provides progression opportunities to the next stage and, through the ranks, to captain (master) or chief engineer officer depending on ability and ambition. The routes are:

- Marine Traineeship: structured training for seafarers employed, usually, as ratings, in the deck or engineering departments in support of the officers of the watch. Entrants must show an aptitude to succeed to at least NVQ level 2. As a guide, they are expected to have attained three GCSEs or equivalent.
- Marine Apprenticeship: provides an enhanced level of training for those employed initially as ratings in the deck or engineering departments while following a programme of learning leading to NVQ level 3 and qualification as officer of the watch. As a guide, entrants are expected to have attained a minimum of four GCSEs, including English, mathematics and science (or equivalents).
- Officer cadet: provides structured learning for those aiming to progress to captain (master) or chief engineer officer, and achieve qualifications at HND or degree level in addition to professional certificates of competency. Entry standards may vary from company to company, and according to whether the degree or HND option is chosen. As a guide, candidates are expected to have attained A levels and a minimum of four GCSEs at grades A–C, or equivalents, including mathematics, English and science. Entry with GCSEs only may be possible for suitably motivated candidates.
- Postgraduate entry: accelerated programmes have been developed for new entrants with suitable science-based degrees. This is similar to the cadet programme but recognises prior qualification and maturity of applicants.

Personal Qualities and Skills

All candidates must be in good health and pass a statutory medical examination, with a good standard of eyesight required for prospective deck personnel. The ability to get on well with other people and adapt to new conditions is also important.

info

Careers in Shipping, Carthusian Court, 12 Carthusian Street, London EC1M 6EZ; general information on all Merchant Navy careers and list of shipping companies providing sponsorship; 0800 085 0973; www.gotosea.org.uk; e-mail: careers@gotosea.org.uk

Marine Society, 202 Lambeth Road, London SE1 7JW; 020 7261 9535; fax: 020 7401 2537; www.marine-society.org; e-mail: enq@marine-society.org

Merchant Navy Training Board (MNTB), Carthusian Court, 12 Carthusian Street, London EC1M 6EZ; 020 7417 2800; fax: 020 7726 2030; www.mntb.org.uk; e-mail: enquiry@mntb.org.uk. For careers information pack call 0800 085 0973.

Listings of individual shipping companies

Starting Salary

Starting salaries vary between sponsoring companies. Food, accommodation and other allowances often go with the job.

METALLURGIST

Metallurgists are involved with the extraction of metals from ores, their purification, and with reclaiming them from scrap. They are also concerned with developing new alloys and processing metals during manufacture.

Qualifications and Training

GCSE passes in a science subject, maths and English or equivalent are required for entry to Edexcel (BTEC) and SQA two-year courses for a certificate or diploma in metallurgical studies. Candidates who have successfully completed the two-year course and those with A levels or equivalent in maths, physics or chemistry may study for the Edexcel (BTEC)/SQA Higher Certificates and diplomas, or qualify for entry to full-time, sandwich or part-time courses leading to degrees in metallurgy.

Personal Qualities and Skills

Metallurgy demands an interest in scientific and technological subjects, an ability to solve practical problems and work with other people on specific projects.

Starting Salary

New graduates earn between £18,000 and £25,000. With a few years' experience earnings rise to between £30,000 and £37,000.

Institute of Cast Metal Engineers (ICME), National Metalforming Centre, 47 Birmingham Road, West Bromwich, West Midlands B70 6PY; 0121 601 6979; www.icme.org.uk

Institute of Materials, Minerals and Mining (IOM3), 1 Carlton House Terrace, London SW1Y 5DB; 020 7451 7300; www.iom3.org

Metals Industry Skills and Performance, 5/6 Meadowcourt, Amos Road, Sheffield S9 1BX; 0114 244 6833; www.metskill.org.uk

Proskills UK, Centurion Court, 85b Milton Park, Abingdon, Oxfordshire OX14 4RY; 01235 833844; www.proskills.co.uk

Info

METEOROLOGIST

The Meteorological Office is an executive agency within the Ministry of Defence. It is a centre of excellence for the production of numerical weather forecasts, climate prediction and related studies. It serves the different and varying needs of defence, other areas of government, civil aviation, industry, commerce and the general public. A wide range of jobs is available such as researching, developing and delivering weather and environmental information.

Qualifications and Training

From time to time there are vacancies in administration, for which a minimum of five GCSEs to include English are required. Most vacancies arise in the forecasting, research and IT areas, for which a first or upper second-class degree is necessary in maths, one of the physical sciences, computer science or meteorology.

Personal Qualities and Skills

Candidates need to be adaptable and prepared to work in more than one specialist area. Good communication and computing skills are necessary.

Starting Salary

Graduates can earn between £15,500 and £24,000.

info

Local Job Centre Plus and Careers/ Connexions Centres

Meteorological Office, FitzRoy Road, Exeter, Devon EX1 3PB;
0870 900 0100; fax: 0870 900 5050;
www.metoffice.com;
e-mail: enquiries@metoffice.gov.uk

Royal Meteorological Society,
104 Oxford Road, Reading RG1 7LL;
0118 956 8500; fax: 0118 956 8571;
www.royal-met-soc.org.uk

A list of relevant courses at UK universities is available by post from the Royal Meteorological Society.

MICROBIOLOGIST

Microbiology is the study of tiny living organisms (bacteria, viruses, fungi, protozoa and algae) and the massive impact they have on almost every aspect of our lives. There are good job opportunities for microbiologists in the human and animal healthcare sector, medical research, and the food production and agricultural industries. Microbiologists are employed in hospitals, research institutes, industrial research and development and manufacturing sites, universities and environmental companies. Their skills and knowledge are vital to the rapidly growing biotechnology industry, where gene technology, fermentation and bioprocessing play an important part in developing products of the future.

Qualifications and Training

Minimum requirements for entry to a full-time first degree course are five GCSE passes (grades A–C) and two A level science passes. Some courses concentrate on specific areas of microbiology, others are more general and allow specialisation at a later stage. Some courses offer a period of industrial training. It is also possible to obtain qualifications via part-time study while working in a laboratory.

Personal Qualities and Skills

Microbiologists have enquiring minds, are good problem solvers and can work accurately. Good communication skills are vital as microbiologists have to describe their work to other people. Most scientists work in a multidisciplinary group so it helps to be a good team worker.

Starting Salary

Graduate starting salaries are usually in the range of £13,000 to £19,000, depending on the area chosen.

Society for General Microbiology, Marlborough House, Basingstoke Road, Spencers Wood, Reading RG7 1AG; 0118 988 1800; fax: 0118 988 5656; www.socgenmicrobiol.org.uk; e-mail: careers@sgm.ac.uk

www.microbiologyonline.org.uk

'Microbiologists make a difference' (free leaflet from the above)

'Your career in microbiology' (free booklet from the above)

info

MILK ROUNDSPERSON

see Roundsperson

MODELMAKER

Models can be made to represent almost anything: towns, office blocks, oil terminals, shopping centres, motorways, houses, cars and planes. They are often scaled-down versions of the real thing, but sometimes they can be enlargements. They are used to show what the real thing will look like, and if they are working models, may be used as testers. Models are often used too in television and films. Modelmakers work for firms specialising in such work, or sometimes branch out on their own.

Qualifications and Training

Formal academic qualifications are not necessary. Modelmakers may teach themselves or learn at evening class; some large firms offer apprenticeships. Edexcel (BTEC) courses in modelmaking are available at some FE colleges and some art colleges.

Personal Qualities and Skills

Patience, manual dexterity, a good sense of design, shape and colour are necessary. Modelmakers must be prepared to do one job for a considerable length of time; a project such as a model town could take up to a year to complete.

Starting Salary

Low when training; with experience £200+ a week; good modelmakers may earn much more.

Local Job Centre Plus and Careers/Connexions Centres

MOTOR INDUSTRY

The motor industry provides a range of job opportunities, from technical to sales and management roles. A common theme for all these jobs is that you have to have a real interest in motor vehicles. The following section gives details of the most commonly found job titles and training routes within this industry.

Auto electrician

Auto electricians are motor vehicle technicians who have highly specialised knowledge of and skill in the complex electrical and electronic systems that are part of modern motor vehicles.

Qualifications and Training

To be an auto electrician, you need to do an apprenticeship. To start an apprenticeship you must have five GCSEs grades A–C, including maths and English. The apprenticeship combines on-the-job training with your employer and college-based learning. Through your apprenticeship you can gain an NVQ certificate.

Personal Qualities and Skills

You must be good at working with your hands and able to solve problems. You must be good at working as part of a team.

Automotive engineer

see Engineering

Body repairer and refinisher

Body repairers and refinishers restore cars, vans, trucks and motorcycles to their original condition after accidents, damage or other wear and tear. This includes replacing windscreens and other glass, hammering out dents or rubbing away patches of rust. Repair and refinishing covers several different roles including body repair, electrical, mechanical and trim repair, and vehicle valeting.

Qualifications and Training

For any job in body repair and refinishing, apart from car valeting, you need to do an apprenticeship. To be accepted for an apprenticeship you must have five GCSEs grades A–C, including maths and English. The apprenticeship combines on the job training with your employer and college-based learning. Through your apprenticeship you can gain relevant NVQ certificates.

Personal Qualities and Skills

These vary according to exactly which aspect of body repair and refinishing you have chosen, but they all demand that you pay great attention to fine detail, that you can find ways to solve problems and that you are able to work as part of a team.

Roadside assistance and recovery technician

Roadside assistance and recovery workers are called to the scene of vehicle breakdowns. They have to make quick, accurate assessments as to whether they can repair the vehicle on the spot or whether it will have to be towed away. They also have to reassure vehicle drivers and passengers and explain to them clearly what the best course of action is.

Qualifications and Training

For this work you must be 21 years old and hold a full clean driving licence. Most successful applicants will already have worked for three years or more with motor vehicles, usually as a vehicle technician. Most technicians qualify through an apprenticeship.

Personal Qualities and Skills

You need to be extremely responsible, with good technical skills and knowledge. You must be able to take decisions on your own and to solve problems. You must have good people skills, be polite, friendly and reassuring, and good at explaining technical problems.

Vehicle parts operative

Vehicle parts operatives deal with the ordering and management of the hundreds of separate parts that need to be replaced in every type of vehicle. Vehicle parts operatives have to be able to recognise any vehicle part and know that part's place in a vehicle. They have to liaise with customers, with technicians, with manufacturers and with distributors. The work involves ordering and finding stock, controlling stock levels and advising customers.

Qualifications and Training

To work as a parts operative, you need to do an apprenticeship. To be accepted on an apprenticeship you must have five GCSEs grades A–C, including maths and English. The apprenticeship combines on-the-job training with your employer and college-based learning. Through your apprenticeship you can gain relevant NVQ certificates.

Personal Qualities and Skills

You must be really interested in vehicles, be very well organised, able to work under pressure and good at dealing with people. You must be good at handling a lot of detailed information.

Vehicle salesperson

People working in vehicle sales, often described as sales executives, sell cars and other vehicles to private and business customers. They have to know a great deal about cars, not just those they are trying to sell, but those they may be purchasing or taking in part exchange.

Qualifications and Training

There are no formal entry qualifications for this job. Many vehicle sales people have worked as vehicle technicians or in other roles in the automotive industry. Some have come from a selling background in other sectors.

Personal Qualities and Skills

Sales executives have to combine good technical knowledge with excellent people skills. You must be polite, friendly, prepared to answer detailed questions and able to offer clear explanations.

Vehicle technician

Vehicle technicians work to repair and maintain cars, vans, trucks and motorcycles. It is usual for technicians to specialise in just one of these groups of vehicles. Vehicle technicians also work at the many fast fit centres which fit tyres, exhausts or other parts and systems. Some technicians specialise in MOT testing or in converting petrol cars to run on liquid petroleum gas (LPG).

Qualifications and Training

To become a motor vehicle technician (with the exception of fast tyre fitting) you need to do an apprenticeship. To start an apprenticeship you must have five

GCSEs grades A–C, including maths and English. The apprenticeship combines on-the-job training with college-based learning. Through your apprenticeship you can gain relevant NVQ certificates.

Personal Qualities and Skills

All motor vehicle technicians have to have a real interest in working with vehicles and be good at working with their hands. You often need to be a good problem solver and patient too – sometimes why something won't work is not obvious.

Vehicle valeter

Vehicle valeters clean and polish vehicles for individual customers and for car show rooms, and vehicle leasing and rental companies. Valeters clean the inside and the outside of vehicles. They may have to vacuum, clean windows and other glass, steam clean, wash, use high pressure hoses and wax and polish vehicles. Some vehicle valeters combine vehicle pick up and delivery with their valeting work.

Qualifications and Training

There are no formal entry qualifications for this work, but if your job involves driving, you must have a full, clean driving licence. A mature attitude is important, and some experience in customer care work can be an advantage.

Personal Qualities and Skills

You must be very thorough, good at paying attention to detail and you should be reasonably physically fit. You should be polite, friendly and trustworthy.

Automotive Skills: The Sector Skills Council for the Automotive Industry, 93 Newman Street, London W1T 3DT; 0800 093 1777; www.automotiveskills.org.uk/careers

The Sector Skills Council for the retail motor industry, which supplies impartial careers information for the entire sector.

Automotive Distribution Federation, www.adf.org.uk

British Vehicle Rental and Leasing Association, www.bvrla.co.uk

City & Guilds, www.city-and-guilds.co.uk

The Institute of the Motor Industry, Fanshaws, Brickendon, Hertford SG13 8PQ; 01992 511521; www.motor.org.uk

Society of Motor Manufacturers and Traders, www.smmt.co.uk

Vehicle Builders and Repairers Association, Belmont House, 102 Finkle Lane, Gildersome, Leeds LS27 7TW; 0113 253 8333; www.vbra.co.uk

Info

Are you up for a career that's loaded with opportunity?

Take a virtual tour of **AutoCity**™, our game-based interactive CD-ROM and you'll discover a world of possibilities. Have you thought about all the different jobs you could be doing?

The modern motor industry is an exciting place, where use of the latest technology drives every activity from sales and rental through to parts and repair – and financial awareness and sales skills are every bit as important as the technical expertise needed in the workshop. It's an industry for smart people, where there's room for women and men alike, and lots of opportunities to progress.

Want to find out more? Visit our website **www.automotiveskills.org.uk/careers** to order **AutoCity**™ and other resources. Have a flick through **Career Driven**, our lifestyle magazine. Or you can also try our freephone helpline on **0800 093 1777**.

You'll soon see how you can get your career moving in the motor industry.

WELCOME TO
AutoCity

automotive skills

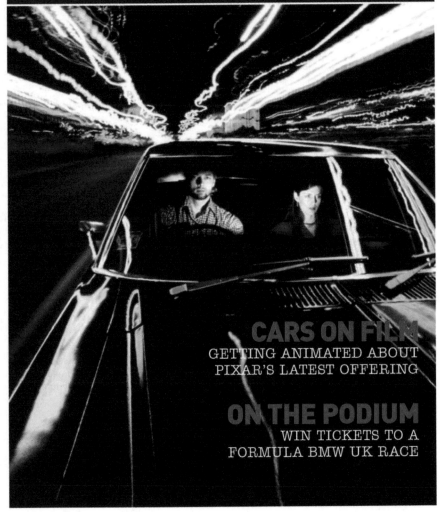

Starting Salary

At the start of a motor vehicle apprenticeship earnings are around £7,000 to £10,000, rising to £15,000 on completing training. Experienced technicians can earn more than this. Car valeters earn between £10,000 and £14,000. Sales staff are normally paid a basic salary plus a percentage or commission for each vehicle they sell. Basic salaries for salespersons start at around £13,000 with a possible extra £4,000 to £5,000 in commission and bonuses.

Many people with technical qualifications and some experience in the industry decide to set up their own businesses.

MUSIC

(*see also* Performing Arts)

Occupations in music range from composing and performing, to making and repairing instruments, to teaching.

info

Incorporated Society of Musicians, 10 Stratford Place, London W1C 1AA; 020 7629 4413; fax: 020 7408 1538; www.ism.org.uk; e-mail: membership@ism.org.uk

Composer

Very few composers earn a living solely by composition; most also perform or teach. The most lucrative area of composition is writing music for television, films, videos and the commercial market, but some composers also find time to write their own music and get it performed. Professional advice on copyright (from a solicitor or professional association) is essential.

Musical instrument technologist

The instrument technologist is concerned with making and repairing instruments of all kinds, from pianos to guitars. Good training and practical skill are essential and ensure plenty of work for the technologist.

Qualifications and Training

The Department of Communications and Music Technology at the London Guildhall University offers courses in almost every aspect of instrument technology through its City & Guilds Certificate, BTEC National Diploma, HND and degree courses. Full- and part-time courses are also offered by Leeds College of Music, Morley College, West Dean College, Merton Technical College and Newark Technical College. The Institute of Musical Instrument Technology awards a diploma and can provide further advice and information.

Personal Qualities and Skills

Instrument technologists need some musical ability, at least an ear for tuning, and relevant technical skills – woodwork, electronics and metalwork.

Starting Salary

Average earnings when starting out are around £12,000 a year. With highly specialised technical knowledge and experience, or experience of electronics, incomes can be between £16,000 and £23,000.

Incorporated Society of Musicians (ISM), 10 Stratford Place, London W1A 1AA; 020 7629 4413; www.ism.org

Society for the Promotion of the New Music, Francis House, Francis Street, London SW1P 1DE; 020 7828 9696; www.spnm.org.uk

National Association of Musical Instrument Repairers; www.namir.org.uk

Skillset, Sector Skills Council for Advertising, Culture and the Arts, Prospect House, 80–110 New Oxford Street, London WC1A 1HB; 020 7520 5757; www.skillset.org

Musician

see Performing Arts

Music teacher

With music now placed as one of the foundation subjects in the National Curriculum there is an increasing demand for music teachers. Opportunities range from private instrumental teaching to class teaching at primary, secondary and tertiary levels. Class teachers and some visiting instrumental teachers working in state schools require Qualified Teacher status.

Private teachers set up and develop their own independent, studio-based business. The Incorporated Society of Musicians (ISM) sets professional standards for members who are listed in their Register of Professional Private Music Teachers. They set minimum hourly tuition fees, so that a reasonable income can be assured, and advise on business matters such as tuition contracts.

Qualifications and Training

Entry to undergraduate courses of study usually requires a minimum of five GCSEs and one or more A levels, preferably including music. Full-time courses of study over three or four years, usually leading to a degree, are available at conservatoires (performance-based), universities (more academic) and colleges of higher education (more broad spectrum). Singers require a longer training, often over six years. Conservatoires and universities also offer a range of postgraduate courses. Teachers require an appropriate teaching qualification, such as a PGCE (Postgraduate Certificate in Education). Details of courses in performance, composition, musicology and teaching are available from the Incorporated Society of Musicians' website. The government has introduced a training scheme for the music industry under the 'New Deal' initiative; details are available from Job Centre Plus centres.

Personal Qualities and Skills

A love of music, a positive and persuasive personality, robust physical and mental health, stamina, patience and excellent communication skills are essential for any career in music. Competition is fierce for performers, and only a very few talented musicians can establish a successful solo career. The ability to get on well with others helps to ensure good relationships with colleagues, managers and promoters to support career development.

Starting Salary

Salaries vary enormously. Guidance on rates of pay is available from the Incorporated Society of Musicians. Hourly rates of £16–£20 are usual.

Music therapist

see Therapy

Piano tuner

Piano tuners or technicians are able both to tune a piano evenly throughout the scale, and to discover and put right any fault. They work with a kit of specialised tools, and are employed in piano factories and by piano dealers. Some also work for themselves.

Qualifications and Training

Courses are available at three institutions: London Guildhall University, Newark and Sherwood College and the Royal National College for the Blind, Hereford. No formal entry qualifications are required. The Piano Tuners' Association will accept a candidate for membership after five years from the start of training – at least two years training and at least two years working as a piano tuner.

Personal Qualities and Skills

Musical ability, while not essential, is an advantage. Patience and deftness are required, together with an aptitude to be able to use woodworking, home-improvement and DIY tools. As tuners are mostly self-employed, the ability to work alone, competence in managing a small business and self-motivation are also important.

Starting Salary

Salaries vary greatly: the average is £250–£300 a week when trained but lower without experience. Established, self-employed piano tuners may earn up to £800 a week.

Pianoforte Tuners' Association, www.pianotuner.org.uk;
e-mail: enquiries@pianotuner.org.uk

info

NAVAL ARCHITECT

Naval architects are professional engineers who play a key role as project leaders and specialists in the design, building and marketing of all systems that have to move just above, on or under the sea, including merchant ships, warships, offshore structures, submarines, hovercraft, yachts and other small craft. They also have to ensure that a safe, economic and seaworthy design is produced. The workplace may be a large company, a small group, a consultancy or a government department.

Qualifications and Training

The usual way to become a naval architect is with a degree or diploma accredited by the Royal Institute of Naval Architects (RINA). Approved subjects include naval architecture, marine engineering and ocean engineering. You need A levels in maths, physics and one other subject to study any of these accredited courses. Anyone with a qualification in another engineering discipline should check with the RINA to see whether it is acceptable, or what further qualifications and training they need to undertake. Without a degree or diploma it may be possible to take equivalent Engineering Council qualifications. Several companies are accredited to provide training. This training covers three areas: design, engineering practice and management services. After a minimum of two years' work experience you can apply to become a chartered or incorporated engineer with the RINA.

info

Royal Institute of Naval Architects (RINA),10 Upper Belgrave Street, London SW1X 8BQ; 020 7235 4622; www.rina.org.uk

SEMTA, 14 Upton Road, Watford, Hertfordshire WD18 0JT; 0808 100 3682; www.semta.org.uk

Engineering Council, 10 Maltravers Street, London WC2R 3ER; 020 7240 7891; www.engtech.co.uk

Personal Qualities and Skills

A genuine interest in ships, boats and other vessels is a good starting point. You must have good technical engineering knowledge and a creative attitude to problem solving. Naval architects need good report-writing skills and the confidence and clarity to explain technical problems to non-technical people.

Starting Salary

Graduate trainees earn between £21,000 and £23,000. Qualified and experienced naval architects earn from £35,000.

NEUROPHYSIOLOGY TECHNOLOGIST

A more familiar name for the neurophysiology technologist is the EEG (electro-encephalography) technologist, who is responsible for setting up and operating electronic equipment that records electrical activity in the brain and nervous system. These tests often include visual, auditory or other types of evoked potentials (EPs), which are the responses of the brain to specific stimuli. EEG and EP tests are performed to help in the diagnosis of patients with epilepsy, cerebral tumours, strokes, dementias or multiple sclerosis.

In many departments, the technologist is also required to assist the clinician with electromyography (EMG) and nerve conduction studies (NCS). These tests look at the way in which nerves and muscles in the body are working, and help in the diagnosis of diseases such as dystrophies and nerve dysfunction. All these procedures are carried out either in the department, wards, intensive care units or operating theatres. Both outpatients and in-patients come to the department, and the tests are performed on all ages. Heart rate and respiration may also be recorded. The neurophysiology technologist works as part of the hospital team in the surgical, neurological or psychiatric department.

Qualifications and Training

Five GCSEs, grade C or above, are normally required, including maths, English and combined science. Many entrants have A levels or equivalent. There are two main ways of entering the profession: as a student technologist employed by a hospital in an EEG clinical neurophysiology department; or as a student supernumerary technologist employed by a regional health authority. Training takes place mostly on the job with day-release facilities to study for an Edexcel (BTEC) qualification/NVQ award, level 3.

Personal Qualities and Skills

A medical technologist needs to be willing to take responsibility, able to keep calm under pressure and must be meticulous. In addition, a pleasant manner to put patients at their ease is essential.

Starting Salary

Trainee £9,600+ plus London allowance where appropriate; once qualified £12,400–£16,900, potentially rising to £35,000+ for senior posts.

info

www.nhscareers.nhs.uk/
nhs-knowledge_base/data/4861.html

Electrophysiological Technologists'
Association, c/o EEG Department,
Staffordshire General Hospital,
Weston Road, Stafford ST16 3SA
(enclose sae)

British Society for Clinical
Neurophysiology,
Middlesex Hospital, Mortimer Street,
London W1T 3AA; www.bscn.org.uk;
e-mail: bscn@bscn.org.uk

NURSING, HEALTH VISITING AND MIDWIFERY

Nurses are employed in a wide variety of settings in hospitals, institutions (such as prisons and colleges), the armed forces, schools, industry and private organisations. There are four specialisms or 'branches' within nursing: adult nursing, children's nursing, mental health nursing and learning disability nursing. Midwifery and health visiting are regarded as separate professions although still part of the nursing family. Healthcare assistants now work with nurses and other healthcare professionals.

Applicants must decide which branch of nursing they want to qualify in before training. Specialist training within community nursing or other areas of nursing can be pursued once registration as a general nurse has been achieved. Specialist qualifications in district nursing, health visiting, community psychiatric nursing, learning disability nursing (community practice), occupational health nursing, school nursing and practice nursing can be taken at degree or diploma level.

Nurses working in the 'adult nursing' branch spend time not only working on hospital wards but also in outpatient departments, operating theatres, intensive care and with elderly patients. They also work in the community under the supervision of district nurses, health visitors and community midwives. A qualification in adult nursing could lead to specialising in areas such as accident and emergency, practice nursing or health visiting.

Children's nursing, usually referred to as 'paediatric nursing', covers community care, surgical nursing, medical nursing and caring for children with physical and learning disabilities. Children's nurses need to be able to deal with the fears and anxieties of sick children and provide support for their family. Communication skills are very important in this branch of nursing. A children's nurse will care for newborn babies and teenagers, support the child's family and help them care for the child, work with the family to plan care, and work within the paediatric team. Specialisms following on from qualification in children's nursing might be in intensive care, child protection or cancer care.

The mental health nurse will care for people who are mentally ill. Mentally ill people are increasingly being cared for at home or in homes within the community setting. Mental health nurses care for patients suffering from a wide range of illnesses. Some patients simply require help, counselling and support from the nurse. Others with more serious mental health illnesses will require monitoring and help with medication. The mental health nurse assesses individual needs and works with the patient to develop a plan of care; monitors the effectiveness of planned care; administers and monitors the dosage of prescribed medicine; and explains the effects of medication to the individual. He or she works as part of a team of professionals and acts as 'key worker' coordinating the care of an individual. The mental health nurse will require skill, tact and patience in caring for people.

A nurse working within the learning disability branch of nursing assesses each individual and works with the person to develop a plan of care. Some people need to be taught basic skills such as bathing, and the nurse breaks each skill into a series of small tasks and works with the individuals. People with learning disabilities often have physical handicaps, and nurses work with other professionals such as physiotherapists, occupational therapists and doctors in providing care and promoting independence. More people with learning disabilities are cared for at home and in the community than ever before, and increasing numbers of nurses are undergoing specialist training to offer care in the community.

Qualifications and Training

To qualify as a nurse you need to complete a degree or diploma course that is approved by the Nursing and Midwifery Council (NMC). At the point when you apply for a course, you must choose the type of nursing in which you wish to specialise – care of adults, children, patients with mental health needs, or patients with learning disabilities. Institutions offering nurse training can set their own academic entry requirements, but there are broad general guidelines. For nursing diploma courses you need five GCSEs grades A–C, including English, maths and a biological science. For degree courses the same GCSE requirements apply, but you also need two A levels. Applicants must be aged 17.5 in England and Wales, 17 in Scotland and 18 in Northern Ireland. In England you must apply through the Nursing and Midwifery Admissions Service (NMAS) – the contacts for Scotland, Wales and Ireland are listed in the info panel. Applicants who do not meet these entry requirements may be successful if they can demonstrate literacy and numeracy skills and provide some evidence that they have recently undertaken successful study of some kind.

There are other routes to qualification. If you are between 16 and 19 you can train through a cadet scheme and healthcare assistants and other healthcare support workers may be able to achieve GNVQ level 3 qualifications which are normally accepted for entry onto nursing diploma and degree courses. All applicants to nursing will have to undergo a Criminal Records Bureau (CRB) check, to ensure that they can work with children and/or vulnerable adults.

Personal Qualities and Skills

Nurses have to have very good interpersonal skills, and be able to be sympathetic and calm when working with patients. They have to be practical and physically and emotionally resilient. Nurses have to work as part of a team and often have to work in highly pressured and stressful situations.

Starting Salary

(These figures are based on working for the NHS.) Newly qualified nurses earn between £19,000 and £25,000. With experience, specialist knowledge and management responsibilities, this rises to between £25,000 and £32,000. A few nurses in consulting roles will earn higher salaries than these.

Healthcare assistant

Healthcare assistants work alongside nurses and provide basic care for patients. They help with treatments, keep wards tidy and complete basic paperwork. They work on general hospital wards, in clinics and outpatient departments, psychiatric hospitals, hospices and care homes. There are also opportunities for community-based work, providing physical care to individuals who might otherwise have needed to go into hospital or residential care homes.

Qualifications and Training

No prior qualifications are needed to start work as a healthcare assistant, but hospitals, care homes and other organisations do provide training and there is currently a drive to ensure that everyone doing this work will achieve at least NVQ level 2.

Personal Qualities and Skills

Like qualified nurses, healthcare assistants must have patience, tact, tolerance and an ability to communicate with the patients in their charge. Physical fitness is essential as the job sometimes involves heavy work (such as lifting and turning patients).

Starting Salary

Health care assistants in the NHS aged 18 or over start on a salary of between £11,100 and £13,300. More experienced staff with a relevant NVQ level 2 or 3 can earn up to £17,000. There are also allowances for antisocial hours, and some overtime payments are possible.

info

Nursing and Midwifery Council (NMC), 23 Portland Place, London W1B 1PZ; 020 7637 7181; registration contacts: overseas 020 7333 6600; general 020 7333 9333; www.nmc-uk.org

Nursing and Midwifery Admissions Service, Rosehill, New Barn Lane, Cheltenham, Gloucestershire GL52 3LZ; 0870 112 2206 for general enquiries; 0870 112 2200 for application packs; www.nmas.ac.uk

NHS Careers, PO Box 376, Bristol BS99 3EY; 0845 606 0655; www.nhscareers.nhs.uk

NHS Education for Scotland, Careers Information Service, 66 Rose Street,

Edinburgh EH2 2NN; 0131 225 4365; www.nes.scot.nhs.uk

National Leadership and Innovation Agency for Healthcare (Wales), Innovation House, Bridgend Road, Llanharan CF72 9RP; 01443 233333; www.wales.nhs.uk/sites3/home.cfm?OrgID-484

Northern Ireland Practice & Education Council for Nursing & Midwifery, Centre House, 79 Chichester Street, Belfast BT1 4JE; 028 9023 8152; www.n-i.nhs.uk/nipec/index.htm

Nursing Careers Centre (NCC), 31/32 Fitzwilliam Square, Dublin 2; 01 639 8500; www.nursingcareers.ie

Health visitors

Health visitors promote health and contribute to the prevention of mental, physical and social ill health in the community. This involves educating people in ways of healthy living and making positive changes in the environment. Education may be achieved by teaching individuals or families in their own homes, in health centres, clinics, in informal groups, or through campaigns for the promotion of good health practices through local or national mass media.

The health visitor may work with people who are registered with a GP or who live within a defined geographical area. The work includes collaboration with a wide range of voluntary and statutory organisations.

Qualifications and Training

Applicants must hold a first-level nurse or midwifery qualification with post-registration experience. One-year health visitor courses are provided at institutions of higher education.

All approved programmes now lead to the award of Specialist Practitioner (Public Health Visiting/Health Visiting). These programmes are at a minimum of first degree level.

Personal Qualities and Skills

Health visitors must be excellent communicators, able to convey information to all types of people without being patronising. They must have self-confidence, tact and a lot of common sense. They must be able to work alone, yet know when to seek advice. They should be confident, articulate public speakers.

Starting Salary

Approximately £18,000, rising to £25,000.

NHS Careers; Careers Helpline: 0845 606 0655; www.nhscareers.nhs.uk

Community Practitioners and Health Visitors Association,

40 Bermondsey Street, London SE1 3UD; 020 7939 7000; fax: 020 7403 2976; www.msfcphva.org; e-mail: infocphva@amicustheunion.org

info

Midwifery

Midwives (who may be female or male) provide care and advice to mothers and fathers before, during and after birth; they are either employed by the NHS in hospital and/or community settings, including home births, by private hospitals, or work independently. The midwife provides care during normal pregnancy and birth, and up to 28 days following the birth. The midwife will also care for women who have complications. The midwife is an integral part of the multidisciplinary team responsible for delivering care, working closely with obstetricians and other health professionals in ensuring the wellbeing of mothers and babies.

Qualifications and Training

To qualify as a midwife you need to complete a degree or diploma course in midwifery that is approved by the Nursing and Midwifery Council (NMC). Institutions running courses can set their own academic entry requirements, but there are broad general guidelines. For nursing diploma courses you need five GCSEs grades A–C, including English, maths and a biological science. For degree courses the same GCSE requirements apply, but you also need two A levels. Applicants must be aged 17.5 in England and Wales, 17 in Scotland and 18 in Northern Ireland. In England you must apply through the Nursing and Midwifery Admissions Service (NMAS) – the contacts for Scotland, Wales and Ireland are listed in the info panel. Applicants who do not meet these entry requirements may be successful if they can demonstrate literacy and numeracy skills and provide some evidence that they have recently undertaken successful study of some kind. If you have a nursing degree or diploma (adult branch) you can do a 12 to 18 month midwifery diploma.

Personal Qualities and Skills

Midwives must have extremely good interpersonal skills, be caring, practical, friendly and encouraging. They must be able to work as part of a team, but also to take responsible decisions on their own.

info

Nursing and Midwifery Council (NMC), 23 Portland Place, London W1B 1PZ; 020 7637 7181; registration contacts: overseas 020 7333 6600, general 020 7333 9333; www.nmc-uk.org

Nursing and Midwifery Admissions System, Rosehill, New Barn Lane, Cheltenham, Gloucestershire GL52 3LZ; 0870 112 2206 for general enquiries, 0870 112 2200 for application packs; www.nmas.ac.uk

NHS Careers, PO Box 376, Bristol BS99 3EY; 0845 606 0655; www.nhscareers.nhs.uk

NHS Education for Scotland, Careers Information Service, 66 Rose Street, Edinburgh EH2 2NN; 0131 225 4365; www.nes.scot.nhs.uk

National Leadership and Innovation Agency for Healthcare (Wales), Innovation House, Bridgend Road, Llanharan CF72 9RP; 01443 233333; www.wales.nhs.uk/sites3/home.cfm?OrgID-484

Northern Ireland Practice & Education Council for Nursing & Midwifery, Centre House, 79 Chichester Street, Belfast BT1 4JE; 028 9023 8152; www.n-i.nhs.uk/nipec/index.htm

Nursing Careers Centre (NCC), 31/32 Fitzwilliam Square, Dublin 2; 01 639 8500; www.nursingcareers.ie

Starting Salary

Newly qualified midwives earn between £19,000 and £25,000. With experience, specialist knowledge and management responsibilities, this rises to between £25,000 and £32,000.

OIL/GAS RIG WORK

There are various openings for personnel working on oil or gas drilling rigs, both onshore (on land) and offshore (such as in the North Sea). Opportunities in all fields are generally limited to experienced and/or highly qualified applicants. An offshore rig has to be self-sufficient and is a combination of a factory, hotel and heliport. The catering and accommodation are similar to the provision onshore. Many of the routine factory tasks (such as cleaning and maintenance) are carried out by outside contractors and service companies.

Divers

(*see also* Diver)

Divers are employed in exploration and production work, as well as underwater repair work such as welding.

Drilling crew

The drilling crew is responsible for the drilling of wells, and the operation and maintenance of a variety of heavy machinery. The crew consists of a toolpusher who manages the team and is responsible for the safety and integrity of the operation, and a team of people including a driller, assistant driller, derrickman, roughnecks and roustabouts. A typical drill crew will number around 10 people. Progression to the role of driller is hierarchical, with people working through general labouring jobs (roustabouts), working on the drill floor (roughnecks) or at the top of the derrick (derrickman). The work is physical, from the operation of the drilling equipment to the cleaning and maintenance of pumps and equipment. A graduate drilling engineer and a range of other specialists such as logging engineers, directional drilling specialists and mudloggers will also work with the drill crew.

Engineers

(*see also* Engineering)

A production engineer supervises activities ranging from production and storage, gas compression and injection (to assist in the recovery of the oil), to tanker loading. The reservoir engineer is concerned with the behaviour of the oil accumulation or reservoir, and has to attempt to discover how much oil remains below ground and what are the most effective methods of recovery. Economics plays an important role. The maintenance engineer must ensure that all equipment is functioning properly, selecting and monitoring the companies under contract.

Geologist

(*see also* Geologist)

The oil companies employ technical experts such as geologists, geophysicists and drilling and petroleum engineers. Geologists collect and analyse data from a variety of sources to determine whether drilling might prove successful at a particular site, and to optimise production from existing oilfields. There are opportunities around the world.

Geophysicist

Geophysicists use remote sensing to study the composition and structure of the sub-surface. A major element of this is computer-aided analysis of seismic data.

Qualifications and Training

Geologist: a good honours degree is the minimum required; many companies prefer postgraduate training. Geophysicist: an honours degree in geology or geophysics or other numerate discipline, such as maths or physics. Postgraduate training may be an advantage. Drilling crew: trainees are normally sponsored by drilling companies. Roughneck courses last four weeks. Drillers, toolpushers and drilling engineers will receive further training, including statutory well-control, safety and emergency response training. Divers: must be trained on courses approved by the Health and Safety Executive. Training is expensive; candidates may be sponsored by employers. Engineers: oil companies recruit engineering graduates for trainee posts.

Personal Qualities and Skills

Geophysicists need scientific aptitude, numeracy, a good eye for detail, an enquiring mind and the ability to work in a team under pressure. Drilling crew members must be physically fit, as the work is arduous. Good team-work skills are essential. Divers must be physically fit and able to stay calm in a crisis. Everyone must be able to cope with harsh environments and long periods away from home.

info

Cogent, the Sector Skills Council for the oil and gas extraction, chemicals manufacturing and petroleum industries; www.cogent-ssc.com

Institute of Petroleum, 61 New Cavendish Street, London W1G 7AR; 020 7467 7100; www.petroleum.co.uk; e-mail: ip@petroleum.co.uk; *Energy: Careers in the oil and gas industry* available from website

Institute of Materials, Minerals and Mining, 1 Carlton House Terrace, London SW1Y 5DB; 020 7451 7300; www.iom3.org; www.materials-careers.org.uk

Engineering Careers Information Service, SEMTA, 14 Upton Road, Watford, Hertfordshire WD1 7EP; 0800 282 167; www.semta.org.uk/enginuity; e-mail: ecis@emta.org.uk

Starting Salary

New members of a drilling crew earn around £20,000 and this rises quickly to around £25,000. Periods of leave are also quite generous. Engineers start on between £20,000 and £30,000, and the range is similar for geologists and geophysicists.

OPTOMETRY

Dispensing optician

Dispensing opticians do not examine eyes or test sight, but supply and fit spectacles and other aids prescribed by an optometrist. They usually work in general practice, including independent businesses, partnership, as an employee of corporate bodies or as a franchisee. There are also job opportunities in hospitals and clinics. Once registered, dispensing opticians can undertake further training to enable them to fit contact lenses.

Qualifications and Training

To practise as a dispensing optician, you must complete a training course approved by the General Optical Council (GOC) and pass a professional examination administered by the Association of British Dispensing Opticians (ABDO). There is a choice of four methods to achieve this: a two-year full-time diploma; a three-year day-release course; a three-year distance learning course; or a three-year full-time degree course in dispensing optics or ophthalmic dispensing management. Degree courses require you to have five GCSEs and two A levels, but entry requirements are a little more flexible if you choose the other routes. From 2007 dispensing opticians will have to demonstrate to the ABDO that they have undertaken appropriate continuing education and will have to register annually. There is a lot of on-the-job training, academic study and practical placements involved in qualifying for this profession.

Personal Qualities and Skills

You must be pleasant, friendly, approachable and patient. You must also be good at handling delicate equipment and have reasonable mathematical skills for taking measurements and making calculations. It is also useful to have a grasp of fashion and style, since this is very important to many of your clients when they choose spectacles or lenses.

Starting Salary

On registration you will earn around £16,000 to £17,000; with a few years experience this rises to £18,000 to £29,000.

Association of British Dispensing Opticians, 199 Gloucester Terrace, London W2 6LD, 020 7298 5100; fax: 020 7298 5111; www.abdo.org.uk; e-mail: general@abdo.org.uk

ABDO College of Education, Godmersham Park Mansion, Godmersham, Canterbury, Kent CT4 7DT; 01227 738829;

www.abdo.org.uk; e-mail: education@abdo.org.uk

General Optical Council, 41 Harley Street, London W1G 8DJ; 020 7580 3898; www.optical.org

A Career in Vision Care is available for download from www.college_optometrists.org

Optometrist

Optometrists are trained to examine eyes and test sight, detect and measure defects in healthy eyes and prescribe spectacles, contact lenses or other appliances to correct or improve vision. They must carry out whatever tests are clinically necessary to detect signs of injury or disease to the eye or elsewhere, and must refer these patients to a medical practitioner. Most optometrists work in general practice in a variety of arrangements, including independent businesses, partnership, as an employee of corporate bodies, as a franchisee or in the hospital eye service. There are also job opportunities in research organisations, academic departments, ophthalmic hospitals and clinics.

Qualifications and Training

Optometrists must be registered with the General Optical Council before being permitted to practise in the UK. To obtain registration they must pass the professional qualifying exam run by the College of Optometrists. The exam is in two parts. For Part I the candidate must gain a BSc honours degree in optometry after three years of study at an accredited institution (or four years in Scotland). Part II is taken after the candidate has completed a pre-registration year of supervised practise. The professional qualifying exam combines practical and oral assessment of the candidate's ability to manage patients and practise safely as an independent optometrist.

For acceptance on to a university course students normally need three A levels, two of which must be maths or science. GCSEs should include English and physics if not gained at A level. Average entry grades vary but are usually 320 A level points.

Personal Qualities and Skills

Opticians need mathematical and scientific skills to make accurate observations and calculations. They also need an ability to get on with and communicate effectively with patients of all ages and backgrounds and to be able to put them at their ease.

Starting Salary

Pre-registration salaries are £11,000–£12,000; post-registration: £25,000–£35,000.

College of Optometrists,
42 Craven Street, London WC2N 5NG;
020 7839 6000; fax: 020 7839 6800;
www.college-optometrists.org;
e-mail: optometry@college-optometrists.org

General Optical Council,
41 Harley Street, London W1G 8DJ;
020 7580 3898; fax: 020 7436 3525;
www.optical.org

Scottish Committee of Optometrists,
7 Queens Buildings, Queensferry
Road, Rosyth, Fife KY11 2RA;
01383 419444;
www.scottishoptometry.co.uk;
e-mail: secretarysco@aol.com

A Career in Vision Care available for download from
www.college-optometrists.org

Orthoptist

Orthoptists diagnose and treat various abnormalities and weaknesses in the eye, such as a squint or double vision. Many patients are children, and special equipment and exercises are used to help correct any defects while they are still young. They work closely with medical eye specialists and, where operations are necessary, with ophthalmic surgeons. Most orthoptists work within the NHS, in hospitals and clinics (including school clinics). There are also opportunities in private practice and teaching.

Qualifications and Training

To practise as an orthoptist you must pass a degree approved by the Health Professionals Council (HPC). Details of approved degree courses are available from the HPC and also from the British and Irish Orthoptic Society. For these degree programmes you normally require five GCSEs grades A–C including English, maths and two sciences. You also need two or three A levels, one of which must be in biology.

Personal Qualities and Skills

You need to enjoy working with people, be good at putting them at ease, patient and reassuring, especially when working with children. You need good powers of observation, good manual dexterity and good numeracy skills.

Starting Salary

Newly qualified orthoptists earn between £19,000 and £25,000. With experience you can earn more than £30,000. (These figures are based on working for the NHS.)

NHS Careers, PO Box 376, Bristol BS99 3EY; 0845 606 0655; www.nhscareers.nhs.uk

Health Professionals Council, Park House, 184 Kennington Park Road, London SE11 4BU; 020 7582 0866; www.hpc-uk.org

British and Irish Orthoptic Society, Tavistock House North, Tavistock Square, London WC1H 9HX; 020 7387 7992; www.orthoptics.org.uk

PAINTER AND DECORATOR

see Construction

PATENTS

A patent is a legal document that gives an inventor the right to claim an invention as his or her own work and to produce, sell or make the invention. It also protects the inventor from having his or her work and/or ideas copied by others.

Patent agent/patent attorney

Patent agents/patent attorneys (these terms are interchangeable) have expertise in the area of intellectual property, advise individual clients and companies on matters relating to patent law, and act on their behalf if they wish to patent an invention, or to register a trademark or a design in the UK or abroad. First, records are searched to gauge the likelihood of a patent being granted. The patent agent then draws up the particulars of the client's invention clearly and concisely, ensuring it neither infringes another patent nor is liable to be copied without infringing its own patent. In cases where a client's patent has been infringed, the agent advises as to the best course of action. Patent agents are employed by private practice firms of patent agencies, industrial companies with a patent department and the government.

Patent examiner

These are civil servants who examine the applications for patents submitted by patent agents and others. The principal task is to establish the originality or otherwise of the invention and whether or not the applicant is entitled to the protection claimed. There is some opportunity to work abroad in the European Patent Office.

Patent officer

These are civil servants employed in protecting Crown rights in new inventions and developments, compensating the owners of patents used by the Crown and generally advising government departments on matters relating to patents.

Qualifications and Training

The minimum educational requirement for an agent is a degree in a science or a technology-related subject. It is usually necessary to register as a patent agent in the European Patent Office. This involves taking the European qualifying exams, for which a degree is necessary.

Patent examiners and officers need a first- or second-class honours degree in engineering, physics, chemistry, maths or an equivalent professional qualification.

Personal Qualities and Skills

Curiosity, the ability to assimilate new ideas, good analytical and critical skills, clear and concise thinking and the capacity for logical and clear expression both in speech and writing are all essential.

Starting Salary

Trainees (no examinations passed) £15,000–£25,000; technical assistants (close to qualification) £25,000–£45,000; newly qualified attorneys £50,000–£70,000; attorneys with three to five years' post-qualification experience £65,000–£90,000.

Chartered Institute of Patent Agents, 95 Chancery Lane, London WC2A 1DT; 020 7405 9450; www.cipa.org.uk; e-mail: mail@cipa.org.uk

Patent Office, Concept House, Cardiff Road, Newport, South Wales NP10 8QQ; 0845 950 0505; fax: 01633 813600; www.patent.gov.uk

Inside Careers, Unit 3, The Quadrangle, 49 Atalanta Street, London SW6 6TR; 020 7565 7900; fax: 020 7565 7938; www.insidecareers.co.uk – downloadable guide to becoming a patent attorney

PERFORMING ARTS

Performing arts cover the range of occupations in the world of entertainment.

Actor

Acting mainly involves the interpretation of someone else's work and the communication of it to an audience, although there are opportunities for actors to write their own material. Actors are employed in various types of theatre (commercial, subsidised, community, fringe theatre and theatre-in-education), and also in television, film, radio, and television and radio commercials.

Competition is keen and, because it is such a precarious profession, those entering it must be prepared for long periods of unemployment.

Qualifications and Training

Most potential actors attend drama school. The National Council for Drama Training is a useful source for information on accredited courses. A good general education is important, and some schools require GCSEs and A levels or equivalent. Training courses at established schools usually last two or three years. Entrance is by audition and is competitive. Further experience may be gained from working in a repertory company or in fringe theatre. This may be an alternative way of entering the profession, but it is becoming increasingly difficult to enter solely by this method.

Personal Qualities and Skills

Acting requires a combination of intelligence, sensitivity and imagination, together with a good memory, determination and physical stamina.

Starting Salary

Comparatively low: minimum weekly salaries are set by theatre employers after negotiations with Equity, which has a number of different agreements for theatre, television and film work. Actors often need to take on other work to make a living, especially while they are getting established.

info

Creative and Cultural Skills, 4th Floor, Lafone House, The Leathermarket, Weston Street, London SE1 3HN; 020 7015 1800; www.ccskills.org.uk

Equity – The British Actors Union, Guild House, Upper St Martins Lane, London WC2H 9EG; 020 7379 6000; www.equity.org.uk

National Association of Youth Theatres, Arts Centre, Vane Terrace, Darlington DL3 7AX; 01325 363330; www.nayt.org.uk

National Council for Drama Training, 1–7 Woburn Walk, Bloomsbury, London WC1H 0JJ; 020 7387 3650; www.ncdt.org.uk

Dancing

Dance can be divided into the two main categories of theatre dance (ballet, modern and contemporary dance, jazz and tap) and social dance (ballroom, folk dance and disco). However, there are no hard and fast divisions between the different forms. The profession of dancing consists of two main areas: performing and teaching. Choreography, notation, dance animation and dance therapy are related areas of work.

Choreographer

Choreographers create and plan dance routines and oversee the execution of their plans by the dancers. Choreographers are often former dancers.

Dance animateur

Dance animateurs work in the community or education to encourage participation and involvement and to raise the profile of dance activity locally. Their precise role is dependent on the funding organisation and the needs of the community in which they work. Animateurs are often qualified dance teachers.

Dance notator

Notators are employed by dance companies to record their repertoire, and assist choreographers and rehearsal staff in the revival of choreographic works. Most notators are graduates of vocational dance schools or ex-professional dancers, as the work involves close and informed observation of the choreography, the ability to demonstrate the movement accurately and the ability to work effectively with professional dancers.

Dance performer

Many of those who wish to perform have had early training in ballet and/or other forms of theatre dance. Opportunities in ballet and contemporary companies are limited, and many dancers find their first employment in companies abroad. Dancers also work in pantomimes, shows and musicals, and on cruise ships. Professional performers find it useful to be members of Equity, the British Actors' Union.

Dance teacher

Teachers of dance can specialise in one area of dance teaching or teach in a variety of areas. The demand for teachers is high, especially as dance is now seen as a form of recreation. Teachers may work in commercial dance studios and professional dance schools both in the UK and abroad.

Qualifications and Training

Ideally, ballet students should attend a recognised residential establishment such as the Royal Ballet School from the age of 11 to 18. Means-tested financial assistance may be available to UK students. Dancers who want to become teachers must obtain the relevant qualifications, for which full-time or part-time courses are available. These generally have an entry requirement of four to five GCSEs at grade C and above. The Royal Academy of Dancing offers certificates, diplomas and degrees in classical ballet teaching. The courses are available on a part-time and full-time basis.

Personal Qualities and Skills

Dancers need to be hard working, self-disciplined both physically and mentally, dedicated and determined. They must be imaginative, able to express themselves artistically, have a good sense of timing and an ear for music.

Starting Salary

Dancers who belong to Equity earn a minimum of £285 per week. Non-Equity members earn much less and some dancers will work voluntarily to help gain contracts. Teachers earn £18,000+ and possibly more in the private sector. Choreographers and notators are reasonably well paid. You can only work as a dancer for a limited period of time, while you are at the peak of physical fitness, so this can affect your long-term income.

info

British Association of Teachers of Dance, 23 Marywood Square, Glasgow G41 2BP; 0141 423 4029; www.batd.co.uk

British Dance Council, Terpsichore House, 240 Merton Road, South Wimbledon, London SW19 1EQ; www.british-dance-council.org

Council for Dance Education & Training (CDET), Toynbee Hall, 28 Commercial Street, London E1 6LS; 020 7247 4030; www.cdet.org.uk

Dance UK, Battersea Arts Centre, Lavender Hill, London SW11 5TF; 020 7228 4990; www.danceuk.org

Laban Centre for Movement and Dance, Creekside, London SE8 3DZ; 020 8691 8600; www.laban.org

National Dance Teachers Association, 47 Grove Hill Road, London SE5 8DF; www.ndta.org.uk

Royal Academy of Dance, 36 Battersea Square, London SW11 3RA; 020 7326 8000; www.rad.org.uk

Musician

(*see also* Music)

A musical training, leading to a degree or equivalent qualification, opens the door to a wide range of careers in music, including performing, teaching, administration, management, broadcasting, recording, journalism, publishing, promotion, librarianship and the retail trade.

Many professional musicians work on a freelance basis as soloists, orchestral players, commercial session musicians and in a variety of chamber music ensembles including classical, rock, dance and jazz groups. A performer's working life often includes some teaching, master classes or community education work alongside regular and vital practice.

Some musicians arrange their own engagements, others have agents or use a diary service to find work. For all performers, membership of a professional association or union is desirable.

There are opportunities, particularly for those who already play an instrument, to join the Army, the RAF or Royal Marines as a bandsman.

Qualifications and Training

Entry to undergraduate courses of study usually requires a minimum of five GCSEs and one or more A levels, preferably including music. Full-time courses of study over three or four years, usually leading to a degree, are available at conservatoires (performance-based), universities (more academic) and colleges of higher education (more broad spectrum). Singers require a longer training, often over six years. Conservatoires and universities also offer a range of post-graduate courses. Details of courses in performance, composition, musicology and teaching are available from the Incorporated Society of Musicians' website. The government has introduced a training scheme for the music industry under the 'New Deal' initiative; details are available from Job Centre Plus centres.

Personal Qualities and Skills

A love of music, a positive and persuasive personality, robust physical and mental health, stamina, patience and excellent communication skills are essential for any career in music. Competition is fierce for performers, and only a very few talented musicians can establish a successful solo career. The ability to get on well with others helps to ensure good relationships with colleagues, managers and promoters to support career development.

Starting Salary

Salaries vary enormously. Guidance on rates of pay is available from the Incorporated Society of Musicians.

Incorporated Society of Musicians, 10 Stratford Place, London W1C 1AA; 020 7629 4413; fax: 020 7408 1538; www.ism.org; e-mail: membership@ism.org	Local Job Centre Plus and Careers/ Connexions Centres

info

Singer

Singers are performers that use certain styles of music, such as pop, rock, jazz, folk, country and western, world or 'easy listening' music. Singers sometimes play musical instruments, record music in a studio, for albums or 'session' work, work as a solo artist or as part of a duo or group, and write songs for themselves or other musical artists.

Singers need to practise for many hours at a time and attend regular rehearsals. They enjoy listening to as much varied music as possible, at gigs, concerts and clubs and on the radio, Internet and CD.

Some singers include dance and movement as part of their performance. If a singer is successful, it is possible to appear in videos or on television. To be a successful singer really depends on an individual's talent, determination and hard work.

Qualifications and Training

The more experience of performing the better; a singer can start at parties and public events. If a singer is then spotted by a recording company it could be possible to get a recording contract. Alternatively, singers can contact record and music publishing companies directly by sending them a 'demo' tape recording. BTEC and SNCC courses in music are available, as are degrees in popular music. In addition, HND and HNC courses are also available in a wide range of relevant subjects. Entry requirements usually start with one A level/H grade or equivalent. Strong evidence of ability and interest in music are normally required.

There are many other full-time and part-time courses, both privately and state funded, and popular music courses offered by adult education institutes and local community organisations.

Personal Qualities and Skills

Success depends largely on musical talent and individuality. A passion for music and the ability to perform to an audience are good qualities for a singer. A certain level of discipline, focus and determination is required.

Starting Salary

Only a small minority of singers earn high incomes. Many singers supplement their earnings with full-time work because they often earn less than the national average wage. The Musicians Union sets minimum rates for musicians. Singers performing live often earn the national minimum rate of £47.50 for up to two hours before midnight. A very experienced singer making backing tracks on an album might earn about £350 per three-hour session.

A solo musician on tour could earn between £500 and £2,000 per week, depending on experience. Equity (the performers' union) sets minimum rates for singers appearing in stage or television productions. The minimum rate for performances in London's West End is £320 per week for eight shows.

info

Brit School for Performing Arts and Technology, 60 The Crescent, Croydon CR0 2HN; 020 8665 5242; fax: 020 8665 5197; www.brit.croydon.sch.uk

British Phonographic Institute (BPI), Riverside Building, County Hall, Westminster Bridge Road, London SE1 7JA; 020 7803 1300; fax: 020 7803 1310; www.bpi.co.uk

Equity, Guild House, Upper St Martins Lane, London WC2H 9EG; 020 7379 6000; fax: 020 7379 7001; www.equity.org.uk; e-mail: info@equity.org.uk

Incorporated Society of Musicians, 10 Stratford Place, London W1C 1AA; 0207 629 4413; fax: 020 7408 1538; www.ism.org; e-mail: membership@ism.org

Musicians Union, 60/62 Clapham Road, London SW9 0JJ; 020 7582 5566; fax: 020 7582 9805; www.musiciansunion.org.uk

Rockschool, 245 Sandycombe Road, Kew TW9 2EW; 020 8332 6303; fax: 020 8332 6297; www.rockschool.co.uk

Scottish Arts Council, 12 Manor Place, Edinburgh EH3 7DD; 0131 226 6051; fax: 0131 225 9833; www.scottisharts.org.uk

PHARMACY

Pharmacists are involved in the dispensing of medicinal drugs, usually prescribed by doctors. There are three branches of the profession: community pharmacists, hospital pharmacists, and industrial and research pharmacists.

Community pharmacist

Community pharmacists work from the high street, health centre and rural pharmacies as part of the NHS. They dispense prescriptions and ensure that medicines ordered on prescription or bought over the counter are correctly and safely supplied, with all necessary advice on their use. They keep a poisons register, and act as a link between the doctor and the pharmaceutical manufacturer, being prepared to discuss developments with both. They are readily accessible health advisers to the public. In addition, they sell a wide range of non-pharmaceutical articles.

Hospital pharmacist

They dispense drugs for hospital in- and outpatients and work side by side with nurses, doctors and other health professionals to ensure NHS patients receive the most appropriate medicines in the most effective way. In addition, in some hospitals, pharmacists manufacture their own products, take part in research work and come into direct contact with in-patients by accompanying medical staff on their ward rounds.

Industrial and research pharmacist

They work as part of a team of scientists researching diseases, developing new drugs and carrying out clinical trials. Industrial pharmacists are also recruited to work in the areas of manufacturing, regulatory and medical affairs, sales and marketing and computer science/information technology.

Qualifications and Training

Pharmacists must complete a four-year Master of Pharmacy degree, followed by one year's paid competency-based training and a registration examination. Entry to degree courses is with A level chemistry plus two other A levels or equivalent; maths and biology are preferred.

Personal Qualities and Skills

On top of excellent relevant medical knowledge and the need to be very careful and accurate, it is also important that you get on well with people and can be patient and understanding. Pharmacists already have responsibility for handling dangerous drugs, and it seems likely that they will be given greater prescribing rights in the near future, when responsibility and decision making will be extremely important aspects of their skills mix.

Starting Salary

In hospitals newly qualified pharmacists start on a range of between £19,000 and £25,000. Community (retail) pharmacists earn between £25,000 and £33,000. The highest salaries are paid in geographical locations where there is a recruitment problem. Industrial pharmacists start on between £20,000 and £30,000.

info

Association of the British Pharmaceutical Industry, 12 Whitehall, London SW1A 2DY; 020 7930 3477; fax: 020 7747 1414; www.abpi.org.uk; www.abpi-careers.org.uk

Guild of Healthcare Pharmacists, 40 Bermondsey Street, London SE1 3UD; 020 7939 7042; www.ghp.org.uk

National Pharmaceutical Association (trade association for community pharmacists), Mallinson House, 38–42 St Peter's Street, St Albans, Hertfordshire AL1 3NP; 01727 832161; fax: 01727 840858; www.npa.co.uk; e-mail: npa@npa.co.uk

Royal Pharmaceutical Society of Great Britain, 1 Lambeth High Street, London SE1 7JN; 020 7735 9141; fax: 020 7735 7629; www.rpsgb.org.uk; e-mail: careers@rpsgb.org.uk; Scottish Department: 36 York Place, Edinburgh EH1 3HU; www.rpsgb.org.uk/scotland/index.html; e-mail: info@rpsis.com

NHS Careers, 0845 606 0655; www.nhscareers.nhs.uk

A Future in Pharmacy (Royal Pharmaceutical Society of Great Britain)

Pharmacy technician

Pharmacy technicians work as part of the pharmacy team and are supervised by a pharmacist. Their duties can include the dispensing of medicines from prescriptions, preparing sterile medicines, assessing stocks of drugs, patient counselling, advising on health promotion issues and collecting and collating information on drugs from a variety of sources. Pharmacy technicians can work in chemists, hospitals, the armed forces, the prison service, or within the pharmaceutical industry.

Qualifications and Training

A nationally recognised qualification is the NVQ Pharmacy Services at level 3 which is available from approved centres. Entry requirements for this are generally four GCSEs at grade C or above, including English, mathematics and chemistry plus one other science. Mature applicants are welcome, and previous education and work experience are considered.

life
inspiring
ideas

As one of the world's leading pharmaceutical companies, AstraZeneca is focused on turning good ideas into innovative, effective medicines that make a real difference in important areas of healthcare.

Our success depends on providing people with a culture that inspires exceptional performance. That means creating an environment in which each individual feels valued, energised and rewarded – and is free to challenge, to solve and to improve.

The diversity of skills and perspectives within our global team is our greatest creative strength. What unites our 65,000 people across 45 countries is a commitment to innovation, and our shared values of integrity, respect, openness and leadership.

To find out more and to apply, visit careers.astrazeneca.co.uk

AstraZeneca

AstraZeneca discovers new medicines that are designed to improve the health and quality of life of patients around the world – medicines which are innovative, effective and which offer added benefits such as reduced side effects or better ways of taking the treatment. We also focus on getting the best from every medicine we make by exploring all the ways it can be used or improved.

We think you'll be excited by the quality and diversity of the opportunities we have to offer at AstraZeneca. Our excellent reputation makes us the natural choice for many candidates from a science background, although our strengths in manufacturing and commerce mean we can also provide challenges to candidates from other disciplines. Your career will progress through an integrated range of flexible training activities and blended learning ideas, and we are looking to recruit to all levels; so whatever your experience, AstraZeneca could have the right role for you.

From day-one induction and personal mentoring to management and global leadership programmes, we will provide the resources and support you need to reach your full potential; while cross-functional moves, secondments and international assignments can broaden the experience.

Ours is a performance-based culture, with competitive salaries and bonuses that are linked to overall progress. But we also believe that quality of life and quality of work go hand-in-hand, which is why we actively pursue opportunities for flexible working arrangements. Core benefits include a minimum level of pension contribution and healthcare provision, and the additional range of "rewards options" is considerable.

However, what also excites many candidates is the opportunity to develop their skills within a truly global business, and one that's setting the standards in an industry rich in challenges and rewards.

Personal Qualities and Skills

As a pharmacy technician you should have a real interest in science and the ability to be accurate and careful. You should be able to deal sensitively and tactfully with people, be good at working as part of a team, and in some posts you may have to use sales skills as well.

Starting Salary

The starting salary for a pharmacy technician is around £11,000 to £13,000 a year. Technicians with experience are likely to earn around £15,000 to £16,000 a year.

Association of Pharmacy Technicians; www.aptuk.org

Royal Pharmaceutical Society of Great Britain, 1 Lambeth High Street, London SE1 7JN; 020 7735 9141; fax: 020 7735 7629; www.rpsgb.org.uk; e-mail: careers@rpsgb.org.uk;

Scottish Department: 36 York Place, Edinburgh EH1 3HU; www.rpsgb.org.uk/scotland/index.html; e-mail: info@rpsis.com

NHS Careers, 0845 606 0655; www.nhscareers.nhs.uk

Info

PHOTOGRAPHY

Photographers produce visual images of many different kinds, either working to a brief given them by a client, or exploring subject matter they have chosen themselves. Photographers use a range of photographic equipment, including conventional and digital cameras, lighting systems and computer programmes developed to manipulate photographs. Some photographers also develop their own work, using either traditional darkroom methods or digital processing. The subject matter you work with is determined by the field of photography in which you work. Typical aspects of the job include choosing locations and subjects, selecting appropriate cameras and accessories, and setting up lighting and background. Photographers also have to compose the picture, whether this is discussing a pose with a model or arranging still life objects.

Advertising/editorial photographer

Advertising photographers take pictures for magazines and brochures. These pictures either advertise a product or illustrate a story. Many advertising photographers specialise in particular subjects such as food, cars, portraiture or landscapes.

Corporate photographer

Corporate photographers work for large businesses and other organisations taking pictures for annual reports, promotional brochures or in-house journals.

Some people working in this field become specialist industrial photographers, taking pictures of the manufacturing process as well as finished products.

Fashion photographer

Fashion photographers take pictures of models promoting clothes, shoes, jewellery, cosmetics and hairstyles. At the top end of the market they work for well-known magazines, taking pictures of models who people have heard of. At the other end of this market, photographers take hundreds of pictures for mail-order catalogues.

General practice photographer

General photographers take pictures for a range of clients in their local communities. A great deal of the work involves wedding photography, but these photographers often cover community events and family occasions. Many do some work for local newspapers that don't employ in-house press photographers. Those photographers who do specialise mainly in weddings or other special occasions are sometimes described as social photographers rather than general practice photographers.

Medical photographer

see Medical illustration

Scientific/technical photographer

Some photographers specialise in taking pictures for scientific journals and research papers. They may have to work with microscope slides as well as living subjects. The work of the wildlife photographer is a highly specialised aspect of this type of photography.

Qualifications and Training

While there are no formal entry requirements, this is a very competitive field. There are several courses you can do, and being able to combine a course with a good portfolio of your work and some relevant work experience is the best way to improve your chances of success. Courses are available at many levels, including City & Guilds, BTEC Certificates and Diplomas, A levels and degree courses. Many people start work as a photographer's assistant to gain basic skills and knowledge. The British Institute of Professional Photography (BIPP) awards the Professional Qualifying Examination (PQE) to photographers – the award is based on assessing a photographer's portfolio to ensure that it is of a good professional standard.

Personal Qualities and Skills

These vary according to your chosen specialism, but all photographers must have the ability to perceive and recreate visual impact in a creative way. They must all be competent with technical equipment and normally need great patience. For most jobs, photographers must be able to work well with people, whether it is as subjects, or as fellow members of a work team. They also need good business management skills.

Starting Salary

Many photographers end up running their own businesses or working free-lance, so salary data only act as a very rough guide. Assistants earn between £10,000 and £12,000, photographers between £15,000 and £30,000. Freelance rates may be calculated on a daily or hourly basis or based on a contract for a particular job of work.

Association of Photographers, 81 Leonard Street, London EC2A 4QS; 020 7739 6669; www.the-aop.org

British Institute of Professional Photography (BIPP), Fox Talbot House, 2 Amwell End, Ware, Hertfordshire

SG12 9HN; 01920 464011; www.bipp.com

Skillset, Prospect House, 80–110 New Oxford Street, London WC1A 1HB; 020 7520 5757; www.skillset.org

info

Photographic production

There is a range of jobs associated with the production of photographs and images.

Manufacturing, retailing and service trades

Large quantities of film, photographic and non-photographic papers and chemicals are manufactured in the UK. Opportunities exist for technicians to research and develop new products; this sector of the industry also employs engineers and sales personnel.

Photographic laboratories/imaging centres

Professional laboratories/imaging centres can be divided into two major segments: social and commercial. The social laboratories cover printing (hand and machine), processing (paper and film), colour negative/colour transparency, and black and white photography, and mostly deal with wedding photographs and portraits. Digital imaging techniques have had a significant effect on the work of commercial laboratories, and use of imaging software is now common.

Photographic laboratory technician

Photographic laboratory technicians work in one of three areas: film processing, digital imaging or print finishing. They work for processing laboratories and imaging centres, which specialise either in commercial or social photography. Film processing technicians process films to produce either prints or images on a disk; they can adjust lighting, colour, etc, to produce the best possible results. Digital imaging technicians acquire specialised knowledge and skill in layout and design of pictures. They use computer software to enhance images, change colours, move subjects, blend two pictures into one, etc. Print finishers learn to finish prints well and show them off to best effect; they become skilled at using precise cutting equipment and laminating machines. They prepare large prints for exhibitions, for example.

Qualifications and Training

In most instances, an interest in photography is more important than formal qualifications, though a good general education including GCSEs in maths and a science can be useful, and larger professional laboratories may set their own entry requirements. Anyone interested in digital imaging should have some experience of desktop publishing. Macintosh (Mac) computers, rather than PCs, are the industry standard. It is possible to take NVQs levels 2 and 3 in photo processing, photo imaging, mini-lab processing and laboratory operations. An apprenticeship in photo laboratory work is sometimes an option, if you are aged between 16 and 24, but these are not all that widely available in this profession. There are also design courses available at every level, from BTEC certificate to a university degree. Most of the training for this work is on-the-job, with frequent requirements to update on new techniques and new equipment.

Personal Qualities and Skills

You should have a genuine interest in photography and design and some creative flair. You need to work with great accuracy and be able to pay attention to small detail. You should be practical and interested in using computers or other professional equipment. You also need good communication skills and you should enjoy working in a team.

Starting Salary

Salaries start between £9,000 and £15,000, rising to £16,000 to £25,000 with three or four years' experience. Digital imaging work offers the highest salaries and good, experienced operators can earn up to £35,000.

Skillset, Prospect House, 80–110 New Oxford Street, London WC1A 1HB; 020 7520 5757; www.skillset.org

British Institute of Professional Photographers (BIPP), Fox Talbot House, 2 Amwell End, Ware, Hertfordshire SG12 9HN; 01920 464011; www.bipp.com

PHYSICIST

Physics deals with the interrelation of matter and energy. Physicists are needed wherever the physical properties of materials have to be studied. They are employed in the fields of electronics, nuclear power, computing, aerospace, optics, telecommunications, engineering and instrument manufacture. In addition, hospitals employ medical physicists whose work includes support for medical use of radiation, and design and implementation of new equipment for diagnosis and treatment of disease. Some physicists lecture in universities or teach in schools. Physics technicians assist fully qualified physicists.

About one-third of all physicists work in public service industries, one-third in private industry and one-third in secondary and higher education. Some physicists work on problems at the frontiers of knowledge; others tackle the problems which arise in the application of physical ideas to industrial and engineering problems. Physics graduates also find themselves employed in occupations such as medicine, computing and even finance.

Qualifications and Training

To continue with science at A level, students must choose either a double award in science (England, Wales and Northern Ireland), which combines the three subjects and leads to two science GCSE qualifications, or a combination of the individual sciences (biology, chemistry, physics), at GCSE or equivalent.

Entry to most degree courses requires two or three A levels (or a suitable combination of A and AS levels) or equivalent, including maths and physics. Since there is a shortage of applicants, grade requirements in some universities are not high, but all departments will consider good grades in maths to be equally as important as good grades in physics. A National Diploma with several merits and distinctions may be considered if it has suitable maths and physics content.

Junior technicians need a good education to GCSE level with particular attention to maths, a science and a subject showing the use of English in order to take an Edexcel (BTEC)/SQA national certificate. There are special certificate courses for medical junior physics technicians. For senior technicians an Edexcel (BTEC)/SQA HND award is available; the requirements are an A level in physics and GCSE maths, chemistry and English. An Edexcel (BTEC)/SQA NC or ND award is acceptable in place of A/H levels. Training for technicians is generally on the job, such as Modern Apprenticeships, with time off to attend courses.

Personal Qualities and Skills

Those working in physics must be able to recognise a problem and plan an experiment or set of experiments to solve it. They should be imaginative, persevering, have good powers of concentration and adopt a sound, logical approach. Technicians should have the practical skills necessary to carry out experiments, be responsible, accurate and caring in their attitude to work.

Starting Salary

Junior technicians earn between £10,500 and £12,000. Senior technicians earn between £15,000 and £17,000. Graduates start on £18,000 to £20,000. Senior physicists doing key research can earn up to £40,000.

info

Institute of Physics, 76 Portland Place, London W1B 1NT; 020 7470 4800; fax: 020 7470 4848; www.iop.org; e-mail: physics@iop.org

Institute of Physics and Engineering in Medicine, Fairmount House, 230 Tadcaster Road, York YO24 1ES; 01904 610821; fax: 01904 612279; www.ipem.ac.uk; e-mail: office@ipem.ac.uk

PHYSIOTHERAPIST

Physiotherapists treat patients suffering from a wide variety of diseases, conditions or injuries by physical means. They help people who have had strokes to regain the use of lost functions, treat sports injuries and people with arthritis, and help children with cerebral palsy to learn to walk. The techniques used include massage and manipulation, exercise, electrotherapy and hydrotherapy. Most physiotherapists work in the Health Service but there are many opportunities now for employment in industry, sports clinics, schools and private practice.

Sports physiotherapist

The increasing number of opportunities to work with sportsmen and women, both professional and amateur, has become a rather specialised and growing area within physiotherapy. Sports physiotherapists must hold first aid certificates and be chartered physiotherapists. There is a special interest group within the Chartered Society of Physiotherapy (CSP) for therapists who specialise in treating sporting injuries. There are also several postgraduate diplomas and Master's courses available in sports physiotherapy.

Qualifications and Training

To be registered with the Health Professionals Council and the Chartered Society of Physiotherapy you must complete an approved degree in physiotherapy.

Entry requirements for these degrees in England, Wales and Northern Ireland usually include four AS levels at grade B, followed by three A levels at grade C or above, including a biological science. You also need five GCSEs grades A–C including maths, English and a range of science subjects. In Scotland, you need five H grades (AABBB) with at least two science subjects. Appropriate access to higher education courses may also be accepted.

Personal Qualities and Skills

You must enjoy working with people, putting them at ease, explaining treatments and teaching exercises. You must have a good grasp of physiology and have good manual dexterity. You should be good at observing people and you also need to be able to work well as part of a team.

Starting Salary

In the NHS salaries start at between £19,000 and £21,000. With experience and responsibility this can rise to £26,000 to £31,000.

Chartered Society of Physiotherapy, 14 Bedford Row, London WC1R 4ED; 020 7306 6666; www.csp.org.uk

Association of Chartered Physiotherapists in Sports Medicine; www.acpsm.org

NHS Careers, PO Box 376, Bristol BS99 3EY; 0845 606 0655; www.nhscareers.nhs.uk

Health Professionals Council, Park House, 184 Kennington Park Road, London SE11 4BU; 020 7582 0866; www.hpc-uk.org

Info

PLUMBER

see Construction

POLICE SERVICE

Police Community Support Officer

Police Community Support Officers (PCSOs) are a recent introduction to the Police Service. This work is done by civilians, rather than serving police officers, but they support and report to local police. They patrol public areas, providing a visible presence to reassure the public. In some areas they have powers to direct traffic or issue arrest warrants, and they often work at events such as football matches or public demonstrations.

Qualifications and Training

There are no formal academic requirements or age restrictions for applying to become a PCSO. Applicants must be UK, EC or Commonwealth citizens. Foreign nationals who have indefinite leave to remain in the UK and the right to work here are also eligible. While each police force sets its own entry requirements for PCSOs, they all tend to use similar selection criteria. You apply via an application form and after an initial screening of these forms you will be invited to an interview. You will also have to sit a written test and take part in role-play exercises to assess how you would cope with the range of situations the job throws up. Many forces set fitness tests, because you may have to undertake long foot patrols. Thorough background and security checks are made on all successful applicants. Having a criminal record does not necessarily exclude you from applying, but any convictions for violent or public order offences will certainly disqualify an applicant. Training takes between three weeks and three months, and is mainly classroom-based; it covers many aspects of the work including using computer systems, first aid, radio communications and patrolling.

Personal Qualities and Skills

You need very good people skills, and to be confident dealing with difficult or sensitive situations. You need to be able to work on your own or as part of a team, to take decisions or seek support as appropriate. You must be able to keep calm in pressured situations and you should be able to remain alert and observant.

Starting Salary

Each police force sets its own salaries for PCSOs, but an average is just over £16,000 rising to between £19,000 and £20,000, more in London. It may be possible to earn more through shift work allowances.

Police officer

Police officers are recruited as trainee police constables (PCs). PCs work in all aspects of policing, including preventing and investigating crime, maintaining public order and protecting people and property. PCs work from police stations or out on the beat, either on foot or in patrol cars. There are many opportunities to specialise in particular areas of police work once you have completed your probationary period.

There is a separate British Transport Police Force, which operates on passenger transport services to prevent crime, protect public safety and maintain public order.

Qualifications and Training

Each police force does its own recruiting, but they all work to a nationally agreed competency framework. While there are no formal educational requirements for joining the police service, there is a demanding selection procedure. Joining the police service is open to British or Commonwealth nationals and also to other foreign nationals who have no restrictions on their right to work in the UK. Applicants must be aged 18 or over. The first stage is to complete an application form and a medical questionnaire. If you are successful at this stage, you are invited to a selection centre to sit a variety of physical and psychometric tests. The physical fitness tests relate to tasks you would have to perform as a serving police officer. Sessions to help you prepare for these tests and to know what to expect are run throughout the UK several times a year.

The psychometric tests include written numeracy, literacy, information handling and reasoning tests, plus personality tests to assess your suitability for the demands of the job. The selection centre also includes an interview and a full medical, with eyesight and hearing tests. You must have good vision and colour vision and be physically fit. If you pass the selection centre, references are followed up and security checks including your financial status are made. Minor convictions or cautions do not necessarily preclude you from joining the police, but you must declare these.

There is an accelerated training scheme for graduates, the Graduate Development Programme (GDP). This is extremely competitive and many graduates wishing to join the police do so through the ordinary route.

New recruits work a probationary period of two years. During this time, training is a mixture of on the job training with the local police service and college-based learning. Everyone goes through the Initial Police Learning and Development Programme. During this period trainees work towards the NVQ level 3 in Policing and either during or shortly after this two-year period they are also expected to complete the NVQ level 4 in Policing. All policemen and women will undergo a wide variety of training throughout their careers enabling them to cope with changes in the law, social policy, information management and technology.

Personal Qualities and Skills

You need a mature attitude and the ability to assess and weigh up situations quickly and then take appropriate action. You must be able to follow orders and have the confidence to instruct others. You must be able to stay calm in difficult situations and you must be emotionally resilient. You need excellent and varied people skills, able to be confident, assertive, diplomatic, reassuring, patient or firm as the occasion demands. You must be effective as part of a team, but also capable of working on your own.

Starting Salary

Salaries are set by individual police forces but the average starting salary is around £20,000 with incremental rises for each year of service. With experience, earnings can reach around £32,500 a year and inspectors earn up to £43,000 a year. Salaries may also be higher than this in London and it is often possible to earn more by doing some overtime.

Police Recruitment,
www.policecouldyou.co.uk

Skills for Justice, 9 Riverside Court,
Don Road, Sheffield S9 2TJ;
0114 261 1499;
www.skillsforjustice.com

British Transport Police,
15 Tavistock Place, London WC1H 9SJ;
020 7830 8800; www.btp.police.uk

Central Police Training and
Development Authority (CENTREX),
Bramshill, Hook, Hampshire
RG27 0JW; 01256 602100;
www.centrex.police.uk

The High Potential Development
Scheme, Home Office,
Police Leadership and Powers Unit,

5th Floor, 50 Queen Anne's Gate,
London SW1H 9AT;
020 7273 3374/3353;
www.policecouldyou.co.uk

Home Office, Direct Communications
Unit, 2 Marsham Street, London
SW1P 4DF; 0870 000 1585;
www.homeoffice.gov.uk

Scottish Executive Justice
Department, The Scottish Executive,
Regent Road, Edinburgh EH1 3DG;
0131 556 8400; www.scotland.gov.uk

Careers and Jobs in the Police Service
(Kogan Page)

*How to Pass the New Police Selection
System* (Kogan Page)

POLITICAL WORK

Though politics offers relatively few career opportunities, there are a number of jobs in politics associated with supporting political parties, undertaking political research and lobbying political bodies on behalf of interest groups.

Politician

Politicians for the House of Commons, the Scottish Parliament, the Welsh Assembly and the European Parliament are all elected, so they don't 'apply' for their jobs in the traditional sense. Their work involves representing the concerns of their constituents and contributing to the process of decision making by joining in debates, asking questions and voting.

Political party agent

Only large political parties employ full-time agents. The agents are responsible for organising and motivating party activity at a local level, whether this is training volunteers, organising meetings or maintaining contact between local party members and their MP.

Political researcher

Many different kinds of organisations employ political researchers; MPs, political parties, trade unions, public relations consultancies and non-government organisations are the most likely employers. The work involves detailed research, by monitoring the media, the daily work of both Houses of Parliament and the institutions of the European Union. Researchers also provide detailed answers to questions on almost every topic imaginable.

Public affairs consultant/lobbyist

This very specialised field of public relations employs researchers and lobbyists to monitor political information and to lobby government on behalf of their clients. Clients may be businesses, trade unions or pressure groups, or any organisations that wish to influence the decision-making processes of government.

Qualifications and Training

Politicians do not need specific qualifications and come from many different career backgrounds; law is one of the more common. Other political jobs require at least a good 2.1 degree in a relevant subject, such as economics, law, politics or social policy. Many successful applicants also have postgraduate qualifications.

Personal Qualities and Skills

Politicians have to be good communicators who are well organised and able to balance the needs of their constituency work with demands in Westminster, or wherever they are based. Good organisational and interpersonal skills as well as a rigorous attitude to information research are essential for other political jobs.

Starting Salary

MPs earn £55,000 with various additional allowances. Salaries for other political work are more wide ranging. Junior research jobs pay £10,000+; an experienced lobbyist can earn £25,000 to £30,000.

Local constituency parties

Conservative Central Office,
32 Smith Square, London SW1P 3HH;
020 7222 9000;
www.conservatives.com

Labour Party, Millbank Tower,
Millbank, London SW1P 4GT;
0870 590 0200; www.labour.org.uk

Liberal Democrats, 4 Cowley Street,
London SW1P 3NB; 020 7222 7999;
www.libdems.org.uk;
e-mail: info@libdems.org.uk

A list of all other UK political parties is available from
http://bubl.ac.uk/uk/parties.htm

Association of Professional Political Consultants (APPC),
c/o Citigate Public Affairs,
26 Grosvenor Gardens, London SW1Y 0GT; 020 7838 4883;
www.appc.org.uk

Parli-training, Suite 49,
34 Buckingham Palace Road, Belgravia, London SW1W 0RD; 020 7898 1103;
www.parli-training.co.uk;
e-mail: enquiries@parli-training.co.uk

Parliamentary Communications Ltd,
14 Great George Street, Westminster, London SW1P 3RX; 020 7878 1576

Info

POSTMAN/WOMAN

Postmen and women deliver mail to private and business addresses. They each have a round including several hundred addresses which they visit on foot, by bicycle or by van. Postmen and women also sort the mail for their own rounds and some mail is still sorted by hand. Postmen and women may also be responsible for collecting mail from post boxes, local post offices and from business addresses.

Some postmen and women work at district or central offices sorting mail to be sent to other areas of the UK or overseas.

There are many other delivery and administrative opportunities within the Post Office, including work for Parcelforce and work behind post office counters.

Qualifications and Training

There are no formal entry qualifications, but applicants have to pass an aptitude test which assesses their suitability for postal work. Once employed it is possible to work towards NVQ level 2 in mail delivery services. This covers mail sorting, mail handling and working with automated systems. Apprenticeships are available for applicants aged 16–18, but many postmen and women are taken on at age 18 or over. If your job involves driving, you must have a full, clean driving licence.

Personal Qualities and Skills

You need good basic literacy and numeracy skills and you must not mind doing repetitive tasks. It is essential to be physically fit, reliable and honest. You need to be polite and friendly, but not mind working on your own.

Starting Salary

At age 16, salaries are around £10,000, rising to £15,000 by the time you are aged 18.

Royal Mail Group plc, 148 Old Street, London EC1V 9HQ; www.royalmailgroup.com

For local vacancies contact your nearest Royal Mail Delivery Office or check the Royal Mail website.

PRINTING

The purpose of printing is communication, whether the printed matter is books, magazines, newspapers, security documents or bank cards. Printers are also involved in other products, from wallpaper and floor coverings to advertising slogans on milk cartons. The printing industry covers a wide range of jobs in both factories and offices. The printing industry employs 200,000 people in 12,000 companies.

Camera/scanner operator

The reproduction of colour photographs is largely done by electronic scanners, requiring technical ability rather than the craft skills of the past.

Finishing department

Printed products are usually produced in large flat sheets or reels. To convert and finish sheets or reels into books, brochures or magazines, the material must be folded, stitched, sewn and trimmed. A range of specialised machinery is used to produce the finished product at high speed. Great care is needed at this stage to avoid faults, which could result in scrapping the product and financial loss to the company.

Graphic design

(*see also* Art and Design)

This is the most artistic job in the printing industry. Designers liaise with clients, understand their needs and transform ideas into high-quality printed products. A mastery of computers, complete understanding of processes, techniques, typography and colour is required. Applicants normally enter the industry after a National Certificate diploma or higher-level course in graphic design.

Office jobs

Account executives look after individual printing jobs; they write instructions for each department and check the product's arrival into and departure from each section. Estimators work out how much a job will cost. Cost clerks go through the costs item by item and discover where and why the money was spent. Sales staff find customers.

In large companies production controllers manage a team of estimators and production control staff. They interpret sales orders, estimate costs, plan materials purchase, arrange time on appropriate machines, set priorities and advise customers on the progress of their order.

Pre-press department

Most setting is via electronic transfer or CD. The pre-press operator uses a computer keyboard and mouse to set type and arrange the page, which is output to film or direct to the printing plate. An error in the pre-press department could result in the scrapping of thousands of books or products.

Printing department

This is where ink is applied to paper or other materials, by a variety of large and small printing machines. Such machines are complex and often computer controlled. They are managed by one or more craftspeople who control the physics and chemistry of the press to ensure that each copy produced is perfect.

Proofreader

Proofreaders check customers' proofs for spelling mistakes and incorrect typefaces before returning them. When setting to disk, proofreading is done automatically.

Printing Industry

Printing is carried out on a variety of scales – industrial scale printing of huge volumes of newspapers, books, magazines, etc, low to medium volumes (generally at a local level), and small volume, "quick" printing in high street premises (usually for the general public or small businesses).

The major sub-divisions of the print industry are:
- Printing of newspapers, journals and magazines
- Printing of advertising catalogues, brochures, calendars, greeting cards, maps, music, postage stamps and timetables
- Bookbinding – the assembling and collating of books and brochures, gold blocking and stamping, heraldic engraving and book stitching
- Pre-press activities such as electrotyping, engraving, etching, photo engraving and preparation and linkage of digital data
- Ancillary activities related to printing – aero-graphing, Braille copying, embossing, laminating, lithography and print colouring.

The big print companies are: De la Rue, Chesapeake UK Holdings, The Polestar Group, St. Ives, and British Polythene Industries.

The industry provides excellent opportunities for career development and some of the jobs available are: pre-press operatives, machine printers, print estimators, graphic designers, print finishers, sales and marketing, accountants and many more! To find out more about jobs, careers qualifications and skills required in the print industry visit our web site on: **www.prospect4u.co.uk**

Coatings Industry

The coatings industry is probably one of the most technologically advanced of UK industrial activities. Comprising the manufacture of decorative and protective paints, varnishes, wood care products, wall coverings and powder coatings, its manufacturers are at the leading edge of scientific and technical advances.

The coatings industry also produces advanced printing inks which are essential to the production of our newspapers, books and magazines and, of course, are used daily in all types of businesses to produce letters, reports and contracts.

Larger employers ICI, Sun Chemicals, Akzo Nobel, and Sigma Kalon.

The coatings industry is not just about producing emulsion and gloss paints. A number of specialist coatings are produced for a wide variety of applications. For example, coatings for tubes and wires, and protective coatings for high-tech equipment such as satellite dishes and mobile telephone and micro-wave transmitters. The coatings required for underground water, gas and electrical wires (especially for fibre-optic links) are at the leading edge of technological developments.

There are range of jobs and careers within the sector. For more details on jobs and qualifications visit Proskills web site on: **www.prospect4u.co.uk**

Qualifications and Training

Academic qualifications are not mandatory for craft workers but the following subjects studied to GCSE level are preferred: English, maths, computer studies and science. Training is to NVQ levels 2 and 3, with time off to attend courses.

Office staff have qualifications ranging from GCSEs to a degree. GCSEs are preferred for junior clerks and there are opportunities to gain further qualifications through Edexcel (BTEC)/SQA or City & Guilds awards. To take the higher diploma in printing on a two- or three-year basis, four GCSEs to include English, maths and a science plus one A level are necessary, or an Edexcel (BTEC)/SQA or NC/ND in printing. There are in addition three print-related degree courses, for which two A levels are necessary.

NVQs at levels 2 and 3 are available in print production and print administration. Modern Apprenticeships are available for production and office trainees.

Personal Qualities and Skills

A responsible attitude and a pride in what is being produced are necessary. Production workers need good colour vision and manual dexterity. Applicants must provide evidence of careful work and attention to detail. They must possess dexterity. The work requires images to be manually or computer manipulated to a high degree of accuracy. Applicants for jobs in the finishing department need physical strength, an affinity with machinery, concentration and the ability to work as a team.

Starting Salary

The range of starting salaries is very wide, but many production jobs start at between £12,000 and £17,000. It is possible to earn more than this with payments for shift work and if you develop highly specialised technical knowledge. Management jobs pay up to £23,000.

British Printing Industries Federation (BPIF), Farringdon Point, 29–35 Farringdon Road, London EC1M 3JF; 0870 240 4085; www.britishprint.com

Proskills UK Ltd, Centurion House, 85B Milton Park, Abingdon, Oxon OX14 4RY; 01235 833844; www.proskills.co.uk

Scottish Print Employers' Federation, 48 Palmerston Place, Edinburgh EH12 5DE; www.spef.org.uk

Get into Print; www.getintoprint.org

info

PRISON OFFICER

Prison officers are employed in prisons, detention centres, young offender institutions and remand centres. The work involves supervising prisoners inside the place of detention, escorting them to courts and other prisons and, if relevant, teaching a skill or trade. Officers also deliver programmes that help prisoners address their offending behaviour. Some specialist prison officers are employed as hospital officers, dog handlers, security experts and caterers.

Qualifications and Training

Five GCSEs, including maths and English, are required and applicants must pass an aptitude test and an interview. Training is a mixture of time spent at a local prison and residential courses at an officers' training school. In Scotland, the requirement is five standard grades (1, 2 or 3) or equivalent (including maths and English) or three years' experience managing people. A good level of physical fitness is required. NVQs in custodial care are available at levels 2 and 3, as is custodial healthcare level 3 and youth justice levels 3 and 4. There is special training for caterers, dog handlers, physical education instructors and medical staff. An accelerated promotions scheme exists for graduate entrants.

Personal Qualities and Skills

Officers should be positive thinkers with humanity and common sense; they must be good listeners, assertive, have excellent communication skills and the ability to mix with a wide range of people.

Starting Salary

Salaries in England and Wales are between £17,500 and £25,500. This can be increased by local allowances ranging from £1,000 to £4,000 depending on location. There are also long-service payments for anyone who has worked in the service for 12 years or more. Starting salaries in Scotland are between £12,000 and £14,000.

info

HM Prison Service, Headquarters, Cleland House, Page Street, London SW1P 4LN; 020 7217 3000; www.hmprisonservice.gov.uk

Home Office, Direct Communications Unit, 2 Marsham Street, London SW1P 4DF; 0870 000 1585; www.homeoffice.gov.uk

Prison Officers Association, Cronin House, 245 Church Street, London N9 9HW; 020 8803 0255; www.poauk.org.uk

Scottish Prison Service, Calton House, 5 Redheughs Rigg, Edinburgh EH12 9HW; 0131 244 8745; www.sps.gov.uk

Skills for Justice, 9 Riverside Court, Don Road, Sheffield S9 2TJ; 0114 261 1499; www.skillsforjustice.org.uk

PRIVATE INVESTIGATOR

Private investigators work with individuals, businesses, insurance companies, solicitors and other organisations. They are often self-employed, but may be employed by organisations such as law firms or insurance companies. The work is very varied, including tracing missing persons, investigating insurance claims and presenting legal or financial documents to private individuals and to businesses. Private investigators also investigate commercial piracy and fraudulent activities. Work activities are varied, including interviewing people, carrying out detailed research and surveillance operations.

Qualifications and Training

There are no formal entry qualifications, but many private investigators have worked in other security roles – it is normally a second career. A good standard of general education is important. All private investigators must be licensed by the Security Industry Authority (SIA) and the SIA is in the process of developing both a licensing system and appropriate qualifications. Currently details of training courses and providers are available from the Institute of Professional Investigators (IPI) and the Association of British Investigators (ABI) – check websites for details.

Personal Qualities and Skills

You must have excellent powers of observation and concentration. You need good people skills, to be able to talk to people and encourage them to share information with you. You need good research and information gathering abilities and some knowledge of IT. You should be self-confident with good business awareness.

Starting Salary

New entrants earn around £12,000. Private investigators on regular salaries earn between £15,000 and £20,000. It is harder to predict incomes for those who are self-employed, but £20,000 to £25,000 is a reasonable estimate.

Association of British Investigators (ABI), 27 Old Gloucester Street, London WC1N 3XX; 0871 474 0006; www.theabi.org.uk

Institute of Professional Investigators, 83 Guildford Street, Chertsey, Surrey KT16 9JL; 0870 330 8622; www.ipi.org.uk

Security Industry Authority (SIA), PO Box 9, Newcastle Upon Tyne NE82 6YX; 0870 243 0100; www.the-sia.org.uk

info

PSYCHOLOGY

Psychologists work in many different settings, in hospitals and healthcare, in schools and for Local Education Authorities, in industry, in marketing and business, for the police and criminal justice system and in sport. While these settings may be very different, all psychologists work to measure, understand, predict and assess human behaviour.

Qualifications and Training

For most branches of psychology, you must obtain Graduate Basis for Registration (GBR) with the British Psychological Society (BPS). This means completing a three- or four-year degree in psychology, accredited by the BPS, and it is important to check the status of any psychology degree before you begin your studies, if you think you may wish to register as a chartered psychologist. If your undergraduate degree is not in psychology you can start by doing a BPS approved Conversion Course and sitting a qualifying examination. Consult the BPS website for details of these courses. Further detail on specific qualifications for the different branches of psychology is given in the following sections.

Clinical psychologist

Clinical psychologists work mainly in health and social care settings with clients of all ages who are facing a variety of mental health and emotional problems. Clinical psychologists work as part of a multidisciplinary team devising programmes to help people who are suffering such conditions as severe anxiety or phobias, depression, addictive behaviour, or behaviours resulting from neurological or physical injury. They assess their client's mental and emotional states and may offer advice, counselling or therapy.

Qualifications and Training

In addition to a BPS accredited degree, clinical psychologists must complete a three-year NHS funded doctorate programme in clinical psychology. Places on these programmes are highly sought after, so you normally need a First or 2.1 degree plus some relevant work experience. Work as an assistant in a clinical psychology department is most useful, but course providers will give you advice on what work experience is suitable.

Consumer psychologist

Consumer psychologists do not have to be chartered with the BPS. They work in marketing in commercial businesses and other organisations, trying to understand and make use of the psychological basis of the choices that consumers make and why they choose to buy a certain product or service. Much of their work involves interviewing people or organising focus groups. They interpret the results of these interviews and discussions to help marketers understand and exploit trends in consumer behaviour.

Qualifications and Training

Most consumer psychologists have degrees either in psychology or in a marketing discipline where the course has covered consumer psychology in some depth. Some consumer psychologists start their careers in other roles in marketing departments.

Counselling psychologist

Counselling psychologists work with children and adults of all ages, helping them to deal with difficulties of many kinds. These could include psychological conditions such as anxiety or depression. Problems may be associated with life situations such as domestic violence or bereavement. Sometimes the problems are associated with substance abuse or eating disorders. Counselling psychologists advise their clients on ways of coping with situations and moving on.

Qualifications and Training

In addition to the BPS accredited degree, counselling psychologists need to complete a postgraduate qualification in counselling psychology, also approved by the BPS. There is an alternative 'independent route' into this field of psychology. This entails the equivalent of three years' full-time study, supervised work, the submission of a portfolio and an oral examination by the BPS.

Educational psychologist

Educational psychologists work with school students and other young people who are experiencing difficulties in learning and making progress with their education. Students may encounter difficulties because they have a learning disability, a sensory impairment or some emotional problem which is getting in the way. Educational psychologists work with individual students, with parents, teachers and other professionals, to try to find ways round the problem. They may advise students on new ways to learn, encourage them to talk about problems or set up particular programmes of study and activities.

Qualifications and Training

In addition to a BPS accredited degree, educational psychologists in England, Wales and Northern Ireland must complete a three-year Doctorate in Educational Psychology; in Scotland they must complete a two-year Master's in Educational Psychology plus one year of supervised practice.

Forensic psychologist

Forensic psychologists work mainly in the prison and probation services. The aim of their work is to try to develop interventions that stop offenders from re-offending and help them find ways to change their behaviours. Work may be one-to-one or in groups. They also advise prison governors and other prison and probation staff on what treatment programmes and institutional policies might be most effective in helping reduce offending. They work closely with the court system, with victims and with witnesses. They have to evaluate the programmes they have set up to measure their effectiveness.

Qualifications and Training

In addition to a BPS accredited degree, forensic psychologists must complete a Master's degree in forensic psychology (one year full time, two years' part time) and then undergo two years' supervised practice.

Health psychologist

This is a new and evolving area, and is the practice and application of psychological methods to the study of behaviour relevant to illness and healthcare. Health psychologists work in community, social care and healthcare settings examining the psychological aspects of illness. They help people implement programmes of behaviour that might prevent health problems and they also work with people learning to cope with various aspects of chronic and acute illnesses. At present, only a small number of health psychologists are employed by the NHS.

Qualifications and Training

In addition to a BPS accredited degree in psychology, health psychologists must complete a Master's degree in health psychology and two years' supervised work experience.

Occupational psychologist

Occupational psychologists work in organisations of many kinds or for private consultants. They examine how particular work tasks affect the well-being or performance of workers and they also determine which personal characteristics allow someone to perform tasks well. A major part of their work is in designing recruitment tests that will help employers select the most likely candidates to succeed in particular work roles. Occupational psychologists also work with organisations to solve issues of conflict within a work team, or to identify possible new management strategies.

Qualifications and Training

In addition to a BPS accredited degree in psychology, occupational psychologists need to complete a Master's degree in occupational psychology plus two years' supervised practice. An alternative route is to undertake three years' supervised practice and study for the BPS Certificate in Occupational Psychology.

Sports psychologist

Sports psychologists work with sportsmen and women helping them to improve their performance by examining the psychological aspects of their games and strategies. Sports psychologists teach techniques like relaxation and visualisation, which should help people to perform better. They also undertake research on the general effects of taking part in sport and physical exercise. Sports psychologists are often self-employed, though some are employed by sports teams or by umbrella organisations for particular sports.

Qualifications and Training

This is a very new branch of psychology, so there is no formal training route in place yet. Most entrants will have a degree in psychology or in sports science, followed by a Master's degree in sports psychology. This is followed by a period of supervised work experience.

Personal Qualities and Skills

Psychologists have to have excellent interpersonal skills, and be easily able to work with and listen to people who may be very distressed. They have to be good at observing and highly perceptive. In many roles they need good numeracy skills and the ability to write good reports.

Starting Salary

In the National Health Service (NHS) clinical psychologists and counselling psychologists start on around £25,000. Outside the NHS salaries vary considerably and some counselling psychologists are self-employed. The salary for newly qualified educational psychologists is in the range £30,000 to £40,000. Trainee forensic psychologists start on £16,500 rising to £19,000 at the end of the two-year training period. Occupational psychologists earn between £25,000 and £42,000. Most experienced psychologists in all branches of the profession earn between £25,000 and £40,000.

British Association for Counselling and Psychotherapy (BACP), BACP House, 35–37 Albert Street, Rugby, Warwickshire CV21 2SG; 0870 443 5252; www.bacp.co.uk/

British Psychological Society (BPS), St Andrews House, 48 Princess Road East, Leicester LE1 7DR; 0116 254 9568; www.bps.org.uk

Division of Counselling Psychology (DCoP), c/o British Psychological Society (BPS), St Andrews House, 48 Princess Road East, Leicester LE1 7DR; www.counsellingpsychology.org.uk

NHS Careers, PO Box 376, Bristol BS99 3EY; 0845 606 0655; www.nhscareers.nhs.uk

National Probation Service of England and Wales, National Probation Directorate, 1st Floor, Abell House, John Islip Street, London SW1P 4LH; www.probation.homeoffice.gov.uk/

Probation Board for Northern Ireland, 80–90 North Street, Belfast BT1 1LD; 028 9026 2400; www.pbni.org.uk/

info

PSYCHOTHERAPIST

Psychotherapy is a generic term, within which there are many specialist disciplines. People may practise as psychoanalytic psychotherapists, as cognitive or behavioural psychotherapists, or as counsellors, with varying degrees of training and experience; however, there are plans to introduce greater regulation.

Psychotherapists may work with individuals of any age, couples and families, or groups resolving problems such as over-shyness, over-aggression, sleeping disorders, separation difficulties, behavioural problems, eating difficulties, self-harm and depression. They work in hospitals, in- and out-patient clinics, child and family consultation centres, GPs' surgeries, special schools for disturbed children and in private practice.

Qualifications and Training

Psychotherapists come from varying professional backgrounds, but will usually have a degree in medicine, psychology, social sciences or a qualification in one of the core professions of the Health Service plus appropriate experience of working with people with mental health problems. Training then takes a further four years and involves academic study, personal analysis, workshops and supervised therapeutic treatment. There are several different training organisations. Most courses lead to national registration with either the British Confederation of Psychotherapists (BCP) or the UK Council for Psychotherapy.

Personal Qualities and Skills

Psychotherapists must have a genuine interest in the problems of children and adults, and a desire to help. They must themselves be emotionally well balanced.

Starting Salary

Salaries vary depending on the experience and professional background of the individual therapist. Self-employed therapists charge between £30 and £100 an hour.

info

British Association of Psychotherapists, 37 Mapesbury Road, London NW2 4HJ; 020 8452 9823; fax: 020 8452 0310; www.bap-psychotherapy.org; e-mail: mail@bap-psychotherapy.org

British Confederation of Psychotherapists, West Hill House, 6 Swains Lane, London N6 6QS; 020 7267 3626; fax: 020 7267 4772; www.bcp.org.uk; e-mail: mail@bcp.org.uk

UK Council for Psychotherapy (UKCP), 2nd Floor, Edward House, 2 Wakley Street, London EC1V 7LT 020 7014 9955; fax: 020 7014 9977; www.psychotherapy.org.uk; e-mail: info@psychotheraphy.org.uk

NHS Careers, Careers helpline: 0845 606 0655; www.nhscareers.nhs.uk

PUBLIC RELATIONS OFFICER

The chief aim of the public relations (PR) officer/executive is to ensure that the correct information about his or her employer or client is made known to the right people in order to establish and maintain goodwill and mutual understanding between an organisation and its public. This is done by a variety of means, including media relations, internal and external communication, company literature, exhibitions and events. Corporate PR work is concerned with effectively putting across an organisation's policy and activities to a variety of people, including government departments, employees, shareholders and other stakeholders. Consumer PR is concerned with giving information about a product; it is closely allied with marketing and advertising. Other areas of PR include community relations, sponsorship and financial PR. PR executives are employed by organisations, PR consultancies, or work as freelance consultants.

Qualifications and Training

Most entrants to the profession are graduates. The Institute of Public Relations (IPR) has approved 15 courses at various levels as qualifications for associate membership. Entry requirements for degree courses vary according to the institution, but most require five GCSEs and A levels or equivalents. The IPR runs its own postgraduate foundation and diploma courses, available at eight centres across Britain.

Personal Qualities and Skills

Public relations officers must understand people and what motivates them, and have the ability to get on well with people from different backgrounds. They must be imaginative, creative, reliable and have good managerial skills. Excellent written and oral communication skills are essential.

Starting Salary

Trainees in PR earn around £15,000. Salaries vary across the business sectors but the average for a PR account executive is £23,000+.

Institute of Public Relations,
The Old Trading House,
15 Northburgh Street, London
EC1V 0PR; 020 7253 5151;
fax: 020 7490 0588;
www.ipr.org.uk;
e-mail: info@ipr.org.uk

Public Relations Consultants
Association (PRCA), Willow House,
Willow Place, London SW1P 1JH;
020 7233 6026; fax: 020 7828 4797;
www.prca.org.uk

*Careers in Marketing, Advertising
and Public Relations* (Kogan Page)

info

PUBLISHING

Publishing houses differ in their structure, but most have three main departments: editorial, production/design, and sales and marketing. Additionally, there are the service departments found in most commercial offices: accounts, reception, personnel, warehousing and distribution.

Book publishing: editorial

This is the department which attracts the most applicants although editors are a very small percentage of the total publishing labour force. Editors liaise with those involved in the design, planning and production of each book. They read and edit the manuscript, prepare it for the typesetter, check the proofs and are responsible for assembling all the various parts, paginated in the correct order, for the printer. There is no automatic promotion system or salary structure. In a small company the only way to move up may be to move out.

The editorial director or managing editor runs a centralised copy-editing department, and commissions and supervises freelance editorial workers.

Acquisitions or commissioning editors (also known as publishers) build lists and find authors and books of quality. They may have specialist knowledge or contacts. They buy book rights, commission translations, find new authors, read and report on commissioned and unsolicited manuscripts and proposals, keep established authors happy and negotiate with literary agents. They must manage the editorial team and deliver books within budget and on time. They are also responsible for spotting and capitalising on new buying trends and markets.

Desk editors, also known as sub-editors or copy editors, read a manuscript several times, check it for copyright material and prepare it for the printer. They check references and facts, correct grammar, spelling and punctuation, discuss revisions with the author, decide picture content, design and produce schedules, choose the illustrations, and draft the jacket blurb and catalogue copy. They hand the edited manuscript to the design department for production. Once the manuscript has been set in type, they send a set of proofs to the author, proofread one themselves, collate the two sets of corrections and return the proofs (via the production department) to the printer.

Editorial assistants are publishing novices. Most of them have secretarial skills and, under the guidance of a senior editor, perform basic editorial tasks such as preparing captions for illustrations, researching bibliographic information, obtaining pictures and so on.

The copyright/permissions editor deals with requests from individuals and other publishers to reproduce passages or illustrations from its copyright works.

Picture researchers are briefed on the pictures needed for a book and asked to acquire them within a set budget. Picture researchers need to have an eye for detail and good negotiation skills.

Training and Qualifications

Editorial entrants will normally be expected to have degrees. Work experience and/or postgraduate vocational qualifications are also desirable. Specialist titles, such as science and technical publishing, will require appropriate degrees.

Personal Qualities and Skills

Commissioning editors will need to have good communication skills and exercise tact and diplomacy when dealing with authors. They will need to have an enquiring mind and a good knowledge of the field in which they specialise. Good management and team leader skills are also important.

Desk editors will need to be meticulous and have a good eye for detail. They will be expected to have excellent literacy skills and be able to communicate well with both authors and other members of the publishing team.

Editorial assistants should have good secretarial and organisational skills.

Starting Salary

Editorial assistants start on around £16,000 to £19,000, and after this you are likely to take on a different editorial role, rather than get a higher salary as an assistant. Commissioning editors get between £20,000 and £26,000 and salaries can be higher than this for anyone with wide commissioning responsibilities. Picture researchers/editors get between £16,000 and £22,000. Publishing is a field where there are many opportunities for short-term contracts, where you receive a fixed sum per contract.

Production controller: books

The production controller draws up an accurate specification for the book and invites tenders from typesetters, printers, paper suppliers and binders. When all the estimates have been received, the production controller places orders and ensures that all the production stages are carried out to the required standard, and on schedule. Undemanding production work on, for example, leaflets or reprints, is often given to a production assistant, who is regarded as a trainee.

Designer: books

(*see also* Art and Design)

Designers prepare layouts, sketches, specimen pages and dummies, and mark up all the manuscripts for the typesetter after they have been edited. All the activities of the design department are managed by the design director. Directors discuss illustrated or complicated technical books with the author and the editor, commission freelance artwork, arrange the in-house preparation of artwork and impose a visual style on the company product.

Training and Qualifications

Production and design staff tend to be graduates and will be expected to have a vocational diploma or relevant qualification.

Personal Qualities and Skills

Production and design professionals will need to be able to work under pressure and to tight deadlines. Being able to work well in a team and to interpret editorial briefs is also a quality expected in this area. Good planning skills are also essential. Production staff will also be expected to negotiate with printers and freelance designers for good deals.

Starting Salary

Production assistant £14,000+, production controller £18,000+, production manager £25,000+.

Sales, marketing and publicity executives: books

(*see also* Marketing, Public Relations Officer and Sales Representative)

Depending on the size of the company, there will be one, two or three departments working on the promotion and selling of the books. Applicants are usually graduates and should be creative and write lively and informative copy.

Sales representatives will spend a considerable amount of time travelling to booksellers both in the UK and abroad. They will present details of new publications in order to secure orders for the books, and continue to present the back catalogue to potential purchasers.

Training and Qualifications

Marketing and publicity executives are expected to have good literacy skills and are normally graduates. A postgraduate marketing qualification is also expected in more experienced marketing professionals. Sales representatives are also expected to have had experience within the book trade, and international sales representatives are expected to have a language degree or equivalent qualification.

Personal Qualities and Skills

Staff in this field need to be able to work in a team, and to develop and stick to marketing plans and budgets. They should have an interest in the field and the ability to pick up leads, and require good communication and literacy skills.

Starting Salary

Sales and marketing assistant £14,000+, marketing executive £18,000+, publicity manager £22,000+, sales representatives £20,000+, marketing manager £24,000+.

Indexers: books

Indexers provide a systematic arrangement of the terms appearing in a book, journal or other publication, which could be electronic or paper-based. They also work with page numbers or other locators in order to ensure the information can be easily found. Indexers are generally employed by publishers or authors. Most are freelancers working from home.

Qualifications and Training

No formal qualifications are required but a good education, normally to degree level, is necessary plus subject knowledge in the case of specialist books. Training is by open-learning course leading to accreditation. Registered indexers prove their experience and competence through an assessment procedure and admission to the Register of Indexers.

Personal Qualities and Skills

An ability to analyse a text and meticulous attention to detail are essential, plus the ability to work to set requirements and time limits.

Starting Salary

Payment may be per contract or by the hour. The Society of Indexers recommends rates of £16–£30 per hour or £1.20–£5.00 per page.

Society of Indexers, Blades Enterprise Centre, John Street, Sheffield S2 4SU; 0114 292 2350; fax: 0114 292 2350; www.socind.demon.co.uk; e-mail: admin@indexers.org.uk

Careers and Jobs in the Media (Kogan Page)

info

Magazines and newspapers

(*see also* Journalism)

The organisation of periodical publishing differs from that of book publishing and has much in common with newspapers. The main areas of activity outside the service departments are editorial, advertisement sales and circulation. Editorial jobs within the magazine and newspaper industry are covered in 'Journalism'.

However, in addition to editorial opportunities a number of alternative career paths can be found in magazine and newspaper publishing. Advertising sales are crucial to the majority of magazines and newspapers, and represent just one of the opportunities available to those who wish to work in these fields of publishing but are not seeking a job as a journalist.

Advertisement sales representatives: magazines

Commercial magazines depend on advertising revenue for survival. Graduates are often recruited straight from university to sales posts and are trained on the job. Sales staff must know the magazine's readership and build up advantageous contacts with potential advertisers. They spend a lot of time researching, analysing and planning, and need a persuasive manner and numerical skills.

Qualifications and Training

Requirements for trainees vary and many sales reps learn through work experience.

Personal Qualities and Skills

Sales staff need an outgoing personality and good communication skills, the ability to work under pressure and to meet deadlines.

Starting Salary

Many advertising reps earn a basic salary of approximately £12,000 and then are expected to earn the rest on commission. Successful advertising sales reps can earn £40,000+.

Design: magazines

(*see also* Art and Design)

The range of work includes cover design, typographical design, layout, design of advertisements and direct mail material. Entrants will need a design qualification. Entrants need to have a good working knowledge of current design software used within the industry.

Production manager: magazines

Production staff are trained in the printing trade. It is their responsibility to see the magazine is available at point of sale on publication day, and this involves meticulous planning and a tolerance of stress.

Training and Qualifications

Production and design staff tend to be graduates and are expected to have a vocational diploma or relevant qualification.

Personal Qualities and Skills

Production and design professionals need to be able to work under pressure and to tight deadlines. Being able to work well in a team and to interpret editorial briefs is also a quality expected in this area. Good planning skills are also essential.

Starting Salaries

Production assistant £15,000+, designers £18,000+.

info

PURCHASING OFFICER/INDUSTRIAL BUYER

Purchasing careers exist in all large organisations, whether profit-making or not. Essentially, purchasing and supply management involves identifying the requirements of the company's internal customers and then obtaining the necessary products and services by negotiation and agreement with suppliers. The primary objective is to obtain value for money. This does not always mean achieving the very lowest price – sometimes other commercial considerations are more important. For example, the flexibility and speed of response of the supplier might be the deciding factor, or the need to minimise risk by choosing a vendor with a good business record.

In a manufacturing environment such as a car plant, the purchaser is directly involved in buying components such as wheels, lights and shock absorbers for the production line. In a financial services company, purchases might well be for telecommunications systems, catering services and marketing services, including advertising and design. In retail purchasing the role is slightly different as buyers are more involved in merchandising, selecting product lines which appeal to the consumer and sell quickly.

Qualifications and Training

Most companies require a minimum of four or five GCSE passes. Graduates or individuals with A levels usually enter as trainee buyers, working with experienced personnel and continuing their training in the workplace. The minimum requirement for individuals wishing to study for the Foundation Stage of the CIPS Graduate Diploma is two A levels and three GCSEs (or equivalent). The Certificate in Purchasing and Supply Management is offered to those with no A levels.

Personal Qualities and Skills

You need good written and spoken communication skills and a high level of numeracy. You have to have the confidence to negotiate firmly and the temperament to take risks at times. You should be able to build good relationships with people and you need a good all round business awareness.

Starting Salary

Salaries start between £19,000 and £26,000, but senior purchasing managers will earn between £30,000 and £45,000.

info

Account Planning Group,
16 Creighton Avenue, London
N10 1NV; 020 8444 3692;
www.apg.org.uk

Chartered Institute of Purchasing and
Supply (CIPS), Easton House,
Easton on the Hill, Stamford, Lincs

PE9 3NZ; 01780 756777;
www.cips.org

Skillsmart Retail: The Sector Skills
Council for Retail, 40 Duke Street,
London W1A 1AB; 020 7399 3450;
www.skillsmartretail.com

QUARRYING

Quarrying is opencast mining for clay, sand, limestone, slate and other materials that are just below the layer of topsoil. Quarry workers or quarry operatives are involved in the operations connected with this extraction process. Modern quarrying involves using very heavy machinery to excavate, transport, cut and crush the different products, and quarry workers operate this machinery.

Qualifications and Training

There are no specific academic entry qualifications, but you must be fit, and having an LGV (light goods vehicle) driving licence or experience of using heavy plant and machinery can be an advantage. If you are between 16 and 24 years old, you may be able to do an apprenticeship; availability of these varies according to locality. Some employers will expect you to have four GCSEs to do an apprenticeship; these should include, English, maths and technology. The industry offers the chance to do NVQs at levels 2 and 3 in drilling operations, plant operations and process operations. There is also an NVQ level 3 in working with explosives, and there are higher-level courses in sampling. The majority of training is on-the-job.

Personal Qualities and Skills

You need to be physically fit and confident in handling highly specialised technical equipment. You should have good numeracy skills for calculating quantities and you must be able to work as part of a team. You should have an acute awareness of health and safety issues.

Starting Salary

New entrants start on around £12,000; this rises to £17,000 after two or three years' experience. Senior quarry workers earn between £20,000 and £25,000. There are often opportunities to increase earnings with overtime and shift-work payments.

EPIC Training Ltd, Alban Row,   www.careersinquarrying.co.uk
27–31 Verulam Road, St Albans, Herts
AL3 4DG; 01727 869008;
www.epicltd.com

info

RADIOGRAPHER

Radiography is a caring profession which calls for considerable technological expertise. There are two branches: diagnostic radiography and therapeutic radiography. Diagnostic radiographers are responsible for producing high-quality images on film and other recording materials which help doctors to diagnose disease and the extent of injuries. Therapeutic radiographers help to treat patients, many of whom have cancer, using X-rays, ionising radiation and sometimes drugs.

Qualifications and Training

All radiography qualifying courses are now at degree level. Courses are normally based in a university or higher education institution affiliated to a university, with half the time spent on clinical education in hospital departments associated with the university.

On graduation, entrants are eligible for State Registration by the Radiographers Board of the Council for Professions Supplementary to Medicine, which is an essential requirement for employment in the National Health Service. The requirements for entry to radiography courses are two A levels and three GCSEs at grade C or above, or equivalent. Entry is also possible through validated access courses, and applications from mature candidates are welcomed by many radiography education centres.

Personal Qualities and Skills

As well as having an interest in science, radiographers should be caring and compassionate but sufficiently level-headed not to get upset when dealing with sick people. They need to be patient and calm when faced with patients who

Society and College of Radiographers, 207 Providence Square, Mill Street, London SE1 2EW; 020 7740 7200; fax: 020 7740 7204; www.sor.org

NHS Careers, PO Box 376, Bristol BS99 3EY;
Careers helpline: 0845 606 0655;
www.nhscareers.nhs.uk/index.html

A Factsheet 'What is a radiographer?' is available from NHS Careers may be frightened or difficult. Good health and reasonable strength are needed for lifting people and heavy equipment. In addition, radiographers should be good humoured, able to work well in a team and assume responsibility.

Starting Salary

Starting salary varies from around £19,000 to £25,000 in the NHS rising to a top level of £35,000+.

RAILWAY WORK

The rail industry employs a vast number of people: drivers, revenue protection inspectors, customer service assistants, signal operators, engineers, fitters, clerical workers, technicians and managers. The latter are responsible for the day-to-day running of the railways or are in charge of departments such as planning, engineering, marketing and accounts.

Qualifications and Training

Train drivers must be aged 21 with a good general education. Train companies set their own entrance requirements, but often use aptitude tests including tests on train cab simulators. Training takes between nine and 18 months and includes work towards NVQ level 2 in Rail Transport Operations (Driving). It is likely that a licensing system for train drivers will be introduced in the near future.

Electricians, fitters and mechanics often have experience as technicians or electricians in other sectors before they join the railway. Apprenticeships may be an option for school leavers; those with four or five GCSEs grades A–C including maths, English and a science are able to join. All technicians and engineers are put through Personal Track Safety (PTS) training by their employers before they are allowed to work on railway tracks.

Station assistants, booking clerks and other customer service staff need no formal entry qualifications. Engineers and managers normally have degrees in relevant subjects: electrical or mechanical engineering, or business subjects respectively.

Personal Qualities and Skills

An interest in railways is a good starting point. Roles such as driving and signal work require good concentration, and safety awareness at all times is essential. Many positions entail a great deal of customer contact or team work so good interpersonal skills are extremely important.

Starting Salary

Trainee drivers earn around £15,000–£25,000, and up to £35,000 once training is completed. Trainee fitters/electricians start on £13,000, less for apprentices. After training, earnings are between £17,000 and £20,000.

Network Rail, 40 Melton Street, London NW1 2EE; 020 7557 8000; www.networkrail.co.uk

GoSkills, Concorde House, Trinity Park, Solihull, Birmingham B37 7UQ; 0121 635 5520; www.goskills.org

RECEPTIONIST

see Hospitality and Catering, *and* Business Administration

RECRUITMENT CONSULTANT

The aim of recruitment/employment consultants is to fit people to jobs. Agencies deal with all types of staff, from office and secretarial to highly complex and specialist technical roles. Much of the work involves selling to potential users and matching clients' demands. This includes interviewing prospective job candidates, keeping records of their details and matching them to employers' requirements.

Qualifications and Training

Many recruitment consultants have come into the industry after some experience of another job, for example sales, personnel or office work. They are trained either in-house or on courses run by the Recruitment and Employment Confederation (REC). The REC offers two levels of qualification: the Foundation Award, suitable for those in their first year in the industry, and the Certificate in Recruitment Practice for those with more than one year's experience. Both qualifications can be studied by distance learning or at an evening class.

Personal Qualities and Skills

Recruitment consultants must be able to relate to people at different organisational levels, have good communication skills, work quickly and calmly under pressure and be organised and resilient.

Starting Salary

Trainees earn between £11,500 and £18,000. With experience, earnings range from £23,000 to £35,000. Some consultants are self-employed.

Recruitment and Employment Confederation, 15 Welbeck Street, London W1G 9XT; 020 7009 2100; www.rec.uk.com

Chartered Institute of Personnel and Development, 151 The Broadway, London SW19 1JQ; 020 8612 6200; www.cipd.co.uk

REGISTRAR

The local registration service (LRS) is a network of register offices in England and Wales which registers births, stillbirths, marriages and deaths. These are staffed by a mixture of statutory officers and local government employees. The latter are known as 'deputies' to the statutory officers. England and Wales is divided into 366 registration districts, and each district has a Superintendent Registrar based at the register office. Some districts have outstations that are either visited or permanently staffed.

Qualifications and Training

No formal requirements other than a good general education are necessary. Training is on the job but vacancies are few.

Personal Qualities and Skills

Registrars must be able to get on with people, giving advice calmly and sympathetically, and be even-tempered. They should be able to do their job well in situations of excitement, emotion and distress. Confidentiality must be maintained at all times. Good handwriting is important, and the ability to drive may be necessary in rural locations. Entrants must be prepared for weekend work.

Starting Salary

Trainees earn between £16,000 and £18,000. Superintendent Registrars earn from £18,000 to £25,000.

Local Government Careers;
www.lgcareers.com

General Registrar Office for Scotland,
New Register House, 3 West Street,
Edinburgh EH1 3YT; 0131 314 4467;
www.gro-scotland.gov.uk

General Register Office (GRO),
Trafalgar Road, Southport PR8 2HH;
0151 471 4805; www.gro.gov.uk

info

REMOVALS

Removers play a key role in the chain of events leading up to departure from one home and arrival in another – which can be around the corner or on the other side of the world. It is the remover's job to see that all the customer's belongings are professionally packed and transported to their destination. The work may involve packing fragile objects quickly and efficiently, as well as travelling long distances. Some large companies have their own storage facilities, so employees may be involved in ensuring that furniture is stored safely.

Estimators are the technical salespeople in a removals company. They visit customers' homes and estimate the amount of packing space needed, the time it will take and the price.

Qualifications and Training

Employees can work towards NVQs for the removals and storage industry. Progression is also possible to supervisory level. An LGV (large goods vehicle) licence would be beneficial, but is not essential when starting out. Estimators should have a good standard of education with good passes preferably in English, maths, geography and modern languages, hold a full car driving licence and be able to express themselves clearly and persuasively. Training is on the job.

Personal Qualities and Skills

Removers should be fit and strong. They must be honest and have a sense of responsibility towards other people's possessions. Common sense and the ability to work in a team are important.

Starting Salary

Salaries vary from region to region in the UK depending upon the market and competition in the area. There is no set income and salaries are often paid hourly, especially with casual staff. Income varies with experience and skills: a new entrant can earn £10,000 per year; with experience it is possible to earn between £11,000 to £13,000 per year. A senior person earns over £17,000.

info

British Association of Removers Limited, 3 Churchill Court, 58 Station Road, North Harrow, Middlesex HA2 7SA; 020 8861 3331; fax: 020 8861 3332;

www.removers.org.uk; e-mail: info@bar.co.uk

Local Job Centre Plus and Careers/ Connexions Centres

RETAILING

Retailing is a sector offering many different career opportunities. As well as the careers outlined in this section, retailing offers opportunities in distribution management and warehouse work, in finance, in marketing and in human resource management. There are openings at school leaver level through to graduate and senior management opportunities. Retail outlets include small shops, specialising in a particular type of product: shoes, car spares or quality foods, for example. Supermarkets, department stores and discount stores are just some of the other examples of retail outlets.

Checkout operator

Checkout operators work at the tills in supermarkets and other large retail stores. They scan the prices of all the items customers have purchased, process payments whether by cash, cheque or card, and they may also offer some assistance with packing, eg wrapping delicate items or putting frozen foods into separate bags.

Can you see yourself managing the entire floor?

**Don't just think it.
In two years you could be doing it.**

Ready to start your retail management career? Then why not apply for our new **Management Trainee Programme**? After 12 months, you could be running your own section. Within two years, you could be a Commercial Manager. All thanks to a combination of tailored workshops, on-the-job learning, and your own commitment and drive.

Anyone whose highest qualification is two A-levels or equivalent* can apply.

Please visit www.marksandspencer.com/traineemanager for further details.

*Scottish Highers (x3), Advanced Highers (x2), Leaving Certificate (Ireland), AVCE (12 units), NVQ Level 3

  Marks and Spencer plc is an equal opportunities employer.

www.marksandspencer.com/careers

Qualifications and Training

No specific qualifications are necessary, though individual stores may request a good standard of education. Training is provided on the job and it is possible to obtain NVQ level 1 in checkout operations and NVQ levels 2 and 3 in customer service and sales. Career progression is to supervisory roles.

Personal Qualities and Skills

You must be polite and friendly and able to talk to people without losing your concentration or slowing down. You need good numeracy skills in order to spot errors. You must have good stamina and be able to work under pressure in a hectic environment.

Starting Salary

Starting salary is around £10,000 to £12,000 depending on whether you have to work antisocial shifts. Supervisors earn between £12,000 and £16,000.

Skillsmart Retail, 40 Duke Street, London W1A 1AB; 0800 093 5001; www.skillsmartretail.com

Display designer/visual merchandiser

Display designers are responsible for shop windows and displays inside stores. These may be to attract customers into a shop, promote a new product or reinforce a company image. Displays are often seasonal or themed. Some designers work to instructions from head office, others create their own designs. The work may include making props, arranging lighting and general care of the display areas. Some shops also employ visual merchandisers who arrange products according to an organisation's display policy.

Qualifications and Training

While there are no standard, formal entry qualifications, in practice most entrants have a relevant qualification. There are several three- or four-year degree courses in Design Merchandising Management and Exhibition and Retail Design. There are also some two-year foundation degrees available in display design or visual merchandising. Other art-based qualifications may be accepted by some employers. A great deal of training is on the job.

Personal Qualities and Skills

You need real artistic flair and to be good at working with colour and with three-dimensional design. You should be imaginative and practical, able to work as part of a team and able to relate design ideas to commercial impact. You also need good IT skills, preferably able to use CAD (computer assisted design).

Starting Salary

Trainees earn between £10,000 and £12,000, while experienced display designers earn up to £20,000. It is possible for a display manager with a large store to earn more than £35,000.

British Display Society,
146 Welling Way, Welling, Kent
DA16 2RS; 020 8856 2030;
www.britishdisplaysociety.co.uk

Skillsmart Retail, 40 Duke Street,
London W1A 1AB; 0800 093 5001;
www.skillsmartretail.com

Retail store manager

Retail store managers work in department stores, in supermarkets and in small, individually owned stores. In a small store they will run the whole operation. In a supermarket they may be responsible for one area, fresh produce or the checkouts, for example. In a department store they may run one or several departments. Managers are responsible for ensuring that everything runs smoothly. They have to organise work rosters, ensure that sales targets are met, that customer service is of a high standard and that sales staff are fully trained.

Qualifications and Training

There are several ways to become a retail store manager. Large stores or chains may run graduate management training programmes or programmes open to school leavers with two or three A levels. Experience, however, is often as important as qualifications, and many managers start out as sales assistants and work their way up to management positions.

Sales assistant

There are many opportunities for sales staff in retailing. Your responsibilities and tasks depend on what kind of retail outlet you are working in, as well as your level of experience. In general, sales staff are expected to sort stock, sell goods, ensure these goods are attractively displayed and deal with payments for goods. They also answer customers' queries, give information about products and offer advice. Some sales staff process orders for new stock.

Qualifications and Training

While no formal academic qualifications are necessarily needed, GCSEs grades A–C in English and maths are a help as is some experience of working with people. Training is on the job, and large stores or chain stores may offer some structured training programmes. It is possible to work towards several NVQs at levels 2 and 3 in retail, including sales, retail operations and customer service.

The Best of Everything

Life at Tesco is incredibly diverse. So we have more diverse career development opportunities than most. With over 1900 stores, 250,000 employees and group turnover of £41.8 billion, we can offer the potential for rapid progress and plenty of early responsibility.

We have opportunities across all areas of our business – you can take your pick from office, stores and distribution graduate programmes.

Join one of our **Office Management Programmes** and you will develop in-depth knowledge of one of our specialist business areas. 12-18 month development programmes are offered in Corporate & Legal Affairs, Corporate Purchasing, Finance, Information Technology, Property & Engineering, Research & Analysis, Supply Chain or Tesco.com. Alternatively, you may prefer to join Commercial, Marketing, or Personnel.

Our **Store Management Programmes** offer opportunities both in-store and in the support office – if you want to be directly involved in our core business, then these programmes are for you. Within a year you'll either be ready to run a key area in one of our stores, or you'll be working in our Support Office on projects enhancing our customers' shopping experience.

Join our **Distribution Management Programme** and you'll work for the UK's number one Distribution network. The Distribution programme will involve hands-on experience in our Depots where you will learn how to deliver an efficient operation through effective planning and organisation. Within 2 years you could be managing a shift, overseeing 13 other managers and ensuring our customers get the products they want, when they want them.

If you have a passion for working for an innovative blue chip organisation, and have at least a 2:1 degree, one of the Tesco graduate programmes could be for you.

To find out more and apply, visit **www.tesco-graduates.com**

Tesco quality.

Great for graduates as well as customers.

We've 15 specially selected
business programmes.

All ripe with opportunity for a fuller career.

Not to mention a strong whiff
of responsibility.

To find out more, go to
www.tesco-graduates.com

★ Choose from Commercial, Corporate & Legal Affairs,
Corporate Purchasing, Distribution, Finance,
IT, Marketing, Personnel, Pharmacy,
Property & Engineering, Research & Analysis,
Stores, Supply Chain, Support Office or Tesco.com

Many people who start as sales assistants become supervisors for a section of a store, or progress to become store managers.

Personal Qualities and Skills

You must be polite and friendly and enjoy working with people. You need good basic literacy and numeracy skills and must be reasonably physically fit. Being smart and tidy is important, especially in fashion retailing. For anyone interested in supervisory and management responsibility, you have to be very well organised, good at taking decisions and good at leading and motivating other people.

Starting Salary

Sales assistants start on between £10,000 and £13,000. Supervisors earn between £15,000 and £17,000. Salaries for managers range from £14,000 to £20,000 for trainees through to £20,000 to £26,000 for experienced managers.

ROAD TRANSPORT

(*see also* Logistics)

This industry includes road haulage, plus passenger transport and commercial companies that have their own transport and delivery facilities. Passenger transport covers bus and coach services. Commercial companies need to plan the flow of materials or parts for manufacturing and the subsequent delivery of their products to their customers. Similarly, retail organisations need transport to bring merchandise to their outlets. The work divides into loading, moving and unloading, involving a wide range of operative and administrative staff: drivers, warehouse staff, depot managers, mechanics, clerical staff, transport planners and many others. There is a variety of public-sector and private-sector employers.

Qualifications and Training

Jobs range from those needing few formal qualifications to those that require a degree. There are NVQs in road passenger and road freight transport for operative staff; and Edexcel (BTEC)/SQA National Certificates for those with four GCSEs or equivalent; the Institute of Logistics and Transport offers a range of professional qualifications from entry level upwards. In England and Wales the Foundation and Advanced Modern Apprenticeships in road haulage and distribution are available. In Scotland NVQ/SVQ training at level 2 through Skillseekers and at level 3 through Skillseekers Modern Apprenticeships is available. Degrees in transport management are available at a number of universities.

Personal Qualities and Skills

Drivers need to be physically strong, responsible, careful and able to communicate effectively. Transport managers need good numeracy and ICT skills, and to be able to think analytically and plan effectively.

Starting Salary

A newly qualified driver will earn around £10,000–£12,000, while an experienced driver carrying dangerous goods can earn £25,000+. Graduate trainees start between £18,000 and £24,000.

Skills for Logistics, 14 Warren Yard, Warren Farm Office Village, Milton Keynes MK12 5NW; 01908 313360; www.skillsforlogistics.org; e-mail: info@skillsforlogistics.org

British International Freight Association, Institute of Freight Forwarders, Redfern House, Browells Lane, Feltham, Middlesex TW13 7EP; 020 8844 2266; fax: 020 8890 5546; www.bifa.org; e-mail: bifa@bifa.org

Institute of Logistics and Transport, 11–12 Buckingham Gate, London SW1E 6LB; www.iolt.org.uk

Institute of Transport Administration, IoTA House, 7B St Leonards Road, Horsham, West Sussex RH13 6EH; 01403 242412; fax: 01403 242413; www.iota.org.uk

GoSkills, Concorde House, Trinity Park, Solihull, Birmingham B37 7UQ; 0121 635 5520; fax: 0121 635 5521; www.transfed.org

info

ROOFER

see Construction

ROUNDSPERSON

The roundsperson we are all most familiar with is probably the person who delivers milk and other dairy products to people's doorsteps on a daily basis.

In fact, working as a roundsperson can involve delivering and selling goods and services of many kinds to private homes and business premises. Examples include doing a sandwich round to businesses, selling ice cream or fast food and running mobile shops, selling many different kinds of goods. Usually, you work for yourself or you operate a franchise for a franchising company.

Qualifications and Training

You do not need any formal qualifications to do this work, but some companies set their own entry tests, and you need good basic maths skills for calculating prices and making out bills. You need a full driving licence and many companies prefer applicants to be over 21 years old. If you are selling fast food, you will need a licence to trade from your local Environmental Health Department. You could do a number of relevant NVQs in customer service and sales. If you are employed by a retailer or a franchising company, it usually provides specific training about its own products and services.

Personal Qualities and Skills

For most of the time you are working on your own, but you have to enjoy and be good at dealing with customers. You must be well organised with good numeracy skills and usually some computer skills these days. You have to be highly motivated, well organised and not mind working some antisocial hours or being out in all weathers.

Starting Salary

When you start off it is hard to earn more than about £10,000, though with experience this can rise to £15,000 to £20,000 and there are only a few types of round (milk and sandwiches, for example) where you are likely to receive seasonal tips.

info

British Franchise Association, Thames View, Newtown Road, Henley-on-Thames, Oxfordshire RG9 1HG; 01491 578050; www.british-franchise.org.uk

Improve: The Food and Drink Manufacturing and Processing Sector Skills Council, Providence House, 2 Innovation Close, Heslington, York

YO10 52F; 0845 644 0448; www.improveltd.co.uk

Dairy Training and Development Council, 19 Cornwall Terrace, London NW1 4QP; 020 7486 7244; www.dairytraining.org.uk

Local Job Centre Plus and Connexions/Careers Centres

ROYAL AIR FORCE

The Royal Air Force is responsible for the airborne defence of the UK and its allies. It consists of a small flying force, almost exclusively officers, supported by non-commissioned airmen and airwomen working in a variety of trades such as engineering, communication and air traffic control work as well as supporting jobs such as catering, medical and dental support workers, photographers, security guards and musicians. A few non-commissioned officer airmen and airwomen work as crew in specialities such as air signallers, air electronics operators or air loadmasters.

Ground opportunities for officers include air traffic and fighter control, engineering, physical education, intelligence, catering, administration, supply and education. There are also provost (police) officers, medical officers, dental officers, nursing officers, legal officers and chaplains.

Qualifications and Training

Non-commissioned personnel

For some jobs no academic qualifications are needed. For entry to scientific and technical trades, three to five GCSEs, often including science and maths, are required. Musicians need to have passed Grade 8 or have a higher qualification; dental/nursing staff need the appropriate professional qualifications. The minimum age for entry to most trades is 16; the upper age limit is normally 30, but there is some variation between trades.

Ground recruits attend an initial seven-week course covering physical fitness and weapons training which is followed by specialist training. Aircrew have a 12-week basic training course followed by specialist training. Many airmen and airwomen will work towards NVQs or other nationally recognised qualifications throughout their career.

Officers

Minimum academic entry requirements are two A levels and five GCSEs at A–C (including English and maths) or equivalent. The normal upper age limit is 26 (24 for pilots) but qualified specialists can apply up to the age of 39. Graduates are preferred for some specialisms and student sponsorships are available. Those wanting to train as pilots take aptitude tests to assess coordination and speed of reaction. Applicants must meet nationality and residence requirements and pass a medical examination. For some jobs good eyesight and colour vision is essential. Women may apply to all branches except the RAF Regiment.

Training for all new officers starts with an intensive 24-week course which covers operational and leadership skills. This is followed by training relevant to the chosen specialisation, which varies in length from a few weeks to up to three years for pilots.

Personal Qualities and Skills

Air Force personnel must enjoy teamwork and a disciplined regime and be willing to go into combat. They need physical fitness, dedication, commitment, initiative and a sense of responsibility.

Starting Salary

Your salary is based on the job you do, the qualifications you have and your length of service. Some jobs have additional pay for special skills, like parachuting. Typical starting salaries for airmen/airwomen are around £15,000. Graduates entering as commissioned officers may be offered enhanced promotion and can expect higher salaries; for example the starting salary for a Catering Officer is at least £26,350.

Local RAF Careers Offices;
0845 605 5555; www.rafcareers.com

Joint Services Command and Staff
College, Faringdon Road, Watchfield,
Swindon SN6 8TS; 01793 788000;
www.da.mod.uk/JSCSC

Royal Aeronautical Society (RAES),
4 Hamilton Place, London W1J 7BQ;
020 7670 4300; www.raes.org.uk

Info

ROYAL MARINES

The Royal Marines acts as the emergency strike force of the Royal Navy. Its personnel are trained for amphibious assaults and commando operations on land. It has a well-deserved reputation for toughness, and training is arduous. Marines are sent at short notice to deal with emergency situations, which include natural disasters as well as military operations. There are six specialist areas in the Royal Marines. These are Ships Detachment (serving on Royal Navy ships), Air Squadron, Special Boat Squadron, Jungle and Arctic Warfare and Embarked Force (working at sea and forming part of the amphibious Task Force). Most commandos serve as Riflemen but there are some specialist and support trades. The Royal Marines is an all-male service.

Qualifications and Training

Officers

Full career entry is between 17 and a half and 23, and at least two A levels or equivalent are required. Undergraduates may be recruited on a cadetship scheme and sponsored at university. Graduates can enter up to the age of 25. Initial training is 15 months followed by 9 months working in a specialist unit. Officers specialise in particular areas of work such as radio communications, amphibious operations or special reconnaissance work, but are trained in all the activities undertaken by the Marines.

Other ranks

Entry to the Royal Marines is between 17 and a half and 28 and does not require formal qualifications but many recruits have GCSEs and some have A levels. All candidates must pass the Royal Navy selection test. The minimum height requirement is 1.65 m (5 ft 6 in) with appropriate height to weight ratio. Initial training lasts 30 weeks and is followed by a period of more advanced training with the opportunity to work towards the appropriate qualifications. Before returning to civilian life Marines can learn a new trade or supervisory and management skills at a Royal Navy vocational training centre.

Personal Qualities and Skills

The same basic qualities are needed as for the other services: discipline, dedication, fitness, initiative and an ability to work with others. Marines spend long periods away from home, often in difficult and dangerous locations with climates ranging from tropical to arctic. High standards of physical fitness and stamina are essential. Around 900 Marines are recruited each year and entry is competitive.

Starting Salary

Your salary depends on the job you do, the qualifications you have and your length of service. Earnings for new entrants start at just over £12,000 and the top of the scale is around £36,000. Additional allowances are paid for submarine and other special duties. Salaries rise on 1 April every year.

Royal Navy; careers enquiries:	Armed Forces Careers Office (NI),
0845 607 5555;	Royal Navy and Royal Marines,
www.royal-navy.mod.uk	Palace Barracks, Holywood, Co Down
	BT18 9RA; 028 9042 7040

ROYAL NAVY

Navy personnel work in the nation's combat fleet and at its land bases. Like the other services, the Navy uses many trades and skills. Royal Navy ratings are non-commissioned servicemen and women working in one of six branches: warfare, engineering, supply, medical, Fleet Air Arm and deep navy (submarines). Officers command and are responsible for the welfare of the ranks. They may work in warfare, engineering, supply, aviation or training. Special Officers work as doctors, dentists, nursing officers or chaplains.

Qualifications and Training

Officers

There are two main entry routes – direct entry from school, university or civilian employment or by promotion from the ranks. Some scholarships are available for sixth formers and undergraduates. Minimum entry requirements are two A levels or equivalent.

An increasing number of officers are graduates. Applicants must be under 23 (26 for graduates). Experienced engineers must be under 32 on entry; age limits for Special Officers can be up to 44.

All officers spend two to five terms at the Britannia Royal Naval College at Dartmouth, which will include some time spent at sea. After this they go on to further training which varies in length according to specialism.

Ratings

The minimum age for entry to most jobs is 16. Medical and dental assistants and nurses need to be slightly older. The upper age limit for communications technicians and artificer apprentices is 27; for other trades 32. Academic requirements vary according to the trade but are between two and five GCSEs or equivalent. Medical and dental assistants and nurses may need professional qualifications. All applicants have to pass a test in reasoning, English, numeracy and mechanical comprehension and a medical. Jobs in submarines are not open to women.

Initial basic training is eight weeks followed by specialist training relevant to the trade chosen. Some of this time will be spent at sea.

Personal Qualities and Skills

A liking for the sea is important. Other requirements are the same as for the other services: discipline, dedication, fitness, initiative and an ability to work with others. Different trades demand specific skills – languages are useful for those working in communications, while a knowledge of science and technology is needed by those working with sophisticated equipment.

Starting Salary

Your salary depends on the job you do, the qualifications you have and your length of service. Earnings for new entrants start at just over £12,000 and the top of the scale is around £36,000. Additional allowances are paid for submarine and other special duties. Salaries rise on 1 April every year.

SALES REPRESENTATIVE

A sales representative may work for a manufacturer, wholesale distributor or service industry, persuading potential customers to buy the firm's products and also looking after the needs of existing customers. The representative is usually assigned a geographical area and travels around it on the firm's behalf. It is possible to be a representative for any number of products, from soap powder to pharmaceutical supplies to office equipment, machine tools and beauty products.

Qualifications and Training

Requirements for trainees vary, but most firms look for four GCSEs grades A–C or equivalent and in some companies recruitment is at graduate level. Sales reps may study for examinations set by such bodies as the Chartered Institute of Marketing or the Managing and Marketing Sales Association. Diplomas and certificates are also issued by various trade associations representing particular types of product. Technical sales representatives usually have a degree or equivalent in the relevant subject.

Personal Qualities and Skills

An outgoing, friendly personality, a manner that inspires confidence and the ability to speak forcefully and persuasively, plus persistence and stamina, are all important.

Starting Salary

There is a fairly wide range of salaries for new sales representatives: £11,000 to £19,000, rising to £20,000 to £35,000 with experience. For most jobs, salary is made up of a basic rate of pay supplemented by commission on individual sales made and/or bonuses based on the performance of a sales team.

Managing and Marketing Sales Association (MAMSA), PO Box 11, Sandbach, Cheshire CW11 3GE; 01270 526339; www.mamsasbp.com

Institute of Sales and Marketing Management, Harrier Court, Lower Woodside, Luton LU1 4DQ; 01582 840001; www.ismm.co.uk

info

SCIENTIFIC RESEARCH

Research scientists work in medicine, in physics and in life sciences. They are employed in industry and in academia. The topics and issues they research are extremely wide ranging and are of course determined by the particular field of science in which they work. They may be involved in developing new products, materials or medicines, examining the effects of chemicals on behaviour, or of climate upon plants. Research scientists may be involved in the development of drugs, the study of genetics or stem cell research. In astrophysics they may be tackling questions about the nature of the universe or the structure of asteroids. In whichever scientific specialism researchers work, their main role is to design, carry out and analyse the results of scientific experiments.

Qualifications and Training

Scientific research is a graduate entry profession. While job titles vary, there are basically three levels at which you can get into research. Technician level posts require an undergraduate degree in a science discipline relevant to the field of research. Research assistants usually need to have a Master's degree in the appropriate area of science, and research associates have usually completed a PhD.

Personal Qualities and Skills

Regardless of which field of science you enter, you must have a rigorous and questioning approach to whatever you do. You need good numeracy skills and the ability to interpret data accurately. Many posts require good IT skills and/or the ability to work with highly specialised equipment. You need to be able to work on your own and as part of a team. You may well have to negotiate for funds and you have to be an imaginative problem solver with a real fascination for your subject.

info

Biotechnology and Biological Sciences Research Council (BBSRC), Polaris House, North Star Avenue, Swindon SN2 1UH; 01793 413200; www.bbsrc.ac.uk/

Institute of Biology (IOB); 9 Red Lion Court, London EC4A 3EF; 020 7936 5900; www.iob.org/

Engineering and Physical Sciences Research Council (EPSRC), Polaris House, North Star Avenue, Swindon SN2 1ET; 01793 444000; www.epsrc.ac.uk

Institute of Mathematics and its Applications, Catherine Richards House, 16 Nelson Street, Southend-on-Sea, Essex SS1 1EF; 01702 354020; www.ima.org.uk

Medical Research Council (MRC), 20 Park Crescent, London W1B 1AL; 020 7636 5422; www.mrc.ac.uk

Particle Physics and Astronomy Research Council (PPARC), Polaris House, North Star Avenue, Swindon SN2 1SZ; 01793 442000; www.pparc.ac.uk

Starting Salary

Typical starting salaries are £15,000 to £20,000 at technician level; £20,000 to £25,000 for research assistant level (usually with an MSc or MPhil); and £25,000 to £30,000 at postdoctoral research associate level. Research scientists working in industry or leading a research project or team may earn more than this.

SECURITY WORK

Security guards and security officers work for all kinds of organisations and businesses, where buildings, property and people need protection. They work to prevent theft and other criminal activities and to alert the police when the need arises. Typical tasks for security guards and officers include door supervision, checking people who enter a premises to confirm identity, patrolling buildings on foot or monitoring them from a control room, guarding cash and other valuables as they are delivered or removed or when they are in transit, and checking individuals and observing behaviour at airports or other public places. Many security staff begin as security guards and then progress to becoming security officers or supervisors with responsibility for coordinating security arrangements and training other security staff.

Qualifications and Training

No specific entry qualifications are required, but you must be at least 18 – many companies prefer you to be 21. You often need a driving licence and you may have to pass some written tests and have a medical. Many companies will carry out extensive checks on your past work record to ensure that you are trustworthy and honest.

The Security Industry Association operates a new training scheme that incorporates a security guard qualification and a licence to work as a security guard. The training takes 30 hours and is usually completed over a few days. It is possible to do City & Guilds courses equivalent to GNVQ levels 2 and 3 in security guard work, and many companies provide a range of short courses in relevant skills such as dog handling, or use of electronic monitoring.

Personal Qualities and Skills

You need to be self-confident and mature – able to challenge people when necessary, but also polite and helpful. You should be able to write short reports and also have good basic IT skills. You need to be physically fit, and able to concentrate for long periods while remaining highly observant. You should be able to work on your own, but also work as part of a team and know when to seek help, support or advice.

Starting Salary

New security guards are often paid the minimum wage, or something close to it; £5.35 an hour, or £10,000 to £12,000 depending on the hours you work. Senior security officers with experience and some supervisory responsibility earn between £15,000 and £22,000 a year.

info

British Security Industry Association
Limited, Security House,
Barbourne Road, Worcester WR1 1RS;
01905 21464; fax: 01905 613625;
www.bsia.co.uk;
e-mail: info@bsia.co.uk

National Security Inspectorate,
Queensgate House, 14 Cookham Road,
Maidenhead, Berks SL6 8AJ;
0870 205 0000, fax: 01628 773367,
www.nsi.org.uk;
e-mail: nsi@nsi.org.uk

Security Industry Training
Organisation, Security House,
Barbourne Road, Worcester WR1 1RS;
01905 20004; fax: 01905 724949;
www.sito.co.uk;
e-mail: info@sito.co.uk

Security Industry Authority (SIA),
PO Box 9, Newcastle upon Tyne
NE82 6YX; 0845 243 0100;
www.the-sia.org.uk

SHEET METAL WORKER

see Manufacturing

SHIPBROKER

Shipbrokers act as go-betweens for ship owners, looking for cargo to fill their vessels, and charterers, seeking to ship their dry cargo and tanker requirements. Sale and purchase of vessels is also an important service offered to clients. Brokers are paid commission on the contracts arranged. The Baltic Exchange in London is the centre of the chartering market. It is a self-regulated market and the Exchange maintains a register of those seeking employment, which its member companies may consult. Vacancies are also advertised on the website. Additionally, shipbrokers/ship's agents in ports make arrangements when a ship calls for customs clearance – loading and discharging cargoes, meeting crew requirements and so on. Port agents who attend to cargo liners may also be involved in marketing and documenting cargo. In order to maintain contact with the international scene, shipbrokers tend to work long hours and to travel abroad frequently.

Qualifications and Training

There are no specific academic qualifications needed for ship broking beyond a good general educational background. However, members of a firm who wish to make a career in the shipping business usually study for the examination leading to membership of the Institute of Chartered Shipbrokers. Such study can be part time or by correspondence course, and covers not only shipping practice but more general studies in law, economics and international trade. The Institute also offers a foundation diploma in shipping for those just starting in the business.

Personal Qualities and Skills

A good business sense, the ability to learn through practical experience, and willingness to work long and irregular hours and to travel are all necessary.

Starting Salary

Salaries start at between £16,000 and £21,000, rising to £23,000 to £25,000 after two or three years.

British International Freight Association (BIFA), Redfern House, Browells Lane, Feltham, Middlesex TW13 7EP; 020 8844 2266; www.bifa.org

The Chartered Institute of Logistics and Transport (CILT) UK, 11–12 Buckingham Gate, London

SW1E 6LB; 01536 740104; www.ciltuk.org.uk

Skills for Logistics, 14 Warren Yard, Warren Farm Office Village, Milton Keynes MK12 5NW; 01908 313 360; www.skillsforlogistics.org/

SIGNWRITER

see Art and Design

SOCIAL WORK/SOCIAL CARE

Home carer

Home carers provide emotional and practical support for the elderly, people with physical disabilities, mental health problems and a range of other illnesses.

The role of the home carer includes housework, shopping, dressing, bathing, toileting and supervising medication. Carers are offered training and support by a home care organiser, who also provides team supervision. Most home carers work for local authorities or private agencies.

Home care organiser

Home care organisers undertake assessment of a person's needs and their financial circumstances. They decide whether or not the person is eligible for support and exactly what financial support he or she needs. They then arrange for home care provision. They work in teams alongside social workers and care managers, mainly in local authorities, the voluntary sector or private agencies.

Qualifications and Training

For home carers, NVQs in care are available. For a home care organiser, some relevant experience and NVQs in care or management, a diploma in domiciliary care management, and a certificate/diploma in management studies are all qualifications that are increasingly required.

Personal Qualities and Skills

All individuals working in the area of social work need patience and a warm, sympathetic personality. They need to have excellent communication skills, be good listeners, trustworthy, and have compassion for others.

Starting Salary

For home carers, salaries vary locally but are around minimum wage levels. A home care organiser may earn £13,000 to £19,000 depending on qualifications and experience.

info

British Association of Social Workers, 16 Kent Street, Birmingham B5 6RD; 0121 622 3911; www.basw.co.uk

General Social Care Council, Goldings House, 2 Hay's Lane, London SE1 2HB; 020 7397 5800; Registration helpline: 0845 070 0630; www.gscc.org.uk

Skills for Care (England), Albion Court, 5 Albion Place, Leeds LS1 6JP; 0113 245 1716; www.topss.org.uk

Scottish Social Services Council (SSSC), Compass House, Discovery Quay, 11 Riverside Drive, Dundee DD1 4NY; 01382 207101; www.sssc.uk.com

Care Council for Wales (CCW), 6th Floor West Wing, South Gate House, Wood Street, Cardiff CF10 1EW; 029 2022 6257; www.ccwales.org.uk

Northern Ireland Social Care Council (NISCC), 7th Floor Millennium House, Great Victoria Street, Belfast BT2 7AQ; 028 9041 7600; www.niscc.info

Social Work Admissions System (SWAS), Rose Hill, New Barn Lane, Cheltenham GL62 3LZ; 01242 223707; www.ucas.ac.uk

www.socialworkcareers.co.uk; 0845 604 6404

Probation officer

The aims of the National Probation Service for England and Wales (NPS) are: protecting the public; reducing re-offending; the proper punishment of offenders in the community; ensuring offenders are aware of the effects of crime on the victims of crime and the public; and the rehabilitation of offenders.

All probation work with offenders combines continuous assessment and management of risk with the provision of expert supervision programmes designed to reduce re-offending. Approximately 70 per cent of offenders supervised will be on community supervision orders and 30 per cent in prison.

Probation staff are regularly seconded to work in youth offending teams, prisons and with a range of crime prevention agencies.

In Scotland, the functions of the probation officer are performed by social work departments in local authorities.

Qualifications and Training

To qualify as a probation officer in England and Wales you must gain the Diploma in Probation Studies, which is awarded by Skills for Justice. To be eligible for this course you must be at least 20 years old and be employed by a Probation Service. Entry requirements may vary slightly between Probation Services but in general if you are under 21 you need three GCSEs grade A–C and two A levels. If you are between 21 and 25 you need five GCSE passes. If you are 25 years or older, you may be accepted without formal qualifications if you have relevant experience. In all cases you have to pass a demanding selection test including a written exercise, to ensure that you can study at an advanced level. There are no accelerated or shortened courses open to people who already have a degree. In Scotland you qualify for criminal justice work via a four-year social work degree.

Personal Qualities and Skills

Probation officers need to be able to develop imaginative, relevant strategies to help offenders lead law-abiding lives. They need to be good listeners and have an understanding of different ethnic and cultural backgrounds. They also need to be assertive, able to exercise and maintain authority and cope with aggression.

Starting Salary

Trainee probation officers can earn between £14,500 and £15,500. Main grade probation officers earn around £25,000 to £28,000 a year. Criminal justice social workers in Scotland earn between £17,000 and £28,000. The government is planning to restructure the Probation Service in the next three years and this may alter pay and conditions.

National Probation Service, Horseferry House, Dean Ryle Street, London SW1P 2AW; 020 7217 0659; www.probation.homeoffice.gov.uk

Probation Board for Northern Ireland, 80–90 North Street, Belfast BT1 1LD; 028 9026 2400; www.pbni.org.uk

Skills for Justice, 9 Riverside Court, Don Road, Sheffield S9 2TJ; 0114 261 1499; www.skillsforjustice.com

Scottish Social Services Council (SSSC), Compass House, 11 Riverside Drive, Dundee DD1 4NY; 01382 207101; www.sssc.uk.com

Wales Probation Training Consortium, 4–7 The Broadway, Pontypridd CF37 1BA; 01443 494333; www.probation.walestraining.gov.uk

Info

Social workers and social carers

Social workers and social carers provide support for individuals, families and groups within the community. They work in a variety of settings and with many different client groups, eg, adults with mental health problems or learning disabilities, children, older people, young offenders, drug users – anyone who is disadvantaged in some way. Most social workers are employed by local authorities and work in teams based around particular client groups – children and young people, adults with disabilities, etc. Some work for voluntary organisations and other non-governmental groups.

Social care assistant

Social care assistants work in residential care homes and day centres, providing support to clients and professional staff who may be nurses, social workers or other care professionals. They may help with basic physical, but non-medical care, such as washing and dressing and assisting clients at meal times and with social activities.

Social work assistant

Social work assistants work with social workers and while they don't have responsibility for individual cases they will often meet clients and do a lot of the follow-up work, for example contacting other agencies to arrange support for clients. They set up meetings, follow up enquiries and help keep track of cases.

Qualifications and Training

No specific academic qualifications are required for assistant's posts, but individual authorities or care providers may ask for some GCSEs and certainly will look for a background of dealing with people. There are opportunities to qualify to NVQ level 3 while working and some assistants do progress to management level.

Personal Qualities and Skills

Being warm, friendly and able to deal comfortably with people who face all kinds of difficulties is very important. Being practical, enthusiastic and encouraging is also important.

Starting Salary

For social care assistants the pay is often at or close to the minimum wage. Social work assistants earn from £9,000 to £13,000.

For further information see Social Worker.

Social worker – children and young people

More than half of all social workers work in some way with children. This may be in one of the specific areas outlined below or it may be as part of an area social work team working with local children and families. Child protection is an important part of the social worker's role.

Social worker – day care settings

Day care settings where social workers are employed include day care provision for adults and older people with a range of special needs, which might be emotional, behavioural or physical. It is often a qualified social worker who manages a day care centre.

Social worker – education settings

These social workers are sometimes referred to as 'education welfare officers'. It is their job to work with those school pupils who, for whatever reason, are failing to attend school properly. Education social workers work with the pupils and their families to try to get to the root of the problem and get the pupil back into school.

Social worker – healthcare settings

Social workers attached to hospitals work with patients who are about to be discharged from, or who have just been discharged from hospital, after a long stay. Their main client groups are older people or people who have had major accidents or serious long-term illnesses. The social worker helps clients to plan for their return home and to access whatever support services they need.

Social worker – mental health settings

Working with clients who have mental health problems, these social workers support their clients in the community, in hospitals or in sheltered accommodation. Social workers help assess risks, work out what support needs their clients have and help them to access such services as education, or a return to employment.

Social worker – residential settings

Social workers in residential settings work with clients who are resident in care homes. Their clients may be children, young adults with learning or physical disabilities, or frail elderly people who are unable to continue living in their own homes.

396 Sports and recreation facility management

Qualifications and Training

The main routes to qualifying are either through a three-year social work degree, a two-year postgraduate diploma, or accelerated degree for graduates of other subjects. Preferred degree subjects include social sciences, social policy and psychology. Non-graduates with plenty of relevant experience can do a diploma course. All the courses are a combination of theoretical study and practical placements. Once qualified there are advanced courses in different areas of practice such as childcare, mental health work or social work teaching.

Personal Qualities and Skills

Social workers must be warm and caring, but be able to keep calm and not get upset by potentially distressing situations. They must be comfortable working with many different types of people. They should also be well organised, quick thinking and good at problem solving.

Starting Salary

Starting salaries range from £17,000 to £28,000 depending on qualifications and experience. Slightly lower salaries may be paid in the voluntary sector.

SPORTS AND RECREATION FACILITY MANAGEMENT

Sports and recreation facility managers are responsible for the efficient running of leisure centres, swimming pools, sports halls and associated facilities. Managers usually start their careers as recreation assistants and progress through supervisory and assistant manager positions via on-the-job training and professional development.

Qualifications and Training

There are two routes into this career. You can either start as a junior or management trainee and work for professional qualifications, or you can do a BTEC qualification, foundation degree or degree course. The Institute of Sport and Recreation Management (ISRM) and the Institute of Leisure and Amenity Management (ILAM) run relevant certificate and diploma courses that can be studied on a part-time basis. There is also a wide choice of BTEC, foundation degree and degree courses available in sports and leisure management, leisure studies, sports science and recreation management. Whether you work your way up or join as a graduate trainee, there is a lot of on the job training.

Personal Qualities and Skills

You need excellent interpersonal skills, be able to motivate staff and work well with members of the public. You must be well organised, energetic and able to take responsibility.

Starting Salary

Trainee and assistant managers earn between £14,000 and £17,000. Newly qualified managers earn between £18,000 and £25,000. An experienced manager of a large facility can earn more than £35,000.

SkillsActive, Castlewood House, 77–91 New Oxford Street, London WC1A 1PX; 0800 093 3300; www.skillsactive.com

Institute of Sport and Recreation Management (ISRM), Sir John Beckwith Centre for Sport, Loughborough University,

Loughborough, Leics LE11 3TU; 01509 226474; www.isrm.co.uk

Institute of Leisure and Amenity Management (ILAM), ILAM House, Lower Basildon, Reading, Berks RG8 9NE; 01491 874800; www.ilam.co.uk

SPORT

While relatively few earn a significant living from being a professional sports-person, there are many other occupations within the sports sector.

Coach

Coaches help individuals and teams identify areas for improvement in physical fitness levels and for specific sports skills. They also plan and implement training programmes in a wide variety of sports provided by sports centres, clubs, schools, hotels and swimming baths.

Much coaching is done on a voluntary basis; however, there are opportunities for paid work, and many coaches work in a self-employed capacity. Some local authorities employ coaches to offer facilities for local schools at one or more centres in the authority. Such coaches are expected to be able to coach in most of the following sports: badminton, basketball, climbing (on indoor walls), ice skating, swimming, squash, tennis, trampolining and weight training. Increasingly, there is a need for coaches in the summer months to work in outdoor activity centres.

Qualifications and Training

Coaches must gain recognised coaching qualifications, which are awarded by the governing bodies of the various sports and acquired either at evening class or weekend school. Swimming coaches must also hold a national lifeguard award. All coaches need to have and develop their knowledge of related areas such as injury, sports science and nutrition.

Personal Qualities and Skills

Coaches need the ability to communicate, as well as perseverance, patience and tact. The ability to inspire children or adults of very different abilities is also needed.

Starting Salary

Coaches who are employed full time earn from £12,000 to £20,000. Many coaches work part time, charging hourly rates of between £10 and £20. Earnings can be far higher for anyone working with professional sportsmen and women.

info

Sport England, 3rd Floor, Victoria House, Bloomsbury Square, London WC1B 4SE; 0845 850 8508; www.sportengland.org

Coaching Wales, Coaching Unit, Sport Council for Wales, Sophia Gardens, Cardiff CF11 9SW; 0845 045 0904; www.coachingwales.com

SkillsActive, Castlewood House, 77–91 New Oxford Street, London

WC1A 1PX; 020 7632 2000; www.skillsactive.com

Coaching NI, Queen's PEC, Botanic Gardens, Belfast BT9 5EX; 028 9068 6940; www.coachingni.net

Sports Coach UK, 114 Cardigan Road, Headingley, Leeds LS6 3BJ; 0113 274 4802; www.sportscoachuk.org

Sports Leadership UK; www.bst.org.uk

Physiotherapist

see Physiotherapy

Teacher

see Teaching

Sportsperson

There are opportunities in sport for professional sportspeople and for careers in coaching. Not all sports allow players to be professionals, and there are others, such as snooker, where there is room for only a very few professionals. Sports attracting professionals in relatively large numbers are football, cricket, golf, horse racing, Rugby (League and Union) and tennis.

Sportspeople's careers are generally short, but if, during their careers, they have made a name for themselves, there may be opportunities in journalism, broadcasting or consultancy.

Qualifications and Training

Professional sportspeople naturally need to be excellent at their sport. Those in team games generally begin by playing for their school, town or county side. In this context, a young player may be noticed by professional selectors. In the case of football, it is not necessary to join a local football league club; apprentices are taken on from all over the country. Because a club apprentice has no guarantee that he will ever play for the first side, some clubs allow apprentices time off to obtain academic qualifications.

Personal Qualities and Skills

As well as talent, professional sportspeople must possess dedication, perseverance, commitment and be highly competitive.

Starting Salary

Salaries for professionals are often low initially, but the rewards for top performers may be very high. The amount of money earned varies enormously depending upon the sport. Coaches' salaries vary according to whether the work is full or part time, what type of work they are doing and the number of hours.

SkillsActive, Castlewood House, 77–91 New Oxford Street, London WC1A 1PX; 020 7632 2000; www.skillsactive.com

Sport England, 3rd Floor, Victoria House, Bloomsbury Square, London WC1B 4SE; 0845 8508 508; www.sportengland.org

Sport Scotland, Caledonia House, South Gyle, Edinburgh EH12 9DQ; 0131 317 7200; www.sportscotland.org.uk

Sports Council for Northern Ireland, House of Sport, Upper Malone Road, Belfast BT9 5LA; 028 9038 1222; www.sportni.net/

Sports Council for Wales, The National Sports Centre, Sophia Gardens, Cardiff CF1 9SW; 029 2030 0500; www.sports-council-wales.co.uk

info

STATISTICIAN

Every business and every government department uses the information gathered from statistics to plan its workload, market its products, analyse behaviour, etc. Statisticians are concerned with the collection, analysis and interpretation of numerical data. Statisticians design and plan surveys and use various software packages to help them in their analysis.

Qualifications and Training

Most entrants to this profession have a degree in statistics, mathematics or another degree or postgraduate qualification that has an in-depth level of statistical work as part of the course. Sometimes entrants with A levels or good GCSEs can work their way up from other administrative or routine data management jobs if they have an obvious flair for dealing with and interpreting numbers. The Royal Statistical Society also offers some distance learning and

STATISTICIAN

Every business, government department and much of the health sector uses statistical information to plan workloads, monitor and analyse behaviour, and develop and market products. Statisticians design and plan surveys, and collect, analyse and interpret numerical data in a wide range of contexts.

Qualifications and Training

Most entrants to this profession have a degree or postgraduate qualification in statistics or mathematics or some other discipline where statistics is used. It is also possible for school-leavers (and career changers) to become statistical assistants and work their way up through their organisations. Professional examinations are offered by the Royal Statistical Society.

Personal Qualities and Skills

You need a really good understanding of statistical methodology, sound problem solving and analytical ability plus strong communication, team working and IT skills. You will often work with other specialists and will need to advise others about project design and explain your findings to team members and clients who are not statisticians.

Salaries

Starting salaries range between approximately £19,000 and £29,000 and can rise to £30,000 to £50,000 or more.

INFORMATION

Royal Statistical Society (RSS)	Government Statistical Service (GSS)
12 Errol Street	1 Drummond Gate
London EC1Y 8LX	London SW1V 2QQ
www.rss.org.uk/careers www.mathscareers.org.uk	www.statistics.gov.uk

part-time courses for people already in work, but most candidates studying these already possess a degree.

Personal Qualities and Skills

You need to have a really good understanding of statistical and other numerical ideas, but it is also important that you can interpret them and explain your findings in a way that less mathematically minded colleagues will understand. You need good IT skills and good problem solving and analytical ability.

Starting Salary

Starting salaries range between £17,000 and £29,000. Commerce and industry pay higher salaries than local government, the Civil Service, education and the National Health Service. Salaries rise to £30,000 to £40,000 with experience.

---

info

Biomathematics and Statistics Scotland, The University of Edinburgh, James Clerk Maxwell Building, The King's Buildings, Edinburgh EH9 3JZ; 0131 650 4900; www.bioss.sari.ac.uk/index.html

Eurostat: The Statistical Office of the European Communities, Bâtiment Jean Monnet, Rue Alcide de Gasperi, L-2920 Luxembourg; europa.eu.int/comm/eurostat/

Government Statistical Service (GSS), 1 Drummond Gate, Pimlico, London

SW1V 2QQ; 0845 601 3034; www.statistics.gov.uk

Office for National Statistics (ONS), Customer Contact Centre, Room 1.015, Office for National Statistics, Cardiff Road, Newport NP10 8XG; 0845 601 3034; www.statistics.gov.uk/

Royal Statistical Society (RSS), 12 Errol Street, London EC1Y 8LX; 020 7638 8998; www.rss.org.uk

---

SURVEYING

Surveying covers a wide variety of work within one profession, and a number of professional bodies offer qualifications in the different areas (see below). There are also technician qualifications. Surveying technicians work in all the same fields as surveyors but without being professionally qualified.

Aerial surveying

A specialisation of land surveying (see below), aerial surveying involves photogrammetry – the use of aerial photographs as a basis for calculations. Qualifications are offered by the Architecture and Surveying Institute (ASI) and the Institute of Civil Engineering Surveyors.

Archaeological surveying

This relatively new specialisation involves working on an archaeological dig, making plans, maps and cross-sections of the excavations. It requires the skill of a cartographer as well as that of a land surveyor. The Architects' and Surveyors' Institute has members in this discipline.

Building surveying

The structural surveying of properties and reporting on their condition and valuation is carried out by building surveyors/building engineers. They advise on necessary repairs and maintenance, and prepare plans and specifications for alterations and improvements. Local and central government employ a large proportion of qualified building surveyors, although many are in private practice. Qualifications in this area are available from the Association of Building Engineers (ABE), the ASI and the Royal Institution of Chartered Surveyors (RICS).

General practice

This includes auctioneering, estate agency, valuation and estate management. People working in this area are responsible for the selling or letting, surveying, valuation and management of both urban and rural property. Qualifications in general practice are offered by the ABE, the ASI and the RICS.

Hydrographic surveying

The hydrographer surveys and charts underwater areas, such as ports and harbours and offshore areas where drilling for oil takes place. Hydrographic surveying qualifications are offered by the ASI and the RICS.

Land surveying

The land surveyor measures and charts the earth's physical features so that maps can be drawn. The scale of the work can range from a one-house building site to a whole region of Africa, and there are opportunities in public services (the Ordnance Survey and the Ministry of Defence, for example), as well as in private practice or large commercial organisations. Qualifications are offered by the ASI and the RICS.

Minerals surveying

Minerals surveyors assist in the design, development and surveying of quarries and underground mines, ensuring safety for the workers as well as optimum profitability for the company extracting the minerals. They also value mineral workings for rating and taxation, and therefore need to be all-rounders with knowledge of geology, the management of mineral workings, taxation and planning legislation. This area of surveying is unique in having its qualifications and duties laid down by law. Minerals surveyors must hold the surveyor's certificate granted on behalf of the Secretary of State for Industry by the Mining Qualifications Board. They must be at least 21 and have at least four years' practical experience (including 2,000 hours underground) in order to sit the exam for this certificate. Further qualifications are provided by the RICS and the ASI.

Quantity surveying

In private practice, quantity surveyors work with an architect to draw up design specifications in line with the client's budget. When the finished design is agreed, the quantity surveyor draws up a bill of quantities, detailing the materials and labour that will be needed. Building contractors work on this bill of quantities in preparing their tender for the job; they will use their own quantity surveyors to estimate their costs. Quantity surveyors also monitor costs as the work progresses and is completed. If they train for this work while employed by construction contractors, they usually take the qualification of the RICS. Professional qualifications are also offered by the ASI.

Rural practice

This is often combined with land agency, and concerns the use and development of agricultural land. The qualifying bodies in this area are the ASI and the RICS.

Qualifications and Training

The RICS offers a range of qualifications in the different areas of surveying. Normally entrants need three A levels or equivalent for entry into an RICS-approved degree or diploma course. An alternative is undertaking an HND or HNC in a related surveying discipline, which can give advanced entry to those courses. On successful completion of an RICS-approved degree or diploma, graduates enrol onto the Assessment of Professional Competence (APC), which is two years' practical training while in employment, concluding with an RICS professional assessment interview. Various degree backgrounds are valuable for surveying; one-year full-time and two-year part-time postgraduate conversion courses are available.

Technicians need a relevant HNC/HND or NVQ level 4 followed by the Assessment of Technical Competence. This is two years' RICS structured training while working, which concludes with the RICS technical assessment interview. Those who have gained technical membership of RICS can take a bridging course to become a Chartered Surveyor.

Personal Qualities and Skills

Logical and orderly thinking, ability in figure work and detailed drawings are called for in this precision work. Communication skills and business acumen are essential. Good oral and written English is an asset, and some areas may require specialised mathematical ability.

Starting Salary

Newly qualified surveyors earn between £20,000 and £24,000. Experienced surveyors earn between £25,000 and £38,000. Senior Chartered Surveyors working for large companies can earn far in excess of these figures.

info

Chartered Institute of Building (Faculty of Architecture and Surveying), Englemere, Kings Ride, Ascot, Berkshire SL5 7TB; 01344 630700; fax: 01344 630777; www.ciob.org.uk; e-mail: reception@ciob.org.uk

Association of Building Engineers (ABE), Lutyens House, Billing Brook Road, Weston Favell, Northampton NN3 8NW; 0845 126 1058; fax: 01604 784220; www.abe.org.uk; e-mail: building.engineers@abe.org.uk

Royal Institution of Chartered Surveyors (RICS),

12 Great George Street, Parliament Square, London SW1P 3AD; 0870 333 1600; www.rics.org; e-mail: contactrics@rics.org

Royal Institution of Chartered Surveyors in Scotland, 9 Manor Place, Edinburgh EH3 7DN; 0131 225 7078; fax: 0131 240 0830; www.rics-scotland.org.uk

RICS Contact Centre (for general enquiries), Surveyor Court, Westwood Way, Coventry CV4 8JE; 0870 333 1600; www.rics.org; e-mail: contactrics@rics.org

TAXATION

Those who work in the area of taxation deal with the payment of taxes, which is a source of revenue for public expenditure.

Tax adviser/technician

Tax advisers/technicians work for private firms or independently, offering assistance to other firms/individuals who need guidance through the complications of the tax laws. A tax adviser is able to advise clients on how to plan and present their taxable income so that they legally pay the least tax possible.

Tax technicians work for firms of accountants or solicitors, in clearing banks and for consultancy firms that offer a complete tax service to their clients. However, the largest area of work involves corporate tax in organisations that have their own tax department to prepare corporate tax and VAT returns on behalf of the company.

Qualifications and Training

Many tax advisers qualify first as accountants, but a growing number begin with A levels as tax trainees. The Chartered Institute of Taxation offers a qualifying exam for candidates already qualified as accountants or lawyers. The Association of Taxation Technicians is a starting point for all other tax trainees, and offers an exam. This may be sufficient in itself for those candidates who do not expect to

Chartered Institute of Taxation, 12 Upper Belgrave Street, London SW1X 8BB; 020 7235 9381; fax: 020 7235 2562; www.tax.org.uk; e-mail: post@tax.org.uk

Association of Taxation Technicians, 12 Upper Belgrave Street, London SW1X 8BB; 020 7235 2544; fax: 020 7235 4571; www.att.org.uk; e-mail: info@att.org.uk

For a downloadable guide see: www.insidecareers.co.uk/tax

info

give detailed planning advice in their careers, or provide a stepping stone to the Institute's exam.

Personal Qualities and Skills

Tax advisers/technicians must be prepared for continuous professional development, be able to keep up to date with numerous tax changes, have an analytical mind, be able to apply lateral thinking and have good communication skills.

Starting Salary

The starting salary is similar to others in finance at £15,000+; those with experience earn high salaries.

Tax inspectors

Tax inspectors work for HM Revenue & Customs, formed from the merger of the Inland Revenue and HM Customs & Excise Departments. It is the government department responsible under the direction of the Treasury for the efficient administration of income tax, tax credits, corporation tax, capital gains tax, petroleum revenue tax, inheritance tax, National Insurance contributions and stamp duties. Inspectors are responsible for the tax affairs of businesses and individuals, ensuring they pay the right amount at the right time, helping them to obtain their entitlements and meet their obligations. Inspectors detect and deter non-compliance and encourage voluntary compliance by carrying out enquiry work.

Qualifications and Training

HMRC runs a graduate entry scheme called the Talent Recruitment Programme. For this, you need at least a second class honours degree in any subject. HMRC also recruits graduates through the Civil Service Fast Stream Development Programme (see Civil Service), recruiting graduate management trainees to work on policy development and implementation. Those selected for the Talent Recruitment Programme normally train through the HMRC's Inspector Development Programme (IDP).

If you do not have a degree, you can start as an administrative assistant (two GCSEs grades A–C) or an administrative officer (five GCSEs grades A–C) and become an inspector through promotion and passing internal examinations.

Personal Qualities and Skills

You must be very good at analysing large quantities of information and data. You must be a creative problem solver with an open, enquiring mind. Good written and spoken English, numeracy and IT skills are also essential. You must be a good communicator, calm, fair and able to interpret and apply rules.

Starting Salary

Graduate trainees on the Inspector Development Programme earn £25,000 with an additional £2,000 for working in London. Having completed the programme, salaries start at £30,000 rising to £40,000 plus with appropriate experience and responsibilities.

Her Majesty's Revenue and Customs; www.hmrc.gov.uk

Civil Service Careers; www.careers.civil-service.gov.uk

Financial Services Skills Council, 51 Gresham Street, London EC2V 7HQ; 020 7216 7366; www.fssc.org.uk

Tax Working; www.taxworking.org.uk

info

TEACHING

Most formal teaching is done in schools, while lecturing is carried out in universities and other further and higher education establishments.

Lecturer

Further education

Lecturers in this field may teach anyone over the age of 16. The range of subjects taught in further education is diverse and growing rapidly. Most lecturers have a particular expertise but are increasingly expected to teach outside their specialist area. They may work on vocational and/or academic courses. In order to meet the demands of their clients, further education colleges offer courses on a full- or part-time basis. These include evening courses and short courses.

Higher education

Lecturers in universities and other higher education institutions (HEIs) teach mainly undergraduates. As well as teaching, many carry out research, write articles and books, give outside lectures and broadcasts. Competition is fierce and it is unlikely that a new graduate will be able to enter higher education as a first job.

Qualifications and Training

Lecturers in HEIs must have first- or upper-second class degrees; many have postgraduate qualifications, and some have further degrees. In the new universities, lecturers may be drawn from industry or commerce.

Qualifications for lecturers in further education vary, depending on the subject taught. A degree, a professional qualification and a teaching qualification are all acceptable and desirable. There are one-year full-time and two-year part-time courses available for those intending to teach in further education.

Personal Qualities and Skills

All teachers/lecturers must have a high level of knowledge of, and enthusiasm for, their subject, combined with a desire to communicate this to others. They

If you are passionate about education and enthused by the idea of running a business then join us at Explore Learning...

Explore Learning provides innovative education centres nationwide. We help 5-14 year olds reach their academic and creative potential, through individualised learning programmes which allow us to teach, support and encourage children in low pupil-staff ratios.

Explore Learning is growing from strength to strength. We launched our first centre in 2001 and we now have sixteen centres in operation benefiting over 3000 children. We are scheduled to open a further 6-10 centres in 2007.

Graduates gain significant early responsibility in a management role. Whilst working with children to further their academic and personal development, graduates will develop their business and marketing expertise. Explore has an extensive training programme to ensure that graduates reach their full potential and will work to complete a NVQ level 3 in Childcare and Management.

We are looking for enthusiastic, persuasive candidates who are passionate about education and enthused by the idea of running and marketing a business. Starting as an **Assistant Director** you would help run and launch Explore Learning centres across the UK.

We prefer applicants to have a minimum grade B in GCSE maths and English and a 2:1 degree in any discipline. Experience of working with children is essential.

£19k pa (plus London weighting), £2,800 pa bonus potential & pension scheme. South England/London/Midlands/Scotland

Visit it our Careers page on our website: **www.explorelearning.org.uk**

must have the ability to organise and deliver their material in a way that is understandable to their students.

Starting Salary

In further education, salaries range from £16,000 to £21,000. These are based on rates recommended by the National Association of Teachers in Further and Higher Education, but not all colleges pay at these rates. In higher education, salaries range from £24,500 to £30,000. Senior lecturers earn around £37,000.

info

Lifelong Learning UK (LLUK),
4th Floor, 32 Farringdon Street,
London EC4A 4HJ; 020 7332 9535;
www.lifelonglearninguk.org

The Higher Education Academy,
Innovation Way, York Science Park,
Heslington, York YO10 5BR;
01904 717500; www.heacademy.ac.uk

Association of University Teachers
(AUT), Egmont House,
25–31 Tavistock Place, London
WC1H 9UT; 020 7670 9700;
www.aut.org.uk

Teacher

Teaching offers a wide variety of openings working with children and young people of all ages and backgrounds.

The work of a teacher varies according to the age group being taught. Nursery and Foundation Stage teachers take the under-fives, Key Stage 1 primary teachers take five- to seven-year-olds and Key Stage 2 teachers take 7–11-year-olds. Secondary education (Key Stages 3 and 4) starts at 11 and continues (in some cases) to 18 or 19. In addition, teachers are needed in sixth-form colleges and the numerous further and higher education establishments. Teachers at primary level (up to age 11) generally teach a variety of basic subjects, and specialist subject teachers are not introduced until secondary level, although specialist music or sports teachers may be brought in at an earlier age.

The majority of pupils attend state schools, although there are also openings in private education. There are also opportunities for teachers in special schools: for the handicapped (either boarding or day establishments), for disturbed children (in community homes or approved schools), for those with special educational needs and in children's hospitals, where long-term patients are expected to take lessons.

Qualifications and Training

To teach in state schools, you must attain Qualified Teacher Status (QTS) by undertaking a course of Initial Teacher Training (ITT). This is not essential to work in the independent sector, but many schools prefer it. There are several types of ITT, but there are certain criteria which you must meet for all of them. You must have GCSEs grade A–C in English and maths. If you are teaching beyond Key Stages 2/3 your GCSEs must also include a science at grades A–C. You must pass QTS skills tests in English, maths and information and communications technology (ICT). These tests are computerised and run at more than 40 centres throughout England. In Wales, you do not have to take these. You must have a satisfactory Criminal Records Bureau (CRB) check, and some experience of working with children and young people is a great advantage.

There are a number of different routes to QTS, such as a degree in the subject you want to teach at secondary level or in a subject related to the core curriculum at primary level, followed by a Postgraduate Certificate in Education (PGCE). A PGCE can be one year full time college-based, two years part time college-based, or one year full time school-based. If you already have some relevant teaching experience there is an option to do a flexible tailor-made PGCE programme by distance learning. The Graduate Teacher Training Registry (GTTR) provides details of courses and an online applications system.

Alternatively, you can do a three- or four-year BEd (Bachelor of Education) or a BA or BSc which awards QTS. Most of these degree courses are for primary teachers, but a few are available at secondary level.

A third method is to undertake a School Centred Initial Teacher Training (SCITT) – this is considered to be at PGCE level. Schools run Graduate Teacher Programmes (GTPs) where graduates work as unqualified teachers while undergoing training. You can find details of course providers on the Training and Development Agency for Schools website. On this website you can also find details of other employer-based schemes for people with HNDs, two years of degree level study, or overseas qualifications.

Teach First is a special scheme operating in London and Manchester for graduates with a 2.1 in a curriculum subject who are prepared to work in challenging schools and take part in special leadership training courses.

Personal Qualities and Skills

Teachers must enjoy working with the age group they teach. They must be excellent communicators, able to motivate and encourage their students. They have to have great self-confidence, be able to handle difficult situations and discuss issues with parents as well as students. They must be able to work under considerable pressure, be well organised administrators and come up with imaginative solutions to problems.

Fast Track Teaching Recruitment Team, National College of School Leadership; 0845 058 1066; www.ncsl.org.uk/programmes/fasttrack

Graduate Teacher Training Registry (GTTR), Rosehill, New Barn Lane, Cheltenham, Gloucestershire GL52 3LZ; 0870 112 2205; www.gttr.ac.uk

Teachernet; www.teachernet.gov.uk

Department of Education Northern Ireland, Rathael House, Balloo Road, Bangor BT19 7PR; 028 9127 9279; www.deni.gov.uk

Training and Development Agency for Schools, 151 Buckingham Palace Road, London SW1W 9SZ; 0845 6000 991; www.tda.gov.uk

Starting Salary

New entrants are paid on a scale ranging from £19,000 to £29,000. Incremental points are awarded for taking on particular responsibilities or for working in challenging schools. Senior teachers are paid on a scale of £30,000 to £49,000.

Teaching assistant

Teaching assistants or classroom assistants provide help and support for qualified teachers in the classroom. They can work in any school, but there are more employed at primary school level helping younger children with reading, writing and mathematics. They often provide particular support to children with special needs or whose first language is not English. They also help prepare lesson materials.

If a job ad describes the post as 'Learning Support Assistant' rather than a classroom or teaching assistant, the work involves supporting an individual child who has particular special needs, such as a sensory impairment, or a physical or psychological disability.

Qualifications and Training

At present, this varies from LEA (local education authority) to LEA, though the government does plan to introduce a standard training model. Many LEAs do not ask for any formal qualifications, but some ask for GCSEs in English and mathematics.

Personal Qualities and Skills

Teaching assistants must be able to build good relationships with children and have a lot of common sense. They should be able to work well as part of a team, and being imaginative and creative is also useful.

Starting Salary

Teaching assistants are often paid on an hourly rate and this is sometimes close to the minimum wage, though it can be £6.50 to £8.00 an hour. A lot of the work is part time and available only during term time.

TELECOMMUNICATIONS

The telecommunications industry continues to change and develop rapidly. Although there have been job cuts in this sector, there are still a large range of career opportunities. Deregulation of the industry around the world has resulted in many mergers and alliances to take advantage of the greater need for communications in business, as well as home use of the internet, digital TV and WAP cell phones.

Technicians

The sector recruits large numbers of hardware technicians and software engineers but telecommunications companies also employ people in accountancy, sales and marketing, training, finance, human resources and production planning.

Technicians in the industry are involved in finding faults in telecommunications systems and ensuring that networks and equipment are working properly. This includes installing, setting up, testing and repairing equipment in businesses or people's homes, such as phones, cable, satellite or digital TV, fax machines or computers. Some technicians install and maintain the communications links for power and rail companies. There are also opportunities for such work in the armed services. Engineers and IT specialists combine technical expertise with strategic vision to enhance existing services, particularly in mobile and internet technologies.

Qualifications and Training

Technicians normally need at least four GCSEs grades A–C or equivalent in maths, English, science and technology. Many have other qualifications such as a National Certificate or diploma in electronics or telecommunications technology. Modern Apprenticeships are available, as are NVQs in testing and approval, fitting, maintenance and operation of telecommunications switching, transmission, radio (or mobile telephones), cabling and power systems.

Engineers and IT specialists are normally graduates with relevant degrees in computer science, telecommunications or electronics. Graduates from a range of degree backgrounds are recruited as trainees to commercial posts.

Personal Qualities and Skills

An interest in technological developments, good communication and interpersonal skills and the ability to work as part of a team.

Starting Salary

Technicians start around £11,000 to £15,000 and with experience can earn from £20,000 to £30,000. Graduate trainees' salaries are around £18,000+.

British Telecom, 81 Newgate Street, British Telecom Centre, London EC1A 7AJ; 0207 356 5000; www.bt.com

Vodafone: www.vodafone.co.uk

Orange: www.orange.co.uk

T-Mobile: www.t-mobile.co.uk

Sector Skills Council for IT, Telecoms and Contact Centres, 1 Castle Lane, London SW1E 6DR; 020 7963 8920; fax: 020 7592 9138; www.e-skillsnto.org.uk; e-mail: info@e-skillsnto.org.uk

Info

THEATRE

Theatre comprises much more than the actors and directors who receive the publicity. Many other people are involved in a theatrical production. Lighting and sound effects are created and handled by electricians; scenery and props are built, arranged and moved by technicians; the practical aspects of the production are organised and run by the stage manager and assistants. The designer creates the sets; the wardrobe mistress makes the costumes and the director or producer is responsible for the production as a whole. Other staff include the publicity officer, house manager and box office staff.

Actors

see Performing Arts

Box office

The box office is in charge of ticket sales. The manager is responsible for promotion and marketing, for hiring his or her staff and for checking the takings. Experience of accounts or general management is useful. This office makes a good starting place for anyone interested in arts administration.

Designer

The designer is responsible for sets and costumes, working closely with the director, and produces drawings of sets and costumes. The scenery and costume departments will work from these drawings and also from scale models of the sets.

Director

The director is in charge of the actors, dancers, designers, singers and technicians, working within the managerial brief and, in consultation with producer and playwright, responsible for casting. The director's main work is in taking rehearsals and in turning the play into a theatrical production. The casting director auditions actors and arranges financial details with the actors and their agents.

Lighting designer

The theatre electrician may be in sole charge of the lighting or, in a large company with sophisticated equipment, be part of a team headed by an expert who will design a lighting plan. Appropriate electrician's qualifications are needed.

Press office/marketing

These departments deal with publicity for the theatre. Press officers provide editorial content and liaise with the press, arrange for photo sessions and interviews. Staff often have a background in journalism or advertising. The marketing department produces posters, advertisements and programmes. An arts graduate with secretarial training may find work here. Tact, self-confidence and a pleasant voice are useful qualities.

Producer

The producer chooses the play, rents the theatre, engages the director and actors and is responsible for paying the bills. The producer is responsible for raising the money for the production.

Production manager/technical director

They are responsible for budgets, contracting and scheduling. This is a project management role and is usually a promotion from stage manager posts.

Production staff

A large theatre may have a series of production workshops; smaller theatres may combine several jobs in one:

- Armoury: the armoury is responsible for making armour or weapons, for special effects like gunfire and shells and for decorative metalwork. The members of the team are experts, for example gunsmiths.
- Carpenters' workshop: technical drawing and carpentry skills come in useful for building sets. RADA offers a course for theatre carpentry.
- Metal workshop: here the heavy metalwork is designed and manufactured, for example for steel supports and complex trees. A welding qualification is useful.
- Paint workshop: this is where the sets are painted. Knowing how to create the right textures and effects is part of the scene painter's skill.
- Property-making shop: properties are often bought but in many productions, some props – for example a throne or special upholstery – have to be specially made. An enthusiasm for research and an eye for detail are needed.
- Wardrobe and wigs: although costumes and wigs may be hired, many are made by the wardrobe department. A good knowledge of period fashion and skills in dressmaking and tailoring are needed. Casual help is also needed when there is much sewing for a new production. Special hats are usually produced by a freelance milliner. Accessory making is another specialist job, as is wig and beard making, for which a City & Guilds certificate is a useful qualification. The wardrobe department is also responsible for looking after costumes and repairing and cleaning them.

Stage manager

The stage manager is responsible for the smooth running of rehearsals and productions, ensuring that properties and costumes are ready when required, that actors know when they are needed, for supervising lighting, scene making and scene changes, and responsible for effects, music, curtain calls and prompting. A stage manager will often have assistants (assistant stage managers, ASMs and deputy stage managers, DSMs) and will also be helped by scene shifters. A stage manager may sometimes become a producer or director.

Theatrical agent

Agents try to find work for the actors on their books. Experience and good contacts are essential. Payment is usually 10 to 15 per cent of the client's fee.

Qualifications and Training

Designer
Most designers will have completed a full-time art and design course.

Director
A thorough grounding in the dramatic arts is essential. A degree in drama is useful. There are a few trainee director posts, mostly under the auspices of the Arts Council. A director will have had extensive experience of the theatre, probably as a stage manager or actor. Some directors come to the theatre from film or television, which also offer training.

Production
NVQs are available at levels 1, 2 and 3 for theatre technicians.

Personal Qualities and Skills

Designer
A theatre designer needs a thorough knowledge of period settings and costumes, and what looks effective on stage, as well as a sense of style and an ability to work within a budget and adapt to a variety of stage shapes.

Director
Directors need creativity, strong character, the ability to direct and weld together a team of people and a strong sense of the theatre. The casting director needs tact and the ability to cope with crises.

Producer
Tact, persuasiveness, sound business sense, flair for organisation and knowledge of what 'sells' in the theatre are all necessary.

Stage manager

Managers need organising ability, tact, calmness in a crisis, a good memory, an eye for detail, a practical approach and an interest in the literary and technical aspects of theatrical production.

Starting Salary

Salaries are generally low in this sector. Some of the work is part time, seasonal, or on short contracts, but salaries pro rata start at around £8,000, with £12,000 to £20,000 for more specialised jobs or for people with a lot of experience.

The Conference of Drama Schools, CDS Ltd, PO Box 34252, London NW5 1XJ; 020 7692 0032; www.drama.ac.uk

Creative and Cultural Skills, 4th Floor, Lafone House, The Leathermarket, Weston Street, London SE1 3HN; 020 7015 1800; www.ccskills.org.uk

EQ: Diversity and Opportunity in Creative Industries, Suite E237, Dean Clough, Halifax, West Yorkshire HX3 5AX; 01422 381618; www.thinkeq.org.uk/

Equity – The British Actors Union, Guild House, Upper St Martins Lane, London WC2H 9EG; 020 7379 6000; www.equity.org.uk

National Council for Drama Training, 1–7 Woburn Walk, Bloomsbury, London WC1H 0JJ; 020 7387 3650; www.ncdt.co.uk

Royal Academy of Dramatic Art, 62–64 Gower Street, London WC1E 6ED; 020 7636 7076; www.rada.ac.uk

Royal National Theatre, South Bank, London SE1 9PX; 020 7452 3400; www.nationaltheatre.org.uk

Society of British Theatre Designers, 17 Bermondsey Street, London SE1 1XT; 020 7403 3778; www.theatredesign.org.uk

Info

THERAPY

There is a vast range of therapeutic disciplines and treatments and below is a selection of the most popular and common ones.

Art therapy

Art therapy is used as a treatment for psychological and emotional disorders. Drawing, painting, modelling and sculpture are among the creative activities employed. Art therapy is a State Registered profession. All training courses need to be approved by the Council for Professions Supplementary to Medicine (CPSM) and the British Association of Art Therapists. Details are on the Health Professionals Council website.

Most art therapists work in hospitals, some in special schools and child guidance clinics, and some in prisons, detention centres and community homes. As posts are often part time, therapists usually work for more than one institution within an area.

Qualifications and Training

You normally need a degree in art and design to be eligible to do a postgraduate diploma or Master's in art therapy approved by the British Association of Art Therapists. If you have a degree in psychology or social work, you may be accepted onto one of these postgraduate diplomas. Courses last two years full time or three years part time, and once you have completed the course you must register with the Health Professionals Council (HPC) if you wish to work for the NHS or in social services.

Personal Qualities and Skills

A real ability to communicate and to encourage others to do so has to be combined with imaginative artistic and creative ability. Your clients may be distressed, confused and anxious and you have to be patient, sensitive and calm. You need to be good at working as part of a team and capable of managing your workload effectively.

Starting Salary

Working in the NHS a newly qualified art therapist earns between £23,000 and £25,000, on a scale rising to £37,000.

info

British Association of Art Therapists (BAAT), 24–27 White Lion Street, London N1 9PD; 020 7686 4216; www.baat.org

Health Professionals Council, Park House, 184 Kennington Park Road,

London SE11 4BU; 020 7582 0866; www.hpc-uk.org

NHS Careers, PO Box 376, Bristol BS99 3EY; 0845 606 0655; www.nhscareers.nhs.uk

Dance/movement therapy

This form of therapy uses movement and dance as a medium through which the individual can engage creatively in a process of growth and personal integration. Dance movement therapists work with individuals and groups in health, education and social service settings. Their clients include people who are emotionally disturbed or have learning difficulties, and those who want to use this therapy for personal growth.

Qualifications and Training

A postgraduate qualification in dance movement therapy is required. The University of Roehampton and Goldsmiths College both offer this qualification.

Personal Qualities and Skills

A good understanding of dance and movement and communication skills is needed, as is an understanding of the clinical environment.

Starting Salary

Salaries in the National Health Service are between £23,000 and £25,000. Some other organisations and projects may pay either a little more or a little less than this.

Association of Dance and Movement Therapists (ADMT), 32 Meadfoot Lane, Torquay TQ1 2BW; www.admt.org.uk	Health Professionals Council (HPC), Park House, 184 Kennington Park Road, London SE11 4BU; 020 7582 0866; www.hpc-uk.org

Drama therapist

Drama therapists work with people of all ages who are experiencing emotional or psychological problems, especially in communicating and understanding their own feelings. Drama therapists help people to express their feelings through role play and other drama-based exercises. They encourage clients to be creative and to use their imaginations. Drama therapists work closely with psychologists, social workers and other members of the social and healthcare team.

Qualifications and Training

Drama therapists must be graduates with a degree in drama or theatre studies. Occasionally people with degrees in psychology or social work experience are also able to enter this profession. The main qualification is a postgraduate diploma or Master's course approved by the British Association of Drama Therapists (BADth). Having completed this diploma, if you wish to work in the NHS or for social services you must register with the Health Professionals Council.

Personal Qualities and Skills

Excellent interpersonal skills are essential. You must be sensitive, understanding and yet positive, encouraging and confident. The clients you work with have probably experienced great difficulty or very stressful situations so they will require a lot of patience. You must be imaginative and creative. You should work well as part of a team, but be able to take responsibility for your own caseload.

Starting Salary

In the NHS newly qualified drama therapists earn between £23,000 and £25,000. With experience and responsibility salaries can rise to £37,000.

British Association of Drama
Therapists (BADth),
41 Broomhouse Lane, London
SW6 3DP; 020 7731 0160;
www.badth.org.uk

Health Professionals Council,
Park House,184 Kennington Park Road,
London SE11 4BU; 020 7582 0866;
www.hpc-uk.org

NHS Careers, PO Box 376, Bristol
BS99 3EY; 0845 606 0655;
www.nhscareers.nhs.uk

Music therapist

Music therapy is an interactive, primarily non-verbal intervention. It provides a process through which clients can express themselves, become aware of their feelings and interact more easily. The therapist uses live, improvised music to draw the client into an interactive musical relationship. Therapists work with people of all ages, in a wide variety of settings, including special schools, psychiatric hospitals, hospices and day centres. Music therapy is used in many clinical areas, including communication disorders, developmental delay, learning disabilities, mental health problems, physical difficulties, emotional problems, challenging behaviour and terminal illness.

Qualifications and Training

Music therapy is a State Registered profession and the Council for Professions Supplementary to Medicine recommends that postgraduate students should be at least 23 years old. The training is a postgraduate diploma course lasting between one and two years. Some courses offer a part-time option. Before training as a music therapist, students need first to have completed a three-year musical training leading to a diploma or degree. People from related disciplines, such as psychology or education, may also sometimes be accepted onto a training course if they have sufficient practical musical skills.

Personal Qualities and Skills

Music therapists need to be highly skilled musicians, and be able to use music creatively. Therapists also need to develop an understanding of their own reactions and responses. For this reason, student therapists are required to have their own personal therapy during training. Training courses generally prefer students to be over 25 when they begin training.

Association of Professional Music
Therapists (APMT),
61 Church Hill Road, East Barnet,
Hertfordshire EN4 8SY;
020 8440 4153; www.apmt.org

Health Professionals Council,
Park House, 184 Kennington Park Road,
London SE11 4BU; 020 7582 0866;
www.hpc-uk.org

NHS Careers, PO Box 376, Bristol
BS99 3EY; 0845 606 0655;
www.nhscareers.nhs.uk

Starting Salary

Music therapists start on between £23,000 and £25,000. With experience and responsibility they are paid on a scale that rises to around £37,000.

Occupational therapist

Occupational therapists work with people who have physical, mental or social problems, either from birth or as the result of accident, illness or ageing. Their aim is to enable people to achieve as much as they can for themselves. They start with a thorough assessment of each client and his or her lifestyle, in order to establish what the person wants to achieve. Treatment can involve adapting living and working environments, teaching coping strategies and discovering the most beneficial therapeutic activities.

Although occupational therapists often work as part of a team, they have more autonomy than other healthcare workers in the way they apply their knowledge and expertise. They work in hospitals, social service departments, individuals' homes, residential and nursing homes, schools, universities, charities and prisons. They may also work in private practice.

Employment and promotional opportunities are excellent and all UK-educated occupational therapists receive a qualification that is recognised by the World Federation of Occupational Therapists, giving them opportunities to work abroad.

Qualifications and Training

Entry to the profession is normally on completion of a full- or part-time degree in occupational therapy. Most courses require three A levels or equivalent; mature students will be considered without these academic requirements. Accelerated two-year full-time courses are also available to graduates of other disciplines. Part-time in-service programmes are also available for those employed as occupational therapy support workers or technical instructors. Some part-time courses can be studied irrespective of employment status. Although courses vary, all include the principles and practice of occupational therapy, behavioural, biological and medical sciences, and periods of clinical practice in a variety of hospital and community settings.

Personal Qualities and Skills

In addition to academic ability, potential occupational therapists require sensitivity, tolerance, problem-solving skills and the ability to work as part of a team. Reliability, honesty and patience are also important, as well as enthusiasm, dedication and the desire to help and care for others.

Starting Salary

£20,000 on entry for a graduate, rising to over £36,500 for the highest grade of occupational therapy managers. Additional allowances include London and fringe zone weightings, as well as stand-by and on-call payments.

info

British Association of Occupational Therapists, 106–114 Borough High Street, Southwark, London SE1 1LB; 020 7357 6480; www.baot.org.uk

Health Professionals Council (HPC), Park House, 184 Kennington Park Road, London SE11 4BU; 020 7582 0866; www.hpc-uk.org

Speech and language therapist

Speech and language therapists (SLTs) identify, assess and treat people who have communication and/or swallowing disorders. A large proportion of these will be children but SLTs also help adults who may have communication or swallowing problems caused by disease, accident or psychological trauma. Some SLTs specialise in a particular patient group, for example in the areas of severe learning difficulties, hearing impairment or neurological disorders, while others choose more general, broad-based practice. The NHS is the largest employer of SLTs, working in community clinics, hospitals, special schools and homes for the mentally or physically disabled. Some of the larger voluntary organisations also employ SLTs. Often the SLT works closely in a team which may include members of the medical, teaching, therapeutic, psychological and other caring professions.

Qualifications and Training

Speech and language therapy is a degree-entry profession. Courses leading to professional qualifications are offered at 15 universities and colleges of higher education throughout the UK. There are a number of two-year postgraduate diploma and Master's courses available to candidates with relevant degrees.

Entry qualifications for courses vary from one institution to another, but the minimum is five GCSEs and two A levels or equivalent. A good balance of language and science is expected. Other equivalent qualifications are considered on merit. All courses will consider applications from mature students (over 21), who are encouraged to apply in the normal way.

Students who successfully pass all academic and clinical components of an accredited course are eligible to obtain a certificate to practise and to enter the professional register of the Royal College of Speech and Language Therapists as full professional members.

Opportunities also exist to work as a speech therapist's assistant. An NVQ in care at level 3 is available.

Personal Qualities and Skills

It is essential that speech therapists themselves should have clear speech and be able to listen actively. In addition, they must have an interest in people as individuals, as well as an enquiring mind, initiative, patience, imagination and a willingness to take responsibility.

Starting Salary

£19,000–£24,000.

Royal College of Speech and Language Therapists, 2 White Hart Yard, London SE1 1NX; 020 7378 1200; www.rcslt.org; e-mail: postmaster@rcslt.org

NHS Careers, PO Box 376, Bristol BS99 3EY; Careers helpline: 0845 606 0655; www.nhscareers.nhs.uk

Therapy assistant

Occupational, physiotherapy and speech and language therapy departments in hospitals and clinics employ assistants in each of these three professional areas. The work of assistants varies according to which profession they are working in, but there are many common features of their work. They may carry out introductory interviews with patients, though they cannot make formal assessments or plan treatment programmes. They help patients with programmes of exercises or other activities once these have been planned by a qualified therapist. They observe and monitor patients during exercises or other activities and they may be required to do some administrative work.

Qualifications and Training

These vary between different hospitals and healthcare trusts and within the three disciplines concerned. While there are no standardised formal entry qualifications, most applicants have at least five GCSEs including English, maths and a science. Many have A levels, and some applicants with degrees enter this work. Many people do it after A levels to gain experience of a healthcare profession before progressing to higher education and a career as a healthcare professional. A great deal of training is provided on the job, working with professionals, and there are also a variety of NVQs available at levels 2, 3 and 4.

Personal Qualities and Skills

You need to have excellent interpersonal skills, be kind, patient and understanding, but also able to be firm and positive. You must be practical so that you can handle technical equipment, and be physically fit, emotionally robust and keenly observant. An interest in medicine and science is essential.

Starting Salary

Since the major National Health Service salary review, Agenda for Change, in 2005, there is a lot of variation in individual pay according to your level of skills and experience and your range of responsibilities. A typical starting salary range for assistant is £14,000 to £18,000.

info

Skills for Health, 1st Floor, Goldsmiths House, Broad Plain, Bristol BS2 0JP; 0147 822 1155; www.skillsforhealth.org.uk

Health Professionals Council (HPC), Park House, 184 Kennington Park Road, London SE11 4BU; 020 7582 0866; www.hpc-uk.org

British Association of Occupational Therapists, 106–114 Borough High Street, Southwark, London SE1 1LB; 020 7357 6480; www.baot.org.uk

Chartered Society of Physiotherapists, 14 Bedford Row, London WC1R 4ED; 0207 306 666; www.csp.org.uk

Royal College of Speech and Language Therapists (RCSLT), 2 White Hart Yard, London SE1 1NX; 020 7378 1200; www.rcslt.org.uk

Local hospital occupational therapy, physiotherapy and speech and language therapy departments

TOWN AND COUNTRY PLANNER

Planners are concerned with reconciling the needs of the population for buildings, shopping centres, schools and leisure centres with the necessity of preserving and enhancing the natural and built environment. They collect information about the present use of land, the position of roads and other features, as well as drawing up plans for new schemes. Planners in development control ensure that buildings or developments intended for a particular area are suitable and do not conflict with existing buildings or the surrounding environment. Planners work for local and central government, environmental agencies, and to an increasing extent in private practice. There are also varied opportunities for planning support staff.

Qualifications and Training

To enter a degree or diploma course in town planning, five GCSE passes and two A levels are desirable. Useful subjects include maths, English language, geography and history or a foreign language. Those with Royal Town Planning Institute (RTPI)-accredited degrees or diplomas in town planning have satisfied the academic requirement for election to corporate membership of the Institute. To achieve membership, these candidates also need to be able to demonstrate two years' experience in town and country planning. Planning courses are available at undergraduate and postgraduate levels, full- and part-time and on a distance-learning basis.

Planning support staff are normally expected to have good GCSE grades in English, maths and other appropriate subjects, but relevant experience might be a deciding factor for more mature candidates. There are colleges that offer courses for support staff on a part-time or block-release basis. Qualifications gained are the Edexcel (BTEC) certificate, higher certificate or higher diploma in planning or the SQA certificate or higher certificate in planning. An NVQ at level 3 in town planning support is also available for support staff.

Personal Qualities and Skills

Town planners and support staff need to have a knowledge of many subjects: economics, sociology, architecture and geography. Planners must be able to work in a team and cooperate with experts in other subjects. Planners need to take advice and opinions from many different people, and therefore need to be able to reconcile the conflicting views of various interest groups. They must be good communicators and have imagination, and an interest in, and understanding of, both people and the environment.

Starting Salary

Trainees earn around £20,000, while newly qualified planners earn between £20,000 and £25,000. Town planners with considerable management responsibility earn £35,000 plus.

Local Government Careers; www.lgcareers.com

Royal Town Planning Institute, 41 Botolph Lane, London EC3R 8DL; 020 7929 9494; www.rtpi.org.uk

Royal Town Planning Institute in Scotland, 57 Melville Street, Edinburgh EH3 7HL; 0131 226 1959; www.scotland.rtpi.org.uk

TRADING STANDARDS OFFICER

Trading standards officers are employed by local authorities and are responsible for enforcing a very wide range of legislation aimed at protecting consumers and traders. Laws relate to food and consumer product safety, credit, descriptions of goods and services, prices, animal health and welfare. While most operations are carried out through random inspections, officers are also required to investigate complaints and, where appropriate, take matters to court.

Qualifications and Training

The essential qualification for trading standards officers is the Diploma in Consumer Affairs and Trading Standards (DCATS). The usual way to obtain this qualification is to take a degree in consumer protection or a postgraduate qualification approved by the Trading Standards Institute (TSI); people then apply for trainee trading standards officer posts with a local authority. If you have a lot of previous experience in consumer affairs you may not have to have a degree or postgraduate qualification. Some local authorities may offer sponsorship to applicants interested in doing a degree in consumer protection. Without a degree or relevant experience you can apply for posts as an enforcement officer or consumer adviser in trading standards departments and study for the Foundation Certificate in Consumer Affairs and Trading Standards. The TSI has developed a range of modular courses for trading standards workers at all levels. For all of these you must undergo on the job training and submit a portfolio of your work activities.

Personal Qualities and Skills

You need a broad mix of skills to work in trading standards. You must be a good communicator, confident and persistent, but also patient and tactful at times. You should be able to handle technical equipment and complex technical information. Good IT and numeracy skills and an interest in the law are also important. You should be happy working as an effective member of a team, but also able to work on your own.

Starting Salary

Salaries for trainee trading standards officers and for enforcement officers range from £16,000 to £20,000. Once qualified, earnings are between £23,000 and £36,000 depending on geographical location and your range of responsibilities.

info

Trading Standards Institute, First Floor, 1 Sylvan Court, Sylvan Way, Southfields Business Park, Basildon, Essex SS15 6TH; 0870 872 9000; 0870 872 9017 (careers information); fax: 0870 872 9025; www.tradingstandards.gov.uk; e-mail: institute@tsi.org.uk

Local Government Careers; www.lgcareers.com – for further careers information; www.lgjobs.com – for current job vacancy adverts in local councils all over the country

TRAFFIC WARDEN

Traffic wardens are civilians who work in conjunction with local police forces. They check parking meters and penalise drivers parking on double yellow lines or in other illegal places. They may also be required to do school crossing patrols or traffic control duty, as well as receiving vehicles towed into the police pound and looking out for out-of-date car licences.

Qualifications and Training

Each Police Authority sets its own entry requirements, but there is usually no need to have formal educational qualifications; instead you have to pass a written test, which includes maths and English. Training is on-the-job, sometimes being supervised by a police officer, and many areas send you on a short, introductory course.

Personal Qualities and Skills

You need to be calm, confident and possess a degree of common sense to do this work. You should be a good communicator, able to deal with aggression without becoming aggressive yourself.

Starting Salary

Salaries vary between geographical locations, with London salaries being the highest. The general range is between £15,000 and £18,000.

UK Police Service Portal;
www.police.uk

Metropolitan Police;
www.met.careers.co.uk

Police Recruitment;
www.policecouldyou.co.uk

info

TRAVEL AND TOURISM

Occupations in the travel and tourism sector cover being involved in arranging travel and accommodation for business and pleasure, and providing information on places of interest. It also includes work for airlines.

Airline staff

see also Civil aviation

There are two sides to working for airlines: in front of the public such as with cabin crew and check-in staff, and behind-the-scenes staff such as reservations and cabin crew support.

Cabin crew support collate the information that is required to fly an aircraft. They plan the fuel required, organise crew rosters, book overnight hotels and much more.

A despatcher is employed to make sure the plane leaves on time, and checks that the passengers are alerted and that food and drink has been delivered to the plane. The despatcher also oversees the boarding of passengers.

Ground operations staff load and unload baggage, marshall aircraft into parking positions and oversee toilet and water services.

Cabin crew secure the safety of the passengers and are the most visible element of the airline team. During the flight they serve food and drink and sell duty-free goods.

Training and Qualifications

Most airlines have induction programmes specific to the type of work applied for. Airlines look for students who have taken relevant preliminary training such as the air cabin crew NVQ, languages, or a good marketing or business course. First aid courses are also useful to have on your CV.

Cabin crew need good health and must be over 5 ft 2 in. They also need to be able to swim (a legal requirement). Language qualifications are also essential for most airlines.

Personal Qualities and Skills

Good communication skills and being able to handle the public are essential. Staying calm in stressful situations is also necessary. Cabin crew support staff need to demonstrate reliability.

Starting Salary

Salaries range from £16,000 to £19,000, rising to £20,000 to £26,000 with a few years' experience.

info

GoSkills, Concorde House,
Trinity Park, Solihull, Birmingham
B37 7UQ; 0121 635 5520;
www.goskills.org

People 1st, 2nd Floor,
Armstrong House, 38 Market Square,
Uxbridge, Middlesex UB8 1LH;
0870 060 2550; www.People1st.co.uk

Institute of Travel and Tourism,
PO Box 217, Ware, Hertfordshire
SG12 8WY; 0870 770 7960;
www.itt.co.uk

TTC Training, The Quayside,
4 Furnival Road, Sheffield S4 7YA;
0800 915 9396; www.ttctraining.co.uk

Tour managers

Tour managers are employed by major tour companies as official guides for parties of tourists travelling with them. The manager is responsible for the welfare of the tourists and must deal with any worries or complaints. In addition, managers are responsible for all the paperwork necessary when the party stays overnight in a hotel or crosses a border. Much of the work is seasonal and generally only senior staff are employed on a permanent basis.

Qualifications and Training

While there are no formal entry qualifications, many tour managers do have degrees, HNDs or other qualifications in travel and tourism. Most companies put trainee tour managers through their own induction programmes. These cover all aspects of company policy, procedures, ethos, etc. Many tourism managers also study part time for one of the many certificated courses offered by the Institute of Travel and Tourism.

Personal Qualities and Skills

You need excellent interpersonal skills, must be able to talk to people easily and you should be able to pick up at least a working knowledge of foreign languages very quickly. You must be well organised and ready to take decisions or cope with problems.

Starting Salary

There is a lot of variation between different companies. Salaries are normally calculated as a daily allowance plus free accommodation and food throughout the duration of tours. Annual incomes average out at around £12,000 to £14,000.

Institute of Travel and Tourism,
PO Box 217, Ware, Hertfordshire
SG12 8WY; 0870 770 7960;
www.itt.co.uk

International Association of Tour
Managers (IATM), 397 Walworth Road,
London SE17 2AW; 020 7703 9154;
www.iatm.co.uk

People 1st, 2nd Floor,
Armstrong House, 38 Market Square,
Uxbridge, Middlesex UB8 1LH;
0870 060 2550; www.people1st.co.uk

TTC Training, The Quayside,
4 Furnival Road, Sheffield S4 7YA;
0800 915 9396; www.ttctraining.co.uk

Tourism officer

Tourism officers work for national or regional tourist boards and local authorities with the aim of attracting visitors to Britain or to a particular region. The work includes promoting attractions, working with press and public relations agencies, designers and photographers to advertise local features, researching local history to develop new attractions, and participating in exhibitions both nationally and overseas to promote the area. They work closely with businesses in attracting holidaymakers, tour operators, exhibitions and conferences to the area, and research future trends and needs. They are also responsible for overseeing the council's tourist information offices.

Qualifications and Training

Having a degree or HND in a business- or tourism-related subject can be an advantage, but personal qualities and proven business skills are just as important. NVQs in tourist information at levels 2–3 are available.

Previous tourist information centre experience, paid or voluntary, is invaluable. Marketing, travel agency or other retail experience is advantageous.

Local Government Careers;
www.lgcareers.com – for further
careers information;
www.lgjobs.com – for current job
vacancy adverts in local councils all
over the country

National and local tourist boards

Institute of Travel and Tourism,
Studio 3, Mill Studio, Crane Mead,
Ware, Herts SG12 9PY; 0870 770 7960;
fax: 0870 770 7961; www.itt.co.uk;
e-mail: enquiries@itt.co.uk

TTC Training, The Cornerstone,
The Broadway, Woking, Surrey
GU21 5AR; 01483 727321;
fax: 01483 756698;
www.ttctraining.co.uk;
e-mail: info@ttctraining.co.uk

*Careers and Jobs in Travel and
Tourism* (Kogan Page)

Personal Qualities and Skills

Good communication skills are essential, as are marketing and promotional experience and skills, including the ability to be creative, and write snappy copy to promote the area and various events. Excellent organisational skills and the ability to get on with a wide cross-section of people, from business leaders and councillors to residents and visitors, are important. A knowledge of languages, geography, history or archaeology can be an advantage for some posts.

Starting Salary

£12,000–£14,000 for graduate entrants.

Travel agent

Travel agents sell tickets for travel by air, land and sea on behalf of transport organisations. They make hotel bookings for individual travellers, business people or holidaymakers. Some travel companies deal only with business travel, and are also involved in arranging conferences and trade fairs. However, travel agents are best known for selling package holidays on behalf of tour operators. Many travel agents will also advise travellers on visas, foreign currency and necessary injections.

Qualifications and Training

Modern Apprenticeships and NVQ qualifications are available. No specific qualifications are asked for but GCSEs in maths, English and geography are an advantage. Computer literacy is becoming increasingly important.

Personal Qualities and Skills

Travel agents must enjoy dealing with the general public, and have a responsible attitude regarding the accuracy of information given, and good administrative and ICT skills.

Starting Salary

Varies according to job; assistants earn £8,000–£13,000, managers £15,000+.

info

Local Job Centre Plus and Careers/
Connexions Centres

Institute of Travel and Tourism,
Studio 3, Mill Studio, Crane Mead,
Ware, Herts SG12 9PY;
0870 770 7960; fax: 0870 770 7961;
www.itt.co.uk;
e-mail: enquiries@itt.co.uk

TTC Training, The Cornerstone,
The Broadway, Woking, Surrey
GU21 5AR; 01483 727321;
fax: 01483 756698;
www.ttctraining.co.uk;
e-mail: info@ttctraining.co.uk

*Careers and Jobs in Travel and
Tourism* (Kogan Page)

UNDERTAKER

see Funeral Director

UNDERWRITER

see Insurance

VALUER

see Land and Property

VETERINARY SCIENCE

(*see also* Animals)

Veterinary science is concerned with the care of animals, including both farm animals and domestic pets.

Veterinary nurse

Veterinary nurses (VNs) assist vets during operations and X-rays, sterilise instruments, look after animals recovering from surgery, and keep the animals and their cages clean. After qualification, the work of a veterinary nurse can include practice management, staff supervision, teaching and training other nurses or support staff. Some VNs choose to work outside veterinary practice in research establishments, colleges, zoos and breeding or boarding kennels.

Qualifications and Training

A nationally recognised Veterinary Nursing Scheme (VNS) is administered by the Royal College of Veterinary Surgeons (RCVS), which keeps a register of veterinary practices able to offer training. To train as a veterinary nurse you must be aged 17 or over and have five GCSEs grades A–C including English, maths and two science subjects. You must also be employed by a practice registered to offer training. You can get details of practices approved to provide training from the RCVS website or from the British Veterinary Nursing Association (BVNA). If you particularly want to work with horses you can do specialised training as part of your qualification, but you must be working for a practice that takes on equine work.

If you do not have the required GCSEs, and are working for an approved practice, you can take a day release or distance learning level 2 Certificate for Animal

Nursing Assistants. As an alternative to the Veterinary Nursing Scheme there are several degree and HND courses available in veterinary nursing. If you consider this route, ensure that the course you choose is approved by the RCVS.

Personal Qualities and Skills

You have to love animals and be calm, kind and patient when handling them. You have to be able to deal with sad or distressing situations and you must be able to communicate with people as well as their pets. You need to be practical, with an interest in science, and you can't be the least bit squeamish.

Starting Salary

Salaries start at close to £10,000 and once you are fully qualified and have some experience they rise to £16,000, though only a few veterinary practices would pay at this higher rate.

British Veterinary Nursing Association (BVNA), Suite 11, Shenval House, South Road, Harlow, Essex CM20 2BD; 01279 450567; fax: 01279 420866; www.bvna.org.uk; e-mail: bvna@bvnaoffice.plus.com

Royal College of Veterinary Surgeons, Belgravia House, 62–64 Horseferry Road, London SW1P 2AF; 020 7222 2001; www.rcvs.org.uk; e-mail: admin@rcvs.org.uk

Careers Working with Animals (Kogan Page)

Veterinary surgeon

Most vets work in private practice, usually starting out as a veterinary assistant and working their way up into a partnership or into their own business. Some specialise in small-animal treatment, including pets such as dogs, cats and birds, while others work with particular kinds of animals such as farm animals, racehorses or the more exotic zoo animals. Other vets go into research or industry. The Department of Environment, Food and Rural Affairs, for instance, employs a substantial number to work on disease control, monitoring such epidemics as foot and mouth or swine vesicular disease. Others are employed by animal welfare organisations, such as the PDSA, in animal hospitals. Vets are also needed in the food-processing industries where their job is concerned with checking that conditions are humane and hygienic.

Qualifications and Training

A veterinary surgeon must hold a degree from one of the six veterinary schools in the UK. The six universities offering the course set their own entrance requirements but all demand an extremely high standard of A level passes or equivalent. Chemistry is essential, and other useful subjects are physics, maths, biology and zoology. The course lasts five years (six at Cambridge), and covers a formidable amount of academic and practical work, comparable to that needed to be a doctor.

Personal Qualities and Skills

Vets need to be sympathetic but detached. They must be excellent communicators, explaining and reassuring pet owners and farmers. Patience, calmness and, later on, a good business sense and problem-solving skills are also important.

Starting Salary

A newly qualified vet earns around £20,000 and with a few years' experience this rises to between £25,000 and £30,000. Many vets become partners in a business or run their own business, and can earn more than £45,000.

info

Royal College of Veterinary Surgeons, Belgravia House, 62–64 Horseferry Road, London SW1P 2AF; 020 7222 2001; www.rcvs.org.uk; e-mail: admin@rcvs.org.uk

WATCH AND CLOCK MAKER/REPAIRER

Watch and clock makers make timepieces by hand, sometimes to a design of their own.

Repairers receive watches and clocks from customers for servicing and repair. They must be able to examine a timepiece thoroughly for worn-out parts, clean and regulate a watch or clock, and repair or replace faulty parts. The work involves the use of precision tools and electronic equipment. Restoration is carried out on antique clocks and watches.

Qualifications and Training

The British Horological Institute (BHI) coordinates all watch and clock training organisations. A two-year HND in horology is available from the University of Central England. Applicants need three GCSEs, including maths and English, or to have completed the preliminary year of the BHI course. A one-year course in antique clock repair and restoration is offered by West Dean College in Chichester. St Loye's College in Exeter provides residential training in horology for students with disabilities.

The BHI also offers correspondence courses at preliminary, intermediate and final level which cover all aspects of horology from watch repairs, clocks, electric, electronic to heavy turret and master clocks. These courses lead up to internationally recognised qualifications.

Personal Qualities and Skills

Mathematical and drawing ability as well as dexterity are important. Applicants must have good eyesight, the physical skill and patience to do the intricate work required, and be able to work alone.

Starting Salary

Many horologists are self-employed and earnings vary enormously, starting from £8,000 to over £20,000 for those who have experience and a specialism.

British Horological Institute, Upton Hall, Upton, Newark, Nottinghamshire NG23 5TE; 01636 813795; fax: 01636 812258; www.bhi.co.uk; e-mail: info@bhi.co.uk

info

WELFARE ADVICE WORK

Welfare advice worker

Welfare advice workers are employed by local authorities, by Citizens Advice Bureaux (CAB) and by a wide range of charities and voluntary organisations. Advice workers answer questions and offer confidential advice and practical help (eg help with filling in a form), to members of the public. The work often involves advocacy work, taking up an issue or dealing with bureaucracy on behalf of a client. Some advice workers are generalists, offering advice on many different problems; working for CAB is a good example of this. Other welfare advisers specialise in issues such as debt management, housing questions, consumer concerns, education and career decisions or discrimination of some kind.

Qualifications and Training

While there are no formal entry qualifications, many advice workers are graduates in sociology, psychology or similar subjects. They have often had experience of working with people and many advice workers begin their advice careers in a voluntary capacity. There is a variety of part-time courses available at NVQ levels 2, 3 and 4 in advice and guidance work; many people undertake these once they are working in this field.

Personal Qualities and Skills

You must be very good at listening to people and at explaining documents or rules patiently and carefully. You need good information research skills and good powers of persuasion if your role involves advocacy work of any kind. You need to be well organised and flexible, with good written communication skills.

Starting Salary

Salaries range from £13, 0000 to £20,000 and up to around £25,000 for staff with experience and management responsibilities. Remember that many jobs are part time, so salaries will be on a pro rata basis. In general, salaries are higher in local authorities than in the voluntary sector.

info

Advice UK, 12th Floor,
New London Bridge House,
25 London Bridge Street, London
SE1 9ST; 020 7407 4070;
www.adviceuk.org.uk

National Association of Citizens
Advice Bureaux (NACAB),
Myddelton House,
115–123 Pentonville Road, London
N1 9LZ; www.citizensadvice.org.uk

WINE TRADE

The wine trade has grown beyond the small merchant or importer, and most opportunities are now with large companies which import, retail and deal with the licensed trade, hotels and catering, off-licences, supermarkets and multiple stores. There are posts in marketing, advertising, packaging, promotion, market research, buying and quality control.

Qualifications and Training

Opportunities exist at GCSE, A and degree level for entry into the wine trade. On-the-job training is provided by the Wine and Spirit Education Trust (WSET), a registered educational charity set up by the drinks industry. It offers level 1 Foundation Certificate, Higher Certificate and Diploma courses. The University of Brighton offers a two-year full-time HND in wine studies.

Personal Qualities and Skills

These depend on the area entered, but a love and knowledge of wine are obviously important, plus relevant knowledge about the chief wine-growing areas, and their type of soil and climate. Tasters need a discriminating sense of taste and smell. Language skills can be an advantage.

Starting Salary

Trainee managers start on around £12,000 to £15,000 a year. Experienced wine merchants or managers earn £18,000 to £25,000. A highly successful and knowledgeable wine merchant can earn much more than this.

WRITER

For writers other than journalists, making a living purely from writing can be very difficult, so many writers, especially before they are established, have other careers as well. There are only a handful of people who become successful fiction writers or writers of really popular non-fiction such as biographies. There are some jobs for writers in residence with theatre companies and regional arts organisations, prisons or university departments, but many of these posts are temporary contracts.

Technical authors write user manuals and instruction books for anything from washing machines to computer software, and there are writers who specialise in writing textbooks and other teaching materials. Technical authors are often on permanent, or at least more secure contracts. Many writers of textbooks have other jobs in education.

Qualifications and Training

Generally writers are born, not made. However, it is possible to take courses in both creative and technical writing.

Personal Qualities and Skills

Writers must be self-disciplined, able to work on their own, highly motivated and persevering.

Starting Salary

Earnings vary enormously, but the majority of writers do not support themselves by their writing alone. Writers in residence can expect about £14,000–£20,000. Technical authors earn £13,000–£30,000.

info

Society of Authors,
84 Drayton Gardens, London
SW10 9SB; 020 7373 6642;
fax: 020 7373 5768;
www.societyofauthors.net;
e-mail: info@societyofauthors.net

Writers Guild, 15 Britannia Street,
London WC1X 9JN, 020 7833 0777;
fax: 020 7833 4777;

www.writersguild.org.uk;
e-mail: admin@writersguild.org.uk

Writers' and Artists' Yearbook
(A&C Black); *The Writers' Handbook*
(Macmillan)

YOUTH WORK

Personal adviser (Connexions)

Personal advisers are drawn from a variety of backgrounds, such as careers advice and guidance, youth work, National Health Service, social services, youth justice and education. The Connexions service aims to provide a coherent system of support for young people in their transition to adulthood and working life. It came into operation in all areas of England in 2003 and is staffed by a network of personal advisers whose aim is to help 13- to 19-year-olds achieve their full potential by addressing barriers to learning. Some personal advisers may specialise in working with those who need additional support because of problems such as homelessness, mental illness or substance abuse.

The work of individual advisers will depend on their clients, and involve work with other agencies to broker access to specialist services. Most of an adviser's time will be spent in direct contact with young people, but some time will also be spent liaising with other organisations, working with parents and carers, and promoting links with the local community. There is also a certain amount of administrative work – producing accurate and up-to-date records to be shared with other professionals.

They are based in a variety of settings, including schools, colleges, youth and community centres and Connexions offices. At times, advisers may be called out to deal with crises in young people's lives. Most jobs will involve evening and weekend work. Some Connexions Partnerships will provide services during the evening and overnight, to respond to the needs of young people.

Qualifications and Training

To become a fully qualified personal adviser it is necessary to hold a relevant qualification at S/NVQ level 4, or equivalent, although some personal advisers will be working towards this level during training en route to qualified status. In addition, all personal advisers will be required to attend either the Diploma for Connexions Personal Advisers or the Understanding Connexions training programme.

The minimum age for entry to training is normally 21 and a driving licence is usually required. All candidates undergo police checks, so anyone with a conviction for a crime against children is barred from this type of work.

Personal Qualities and Skills

Advisers need strong communication and relationship-building skills to engage the trust and respect of young people. They need to be able to listen carefully and respond appropriately; a non-judgemental approach is essential. Personal advisers need to empathise with young people's concerns while maintaining professional and emotional detachment. A sense of humour, reliability, flexibility, good time management and team-working skills are also important.

Starting Salaries

Salaries vary between individual Connexions Partnerships. Trainees may start on £14,000 to £15,000; qualified staff with the Diploma for Personal Advisers between £19,000 and £21,000 (£23,000 to £25,500 in London).

Connexions website: www.connexions.gov.uk	Local Connexions Partnership

Youth and community worker

Youth work promotes young people's personal and social development, provides support to help them achieve and progress into independence, and enables young people to have a voice in their communities and in society. This is accomplished through work with individuals, with and in groups, and with communities. In many instances youth workers work in partnership with professionals from other sectors, such as schools and colleges, careers, health organisations, the police and social services.

Youth and community workers work in a range of settings, including youth clubs, schools, colleges, community centres, as personal advisers within the Connexions Service and other specialist agencies offering information, advice and counselling. Some workers also work in mobile centres and with young people on the streets and in cafés. There are currently around 3,000 full-time youth workers employed in England and a far larger number of part-time and volunteer youth workers. The introduction of the Connexions Service in England, which offers advice, information and guidance to young people aged 13–19, has led to substantial numbers of new posts for people with youth work skills.

In Scotland, youth and community work is combined with adult education under the generic term 'community education'.

Qualifications and Training

For those seeking qualification as a full-time, nationally qualified youth worker, various routes, including full-time and part-time diploma and degree courses, postgraduate courses, and distance learning exist. Detailed information on courses can be obtained from the National Youth Agency, directly or via its website. Details of training and employment in Scotland and Wales can be obtained from Communities Scotland and the Welsh Youth Agency, respectively.

NVQs in community work are available at levels 2/3 and 4. There is normally a minimum age requirement varying from 19 to 21 (18 for some degree courses), and applicants are usually expected to have substantial experience of work with young people or adults in community settings. This can be paid or unpaid. Mature entrants may be accepted without formal academic qualifications.

Personal Qualities and Skills

An interest in and understanding of the issues that affect people's lives, plus patience, stamina and a sense of humour are all qualities demanded of youth and community workers. They must also be able to plan, record and evaluate their work.

Starting Salary

Starting salaries are between £15,000 and £19,000, rising to £20,000 to £26,000 with experience. There is often part-time work available in this field.

info

National Youth Agency, Eastgate House, 19–23 Humberstone Road, Leicester LE5 3GJ; www.nya.org.uk

Welsh Youth Agency, Leslie Court, Lon-y-Lyn, Caerphilly CF83 1BQ; 029 2085 5700; www.wya.org.uk/english/home.asp

Youth Council for Northern Ireland, Forestview, Purdy's Lane, Belfast BT8 7AR; 028 9064 3882; www.ycni.org

Communities Scotland, CeVe Unit, Thistle House, 91 Haymarket Terrace, Edinburgh EH12 5HE; 0131 313 0044; www.communitiesscotland.gov.uk

Z

ZOOLOGY

Zoo keeper

see Animals

Zoologist

Zoologists work in either research or teaching. Zoologists study anatomy, physiology, classification, distribution, behaviour and environment of all kinds of animals, from insects to elephants. When working in zoos, they usually coordinate conservation breeding programmes, collection planning and general conservation strategies. A very small number find jobs in industry, mainly in pharmaceutical and animal foodstuff companies. Research zoologists will probably work in one of the many government-backed centres on a variety of projects, including animal behaviour, pest control and the population ecology of birds.

Qualifications and Training

A degree in zoology, available at some universities, is needed for a career as a zoologist. Postgraduate training in specialisations such as entomology or nematology is also available.

Personal Qualities and Skills

Zoologists should have a scientific mind and an interest in research. They should also have keen powers of observation and be patient and confident.

Starting Salary

New graduates working as research or technical assistants earn around £19,000. Zoologists in research posts earn up to £28,000.

Zoological Society of London, Regent's Park, London NW1 4RY; www.zoo.cam.ac.uk/ioz

Index

Index of advertisers